# The Quran With Tafsir Ibn Kathir
## Part 2 of 30:
## Al Baqarah 142 To Al Baqarah 252

# The Quran With Tafsir Ibn Kathir
# Part 2 of 30:
# Al Baqarah 142 To
# Al Baqarah 252

With
Arabic Script, Transliteration of Arabic, Meaning in
English and Ibn Kathir's Abridged Tafsir (Explanation)

Muhammad Saed Abdul-Rahman

BSc, DipHE

© Muhammad Saed Abdul-Rahman, 2012
ISBN 978-1-86179-831-2

All Rights reserved

British Library Cataloguing in Publication Data. A Catalogue record for this book is available from the British Library

Designed, Typeset and produced by:
MSA Publication Limited, 4 Bello Close, Herne Hill,
London SE24 9BW
United Kingdom

Cover design: Houriyah Abdul-Rahman

# TABLE OF CONTENTS

**TABLE OF CONTENTS** .................................................................................................. V

**PRELUDE** ................................................................................................................. XIII

   OPENING SERMAN .................................................................................................... XIII
   OUR MISSION .......................................................................................................... XIV
   BIOGRAPHY OF HAFIZ IBN KATHIR (701 H - 774 H) ................................................. XIV
      Ibn Kathir's Teachers ........................................................................................ xiv
      Ibn Kathir's Students ......................................................................................... xv
      Ibn Kathir's Books ............................................................................................. xvi
      Ibn Kathir's Death ............................................................................................. xvii

**PREFACE** .................................................................................................................. XIX

   ABOUT THIS BOOK ................................................................................................... XIX
   PERFORMING PROSTRATION WHILE READING THE QUR'AN .................................... XIX

**PART 2 FULL ARABIC TEXT** ....................................................................................... 1

**INTRODUCTION TO CHAPTER (SURAH) 2: AL-BAQARAH (THE COW)** .................. 13

   IBN KATHIR'S INTRODUCTION ................................................................................... 13
      The Virtues of Surat Al-Baqarah ....................................................................... 13
      Virtues of Surat Al-Baqarah and Surat Al `Imran ................................................ 15
      Surat Al-Baqarah was revealed in Al-Madinah ................................................... 18

**CHAPTER (SURAH) 2: AL-BAQARAH (THE COW), VERSES 142-252** .................... 19

   *Surah: 2 Ayah: 142 & Ayah: 143* .......................................................................... 19
      Tafsir Ibn Kathir ................................................................................................ 20
         Changing the Qiblah - Direction of the Prayer ............................................... 20
         The Virtues of Muhammad's Nation .............................................................. 23
         The Wisdom behind changing the Qiblah ...................................................... 25
   *Surah: 2 Ayah: 144* ............................................................................................... 27
      Tafsir Ibn Kathir ................................................................................................ 28
         The First Abrogation in the Qur'an was about the Qiblah .............................. 28
         Is the Qiblah the Ka`bah itself or its General Direction ................................. 29
         The Jews had Knowledge that the (Muslim) Qiblah would later be changed ... 29
   *Surah: 2 Ayah: 145* ............................................................................................... 30
      Tafsir Ibn Kathir ................................................................................................ 30
         The Stubbornness and Disbelief of the Jews .................................................. 30
   *Surah: 2 Ayah: 146 & Ayah: 147* .......................................................................... 31
      Tafsir Ibn Kathir ................................................................................................ 31
         The Jews know that the Prophet is True, but they hide the Truth ................... 31
   *Surah: 2 Ayah: 148* ............................................................................................... 32
      Tafsir Ibn Kathir ................................................................................................ 32

| | |
|---|---|
| Every Nation has a Qiblah | 32 |

### Surah: 2 Ayah: 149 & Ayah: 150 ........................................... 33
- Tafsir Ibn Kathir ........................................................... 34
  - Why was changing the Qiblah mentioned thrice ............... 34
  - The Wisdom behind abrogating the Previous Qiblah ......... 35

### Surah: 2 Ayah: 151 & Ayah: 152 ........................................... 36
- Tafsir Ibn Kathir ........................................................... 36
  - Muhammad's Prophecy is a Great Bounty from Allah ........ 36

### Surah: 2 Ayah: 153 & Ayah: 154 ........................................... 38
- Tafsir Ibn Kathir ........................................................... 39
  - The Virtue of Patience and Prayer ................................. 39
  - The Life enjoyed by Martyrs ......................................... 40

### Surah: 2 Ayah: 155, Ayah: 156 & Ayah: 157 ............................ 41
- Tafsir Ibn Kathir ........................................................... 41
  - The Believer is Patient with the Affliction and thus gains a Reward ... 41
  - The Virtue of asserting that We all belong to Allah, during Afflictions ... 43

### Surah: 2 Ayah: 158 ............................................................ 44
- Tafsir Ibn Kathir ........................................................... 44
  - The Meaning of "it is not a sin" in the Ayah .................... 44
  - The Wisdom behind legislating Sa`i between As-Safa and Al-Marwah ... 45

### Surah: 2 Ayah: 159, Ayah: 160, Ayah: 161 & Ayah: 162 .............. 46
- Tafsir Ibn Kathir ........................................................... 47
  - The Eternal Curse for Those Who hide Religious Commandments ... 47
  - Cursing the Disbelievers is allowed ................................ 49

### Surah: 2 Ayah: 163 & Ayah: 164 ........................................... 49
- Tafsir Ibn Kathir ........................................................... 50
  - The Proofs for Tawhid ................................................. 50

### Surah: 2 Ayah: 165, Ayah: 166 & Ayah: 167 ............................ 52
- Tafsir Ibn Kathir ........................................................... 53
  - The Condition of the Polytheists in this Life and the Hereafter ... 53

### Surah: 2 Ayah: 168 & 169 .................................................... 56
- Tafsir Ibn Kathir ........................................................... 56
  - The Order to eat the Lawful Things, and the Prohibition of following the Footsteps of Shaytan ... 56

### Surah: 2 Ayah: 170 & Ayah: 171 ........................................... 58
- Tafsir Ibn Kathir ........................................................... 58
  - The Polytheist imitates Other Polytheists ....................... 58
  - The Disbeliever is just like an Animal ............................ 58

### Surah: 2 Ayah: 172 & Ayah: 173 ........................................... 59
- Tafsir Ibn Kathir ........................................................... 60
  - The Command to eat Pure Things and the Explanation of the Prohibited Things ... 60
  - The Prohibited is Allowed in Cases of Emergency ............ 62

### Surah: 2 Ayah: 174, 2 Ayah: 175 & 2 Ayah: 176 ....................... 63
- Tafsir Ibn Kathir ........................................................... 64

# Table of Contents

- Criticizing the Jews for concealing what Allah revealed ........... 64
- *Surah: 2 Ayah: 177* ........... 66
  - Tafsir Ibn Kathir ........... 67
    - Al-Birr (Piety, Righteousness) ........... 67
- *Surah: 2 Ayah: 178 & Ayah: 179* ........... 71
  - Tafsir Ibn Kathir ........... 72
    - The Command and the Wisdom behind the Law of Equality ........... 72
    - The Benefits and Wisdom of the Law of Equality ........... 74
- *Surah: 2 Ayah: 180, Ayah: 181 & Ayah: 182* ........... 75
  - Tafsir Ibn Kathir ........... 75
    - Including Parents and Relatives in the Will was later abrogated ........... 75
    - The Will for the Relatives that do not qualify as Inheritors ........... 76
    - The Will should observe Justice ........... 77
    - The Virtue of Fairness in the Will ........... 78
- *Surah: 2 Ayah: 183 & Ayah: 184* ........... 78
  - Tafsir Ibn Kathir ........... 79
    - The Order to Fast ........... 79
    - The various Stages of Fasting ........... 80
    - The Fidyah (Expiation) for breaking the Fast is for the Old and the Ailing ........... 81
- *Surah: 2 Ayah: 185* ........... 81
  - Tafsir Ibn Kathir ........... 82
    - The Virtue of Ramadan and the Revelation of the Qur'an in it ........... 82
    - The Virtues of the Qur'an ........... 82
    - The Obligation of Fasting Ramadan ........... 83
    - Several Rulings concerning the Fast ........... 83
    - Ease and not Hardship ........... 85
    - Remembering Allah upon performing the Acts of Worship ........... 86
- *Surah: 2 Ayah: 186* ........... 86
  - Tafsir Ibn Kathir ........... 87
    - Allah hears the Servant's Supplication ........... 87
    - Allah accepts the Invocation ........... 88
    - Three Persons Whose Supplication will not be rejected ........... 90
- *Surah: 2 Ayah: 187* ........... 90
  - Tafsir Ibn Kathir ........... 91
    - Eating, Drinking and Sexual Intercourse are allowed during the Nights of Ramadan ........... 91
    - Time for Suhur ........... 93
    - Suhur is recommended ........... 94
    - There is no Harm in beginning the Fast while Junub (a state of major ritual impurity) ........... 96
    - Fasting ends at Sunset ........... 97
    - Prohibition of Uninterrupted Fasting (Wisal) ........... 98
    - The Rulings of I`tikaf ........... 99
- *Surah: 2 Ayah: 188* ........... 101

| | |
|---|---|
| Tafsir Ibn Kathir | 101 |
|   Bribery is prohibited and is a Sin | 101 |
|   The Judge's Ruling does not allow the Prohibited or prohibit the Lawful | 102 |
| *Surah: 2 Ayah: 189* | *103* |
|   Tafsir Ibn Kathir | 103 |
|     The Crescent Moons | 103 |
|     Righteousness comes from Taqwa | 104 |
| *Surah: 2 Ayah: 190, Ayah: 191, Ayah: 192 & Ayah: 193* | *104* |
|   Tafsir Ibn Kathir | 105 |
|     The Command to fight Those Who fight Muslims and killing Them wherever They are found | 105 |
|     The Prohibition of mutilating the Dead and stealing from the captured Goods | 106 |
|     Shirk is worse than Killing | 107 |
|     Fighting in the Sacred Area is prohibited, except in Self-Defense | 107 |
|     The Order to fight until there is no more Fitnah | 108 |
| *Surah: 2 Ayah: 194* | *111* |
|   Tafsir Ibn Kathir | 111 |
|     Fighting during the Sacred Months is prohibited, except in Self-Defense | 111 |
| *Surah: 2 Ayah: 195* | *112* |
|   Tafsir Ibn Kathir | 112 |
|     The Command to spend in the Cause of Allah | 112 |
| *Surah: 2 Ayah: 196* | *114* |
|   Tafsir Ibn Kathir | 115 |
|     The Command to complete Hajj and `Umrah | 115 |
|     If One is prevented while in Route, He slaughters the Sacrifice, shaves his Head and ends Ihram | 116 |
|     Whoever shaved his Head during Ihram, will have to pay the Fidyah | 118 |
|     Tamattu` during Hajj | 119 |
|     Whoever performs Tamattu` should fast Ten Days if He does not have a Hady | 120 |
|     The Residents of Makkah do not perform Tamattu" | 122 |
| *Surah: 2 Ayah: 197* | *123* |
|   Tafsir Ibn Kathir | 123 |
|     When does Ihram for Hajj start | 123 |
|     The Months of Hajj | 124 |
|     Prohibition of Rafath (Sexual Intercourse) during Hajj | 125 |
|     The Prohibition of Fusuq during Hajj | 125 |
|     The Prohibition of arguing during Hajj | 127 |
|     The Encouragement for Righteous Deeds and to bring Provisions for Hajj | 127 |
|     The Provisions of the Hereafter | 128 |
| *Surah: 2 Ayah: 198* | *128* |
|   Tafsir Ibn Kathir | 128 |
|     Commercial Transactions during Hajj | 128 |
|     Standing at `Arafat | 129 |
|     The Time to leave `Arafat and Al-Muzdalifah | 130 |

# Table of Contents

Al-Mash`ar Al-Haram .................................................................................. 131
*Surah: 2 Ayah: 199* ................................................................................ *132*
   Tafsir Ibn Kathir ................................................................................ 132
      The Order to stand on `Arafat and to depart from it .......................... 132
      Asking Allah for His Forgiveness ........................................................ 133
*Surah: 2 Ayah: 200, Ayah: 201 & Ayah: 202* ........................................ *134*
   Tafsir Ibn Kathir ................................................................................ 135
      The Order for Remembrance of Allah and seeking Good in this Life and the Hereafter upon completing the Rites of Hajj ...................... 135
*Surah: 2 Ayah: 203* ................................................................................ *137*
   Tafsir Ibn Kathir ................................................................................ 138
      Remembering Allah during the Days of Tashriq - Days of Eating and Drinking . 138
      The Appointed Days ........................................................................... 139
*Surah: 2 Ayah: 204, Ayah: 205, Ayah: 206 & Ayah: 207* ...................... *140*
   Tafsir Ibn Kathir ................................................................................ 141
      The Characteristics of the Hypocrites ................................................ 141
      Rejecting Advice is Characteristic of the Hypocrites .......................... 143
      The Sincere Believer prefers pleasing Allah ....................................... 144
*Surah: 2 Ayah: 208 & Ayah: 209* ........................................................... *145*
   Tafsir Ibn Kathir ................................................................................ 145
      Entering Islam in its Entirety is obligated .......................................... 145
*Surah: 2 Ayah: 210* ................................................................................ *146*
   Tafsir Ibn Kathir ................................................................................ 147
      Do not delay embracing the Faith ..................................................... 147
*Surah: 2 Ayah: 211 & Ayah: 212* ........................................................... *147*
   Tafsir Ibn Kathir ................................................................................ 148
      The Punishment for changing Allah's Favor and mocking the Believers ........... 148
*Surah: 2 Ayah: 213* ................................................................................ *150*
   Tafsir Ibn Kathir ................................................................................ 151
      Disputing, after the Clear Signs have come, indicates Deviation ....... 151
*Surah: 2 Ayah: 214* ................................................................................ *153*
   Tafsir Ibn Kathir ................................................................................ 153
      Victory only comes after succeeding in the Trials .............................. 153
*Surah: 2 Ayah: 215* ................................................................................ *155*
   Tafsir Ibn Kathir ................................................................................ 156
      Who deserves the Nafaqah (Spending or Charity) ............................. 156
*Surah: 2 Ayah: 216* ................................................................................ *156*
   Tafsir Ibn Kathir ................................................................................ 157
      Jihad is made Obligatory .................................................................... 157
*Surah: 2 Ayah: 217 & Ayah: 218* ........................................................... *158*
   Tafsir Ibn Kathir ................................................................................ 159
      The Nakhlah Military Maneuvers, and the Ruling on Fighting during the Sacred Months ................................................................................ 159
*Surah: 2 Ayah: 219 & Ayah: 220* ........................................................... *163*

Tafsir Ibn Kathir ................................................................................................ 163
   The Gradual Prohibition of Khamr (Alchoholic Drink) ........................................ 163
   Spending whatever One could spare of his Money on Charity ........................ 165
   Maintaining the Orphan's Property .................................................................... 167
Tafsir Ibn Kathir ................................................................................................ 169
   The Prohibition of marrying Mushrik Men and Women ................................... 169

## Surah: 2 Ayah: 222 & Ayah: 223 ........................................................................ 171
Tafsir Ibn Kathir ................................................................................................ 171
   Sexual Intercourse with Menstruating Women is prohibited ............................ 171
   Anal Sex is prohibited ......................................................................................... 173
   The Reason behind revealing Allah's Statement: "Your Wives are a Tilth for You.
   ................................................................................................................................ 174

## Surah: 2 Ayah: 224 & Ayah: 225 ........................................................................ 177
Tafsir Ibn Kathir ................................................................................................ 178
   The Prohibition of swearing to abandon a Good Deed .................................... 178
   The Laghw (Unintentional) Vows ........................................................................ 179

## Surah: 2 Ayah: 226 & Ayah: 227 ........................................................................ 181
Tafsir Ibn Kathir ................................................................................................ 181
   The Ila' and its Rulings ........................................................................................ 181

## Surah: 2 Ayah: 228 ............................................................................................ 182
Tafsir Ibn Kathir ................................................................................................ 183
   The `Iddah (Waiting Period) of the Divorced Woman ...................................... 183
   The Meaning of Al-Quru ...................................................................................... 183
   A Woman's Statement about Menses and Purity is to be accepted ................ 183
   The Husband has the Right to take back his Divorced Wife during the `Iddah
   (Waiting Period) ..................................................................................................... 184
   The Rights the Spouses have over Each Other ................................................. 184
   The Virtue Men have over Women ..................................................................... 185

## Surah: 2 Ayah: 229 & 2 Ayah: 230 ..................................................................... 186
Tafsir Ibn Kathir ................................................................................................ 187
   Divorce is Thrice ................................................................................................... 187
   Taking back the Mahr (Dowry) ............................................................................ 188
   Allowing Khul` and the Return of the Mahr in that Case ................................. 188
   The `Iddah (Waiting Period) for the Khul" ......................................................... 190
   Transgressing the set limits of Allah is an Injustice ........................................... 190
   Pronouncing Three Divorces at the same Time is Unlawful ............................ 190
   The Wife cannot be taken back after the Third Divorce .................................. 191
   The Curse on the Participants of Tahlil/Halalah ................................................ 192
   When does a Woman who was divorced Three Times become Eligible for Her
   First Husband ........................................................................................................ 193

## Surah: 2 Ayah: 231 ............................................................................................ 193
Tafsir Ibn Kathir ................................................................................................ 194
   Being Kind to the Divorced Wife ........................................................................ 194

## Surah: 2 Ayah: 232 ............................................................................................ 195

## Table of Contents

- Tafsir Ibn Kathir .................... 195
  - The Wali (Guardian) of the Divorced Woman should not prevent Her from going back to Her Husband .................... 195
  - There is no Marriage without a Wali (for the Woman) .................... 196
  - The Reason behind revealing the Ayah (2:232) .................... 196
- *Surah: 2 Ayah: 233* .................... *197*
  - Tafsir Ibn Kathir .................... 198
    - The Suckling Period is only Two Years .................... 198
    - Suckling beyond the Two Years .................... 199
    - Suckling for Monetary Compensation .................... 200
    - No Darar (Harm) or Dirar (Revenge) .................... 200
    - Fitam (weaning) occurs by Mutual Consent .................... 201
- *Surah: 2 Ayah: 234* .................... *202*
  - Tafsir Ibn Kathir .................... 202
    - The `Iddah (Waiting Period) of the Widow .................... 202
    - The Wisdom behind legislating the `Iddah .................... 203
    - The `Iddah of the Slave Mother whose Master dies .................... 203
    - Mourning is required during the `Iddah of Death .................... 204
- *Surah: 2 Ayah: 235* .................... *205*
  - Tafsir Ibn Kathir .................... 206
    - Mentioning Marriage indirectly during the `Iddah .................... 206
- *Surah: 2 Ayah: 236* .................... *208*
  - Tafsir Ibn Kathir .................... 208
    - Divorce before consummating the Marriage .................... 208
    - The Mut`ah (Gift) at the time of Divorce .................... 208
- *Surah: 2 Ayah: 237* .................... *208*
  - Tafsir Ibn Kathir .................... 209
    - The Wife gets half of Her Mahr if She is divorced before the Marriage is consummated .................... 209
- *Surah: 2 Ayah: 238 & Ayah: 239* .................... *210*
  - Tafsir Ibn Kathir .................... 211
    - The Middle Prayer .................... 211
    - The Proof that the `Asr Prayer is the Middle Prayer .................... 212
    - The Prohibition of speaking during the Prayer .................... 214
    - The Fear Prayer .................... 214
    - Prayer during the Times of Peace is performed normally .................... 215
- *Surah: 2 Ayah: 240, Ayah: 241 & Ayah: 242* .................... *216*
  - Tafsir Ibn Kathir .................... 217
    - Ayah (2:240) was abrogated .................... 217
    - The Necessity of the Mut`ah (Gift) at the Time of Divorce .................... 219
- *Surah: 2 Ayah: 243, Ayah: 244 & Ayah: 245* .................... *220*
  - Ibn Kathir's Tafsir .................... 221
    - The Story of the Dead People .................... 221
    - Abandoning Jihad does not alter Destiny .................... 222

The Good Loan and its Reward ................................................................ 223
*Surah: 2 Ayah: 246* ..................................................................................... 224
    Ibn Kathir's Tafsir ................................................................................. 225
        The Story of the Jews Who sought a King to be appointed over Them ............. 225
*Surah: 2 Ayah: 247* ..................................................................................... 226
    Ibn Kathir's Tafsir ................................................................................. 226
*Surah: 2 Ayah: 248* ..................................................................................... 227
    Ibn Kathir's Tafsir ................................................................................. 227
*Surah: 2 Ayah: 249* ..................................................................................... 228
    Ibn Kathir's Tafsir ................................................................................. 229
*Surah: 2 Ayah: 250, Ayah: 251 & Ayah: 252* ............................................... 230
    Ibn Kathir's Tafsir ................................................................................. 231
    Ibn Kathir's Tafsir ................................................................................. 232
        Neither Repentance of the Disbeliever Upon Death, Nor His Ransoming Himself on the Day of Resurrection Shall be Accepted ................................................ 232

# PRELUDE

## Opening Serman

Indeed, all praise is due to Allah. We praise Him and seek His help and forgiveness. We seek refuge with Allah from our soul's evil and our wrong doings. He whom Allah guides, no one can misguide; and he whom He misguides, no one can guide

I bear witness that there is no (true) god except Allah – alone without a partner, and I bear witness that Muhammad (peace and blessings of Allah be upon him) is His 'abd (servant) and messenger.

يَـٰٓأَيُّهَا ٱلَّذِينَ ءَامَنُواْ ٱتَّقُواْ ٱللَّهَ حَقَّ تُقَاتِهِۦ وَلَا تَمُوتُنَّ إِلَّا وَأَنتُم مُّسۡلِمُونَ

O you who believe! Fear Allâh (by doing all that He has ordered and by abstaining from all that He has forbidden) as He should be feared. (Obey Him, be thankful to Him, and remember Him always), and die not except in a state of Islâm (as Muslims (with complete submission to Allâh)).

يَـٰٓأَيُّهَا ٱلنَّاسُ ٱتَّقُواْ رَبَّكُمُ ٱلَّذِى خَلَقَكُم مِّن نَّفۡسٍ وَٰحِدَةٍ وَخَلَقَ مِنۡهَا زَوۡجَهَا وَبَثَّ مِنۡهُمَا رِجَالًا كَثِيرًا وَنِسَآءً ۚ وَٱتَّقُواْ ٱللَّهَ ٱلَّذِى تَسَآءَلُونَ بِهِۦ وَٱلۡأَرۡحَامَ ۚ إِنَّ ٱللَّهَ كَانَ عَلَيۡكُمۡ رَقِيبًا

O mankind! Be dutiful to your Lord, Who created you from a single person (Adam), and from him (Adam) He created his wife (Hawwâ (Eve)) and from them both He created many men and women; and fear Allâh through Whom you demand (your mutual rights), and (do not cut the relations of) the wombs (kinship). Surely, Allâh is Ever an All-Watcher over you.

يُصۡلِحۡ لَكُمۡ أَعۡمَـٰلَكُمۡ وَيَغۡفِرۡ لَكُمۡ ذُنُوبَكُمۡ ۗ وَمَن يُطِعِ ٱللَّهَ وَرَسُولَهُۥ  فَقَدۡ فَازَ فَوۡزًا عَظِيمًا

He will direct you to do righteous good deeds and will forgive you your sins. And whosoever obeys Allâh and His Messenger (peace be upon him), he has indeed achieved a great achievement (i.e. he will be saved from the Hell-fire and will be admitted to Paradise).

Indeed, the best speech is Allah's Book and the best guidance is Muhammad's () guidance. The worst affairs (of religion) are those innovated (by people), for every such innovation is an act of misguidance leading to the Fire

## Our Mission

Our mission is to gather in one place, for the English-speaking public, all relevant information needed to make the Qur'an more understandable and easier to study. This book tries to do this by providing the following:

1. The Arabic Text for those who are able to read Arabic
2. Transliteration of the Arabic text for those who are unable to read the Arabic script. This will give them a sample of the sound of the Qur'an, which they could not otherwise comprehend from reading the English meaning.
3. The meaning of the qur'an (translated by Dr. Muhammad Taqi-ud-Din Al-Hilali, Ph.D. and Dr. Muhammad Muhsin Khan)
4. Explanation (abridged Tafsir) by Ibn Kathir (translated by Safi-ur-Rahman al-Mubarakpuri)

We hope that by doing this an ordinary English-speaker will be able to pick up a copy of this book and study and comprehend The Glorious Qur'an in a way that is acceptable to the understanding of the Rightly-guided Muslim Ummah (Community).

## Biography of Hafiz Ibn Kathir
## (701 H - 774 H)

By the Honored Shaykh `Abdul-Qadir Al-Arna'ut, may Allah protect him.

He is the respected Imam, Abu Al-Fida', `Imad Ad-Din Isma il bin 'Umar bin Kathir Al-Qurashi Al-Busrawi - Busraian in origin; Dimashqi in training, learning and residence.

Ibn Kathir was born in the city of Busra in 701 H. His father was the Friday speaker of the village, but he died while Ibn Kathir was only four years old. Ibn Kathir's brother, Shaykh Abdul-Wahhab, reared him and taught him until he moved to Damascus in 706 H., when he was five years old.

### Ibn Kathir's Teachers

Ibn Kathir studied Fiqh - Islamic jurisprudence - with Burhan Ad-Din, Ibrahim bin `Abdur-Rahman Al-Fizari, known as Ibn Al-Firkah (who died in 729 H). Ibn Kathir heard Hadiths from `Isa bin Al-Mutim, Ahmad bin Abi Talib, (Ibn Ash-Shahnah) (who died in 730 H), Ibn Al-Hajjar, (who died in 730 H), and the Hadith narrator of Ash-Sham (modern day Syria and surrounding areas); Baha

Ad-Din Al-Qasim bin Muzaffar bin `Asakir (who died in 723 H), and Ibn Ash-Shirdzi, Ishaq bin Yahya Al-Ammuddi, also known as `Afif Ad-Din, the Zahiriyyah Shaykh who died in 725 H, and Muhammad bin Zarrad. He remained with Jamal Ad-Din, Yusuf bin Az-Zaki AlMizzi who died in 724 H, he benefited from his knowledge and also married his daughter. He also read with Shaykh Al-Islam, Taqi Ad-Din Ahmad bin `Abdul-Halim bin `Abdus-Salam bin Taymiyyah who died in 728 H. He also read with the Imam Hafiz and historian Shams Ad-Din, Muhammad bin Ahmad bin Uthman bin Qaymaz Adh-Dhahabi, who died in 748 H. Also, Abu Musa Al-Qarafai, Abu Al-Fath Ad-Dabbusi and 'Ali bin `Umar As-Suwani and others who gave him permission to transmit the knowledge he learned with them in Egypt.

In his book, Al-Mu jam Al-Mukhtas, Al-Hafiz Adh-Dhaliabi wrote that Ibn Kathir was, "The Imam, scholar of jurisprudence, skillful scholar of Hadith, renowned Faqih and scholar of Tafsir who wrote several beneficial books."

Further, in Ad-Durar Al-Kdminah, Al-Hafiz Ibn Hajar AlAsqalani said, "Ibn Kathir worked on the subject of the Hadith in the areas of texts and chains of narrators. He had a good memory, his books became popular during his lifetime, and people benefited from them after his death."

Also, the renowned historian Abu Al-Mahasin, Jamal Ad-Din Yusuf bin Sayf Ad-Din (Ibn Taghri Bardi), said in his book, AlManhal As-Safi, "He is the Shaykh, the Imam, the great scholar `Imad Ad-Din Abu Al-Fida'. He learned extensively and was very active in collecting knowledge and writing. He was excellent in the areas of Fiqh, Tafsfr and Hadith. He collected knowledge, authored (books), taught, narrated Hadith and wrote. He had immense knowledge in the fields of Hadith, Tafsir, Fiqh, the Arabic language, and so forth. He gave Fatawa (religious verdicts) and taught until he died, may Allah grant him mercy. He was known for his precision and vast knowledge, and as a scholar of history, Hadith and Tafsir."

## Ibn Kathir's Students

Ibn Hajji was one of Ibn Kathir's students, and he described Ibn Kathir: "He had the best memory of the Hadith texts. He also had the most knowledge concerning the narrators and authenticity, his contemporaries and teachers admitted to these qualities. Every time I met him I gained some benefit from him."

Also, Ibn Al-`Imad Al-Hanbali said in his book, Shadhardt Adh-Dhahab, "He is the renowned Hafiz `Imad Ad-Din, whose memory was excellent, whose forgetfulness was miniscule, whose understanding was adequate, and who had good knowledge in the Arabic language." Also, Ibn Habib said about Ibn Kathir, "He heard knowledge and collected it and wrote various books. He brought comfort to the ears with his Fatwas and narrated Hadith and brought benefit to other people. The papers that contained his Fatwas were transmitted to the various (Islamic) provinces. Further, he was known for his precision and encompassing knowledge."

**Ibn Kathir's Books**

1 - One of the greatest books that Ibn Kathir wrote was his Tafsir of the Noble Qur'an, which is one of the best Tafsir that rely on narrations [of Ahadith, the Tafsir of the Companions, etc.]. The Tafsir by Ibn Kathir was printed many times and several scholars have summarized it.

2- The History Collection known as Al-Biddyah, which was printed in 14 volumes under the name Al-Bidayah wanNihdyah, and contained the stories of the Prophets and previous nations, the Prophet's Seerah (life story) and Islamic history until his time. He also added a book Al-Fitan, about the Signs of the Last Hour.

3- At-Takmil ft Ma`rifat Ath-Thiqat wa Ad-Du'afa wal Majdhil which Ibn Kathir collected from the books of his two Shaykhs Al-Mizzi and Adh-Dhahabi; Al-Kdmal and Mizan Al-Ftiddl. He added several benefits regarding the subject of Al-Jarh and AtT'adil.

4- Al-Hadi was-Sunan ft Ahadith Al-Masdnfd was-Sunan which is also known by, Jami` Al-Masdnfd. In this book, Ibn Kathir collected the narrations of Imams Ahmad bin Hanbal, Al-Bazzar, Abu Ya`la Al-Mawsili, Ibn Abi Shaybah and from the six collections of Hadith: the Two Sahihs [Al-Bukhari and Muslim] and the Four Sunan [Abu Dawud, At-Tirmidhi, AnNasa and Ibn Majah]. Ibn Kathir divided this book according to areas of Fiqh.

5-Tabaqat Ash-Shaf iyah which also contains the virtues of Imam Ash-Shafi.

6- Ibn Kathir wrote references for the Ahadith of Adillat AtTanbfh, from the Shafi school of Fiqh.

7- Ibn Kathir began an explanation of Sahih Al-Bukhari, but he did not finish it.

8- He started writing a large volume on the Ahkam (Laws), but finished only up to the Hajj rituals.

9- He summarized Al-Bayhaqi's 'Al-Madkhal. Many of these books were not printed.

10- He summarized `Ulum Al-Hadith, by Abu `Amr bin AsSalah and called it Mukhtasar `Ulum Al-Hadith. Shaykh Ahmad Shakir, the Egyptian Muhaddith, printed this book along with his commentary on it and called it Al-Ba'th Al-Hathfth fi Sharh Mukhtasar `Ulum Al-Hadith.

11- As-Sfrah An-Nabawiyyah, which is contained in his book Al-Biddyah, and both of these books are in print.

12- A research on Jihad called Al-Ijtihad ft Talabi Al-Jihad, which was printed several times.

**Ibn Kathir's Death**

Al-Hafiz Ibn Hajar Al-Asgalani said, "Ibn Kathir lost his sight just before his life ended. He died in Damascus in 774 H." May Allah grant mercy upon Ibn Kathir and make him among the residents of His Paradise.

# PREFACE

In the name of Allah, Most Gracious, Most Merciful.

## About this book

The previous publication of this book included some background information to the chapters of the Qur'an by an Islamic scholar known as Abul Ala Maududi. This information was used to shed more light on the chapters by giving a summery of why each chapter was given its name, It's period of revelation and the circumstances surrounding its revelatiom. However, some Muslims objected to the inclusion of the contributions of Maududi.

In this new publication of Tafsir Ibn Kathir, we have removed all traces of the contribution of Abul Ala Maududi. Personally, I do not know the reasons for the objections to Maududi, but this work concerns only the tafsir of Ibn Kathir, so we have not included anything from Maududi in it. We have also corrected all the typing and formatting errors found in the previous publication. We have not alter the structure of the book. The reader is still able to read the full Arabic Text of the thirty Parts of the Qur'an and follow its meanings in the English language. The transliteration of the Arabic text should also give the reader a taste of the sound of the original Arabic.

May Almighty Allah accept this effort from us, and make it a source of blessings for us in this world and in the next. I bear witness that there is none worthy of worship but Allah and I bear witness that Muhammad ( may the peace and blessings of Allah be upon him) is the slave and messenger of Allah.

## Performing Prostration While Reading the Qur'an

Question:

Could you please give a list of the Qur'anic verses when a prostration is recommended? What happens if we read these verses and not perform a prostration?

A. Jalil

Answer:

There are 15 verses in the Qur'an that mention prostration before God Almighty as a good action by God-fearing believers. Therefore, it is strongly recommended to perform such a prostration when we read or listen to any of these verses, whether during prayer or in any situation.

Some scholars are of the view that even if one has not performed ablution, one should prostrate oneself. These verses are given here, starting with the Arabic title of the surah which is followed by two numbers, the first indicating the surah, and the second indicating the verse,: Al-Araf 7: 206; Al-Raad 13: 15; Al-Nahl 16: 50; Al-Isra 17: 109; Maryam 19: 58; Al-Hajj 22: 18 & 22: 77; Al-Furqan 25: 60; Al-Naml 27: 26; Al-Sajdah 32: 15; Saad 38: 25; Fussilat 41: 38; Al-Najm 53: 62; Al-Inshiqaq 84: 21 and Al-Alaq 96: 19.

If you do not perform a prostration when you read or listen to any of these verses, you have done badly because you miss out on the reward of performing a prostration for God. You incur no sin and violate no divine order.

Reference:
http://archive.arabnews.com/?page=5&section=0&article=97811&d=1&m=7&y=2007

# Tafsir Ibn Kathir Juz' 2 (Part 2): Chapter (Surah) 2: Al-Baqarah (The Cow) 142 To Chapter (Surah) 2: Al-Baqarah (The Cow) 252

**PART 2 FULL ARABIC TEXT**

## Chapter (Surah) 2: Al-Baqarah 142-252

۞ سَيَقُولُ ٱلسُّفَهَآءُ مِنَ ٱلنَّاسِ مَا وَلَّىٰهُمْ عَن قِبْلَتِهِمُ ٱلَّتِى كَانُواْ عَلَيْهَا ۚ قُل لِّلَّهِ ٱلْمَشْرِقُ وَٱلْمَغْرِبُ ۚ يَهْدِى مَن يَشَآءُ إِلَىٰ صِرَٰطٍ مُّسْتَقِيمٍ ۝ وَكَذَٰلِكَ جَعَلْنَٰكُمْ أُمَّةً وَسَطًا لِّتَكُونُواْ شُهَدَآءَ عَلَى ٱلنَّاسِ وَيَكُونَ ٱلرَّسُولُ عَلَيْكُمْ شَهِيدًا ۗ وَمَا جَعَلْنَا ٱلْقِبْلَةَ ٱلَّتِى كُنتَ عَلَيْهَآ إِلَّا لِنَعْلَمَ مَن يَتَّبِعُ ٱلرَّسُولَ مِمَّن يَنقَلِبُ عَلَىٰ عَقِبَيْهِ ۚ وَإِن كَانَتْ لَكَبِيرَةً إِلَّا عَلَى ٱلَّذِينَ هَدَى ٱللَّهُ ۗ وَمَا كَانَ ٱللَّهُ لِيُضِيعَ إِيمَٰنَكُمْ ۚ إِنَّ ٱللَّهَ بِٱلنَّاسِ لَرَءُوفٌ رَّحِيمٌ ۝ قَدْ نَرَىٰ تَقَلُّبَ وَجْهِكَ فِى ٱلسَّمَآءِ ۖ فَلَنُوَلِّيَنَّكَ قِبْلَةً تَرْضَىٰهَا ۚ فَوَلِّ وَجْهَكَ شَطْرَ ٱلْمَسْجِدِ ٱلْحَرَامِ ۚ وَحَيْثُ مَا كُنتُمْ فَوَلُّواْ وُجُوهَكُمْ شَطْرَهُۥ ۗ وَإِنَّ ٱلَّذِينَ أُوتُواْ ٱلْكِتَٰبَ لَيَعْلَمُونَ أَنَّهُ ٱلْحَقُّ مِن رَّبِّهِمْ ۗ وَمَا ٱللَّهُ بِغَٰفِلٍ عَمَّا يَعْمَلُونَ ۝ وَلَئِنْ أَتَيْتَ ٱلَّذِينَ أُوتُواْ ٱلْكِتَٰبَ بِكُلِّ ءَايَةٍ مَّا تَبِعُواْ قِبْلَتَكَ ۚ وَمَآ أَنتَ بِتَابِعٍ قِبْلَتَهُمْ ۚ وَمَا بَعْضُهُم بِتَابِعٍ قِبْلَةَ بَعْضٍ ۚ وَلَئِنِ ٱتَّبَعْتَ أَهْوَآءَهُم مِّنۢ بَعْدِ مَا جَآءَكَ مِنَ ٱلْعِلْمِ ۙ إِنَّكَ إِذًا لَّمِنَ ٱلظَّٰلِمِينَ ۝ ٱلَّذِينَ ءَاتَيْنَٰهُمُ ٱلْكِتَٰبَ يَعْرِفُونَهُۥ كَمَا يَعْرِفُونَ أَبْنَآءَهُمْ ۖ وَإِنَّ فَرِيقًا مِّنْهُمْ لَيَكْتُمُونَ ٱلْحَقَّ وَهُمْ يَعْلَمُونَ ۝ ٱلْحَقُّ مِن رَّبِّكَ ۖ فَلَا تَكُونَنَّ مِنَ ٱلْمُمْتَرِينَ

۞ وَلِكُلٍّ وِجْهَةٌ هُوَ مُوَلِّيهَا ۖ فَٱسْتَبِقُوا۟ ٱلْخَيْرَٰتِ ۚ أَيْنَ مَا تَكُونُوا۟ يَأْتِ بِكُمُ ٱللَّهُ جَمِيعًا ۚ إِنَّ ٱللَّهَ عَلَىٰ كُلِّ شَىْءٍ قَدِيرٌ ۝ وَمِنْ حَيْثُ خَرَجْتَ فَوَلِّ وَجْهَكَ شَطْرَ ٱلْمَسْجِدِ ٱلْحَرَامِ ۖ وَإِنَّهُ لَلْحَقُّ مِن رَّبِّكَ ۗ وَمَا ٱللَّهُ بِغَٰفِلٍ عَمَّا تَعْمَلُونَ ۝ وَمِنْ حَيْثُ خَرَجْتَ فَوَلِّ وَجْهَكَ شَطْرَ ٱلْمَسْجِدِ ٱلْحَرَامِ ۚ وَحَيْثُ مَا كُنتُمْ فَوَلُّوا۟ وُجُوهَكُمْ شَطْرَهُۥ لِئَلَّا يَكُونَ لِلنَّاسِ عَلَيْكُمْ حُجَّةٌ إِلَّا ٱلَّذِينَ ظَلَمُوا۟ مِنْهُمْ فَلَا تَخْشَوْهُمْ وَٱخْشَوْنِى وَلِأُتِمَّ نِعْمَتِى عَلَيْكُمْ وَلَعَلَّكُمْ تَهْتَدُونَ ۝ كَمَا أَرْسَلْنَا فِيكُمْ رَسُولًا مِّنكُمْ يَتْلُوا۟ عَلَيْكُمْ ءَايَٰتِنَا وَيُزَكِّيكُمْ وَيُعَلِّمُكُمُ ٱلْكِتَٰبَ وَٱلْحِكْمَةَ وَيُعَلِّمُكُم مَّا لَمْ تَكُونُوا۟ تَعْلَمُونَ ۝ فَٱذْكُرُونِى أَذْكُرْكُمْ وَٱشْكُرُوا۟ لِى وَلَا تَكْفُرُونِ ۝ يَٰٓأَيُّهَا ٱلَّذِينَ ءَامَنُوا۟ ٱسْتَعِينُوا۟ بِٱلصَّبْرِ وَٱلصَّلَوٰةِ ۚ إِنَّ ٱللَّهَ مَعَ ٱلصَّٰبِرِينَ ۝ وَلَا تَقُولُوا۟ لِمَن يُقْتَلُ فِى سَبِيلِ ٱللَّهِ أَمْوَٰتٌۢ ۚ بَلْ أَحْيَآءٌ وَلَٰكِن لَّا تَشْعُرُونَ ۝ وَلَنَبْلُوَنَّكُم بِشَىْءٍ مِّنَ ٱلْخَوْفِ وَٱلْجُوعِ وَنَقْصٍ مِّنَ ٱلْأَمْوَٰلِ وَٱلْأَنفُسِ وَٱلثَّمَرَٰتِ ۗ وَبَشِّرِ ٱلصَّٰبِرِينَ ۝ ٱلَّذِينَ إِذَآ أَصَٰبَتْهُم مُّصِيبَةٌ قَالُوٓا۟ إِنَّا لِلَّهِ وَإِنَّآ إِلَيْهِ رَٰجِعُونَ ۝ أُو۟لَٰٓئِكَ عَلَيْهِمْ صَلَوَٰتٌ مِّن رَّبِّهِمْ وَرَحْمَةٌ ۖ وَأُو۟لَٰٓئِكَ هُمُ ٱلْمُهْتَدُونَ ۝ ۞ إِنَّ ٱلصَّفَا وَٱلْمَرْوَةَ مِن شَعَآئِرِ ٱللَّهِ ۖ فَمَنْ حَجَّ ٱلْبَيْتَ أَوِ ٱعْتَمَرَ فَلَا جُنَاحَ عَلَيْهِ أَن يَطَّوَّفَ بِهِمَا ۚ وَمَن تَطَوَّعَ خَيْرًا فَإِنَّ ٱللَّهَ شَاكِرٌ عَلِيمٌ ۝ إِنَّ ٱلَّذِينَ يَكْتُمُونَ مَآ أَنزَلْنَا مِنَ ٱلْبَيِّنَٰتِ وَٱلْهُدَىٰ مِنۢ بَعْدِ مَا بَيَّنَّٰهُ لِلنَّاسِ فِى ٱلْكِتَٰبِ ۙ أُو۟لَٰٓئِكَ يَلْعَنُهُمُ ٱللَّهُ وَيَلْعَنُهُمُ ٱللَّٰعِنُونَ ۝ إِلَّا ٱلَّذِينَ تَابُوا۟ وَأَصْلَحُوا۟ وَبَيَّنُوا۟ فَأُو۟لَٰٓئِكَ أَتُوبُ عَلَيْهِمْ ۚ وَأَنَا ٱلتَّوَّابُ ٱلرَّحِيمُ ۝ إِنَّ ٱلَّذِينَ كَفَرُوا۟ وَمَاتُوا۟ وَهُمْ

كُفَّارٌ أُولَٰئِكَ عَلَيْهِمْ لَعْنَةُ ٱللَّهِ وَٱلْمَلَٰئِكَةِ وَٱلنَّاسِ أَجْمَعِينَ ۝ خَٰلِدِينَ فِيهَا ۖ لَا يُخَفَّفُ عَنْهُمُ ٱلْعَذَابُ وَلَا هُمْ يُنظَرُونَ ۝ وَإِلَٰهُكُمْ إِلَٰهٌ وَٰحِدٌ ۖ لَّآ إِلَٰهَ إِلَّا هُوَ ٱلرَّحْمَٰنُ ٱلرَّحِيمُ ۝ إِنَّ فِى خَلْقِ ٱلسَّمَٰوَٰتِ وَٱلْأَرْضِ وَٱخْتِلَٰفِ ٱلَّيْلِ وَٱلنَّهَارِ وَٱلْفُلْكِ ٱلَّتِى تَجْرِى فِى ٱلْبَحْرِ بِمَا يَنفَعُ ٱلنَّاسَ وَمَآ أَنزَلَ ٱللَّهُ مِنَ ٱلسَّمَآءِ مِن مَّآءٍ فَأَحْيَا بِهِ ٱلْأَرْضَ بَعْدَ مَوْتِهَا وَبَثَّ فِيهَا مِن كُلِّ دَآبَّةٍ وَتَصْرِيفِ ٱلرِّيَٰحِ وَٱلسَّحَابِ ٱلْمُسَخَّرِ بَيْنَ ٱلسَّمَآءِ وَٱلْأَرْضِ لَءَايَٰتٍ لِّقَوْمٍ يَعْقِلُونَ ۝ وَمِنَ ٱلنَّاسِ مَن يَتَّخِذُ مِن دُونِ ٱللَّهِ أَندَادًا يُحِبُّونَهُمْ كَحُبِّ ٱللَّهِ ۖ وَٱلَّذِينَ ءَامَنُوٓا۟ أَشَدُّ حُبًّا لِّلَّهِ ۗ وَلَوْ يَرَى ٱلَّذِينَ ظَلَمُوٓا۟ إِذْ يَرَوْنَ ٱلْعَذَابَ أَنَّ ٱلْقُوَّةَ لِلَّهِ جَمِيعًا وَأَنَّ ٱللَّهَ شَدِيدُ ٱلْعَذَابِ ۝ إِذْ تَبَرَّأَ ٱلَّذِينَ ٱتُّبِعُوا۟ مِنَ ٱلَّذِينَ ٱتَّبَعُوا۟ وَرَأَوُا۟ ٱلْعَذَابَ وَتَقَطَّعَتْ بِهِمُ ٱلْأَسْبَابُ ۝ وَقَالَ ٱلَّذِينَ ٱتَّبَعُوا۟ لَوْ أَنَّ لَنَا كَرَّةً فَنَتَبَرَّأَ مِنْهُمْ كَمَا تَبَرَّءُوا۟ مِنَّا ۗ كَذَٰلِكَ يُرِيهِمُ ٱللَّهُ أَعْمَٰلَهُمْ حَسَرَٰتٍ عَلَيْهِمْ ۖ وَمَا هُم بِخَٰرِجِينَ مِنَ ٱلنَّارِ ۝ يَٰٓأَيُّهَا ٱلنَّاسُ كُلُوا۟ مِمَّا فِى ٱلْأَرْضِ حَلَٰلًا طَيِّبًا وَلَا تَتَّبِعُوا۟ خُطُوَٰتِ ٱلشَّيْطَٰنِ ۚ إِنَّهُ لَكُمْ عَدُوٌّ مُّبِينٌ ۝ إِنَّمَا يَأْمُرُكُم بِٱلسُّوٓءِ وَٱلْفَحْشَآءِ وَأَن تَقُولُوا۟ عَلَى ٱللَّهِ مَا لَا تَعْلَمُونَ ۝ وَإِذَا قِيلَ لَهُمُ ٱتَّبِعُوا۟ مَآ أَنزَلَ ٱللَّهُ قَالُوا۟ بَلْ نَتَّبِعُ مَآ أَلْفَيْنَا عَلَيْهِ ءَابَآءَنَآ ۗ أَوَلَوْ كَانَ ءَابَآؤُهُمْ لَا يَعْقِلُونَ شَيْئًا وَلَا يَهْتَدُونَ ۝ وَمَثَلُ ٱلَّذِينَ كَفَرُوا۟ كَمَثَلِ ٱلَّذِى يَنْعِقُ بِمَا لَا يَسْمَعُ إِلَّا دُعَآءً وَنِدَآءً ۚ صُمٌّ بُكْمٌ عُمْىٌ فَهُمْ لَا يَعْقِلُونَ ۝ يَٰٓأَيُّهَا ٱلَّذِينَ ءَامَنُوا۟ كُلُوا۟ مِن طَيِّبَٰتِ مَا رَزَقْنَٰكُمْ وَٱشْكُرُوا۟ لِلَّهِ إِن كُنتُمْ إِيَّاهُ تَعْبُدُونَ ۝ إِنَّمَا حَرَّمَ عَلَيْكُمُ ٱلْمَيْتَةَ وَٱلدَّمَ وَلَحْمَ ٱلْخِنزِيرِ وَمَآ

أُهِلَّ بِهِ لِغَيْرِ ٱللَّهِ ۖ فَمَنِ ٱضْطُرَّ غَيْرَ بَاغٍ وَلَا عَادٍ فَلَا إِثْمَ عَلَيْهِ ۚ إِنَّ ٱللَّهَ غَفُورٌ رَّحِيمٌ ۝ إِنَّ ٱلَّذِينَ يَكْتُمُونَ مَآ أَنزَلَ ٱللَّهُ مِنَ ٱلْكِتَٰبِ وَيَشْتَرُونَ بِهِۦ ثَمَنًا قَلِيلًا ۙ أُو۟لَٰٓئِكَ مَا يَأْكُلُونَ فِى بُطُونِهِمْ إِلَّا ٱلنَّارَ وَلَا يُكَلِّمُهُمُ ٱللَّهُ يَوْمَ ٱلْقِيَٰمَةِ وَلَا يُزَكِّيهِمْ وَلَهُمْ عَذَابٌ أَلِيمٌ ۝ أُو۟لَٰٓئِكَ ٱلَّذِينَ ٱشْتَرَوُا۟ ٱلضَّلَٰلَةَ بِٱلْهُدَىٰ وَٱلْعَذَابَ بِٱلْمَغْفِرَةِ ۚ فَمَآ أَصْبَرَهُمْ عَلَى ٱلنَّارِ ۝ ذَٰلِكَ بِأَنَّ ٱللَّهَ نَزَّلَ ٱلْكِتَٰبَ بِٱلْحَقِّ ۗ وَإِنَّ ٱلَّذِينَ ٱخْتَلَفُوا۟ فِى ٱلْكِتَٰبِ لَفِى شِقَاقٍ بَعِيدٍ ۝ ۞ لَّيْسَ ٱلْبِرَّ أَن تُوَلُّوا۟ وُجُوهَكُمْ قِبَلَ ٱلْمَشْرِقِ وَٱلْمَغْرِبِ وَلَٰكِنَّ ٱلْبِرَّ مَنْ ءَامَنَ بِٱللَّهِ وَٱلْيَوْمِ ٱلْءَاخِرِ وَٱلْمَلَٰٓئِكَةِ وَٱلْكِتَٰبِ وَٱلنَّبِيِّـۧنَ وَءَاتَى ٱلْمَالَ عَلَىٰ حُبِّهِۦ ذَوِى ٱلْقُرْبَىٰ وَٱلْيَتَٰمَىٰ وَٱلْمَسَٰكِينَ وَٱبْنَ ٱلسَّبِيلِ وَٱلسَّآئِلِينَ وَفِى ٱلرِّقَابِ وَأَقَامَ ٱلصَّلَوٰةَ وَءَاتَى ٱلزَّكَوٰةَ وَٱلْمُوفُونَ بِعَهْدِهِمْ إِذَا عَٰهَدُوا۟ ۖ وَٱلصَّٰبِرِينَ فِى ٱلْبَأْسَآءِ وَٱلضَّرَّآءِ وَحِينَ ٱلْبَأْسِ ۗ أُو۟لَٰٓئِكَ ٱلَّذِينَ صَدَقُوا۟ ۖ وَأُو۟لَٰٓئِكَ هُمُ ٱلْمُتَّقُونَ ۝ يَٰٓأَيُّهَا ٱلَّذِينَ ءَامَنُوا۟ كُتِبَ عَلَيْكُمُ ٱلْقِصَاصُ فِى ٱلْقَتْلَى ۖ ٱلْحُرُّ بِٱلْحُرِّ وَٱلْعَبْدُ بِٱلْعَبْدِ وَٱلْأُنثَىٰ بِٱلْأُنثَىٰ ۚ فَمَنْ عُفِىَ لَهُۥ مِنْ أَخِيهِ شَىْءٌ فَٱتِّبَاعٌۢ بِٱلْمَعْرُوفِ وَأَدَآءٌ إِلَيْهِ بِإِحْسَٰنٍ ۗ ذَٰلِكَ تَخْفِيفٌ مِّن رَّبِّكُمْ وَرَحْمَةٌ ۗ فَمَنِ ٱعْتَدَىٰ بَعْدَ ذَٰلِكَ فَلَهُۥ عَذَابٌ أَلِيمٌ ۝ وَلَكُمْ فِى ٱلْقِصَاصِ حَيَوٰةٌ يَٰٓأُو۟لِى ٱلْأَلْبَٰبِ لَعَلَّكُمْ تَتَّقُونَ ۝ كُتِبَ عَلَيْكُمْ إِذَا حَضَرَ أَحَدَكُمُ ٱلْمَوْتُ إِن تَرَكَ خَيْرًا ٱلْوَصِيَّةُ لِلْوَٰلِدَيْنِ وَٱلْأَقْرَبِينَ بِٱلْمَعْرُوفِ ۖ حَقًّا عَلَى ٱلْمُتَّقِينَ ۝ فَمَنۢ بَدَّلَهُۥ بَعْدَمَا سَمِعَهُۥ فَإِنَّمَآ إِثْمُهُۥ عَلَى ٱلَّذِينَ يُبَدِّلُونَهُۥٓ ۚ إِنَّ ٱللَّهَ سَمِيعٌ عَلِيمٌ ۝ فَمَنْ خَافَ مِن مُّوصٍ جَنَفًا أَوْ إِثْمًا فَأَصْلَحَ بَيْنَهُمْ فَلَآ إِثْمَ عَلَيْهِ ۚ إِنَّ ٱللَّهَ

غَفُورٌ رَّحِيمٌ ۝ يَـٰٓأَيُّهَا ٱلَّذِينَ ءَامَنُوا۟ كُتِبَ عَلَيْكُمُ ٱلصِّيَامُ كَمَا كُتِبَ عَلَى ٱلَّذِينَ مِن قَبْلِكُمْ لَعَلَّكُمْ تَتَّقُونَ ۝ أَيَّامًا مَّعْدُودَٰتٍ ۚ فَمَن كَانَ مِنكُم مَّرِيضًا أَوْ عَلَىٰ سَفَرٍ فَعِدَّةٌ مِّنْ أَيَّامٍ أُخَرَ ۚ وَعَلَى ٱلَّذِينَ يُطِيقُونَهُۥ فِدْيَةٌ طَعَامُ مِسْكِينٍ ۖ فَمَن تَطَوَّعَ خَيْرًا فَهُوَ خَيْرٌ لَّهُۥ ۚ وَأَن تَصُومُوا۟ خَيْرٌ لَّكُمْ ۖ إِن كُنتُمْ تَعْلَمُونَ ۝ شَهْرُ رَمَضَانَ ٱلَّذِىٓ أُنزِلَ فِيهِ ٱلْقُرْءَانُ هُدًى لِّلنَّاسِ وَبَيِّنَـٰتٍ مِّنَ ٱلْهُدَىٰ وَٱلْفُرْقَانِ ۚ فَمَن شَهِدَ مِنكُمُ ٱلشَّهْرَ فَلْيَصُمْهُ ۖ وَمَن كَانَ مَرِيضًا أَوْ عَلَىٰ سَفَرٍ فَعِدَّةٌ مِّنْ أَيَّامٍ أُخَرَ ۗ يُرِيدُ ٱللَّهُ بِكُمُ ٱلْيُسْرَ وَلَا يُرِيدُ بِكُمُ ٱلْعُسْرَ وَلِتُكْمِلُوا۟ ٱلْعِدَّةَ وَلِتُكَبِّرُوا۟ ٱللَّهَ عَلَىٰ مَا هَدَىٰكُمْ وَلَعَلَّكُمْ تَشْكُرُونَ ۝ وَإِذَا سَأَلَكَ عِبَادِى عَنِّى فَإِنِّى قَرِيبٌ ۖ أُجِيبُ دَعْوَةَ ٱلدَّاعِ إِذَا دَعَانِ ۖ فَلْيَسْتَجِيبُوا۟ لِى وَلْيُؤْمِنُوا۟ بِى لَعَلَّهُمْ يَرْشُدُونَ ۝ أُحِلَّ لَكُمْ لَيْلَةَ ٱلصِّيَامِ ٱلرَّفَثُ إِلَىٰ نِسَآئِكُمْ ۚ هُنَّ لِبَاسٌ لَّكُمْ وَأَنتُمْ لِبَاسٌ لَّهُنَّ ۗ عَلِمَ ٱللَّهُ أَنَّكُمْ كُنتُمْ تَخْتَانُونَ أَنفُسَكُمْ فَتَابَ عَلَيْكُمْ وَعَفَا عَنكُمْ ۖ فَٱلْـَٔـٰنَ بَـٰشِرُوهُنَّ وَٱبْتَغُوا۟ مَا كَتَبَ ٱللَّهُ لَكُمْ ۚ وَكُلُوا۟ وَٱشْرَبُوا۟ حَتَّىٰ يَتَبَيَّنَ لَكُمُ ٱلْخَيْطُ ٱلْأَبْيَضُ مِنَ ٱلْخَيْطِ ٱلْأَسْوَدِ مِنَ ٱلْفَجْرِ ۖ ثُمَّ أَتِمُّوا۟ ٱلصِّيَامَ إِلَى ٱلَّيْلِ ۚ وَلَا تُبَـٰشِرُوهُنَّ وَأَنتُمْ عَـٰكِفُونَ فِى ٱلْمَسَـٰجِدِ ۗ تِلْكَ حُدُودُ ٱللَّهِ فَلَا تَقْرَبُوهَا ۗ كَذَٰلِكَ يُبَيِّنُ ٱللَّهُ ءَايَـٰتِهِۦ لِلنَّاسِ لَعَلَّهُمْ يَتَّقُونَ ۝ وَلَا تَأْكُلُوٓا۟ أَمْوَٰلَكُم بَيْنَكُم بِٱلْبَـٰطِلِ وَتُدْلُوا۟ بِهَآ إِلَى ٱلْحُكَّامِ لِتَأْكُلُوا۟ فَرِيقًا مِّنْ أَمْوَٰلِ ٱلنَّاسِ بِٱلْإِثْمِ وَأَنتُمْ تَعْلَمُونَ ۝ ۞ يَسْـَٔلُونَكَ عَنِ ٱلْأَهِلَّةِ ۖ قُلْ هِىَ مَوَٰقِيتُ لِلنَّاسِ وَٱلْحَجِّ ۗ وَلَيْسَ ٱلْبِرُّ بِأَن تَأْتُوا۟ ٱلْبُيُوتَ مِن ظُهُورِهَا وَلَـٰكِنَّ ٱلْبِرَّ مَنِ ٱتَّقَىٰ ۗ وَأْتُوا۟

ٱلْبُيُوتَ مِنْ أَبْوَٰبِهَا ۚ وَٱتَّقُوا۟ ٱللَّهَ لَعَلَّكُمْ تُفْلِحُونَ ۝ وَقَٰتِلُوا۟ فِى سَبِيلِ ٱللَّهِ ٱلَّذِينَ يُقَٰتِلُونَكُمْ وَلَا تَعْتَدُوٓا۟ ۚ إِنَّ ٱللَّهَ لَا يُحِبُّ ٱلْمُعْتَدِينَ ۝ وَٱقْتُلُوهُمْ حَيْثُ ثَقِفْتُمُوهُمْ وَأَخْرِجُوهُم مِّنْ حَيْثُ أَخْرَجُوكُمْ ۚ وَٱلْفِتْنَةُ أَشَدُّ مِنَ ٱلْقَتْلِ ۚ وَلَا تُقَٰتِلُوهُمْ عِندَ ٱلْمَسْجِدِ ٱلْحَرَامِ حَتَّىٰ يُقَٰتِلُوكُمْ فِيهِ ۖ فَإِن قَٰتَلُوكُمْ فَٱقْتُلُوهُمْ ۗ كَذَٰلِكَ جَزَآءُ ٱلْكَٰفِرِينَ ۝ فَإِنِ ٱنتَهَوْا۟ فَإِنَّ ٱللَّهَ غَفُورٌ رَّحِيمٌ ۝ وَقَٰتِلُوهُمْ حَتَّىٰ لَا تَكُونَ فِتْنَةٌ وَيَكُونَ ٱلدِّينُ لِلَّهِ ۖ فَإِنِ ٱنتَهَوْا۟ فَلَا عُدْوَٰنَ إِلَّا عَلَى ٱلظَّٰلِمِينَ ۝ ٱلشَّهْرُ ٱلْحَرَامُ بِٱلشَّهْرِ ٱلْحَرَامِ وَٱلْحُرُمَٰتُ قِصَاصٌ ۚ فَمَنِ ٱعْتَدَىٰ عَلَيْكُمْ فَٱعْتَدُوا۟ عَلَيْهِ بِمِثْلِ مَا ٱعْتَدَىٰ عَلَيْكُمْ ۚ وَٱتَّقُوا۟ ٱللَّهَ وَٱعْلَمُوٓا۟ أَنَّ ٱللَّهَ مَعَ ٱلْمُتَّقِينَ ۝ وَأَنفِقُوا۟ فِى سَبِيلِ ٱللَّهِ وَلَا تُلْقُوا۟ بِأَيْدِيكُمْ إِلَى ٱلتَّهْلُكَةِ ۛ وَأَحْسِنُوٓا۟ ۛ إِنَّ ٱللَّهَ يُحِبُّ ٱلْمُحْسِنِينَ ۝ وَأَتِمُّوا۟ ٱلْحَجَّ وَٱلْعُمْرَةَ لِلَّهِ ۚ فَإِنْ أُحْصِرْتُمْ فَمَا ٱسْتَيْسَرَ مِنَ ٱلْهَدْىِ ۖ وَلَا تَحْلِقُوا۟ رُءُوسَكُمْ حَتَّىٰ يَبْلُغَ ٱلْهَدْىُ مَحِلَّهُۥ ۚ فَمَن كَانَ مِنكُم مَّرِيضًا أَوْ بِهِۦٓ أَذًى مِّن رَّأْسِهِۦ فَفِدْيَةٌ مِّن صِيَامٍ أَوْ صَدَقَةٍ أَوْ نُسُكٍ ۚ فَإِذَآ أَمِنتُمْ فَمَن تَمَتَّعَ بِٱلْعُمْرَةِ إِلَى ٱلْحَجِّ فَمَا ٱسْتَيْسَرَ مِنَ ٱلْهَدْىِ ۚ فَمَن لَّمْ يَجِدْ فَصِيَامُ ثَلَٰثَةِ أَيَّامٍ فِى ٱلْحَجِّ وَسَبْعَةٍ إِذَا رَجَعْتُمْ ۗ تِلْكَ عَشَرَةٌ كَامِلَةٌ ۚ ذَٰلِكَ لِمَن لَّمْ يَكُنْ أَهْلُهُۥ حَاضِرِى ٱلْمَسْجِدِ ٱلْحَرَامِ ۚ وَٱتَّقُوا۟ ٱللَّهَ وَٱعْلَمُوٓا۟ أَنَّ ٱللَّهَ شَدِيدُ ٱلْعِقَابِ ۝ ٱلْحَجُّ أَشْهُرٌ مَّعْلُومَٰتٌ ۚ فَمَن فَرَضَ فِيهِنَّ ٱلْحَجَّ فَلَا رَفَثَ وَلَا فُسُوقَ وَلَا جِدَالَ فِى ٱلْحَجِّ ۗ وَمَا تَفْعَلُوا۟ مِنْ خَيْرٍ يَعْلَمْهُ ٱللَّهُ ۗ وَتَزَوَّدُوا۟ فَإِنَّ خَيْرَ ٱلزَّادِ ٱلتَّقْوَىٰ ۚ وَٱتَّقُونِ يَٰٓأُو۟لِى ٱلْأَلْبَٰبِ ۝ لَيْسَ عَلَيْكُمْ جُنَاحٌ أَن تَبْتَغُوا۟ فَضْلًا مِّن رَّبِّكُمْ ۚ فَإِذَآ أَفَضْتُم مِّنْ

عَرَفَٰتٍ فَٱذْكُرُوا۟ ٱللَّهَ عِندَ ٱلْمَشْعَرِ ٱلْحَرَامِ ۖ وَٱذْكُرُوهُ كَمَا هَدَىٰكُمْ وَإِن كُنتُم مِّن قَبْلِهِۦ لَمِنَ ٱلضَّآلِّينَ ۝ ثُمَّ أَفِيضُوا۟ مِنْ حَيْثُ أَفَاضَ ٱلنَّاسُ وَٱسْتَغْفِرُوا۟ ٱللَّهَ ۚ إِنَّ ٱللَّهَ غَفُورٌ رَّحِيمٌ ۝ فَإِذَا قَضَيْتُم مَّنَٰسِكَكُمْ فَٱذْكُرُوا۟ ٱللَّهَ كَذِكْرِكُمْ ءَابَآءَكُمْ أَوْ أَشَدَّ ذِكْرًا ۗ فَمِنَ ٱلنَّاسِ مَن يَقُولُ رَبَّنَآ ءَاتِنَا فِى ٱلدُّنْيَا وَمَا لَهُۥ فِى ٱلْءَاخِرَةِ مِنْ خَلَٰقٍ ۝ وَمِنْهُم مَّن يَقُولُ رَبَّنَآ ءَاتِنَا فِى ٱلدُّنْيَا حَسَنَةً وَفِى ٱلْءَاخِرَةِ حَسَنَةً وَقِنَا عَذَابَ ٱلنَّارِ ۝ أُو۟لَٰٓئِكَ لَهُمْ نَصِيبٌ مِّمَّا كَسَبُوا۟ ۚ وَٱللَّهُ سَرِيعُ ٱلْحِسَابِ ۝ ۞ وَٱذْكُرُوا۟ ٱللَّهَ فِىٓ أَيَّامٍ مَّعْدُودَٰتٍ ۚ فَمَن تَعَجَّلَ فِى يَوْمَيْنِ فَلَآ إِثْمَ عَلَيْهِ وَمَن تَأَخَّرَ فَلَآ إِثْمَ عَلَيْهِ ۚ لِمَنِ ٱتَّقَىٰ ۗ وَٱتَّقُوا۟ ٱللَّهَ وَٱعْلَمُوٓا۟ أَنَّكُمْ إِلَيْهِ تُحْشَرُونَ ۝ وَمِنَ ٱلنَّاسِ مَن يُعْجِبُكَ قَوْلُهُۥ فِى ٱلْحَيَوٰةِ ٱلدُّنْيَا وَيُشْهِدُ ٱللَّهَ عَلَىٰ مَا فِى قَلْبِهِۦ وَهُوَ أَلَدُّ ٱلْخِصَامِ ۝ وَإِذَا تَوَلَّىٰ سَعَىٰ فِى ٱلْأَرْضِ لِيُفْسِدَ فِيهَا وَيُهْلِكَ ٱلْحَرْثَ وَٱلنَّسْلَ ۗ وَٱللَّهُ لَا يُحِبُّ ٱلْفَسَادَ ۝ وَإِذَا قِيلَ لَهُ ٱتَّقِ ٱللَّهَ أَخَذَتْهُ ٱلْعِزَّةُ بِٱلْإِثْمِ ۚ فَحَسْبُهُۥ جَهَنَّمُ ۚ وَلَبِئْسَ ٱلْمِهَادُ ۝ وَمِنَ ٱلنَّاسِ مَن يَشْرِى نَفْسَهُ ٱبْتِغَآءَ مَرْضَاتِ ٱللَّهِ ۗ وَٱللَّهُ رَءُوفٌۢ بِٱلْعِبَادِ ۝ يَٰٓأَيُّهَا ٱلَّذِينَ ءَامَنُوا۟ ٱدْخُلُوا۟ فِى ٱلسِّلْمِ كَآفَّةً وَلَا تَتَّبِعُوا۟ خُطُوَٰتِ ٱلشَّيْطَٰنِ ۚ إِنَّهُۥ لَكُمْ عَدُوٌّ مُّبِينٌ ۝ فَإِن زَلَلْتُم مِّنۢ بَعْدِ مَا جَآءَتْكُمُ ٱلْبَيِّنَٰتُ فَٱعْلَمُوٓا۟ أَنَّ ٱللَّهَ عَزِيزٌ حَكِيمٌ ۝ هَلْ يَنظُرُونَ إِلَّآ أَن يَأْتِيَهُمُ ٱللَّهُ فِى ظُلَلٍ مِّنَ ٱلْغَمَامِ وَٱلْمَلَٰٓئِكَةُ وَقُضِىَ ٱلْأَمْرُ ۚ وَإِلَى ٱللَّهِ تُرْجَعُ ٱلْأُمُورُ ۝ سَلْ بَنِىٓ إِسْرَٰٓءِيلَ كَمْ ءَاتَيْنَٰهُم مِّنْ ءَايَةٍۭ بَيِّنَةٍ ۗ وَمَن يُبَدِّلْ نِعْمَةَ ٱللَّهِ مِنۢ بَعْدِ مَا جَآءَتْهُ فَإِنَّ ٱللَّهَ شَدِيدُ ٱلْعِقَابِ ۝

زُيِّنَ لِلَّذِينَ كَفَرُواْ ٱلْحَيَوٰةُ ٱلدُّنْيَا وَيَسْخَرُونَ مِنَ ٱلَّذِينَ ءَامَنُواْ ۘ وَٱلَّذِينَ ٱتَّقَواْ فَوْقَهُمْ يَوْمَ ٱلْقِيَـٰمَةِ ۗ وَٱللَّهُ يَرْزُقُ مَن يَشَآءُ بِغَيْرِ حِسَابٍ ۩ كَانَ ٱلنَّاسُ أُمَّةً وَٰحِدَةً فَبَعَثَ ٱللَّهُ ٱلنَّبِيِّـۧنَ مُبَشِّرِينَ وَمُنذِرِينَ وَأَنزَلَ مَعَهُمُ ٱلْكِتَـٰبَ بِٱلْحَقِّ لِيَحْكُمَ بَيْنَ ٱلنَّاسِ فِيمَا ٱخْتَلَفُواْ فِيهِ ۚ وَمَا ٱخْتَلَفَ فِيهِ إِلَّا ٱلَّذِينَ أُوتُوهُ مِنۢ بَعْدِ مَا جَآءَتْهُمُ ٱلْبَيِّنَـٰتُ بَغْيًۢا بَيْنَهُمْ ۖ فَهَدَى ٱللَّهُ ٱلَّذِينَ ءَامَنُواْ لِمَا ٱخْتَلَفُواْ فِيهِ مِنَ ٱلْحَقِّ بِإِذْنِهِۦ ۗ وَٱللَّهُ يَهْدِى مَن يَشَآءُ إِلَىٰ صِرَٰطٍ مُّسْتَقِيمٍ ۩ أَمْ حَسِبْتُمْ أَن تَدْخُلُواْ ٱلْجَنَّةَ وَلَمَّا يَأْتِكُم مَّثَلُ ٱلَّذِينَ خَلَوْاْ مِن قَبْلِكُم ۖ مَّسَّتْهُمُ ٱلْبَأْسَآءُ وَٱلضَّرَّآءُ وَزُلْزِلُواْ حَتَّىٰ يَقُولَ ٱلرَّسُولُ وَٱلَّذِينَ ءَامَنُواْ مَعَهُۥ مَتَىٰ نَصْرُ ٱللَّهِ ۗ أَلَآ إِنَّ نَصْرَ ٱللَّهِ قَرِيبٌ ۩ يَسْـَٔلُونَكَ مَاذَا يُنفِقُونَ ۖ قُلْ مَآ أَنفَقْتُم مِّنْ خَيْرٍ فَلِلْوَٰلِدَيْنِ وَٱلْأَقْرَبِينَ وَٱلْيَتَـٰمَىٰ وَٱلْمَسَـٰكِينِ وَٱبْنِ ٱلسَّبِيلِ ۗ وَمَا تَفْعَلُواْ مِنْ خَيْرٍ فَإِنَّ ٱللَّهَ بِهِۦ عَلِيمٌ ۩ كُتِبَ عَلَيْكُمُ ٱلْقِتَالُ وَهُوَ كُرْهٌ لَّكُمْ ۖ وَعَسَىٰٓ أَن تَكْرَهُواْ شَيْـًٔا وَهُوَ خَيْرٌ لَّكُمْ ۖ وَعَسَىٰٓ أَن تُحِبُّواْ شَيْـًٔا وَهُوَ شَرٌّ لَّكُمْ ۗ وَٱللَّهُ يَعْلَمُ وَأَنتُمْ لَا تَعْلَمُونَ ۩ يَسْـَٔلُونَكَ عَنِ ٱلشَّهْرِ ٱلْحَرَامِ قِتَالٍ فِيهِ ۖ قُلْ قِتَالٌ فِيهِ كَبِيرٌ ۖ وَصَدٌّ عَن سَبِيلِ ٱللَّهِ وَكُفْرٌۢ بِهِۦ وَٱلْمَسْجِدِ ٱلْحَرَامِ وَإِخْرَاجُ أَهْلِهِۦ مِنْهُ أَكْبَرُ عِندَ ٱللَّهِ ۚ وَٱلْفِتْنَةُ أَكْبَرُ مِنَ ٱلْقَتْلِ ۗ وَلَا يَزَالُونَ يُقَـٰتِلُونَكُمْ حَتَّىٰ يَرُدُّوكُمْ عَن دِينِكُمْ إِنِ ٱسْتَطَـٰعُواْ ۚ وَمَن يَرْتَدِدْ مِنكُمْ عَن دِينِهِۦ فَيَمُتْ وَهُوَ كَافِرٌ فَأُوْلَـٰٓئِكَ حَبِطَتْ أَعْمَـٰلُهُمْ فِى ٱلدُّنْيَا وَٱلْـَٔاخِرَةِ ۖ وَأُوْلَـٰٓئِكَ أَصْحَـٰبُ ٱلنَّارِ ۖ هُمْ فِيهَا خَـٰلِدُونَ ۩ إِنَّ ٱلَّذِينَ ءَامَنُواْ وَٱلَّذِينَ هَاجَرُواْ وَجَـٰهَدُواْ فِى سَبِيلِ ٱللَّهِ أُوْلَـٰٓئِكَ يَرْجُونَ رَحْمَتَ ٱللَّهِ ۚ وَٱللَّهُ

غَفُورٌ رَحِيمٌ ۝ ۞ يَسْـَٔلُونَكَ عَنِ ٱلْخَمْرِ وَٱلْمَيْسِرِ ۖ قُلْ فِيهِمَآ إِثْمٌ كَبِيرٌ وَمَنَٰفِعُ لِلنَّاسِ وَإِثْمُهُمَآ أَكْبَرُ مِن نَّفْعِهِمَا ۗ وَيَسْـَٔلُونَكَ مَاذَا يُنفِقُونَ قُلِ ٱلْعَفْوَ ۗ كَذَٰلِكَ يُبَيِّنُ ٱللَّهُ لَكُمُ ٱلْـَٔايَٰتِ لَعَلَّكُمْ تَتَفَكَّرُونَ ۝ فِى ٱلدُّنْيَا وَٱلْـَٔاخِرَةِ ۗ وَيَسْـَٔلُونَكَ عَنِ ٱلْيَتَٰمَىٰ ۖ قُلْ إِصْلَاحٌ لَّهُمْ خَيْرٌ ۖ وَإِن تُخَالِطُوهُمْ فَإِخْوَٰنُكُمْ ۚ وَٱللَّهُ يَعْلَمُ ٱلْمُفْسِدَ مِنَ ٱلْمُصْلِحِ ۚ وَلَوْ شَآءَ ٱللَّهُ لَأَعْنَتَكُمْ ۚ إِنَّ ٱللَّهَ عَزِيزٌ حَكِيمٌ ۝ وَلَا تَنكِحُوا۟ ٱلْمُشْرِكَٰتِ حَتَّىٰ يُؤْمِنَّ ۚ وَلَأَمَةٌ مُّؤْمِنَةٌ خَيْرٌ مِّن مُّشْرِكَةٍ وَلَوْ أَعْجَبَتْكُمْ ۗ وَلَا تُنكِحُوا۟ ٱلْمُشْرِكِينَ حَتَّىٰ يُؤْمِنُوا۟ ۚ وَلَعَبْدٌ مُّؤْمِنٌ خَيْرٌ مِّن مُّشْرِكٍ وَلَوْ أَعْجَبَكُمْ ۗ أُو۟لَٰٓئِكَ يَدْعُونَ إِلَى ٱلنَّارِ ۖ وَٱللَّهُ يَدْعُوٓا۟ إِلَى ٱلْجَنَّةِ وَٱلْمَغْفِرَةِ بِإِذْنِهِۦ ۖ وَيُبَيِّنُ ءَايَٰتِهِۦ لِلنَّاسِ لَعَلَّهُمْ يَتَذَكَّرُونَ ۝ وَيَسْـَٔلُونَكَ عَنِ ٱلْمَحِيضِ ۖ قُلْ هُوَ أَذًى فَٱعْتَزِلُوا۟ ٱلنِّسَآءَ فِى ٱلْمَحِيضِ ۖ وَلَا تَقْرَبُوهُنَّ حَتَّىٰ يَطْهُرْنَ ۖ فَإِذَا تَطَهَّرْنَ فَأْتُوهُنَّ مِنْ حَيْثُ أَمَرَكُمُ ٱللَّهُ ۚ إِنَّ ٱللَّهَ يُحِبُّ ٱلتَّوَّٰبِينَ وَيُحِبُّ ٱلْمُتَطَهِّرِينَ ۝ نِسَآؤُكُمْ حَرْثٌ لَّكُمْ فَأْتُوا۟ حَرْثَكُمْ أَنَّىٰ شِئْتُمْ ۖ وَقَدِّمُوا۟ لِأَنفُسِكُمْ ۚ وَٱتَّقُوا۟ ٱللَّهَ وَٱعْلَمُوٓا۟ أَنَّكُم مُّلَٰقُوهُ ۗ وَبَشِّرِ ٱلْمُؤْمِنِينَ ۝ وَلَا تَجْعَلُوا۟ ٱللَّهَ عُرْضَةً لِّأَيْمَٰنِكُمْ أَن تَبَرُّوا۟ وَتَتَّقُوا۟ وَتُصْلِحُوا۟ بَيْنَ ٱلنَّاسِ ۗ وَٱللَّهُ سَمِيعٌ عَلِيمٌ ۝ لَّا يُؤَاخِذُكُمُ ٱللَّهُ بِٱللَّغْوِ فِىٓ أَيْمَٰنِكُمْ وَلَٰكِن يُؤَاخِذُكُم بِمَا كَسَبَتْ قُلُوبُكُمْ ۗ وَٱللَّهُ غَفُورٌ حَلِيمٌ ۝ لِّلَّذِينَ يُؤْلُونَ مِن نِّسَآئِهِمْ تَرَبُّصُ أَرْبَعَةِ أَشْهُرٍ ۖ فَإِن فَآءُو فَإِنَّ ٱللَّهَ غَفُورٌ رَّحِيمٌ ۝ وَإِنْ عَزَمُوا۟ ٱلطَّلَٰقَ فَإِنَّ ٱللَّهَ سَمِيعٌ عَلِيمٌ ۝ وَٱلْمُطَلَّقَٰتُ يَتَرَبَّصْنَ بِأَنفُسِهِنَّ ثَلَٰثَةَ قُرُوٓءٍ ۚ وَلَا يَحِلُّ لَهُنَّ أَن يَكْتُمْنَ مَا خَلَقَ ٱللَّهُ فِىٓ أَرْحَامِهِنَّ إِن كُنَّ يُؤْمِنَّ بِٱللَّهِ وَٱلْيَوْمِ ٱلْـَٔاخِرِ ۚ وَبُعُولَتُهُنَّ

أَحَقُّ بِرَدِّهِنَّ فِى ذَٰلِكَ إِنْ أَرَادُوٓا۟ إِصْلَٰحًا ۚ وَهُنَّ مِثْلُ ٱلَّذِى عَلَيْهِنَّ بِٱلْمَعْرُوفِ ۚ وَلِلرِّجَالِ عَلَيْهِنَّ دَرَجَةٌ ۗ وَٱللَّهُ عَزِيزٌ حَكِيمٌ ۞ ٱلطَّلَٰقُ مَرَّتَانِ ۖ فَإِمْسَاكٌۢ بِمَعْرُوفٍ أَوْ تَسْرِيحٌۢ بِإِحْسَٰنٍ ۗ وَلَا يَحِلُّ لَكُمْ أَن تَأْخُذُوا۟ مِمَّآ ءَاتَيْتُمُوهُنَّ شَيْـًٔا إِلَّآ أَن يَخَافَآ أَلَّا يُقِيمَا حُدُودَ ٱللَّهِ ۖ فَإِنْ خِفْتُمْ أَلَّا يُقِيمَا حُدُودَ ٱللَّهِ فَلَا جُنَاحَ عَلَيْهِمَا فِيمَا ٱفْتَدَتْ بِهِۦ ۗ تِلْكَ حُدُودُ ٱللَّهِ فَلَا تَعْتَدُوهَا ۚ وَمَن يَتَعَدَّ حُدُودَ ٱللَّهِ فَأُو۟لَٰٓئِكَ هُمُ ٱلظَّٰلِمُونَ ۞ فَإِن طَلَّقَهَا فَلَا تَحِلُّ لَهُۥ مِنۢ بَعْدُ حَتَّىٰ تَنكِحَ زَوْجًا غَيْرَهُۥ ۗ فَإِن طَلَّقَهَا فَلَا جُنَاحَ عَلَيْهِمَآ أَن يَتَرَاجَعَآ إِن ظَنَّآ أَن يُقِيمَا حُدُودَ ٱللَّهِ ۗ وَتِلْكَ حُدُودُ ٱللَّهِ يُبَيِّنُهَا لِقَوْمٍ يَعْلَمُونَ ۞ وَإِذَا طَلَّقْتُمُ ٱلنِّسَآءَ فَبَلَغْنَ أَجَلَهُنَّ فَأَمْسِكُوهُنَّ بِمَعْرُوفٍ أَوْ سَرِّحُوهُنَّ بِمَعْرُوفٍ ۚ وَلَا تُمْسِكُوهُنَّ ضِرَارًا لِّتَعْتَدُوا۟ ۚ وَمَن يَفْعَلْ ذَٰلِكَ فَقَدْ ظَلَمَ نَفْسَهُۥ ۚ وَلَا تَتَّخِذُوٓا۟ ءَايَٰتِ ٱللَّهِ هُزُوًا ۚ وَٱذْكُرُوا۟ نِعْمَتَ ٱللَّهِ عَلَيْكُمْ وَمَآ أَنزَلَ عَلَيْكُم مِّنَ ٱلْكِتَٰبِ وَٱلْحِكْمَةِ يَعِظُكُم بِهِۦ ۚ وَٱتَّقُوا۟ ٱللَّهَ وَٱعْلَمُوٓا۟ أَنَّ ٱللَّهَ بِكُلِّ شَىْءٍ عَلِيمٌ ۞ وَإِذَا طَلَّقْتُمُ ٱلنِّسَآءَ فَبَلَغْنَ أَجَلَهُنَّ فَلَا تَعْضُلُوهُنَّ أَن يَنكِحْنَ أَزْوَٰجَهُنَّ إِذَا تَرَٰضَوْا۟ بَيْنَهُم بِٱلْمَعْرُوفِ ۗ ذَٰلِكَ يُوعَظُ بِهِۦ مَن كَانَ مِنكُمْ يُؤْمِنُ بِٱللَّهِ وَٱلْيَوْمِ ٱلْءَاخِرِ ۗ ذَٰلِكُمْ أَزْكَىٰ لَكُمْ وَأَطْهَرُ ۗ وَٱللَّهُ يَعْلَمُ وَأَنتُمْ لَا تَعْلَمُونَ ۞ ۞ وَٱلْوَٰلِدَٰتُ يُرْضِعْنَ أَوْلَٰدَهُنَّ حَوْلَيْنِ كَامِلَيْنِ ۖ لِمَنْ أَرَادَ أَن يُتِمَّ ٱلرَّضَاعَةَ ۚ وَعَلَى ٱلْمَوْلُودِ لَهُۥ رِزْقُهُنَّ وَكِسْوَتُهُنَّ بِٱلْمَعْرُوفِ ۚ لَا تُكَلَّفُ نَفْسٌ إِلَّا وُسْعَهَا ۚ لَا تُضَآرَّ وَٰلِدَةٌۢ بِوَلَدِهَا وَلَا مَوْلُودٌ لَّهُۥ بِوَلَدِهِۦ ۚ وَعَلَى ٱلْوَارِثِ مِثْلُ ذَٰلِكَ ۗ فَإِنْ أَرَادَا فِصَالًا عَن تَرَاضٍ مِّنْهُمَا وَتَشَاوُرٍ فَلَا جُنَاحَ عَلَيْهِمَا ۗ وَإِنْ أَرَدتُّمْ أَن تَسْتَرْضِعُوٓا۟ أَوْلَٰدَكُمْ فَلَا جُنَاحَ

عَلَيْكُمْ إِذَا سَلَّمْتُم مَّا ءَاتَيْتُم بِٱلْمَعْرُوفِ ۗ وَٱتَّقُوا۟ ٱللَّهَ وَٱعْلَمُوٓا۟ أَنَّ ٱللَّهَ بِمَا تَعْمَلُونَ بَصِيرٌ ۝ وَٱلَّذِينَ يُتَوَفَّوْنَ مِنكُمْ وَيَذَرُونَ أَزْوَٰجًا يَتَرَبَّصْنَ بِأَنفُسِهِنَّ أَرْبَعَةَ أَشْهُرٍ وَعَشْرًا ۖ فَإِذَا بَلَغْنَ أَجَلَهُنَّ فَلَا جُنَاحَ عَلَيْكُمْ فِيمَا فَعَلْنَ فِىٓ أَنفُسِهِنَّ بِٱلْمَعْرُوفِ ۗ وَٱللَّهُ بِمَا تَعْمَلُونَ خَبِيرٌ ۝ وَلَا جُنَاحَ عَلَيْكُمْ فِيمَا عَرَّضْتُم بِهِۦ مِنْ خِطْبَةِ ٱلنِّسَآءِ أَوْ أَكْنَنتُمْ فِىٓ أَنفُسِكُمْ ۚ عَلِمَ ٱللَّهُ أَنَّكُمْ سَتَذْكُرُونَهُنَّ وَلَٰكِن لَّا تُوَاعِدُوهُنَّ سِرًّا إِلَّآ أَن تَقُولُوا۟ قَوْلًا مَّعْرُوفًا ۚ وَلَا تَعْزِمُوا۟ عُقْدَةَ ٱلنِّكَاحِ حَتَّىٰ يَبْلُغَ ٱلْكِتَٰبُ أَجَلَهُۥ ۚ وَٱعْلَمُوٓا۟ أَنَّ ٱللَّهَ يَعْلَمُ مَا فِىٓ أَنفُسِكُمْ فَٱحْذَرُوهُ ۚ وَٱعْلَمُوٓا۟ أَنَّ ٱللَّهَ غَفُورٌ حَلِيمٌ ۝ لَّا جُنَاحَ عَلَيْكُمْ إِن طَلَّقْتُمُ ٱلنِّسَآءَ مَا لَمْ تَمَسُّوهُنَّ أَوْ تَفْرِضُوا۟ لَهُنَّ فَرِيضَةً ۚ وَمَتِّعُوهُنَّ عَلَى ٱلْمُوسِعِ قَدَرُهُۥ وَعَلَى ٱلْمُقْتِرِ قَدَرُهُۥ مَتَٰعًۢا بِٱلْمَعْرُوفِ ۖ حَقًّا عَلَى ٱلْمُحْسِنِينَ ۝ وَإِن طَلَّقْتُمُوهُنَّ مِن قَبْلِ أَن تَمَسُّوهُنَّ وَقَدْ فَرَضْتُمْ لَهُنَّ فَرِيضَةً فَنِصْفُ مَا فَرَضْتُمْ إِلَّآ أَن يَعْفُونَ أَوْ يَعْفُوَا۟ ٱلَّذِى بِيَدِهِۦ عُقْدَةُ ٱلنِّكَاحِ ۚ وَأَن تَعْفُوٓا۟ أَقْرَبُ لِلتَّقْوَىٰ ۚ وَلَا تَنسَوُا۟ ٱلْفَضْلَ بَيْنَكُمْ ۚ إِنَّ ٱللَّهَ بِمَا تَعْمَلُونَ بَصِيرٌ ۝ حَٰفِظُوا۟ عَلَى ٱلصَّلَوَٰتِ وَٱلصَّلَوٰةِ ٱلْوُسْطَىٰ وَقُومُوا۟ لِلَّهِ قَٰنِتِينَ ۝ فَإِنْ خِفْتُمْ فَرِجَالًا أَوْ رُكْبَانًا ۖ فَإِذَآ أَمِنتُمْ فَٱذْكُرُوا۟ ٱللَّهَ كَمَا عَلَّمَكُم مَّا لَمْ تَكُونُوا۟ تَعْلَمُونَ ۝ وَٱلَّذِينَ يُتَوَفَّوْنَ مِنكُمْ وَيَذَرُونَ أَزْوَٰجًا وَصِيَّةً لِّأَزْوَٰجِهِم مَّتَٰعًا إِلَى ٱلْحَوْلِ غَيْرَ إِخْرَاجٍ ۚ فَإِنْ خَرَجْنَ فَلَا جُنَاحَ عَلَيْكُمْ فِى مَا فَعَلْنَ فِىٓ أَنفُسِهِنَّ مِن مَّعْرُوفٍ ۗ وَٱللَّهُ عَزِيزٌ حَكِيمٌ ۝ وَلِلْمُطَلَّقَٰتِ مَتَٰعٌۢ بِٱلْمَعْرُوفِ ۖ حَقًّا عَلَى ٱلْمُتَّقِينَ ۝ كَذَٰلِكَ يُبَيِّنُ ٱللَّهُ لَكُمْ ءَايَٰتِهِۦ لَعَلَّكُمْ تَعْقِلُونَ ۝ ۞ أَلَمْ تَرَ إِلَى

ٱلَّذِينَ خَرَجُواْ مِن دِيَـٰرِهِمْ وَهُمْ أُلُوفٌ حَذَرَ ٱلْمَوْتِ فَقَالَ لَهُمُ ٱللَّهُ مُوتُواْ ثُمَّ أَحْيَـٰهُمْ ۚ إِنَّ ٱللَّهَ لَذُو فَضْلٍ عَلَى ٱلنَّاسِ وَلَـٰكِنَّ أَكْثَرَ ٱلنَّاسِ لَا يَشْكُرُونَ ﴿٢٤٣﴾ وَقَـٰتِلُواْ فِى سَبِيلِ ٱللَّهِ وَٱعْلَمُوٓاْ أَنَّ ٱللَّهَ سَمِيعٌ عَلِيمٌ ﴿٢٤٤﴾ مَّن ذَا ٱلَّذِى يُقْرِضُ ٱللَّهَ قَرْضًا حَسَنًا فَيُضَـٰعِفَهُۥ لَهُۥٓ أَضْعَافًا كَثِيرَةً ۚ وَٱللَّهُ يَقْبِضُ وَيَبْسُۜطُ وَإِلَيْهِ تُرْجَعُونَ ﴿٢٤٥﴾ أَلَمْ تَرَ إِلَى ٱلْمَلَإِ مِنۢ بَنِىٓ إِسْرَٰٓءِيلَ مِنۢ بَعْدِ مُوسَىٰٓ إِذْ قَالُواْ لِنَبِىٍّ لَّهُمُ ٱبْعَثْ لَنَا مَلِكًا نُّقَـٰتِلْ فِى سَبِيلِ ٱللَّهِ ۖ قَالَ هَلْ عَسَيْتُمْ إِن كُتِبَ عَلَيْكُمُ ٱلْقِتَالُ أَلَّا تُقَـٰتِلُواْ ۖ قَالُواْ وَمَا لَنَآ أَلَّا نُقَـٰتِلَ فِى سَبِيلِ ٱللَّهِ وَقَدْ أُخْرِجْنَا مِن دِيَـٰرِنَا وَأَبْنَآئِنَا ۖ فَلَمَّا كُتِبَ عَلَيْهِمُ ٱلْقِتَالُ تَوَلَّوْاْ إِلَّا قَلِيلًا مِّنْهُمْ ۗ وَٱللَّهُ عَلِيمٌۢ بِٱلظَّـٰلِمِينَ ﴿٢٤٦﴾ وَقَالَ لَهُمْ نَبِيُّهُمْ إِنَّ ٱللَّهَ قَدْ بَعَثَ لَكُمْ طَالُوتَ مَلِكًا ۚ قَالُوٓاْ أَنَّىٰ يَكُونُ لَهُ ٱلْمُلْكُ عَلَيْنَا وَنَحْنُ أَحَقُّ بِٱلْمُلْكِ مِنْهُ وَلَمْ يُؤْتَ سَعَةً مِّنَ ٱلْمَالِ ۚ قَالَ إِنَّ ٱللَّهَ ٱصْطَفَىٰهُ عَلَيْكُمْ وَزَادَهُۥ بَسْطَةً فِى ٱلْعِلْمِ وَٱلْجِسْمِ ۖ وَٱللَّهُ يُؤْتِى مُلْكَهُۥ مَن يَشَآءُ ۚ وَٱللَّهُ وَٰسِعٌ عَلِيمٌ ﴿٢٤٧﴾ وَقَالَ لَهُمْ نَبِيُّهُمْ إِنَّ ءَايَةَ مُلْكِهِۦٓ أَن يَأْتِيَكُمُ ٱلتَّابُوتُ فِيهِ سَكِينَةٌ مِّن رَّبِّكُمْ وَبَقِيَّةٌ مِّمَّا تَرَكَ ءَالُ مُوسَىٰ وَءَالُ هَـٰرُونَ تَحْمِلُهُ ٱلْمَلَـٰٓئِكَةُ ۚ إِنَّ فِى ذَٰلِكَ لَـَٔايَةً لَّكُمْ إِن كُنتُم مُّؤْمِنِينَ ﴿٢٤٨﴾ فَلَمَّا فَصَلَ طَالُوتُ بِٱلْجُنُودِ قَالَ إِنَّ ٱللَّهَ مُبْتَلِيكُم بِنَهَرٍ فَمَن شَرِبَ مِنْهُ فَلَيْسَ مِنِّى وَمَن لَّمْ يَطْعَمْهُ فَإِنَّهُۥ مِنِّىٓ إِلَّا مَنِ ٱغْتَرَفَ غُرْفَةًۢ بِيَدِهِۦ ۚ فَشَرِبُواْ مِنْهُ إِلَّا قَلِيلًا مِّنْهُمْ ۚ فَلَمَّا جَاوَزَهُۥ هُوَ وَٱلَّذِينَ ءَامَنُواْ مَعَهُۥ قَالُواْ لَا طَاقَةَ لَنَا ٱلْيَوْمَ بِجَالُوتَ وَجُنُودِهِۦ ۚ قَالَ ٱلَّذِينَ يَظُنُّونَ أَنَّهُم مُّلَـٰقُواْ ٱللَّهِ كَم مِّن فِئَةٍ قَلِيلَةٍ غَلَبَتْ

فِئَةً كَثِيرَةً بِإِذْنِ ٱللَّهِ ۗ وَٱللَّهُ مَعَ ٱلصَّٰبِرِينَ ۝ وَلَمَّا بَرَزُواْ لِجَالُوتَ وَجُنُودِهِۦ قَالُواْ رَبَّنَآ أَفْرِغْ عَلَيْنَا صَبْرًا وَثَبِّتْ أَقْدَامَنَا وَٱنصُرْنَا عَلَى ٱلْقَوْمِ ٱلْكَٰفِرِينَ ۝ فَهَزَمُوهُم بِإِذْنِ ٱللَّهِ وَقَتَلَ دَاوُدُ جَالُوتَ وَءَاتَىٰهُ ٱللَّهُ ٱلْمُلْكَ وَٱلْحِكْمَةَ وَعَلَّمَهُۥ مِمَّا يَشَآءُ ۗ وَلَوْلَا دَفْعُ ٱللَّهِ ٱلنَّاسَ بَعْضَهُم بِبَعْضٍ لَّفَسَدَتِ ٱلْأَرْضُ وَلَٰكِنَّ ٱللَّهَ ذُو فَضْلٍ عَلَى ٱلْعَٰلَمِينَ ۝ تِلْكَ ءَايَٰتُ ٱللَّهِ نَتْلُوهَا عَلَيْكَ بِٱلْحَقِّ ۚ وَإِنَّكَ لَمِنَ ٱلْمُرْسَلِينَ ۝

# INTRODUCTION TO CHAPTER (SURAH) 2: AL-BAQARAH (THE COW)

## Ibn Kathir's Introduction

### The Virtues of Surat Al-Baqarah

The Virtues of Surat Al-Baqarah

In Musnad Ahmad, Sahih Muslim, At-Tirmidhi and An-Nasa'i, it is recorded that Abu Hurayrah said that the Prophet said,

«لَا تَجْعَلُوا بُيُوتَكُمْ قُبُورًا فَإِنَّ الْبَيْتَ الَّذِي تُقْرَأُ فِيهِ سُورَةُ الْبَقَرَةِ لَا يَدْخُلُهُ الشَّيْطَانُ»

(Do not turn your houses into graves. Verily, Shaytan does not enter the house where Surat Al-Baqarah is recited.) At-Tirmidhi said, "Hasan Sahih.

Also, `Abdullah bin Mas`ud said, "Shaytan flees from the house where Surat Al-Baqarah is heard." This Hadith was collected by An-Nasa'i in Al-Yawm wal-Laylah, and Al-Hakim recorded it in his Mustadrak, and then said that its chain of narration is authentic, although the Two Sahihs did not collect it. In his Musnad, Ad-Darimi recorded that Ibn Mas`ud said, "Shaytan departs the house where Surat Al-Baqarah is being recited, and as he leaves, he passes gas." Ad-Darimi also recorded that Ash-Sha`bi said that `Abdullah bin Mas`ud said, "Whoever recites ten Ayat from Surat Al-Baqarah in a night, then Shaytan will not enter his house that night. (These ten Ayat are) four from the beginning, Ayat Al-Kursi (255), the following two Ayat (256-257) and the last three Ayat." In another narration, Ibn Mas`ud said, "Then Shaytan will not come near him or his family, nor will he be touched by anything that he dislikes. Also, if these Ayat were to be recited over a senile person, they would wake him up."

Further, Sahl bin Sa`d said that the Messenger of Allah said,

«إِنَّ لِكُلِّ شَيْءٍ سَنَامًا، وَإِنَّ سَنَامَ الْقُرْآنِ الْبَقَرَةُ، وَإِنَّ مَنْ قَرَأَهَا فِي بَيْتِهِ لَيْلَةً لَمْ يَدْخُلْهُ الشَّيْطَانُ ثَلَاثَ لَيَالٍ، وَمَنْ قَرَأَهَا فِي بَيْتِهِ نَهَارًا لَمْ يَدْخُلْهُ الشَّيْطَانُ ثَلَاثَةَ أَيَّامٍ»

(Everything has a hump (or, high peek), and Al-Baqarah is the high peek of the Qur'an. Whoever recites Al-Baqarah at night in his house, then Shaytan will not enter that house for three nights. Whoever recites it during a day in his house, then Shaytan will not enter that house for three days.) This Hadith was collected by Abu Al-Qasim At-Tabarani, Abu Hatim Ibn Hibban in his Sahih and Ibn Marduwyah.

At-Tirmidhi, An-Nasa'i and Ibn Majah recorded that Abu Hurayrah said, "The Messenger of Allah sent an expedition force comprising of many men and asked each about what they memorized of the Qur'an. The Prophet came to one of the youngest men among them and asked him, `What have you memorized (of the Qur'an) young man' He said, `I memorized such and such Surahs and also Al-Baqarah.' The Prophet said, `You memorized Surat Al-Baqarah' He said, `Yes.' The Prophet said, `Then you are their commander.' One of the noted men (or chiefs) commented, `By Allah! I did not learn Surat Al-Baqarah, for fear that I would not be able to implement it. The Messenger of Allah said,

«تَعَلَّمُوا الْقُرْآنَ وَاقْرَءُوهُ، فَإِنَّ مَثَلَ الْقُرْآنِ لِمَنْ تَعَلَّمَهُ فَقَرَأَ وَقَامَ بِهِ كَمَثَلِ جِرَابٍ مَحْشُوٍّ مِسْكًا يَفُوحُ رِيحُهُ فِي كُلِّ مَكَانٍ، وَمَثَلُ مَنْ تَعَلَّمَهُ فَيَرْقُدُ وَهُوَ فِي جَوْفِهِ كَمَثَلِ جِرَابٍ أُوكِيَ عَلَى مِسْكٍ»

(Learn Al-Qur'an and recite it, for the example of whoever learns the Qur'an, recites it and adheres to it, is the example of a bag that is full of musk whose scent fills the air. The example of whoever learns the Qur'an and then sleeps (i.e. lazy) while the Qur'an is in his memory, is the example of a bag that has musk, but is closed tight.)

This is the wording collected by At-Tirmidhi, who said that this Hadith is Hasan. In another narration, At-Tirmidhi recorded this same Hadith in a Mursal manner, so Allah knows best.

# Chapter 2: Al-Baqarah (The Cow), Verses 142-252

Also, Al-Bukhari recorded that Usayd bin Hudayr said that he was once reciting Surat Al-Baqarah while his horse was tied next to him. The horse started to make some noise. When Usayd stopped reciting, the horse stopped moving about. When he resumed reading, the horse started moving about again. When he stopped reciting, the horse stopped moving, and when he resumed reading, the horse started to move again. Meanwhile, his son Yahya was close to the horse, and he feared that the horse might step on him. When he moved his son back, he looked up to the sky and saw a cloud radiating with light that looked like lamps. In the morning, he went to the Prophet and told him what had happened and then said, "O Messenger of Allah! My son Yahya was close to the horse and I feared that she might step on him. When I attended to him and raised my head to the sky, I saw a cloud with lights like lamps. So I went, but I couldn't see it." The Prophet said, "Do you know what that was" He said, "No." The Prophet said,

»تِلْكَ الْمَلَائِكَةُ دَنَتْ لِصَوْتِكَ وَلَو قَرَأْتَ لَأَصْبَحْتَ يَنْظُرُ النَّاسُ إِلَيْهَا، لَا تَتَوَارَى مِنْهُم«

(They were the angels, they came close hearing your voice (reciting Surat Al-Baqarah), and if you had kept reading, the people would have been able to see the angels when the morning came, and the angels would not be hidden from their eyes.)

This is the narration reported by Imam Abu Ubayd Al-Qasim bin Salam in his book Fada'il Al-Qur'an.

### Virtues of Surat Al-Baqarah and Surat Al `Imran

Imam Ahmad said that Abu Nu`aym narrated to them that Bishr bin Muhajir said that `Abdullah bin Buraydah narrated to him from his father, "I was sitting with the Prophet and I heard him say,

»تَعَلَّمُوا سُورَةَ الْبَقَرَةِ فَإِنَّ أَخْذَهَا بَرَكَةٌ، وَتَرْكَهَا حَسْرَةٌ، وَلَا تَسْتَطِيعُهَا الْبَطَلَة«

(Learn Surat Al-Baqarah, because in learning it there is blessing, in ignoring it there is sorrow, and the sorceresses cannot memorize it.)

He kept silent for a while and then said,

»تَعَلَّمُوا سُورَةَ الْبَقَرَةِ وَآلَ عِمْرَانَ فَإِنَّهُمَا الزَّهْرَاوَانِ، يُظِلَّانِ صَاحِبَهُمَا

يَوْمَ الْقِيَامَةِ كَأَنَّهُمَا غَمَامَتَانِ أَوْ غَيَايَتَانِ أَوْ فِرْقَانِ مِنْ طَيْرٍ صَوَافَّ، وَإِنَّ الْقُرْآنَ يَلْقَى صَاحِبَهُ يَوْمَ الْقِيَامَةِ حِينَ يَنْشَقُّ عَنْهُ قَبْرُهُ كَالرَّجُلِ الشَّاحِبِ فَيَقُولُ لَهُ: هَلْ تَعْرِفُنِي؟ فَيَقُولُ: مَا أَعْرِفُكَ. فَيَقُولُ: أَنَا صَاحِبُكَ الْقُرْآنُ الَّذِي أَظْمَأْتُكَ فِي الْهَوَاجِرِ وَأَسْهَرْتُ لَيْلَكَ وَإِنَّ كُلَّ تَاجِرٍ مِنْ وَرَاءِ تِجَارَتِهِ، وَإِنَّكَ الْيَوْمَ مِنْ وَرَاءِ كُلِّ تِجَارَةٍ فَيُعْطَى الْمُلْكَ بِيَمِينِهِ وَالْخُلْدَ بِشِمَالِهِ وَيُوضَعُ عَلَى رَأْسِهِ تَاجُ الْوَقَارِ، وَيُكْسَى وَالِدَاهُ حُلَّتَانِ لَا يَقُومُ لَهُمَا أَهْلُ الدُّنْيَا، فَيَقُولَانِ: بِمَا كُسِينَا هَذَا؟ فَيُقَالُ: بِأَخْذِ وَلَدِكُمَا الْقُرْآنَ ثُمَّ يُقَالُ: اقْرَأْ وَاصْعَدْ فِي دَرَجِ الْجَنَّةِ وَغُرَفِهَا، فَهُوَ فِي صُعُودٍ مَا دَامَ يَقْرَأُ هَذَّا كَانَ أَوْ تَرْتِيلًا»

(Learn Surat Al-Baqarah and Al `Imran because they are two lights and they shade their people on the Day of Resurrection, just as two clouds, two spaces of shade or two lines of (flying) birds. The Qur'an will meet its companion in the shape of a pale-faced man on the Day of Resurrection when his grave is opened. The Qur'an will ask him, 'Do you know me' The man will say, 'I do not know you.' The Qur'an will say, 'I am your companion, the Qur'an, which has brought you thirst during the heat and made you stay up during the night. Every merchant has his certain trade. But, this Day, you are behind all types of trade.' Kingship will then be given to him in his right hand, eternal life in his left hand and the crown of grace will be placed on his head. His parents will also be granted two garments that the people of this life could never afford. They will say, 'Why were we granted these garments' It will be said, 'Because your son was carrying the Qur'an.' It will be said (to the reader of the Qur'an), 'Read and ascend through the levels of Paradise.' He will go on ascending as long as he recites, whether reciting slowly or quickly.)''

Ibn Majah also recorded part of this Hadith from Bishr bin Al-Muhajir, and this chain of narrators is Hasan, according to the criteria of Imam Muslim.

A part of this Hadith is also supported by other Hadiths. For instance, Imam Ahmad recorded that Abu Umamah Al-Bahili said that he heard the Messenger of Allah say,

## Chapter 2: Al-Baqarah (The Cow), Verses 142-252

«اقْرَأُوا الْقُرْآنَ فَإِنَّهُ شَافِعٌ لِأَهْلِهِ يَوْمَ الْقِيَامَةِ اقْرَأُوا الزَّهْرَاوَيْنِ، الْبَقَرَةَ وَآلَ عِمْرَانَ، فَإِنَّهُمَا يَأْتِيَانِ يَوْمَ الْقِيَامَةِ كَأَنَّهُمَا غَمَامَتَانِ، أَوْ كَأَنَّهُمَا غَيَايَتَانِ أَوْ كَأَنَّهُمَا فِرْقَانِ مِنْ طَيْرٍ صَوَافَّ، يُحَاجَّانِ عَنْ أَهْلِهِمَا يَوْمَ الْقِيَامَةِ»

(Read the Qur'an, because it will intercede on behalf of its people on the Day of Resurrection. Read the two lights, Al-Baqarah and Al `Imran, because they will come in the shape of two clouds, two shades or two lines of birds on the Day of Resurrection and will argue on behalf of their people on that Day.)

The Prophet then said,

«اقْرَأُوا الْبَقَرَةَ فَإِنَّ أَخْذَهَا بَرَكَةٌ وَتَرْكَهَا حَسْرَةٌ وَلَا تَسْتَطِيعُهَا الْبَطَلَة»

(Read Al-Baqarah, because in having it there is blessing, and in ignoring there is a sorrow and the sorceresses cannot memorize it.)

Also, Imam Muslim narrated this Hadith in the Book of Prayer

Imam Ahmad narrated that An-Nawwas bin Sam`an said that the Prophet said,

«يُؤْتَى بِالْقُرْآنِ يَوْمَ الْقِيَامَةِ وَأَهْلِهِ الَّذِينَ كَانُوا يَعْمَلُونَ بِهِ تَقْدَمُهُمْ سُورَةُ الْبَقَرَةِ وَآلُ عِمْرَانَ»

(On the Day of Resurrection the Qur'an and its people who used to implement it will be brought forth, preceded by Surat Al-Baqarah and Al `Imran.)

An-Nawwas said, "The Prophet set three examples for these two Surahs and I did not forget these examples ever since. He said,

«كَأَنَّهُمَا غَمَامَتَانِ، أَوْ ظُلَّتَانِ سَوْدَاوَانِ بَيْنَهُمَا شَرْقٌ، أَوْ كَأَنَّهُمَا فِرْقَانِ مِنْ طَيْرٍ صَوَافَّ، يُحَاجَّانِ عَنْ صَاحِبِهِمَا»

(They will come like two clouds, two dark shades or two lines of birds arguing on behalf of their people.)

It was also recorded in Sahih Muslim and At-Tirmidhi narrated this Hadith, which he rendered Hasan Gharib.

## Surat Al-Baqarah was revealed in Al-Madinah

There is no disagreement over the view that Surat Al-Baqarah was revealed in its entirety in Al-Madinah. Moreover, Al-Baqarah was one of the first Surahs to be revealed in Al-Madinah, while, Allah's statement,

(And be afraid of the Day when you shall be brought back to Allah.) (2:281) was the last Ayah to be revealed from the Qur'an. Also, the Ayat about usury were among the last Ayat to be revealed. Khalid bin Ma`dan used to call Al-Baqarah the Fustat (tent) of the Qur'an. Some of the scholars said that it contains a thousand news incidents, a thousand commands and a thousand prohibitions. Those who count said that the number of Al-Baqarah's Ayat is two hundred and eighty-seven, and its words are six thousand two hundred and twenty-one words. Further, its letters are twenty-five thousand five hundred. Allah knows best.

Ibn Jurayj narrated that `Ata' said that Ibn `Abbas said, "Surat Al-Baqarah was revealed in Al-Madinah." Also, Khasif said from Mujahid that `Abdullah bin Az-Zubayr said; "Surat Al-Baqarah was revealed in Al-Madinah." Several Imams and scholars of Tafsir issued similar statements, and there is no difference of opinion over this as we have stated.

The Two Sahihs recorded that Ibn Mas`ud kept the Ka`bah on his left side and Mina on his right side and threw seven pebbles (at the Jamrah) and said, "The one to whom Surat Al-Baqarah was revealed (i.e. the Prophet ) performed Rami (the Hajj rite of throwing pebbles) similarly." The Two Sahihs recorded this Hadith.

Further, Ibn Marduwyah reported a Hadith of Shu`bah from `Aqil bin Talhah from `Utbah bin Marthad; "The Prophet saw that his Companions were not in the first lines and he said,

《يَا أَصْحَابَ سُورَةِ الْبَقَرَةِ》

(O Companions of Surat Al-Baqarah.) I Think that this incident occurred during the battle of Hunayn when the Companions retreated. Then, the Prophet commanded Al-`Abbas (his uncle) to yell out,

《يَا أَصْحَابَ الشَّجَرَةِ》

(O Companions of the tree!) meaning the Companions who participated in the pledge of Ar-Ridwan (under the tree). In another narration, Al- `Abbas cried, "O Companions of Surat Al-Baqarah!" encouraging them to come back, so they returned from every direction. Also, during the battle of Al-Yamamah, against the army of Musaylimah the Liar, the Companions first retreated because of the huge number of soldiers in Musaylimah's army. The Muhajirun and the Ansar called out for each other, saying; "O people of Surat Al-Baqarah!" Allah then gave them victory over their enemy, may Allah be pleased with all of the companions of all the Messengers of Allah.

# CHAPTER (SURAH) 2: AL-BAQARAH (THE COW), VERSES 142-252

### Surah: 2 Ayah: 142 & Ayah: 143

﴿ ۞ سَيَقُولُ ٱلسُّفَهَآءُ مِنَ ٱلنَّاسِ مَا وَلَّىٰهُمْ عَن قِبْلَتِهِمُ ٱلَّتِي كَانُوا۟ عَلَيْهَا ۚ قُل لِّلَّهِ ٱلْمَشْرِقُ وَٱلْمَغْرِبُ ۚ يَهْدِى مَن يَشَآءُ إِلَىٰ صِرَٰطٍ مُّسْتَقِيمٍ ۝ ﴾

142. The fools among the people (pagans, hypocrites, and Jews) will say, "What has turned them (Muslims) from their Qiblah (prayer direction (towards Jerusalem)) to which they used to face in prayer." Say, (O Muhammad (peace be upon him)) "To Allâh belong both, east and the west. He guides whom He wills to the Straight Way."

﴿ وَكَذَٰلِكَ جَعَلْنَٰكُمْ أُمَّةً وَسَطًا لِّتَكُونُوا۟ شُهَدَآءَ عَلَى ٱلنَّاسِ وَيَكُونَ ٱلرَّسُولُ عَلَيْكُمْ شَهِيدًا ۗ وَمَا جَعَلْنَا ٱلْقِبْلَةَ ٱلَّتِي كُنتَ عَلَيْهَآ إِلَّا لِنَعْلَمَ مَن يَتَّبِعُ ٱلرَّسُولَ مِمَّن يَنقَلِبُ عَلَىٰ عَقِبَيْهِ ۚ وَإِن كَانَتْ لَكَبِيرَةً إِلَّا عَلَى ٱلَّذِينَ هَدَى ٱللَّهُ ۗ وَمَا كَانَ ٱللَّهُ لِيُضِيعَ إِيمَٰنَكُمْ ۚ إِنَّ ٱللَّهَ بِٱلنَّاسِ لَرَءُوفٌ رَّحِيمٌ ۝ ﴾

143. Thus We have made you (true Muslims - real believers of Islâmic Monotheism, true followers of Prophet Muhammad (peace be upon him) and his Sunnah (legal ways)) a just (and the best) nation, that you be witnesses over mankind and the Messenger (Muhammad (peace be upon him)) be a witness over you. And We made the Qiblah (prayer direction towards Jerusalem) which you used to face, only to test those who followed the Messenger (Muhammad (peace be upon him)) from those who would turn on their heels (i.e. disobey the Messenger). Indeed it was great (heavy) except for those whom Allâh guided. And Allâh would never make your faith (prayers) to be lost (i.e. your prayers offered towards Jerusalem). Truly, Allâh is full of Kindness, the Most Merciful towards mankind.

### Transliteration

142. Sayaqoolu alssufahao mina alnnasi ma wallahum AAan qiblatihimu allatee kanoo AAalayha qul lillahi almashriqu waalmaghribu yahdee man yashao ila

siratin mustaqeemin 143. Wakathalika jaAAalnakum ommatan wasatan litakoonoo shuhadaa AAala alnnasi wayakoona alrrasoolu AAalaykum shaheedan wama jaAAalna alqiblata allatee kunta AAalayha illa linaAAlama man yattabiAAu alrrasoola mimman yanqalibu AAala AAaqibayhi wa-in kanat lakabeeratan illa AAala allatheena hada Allahu wama kana Allahu liyudeeAAa eemanakum inna Allaha bialnnasi laraoofun raheemun

## Tafsir Ibn Kathir

### Changing the Qiblah - Direction of the Prayer

Imam Al-Bukhari reported that Al-Bara' bin `Azib narrated: "Allah's Messenger offered his prayers facing Bayt Al-Maqdis (Jerusalem) for sixteen or seventeen months, but he wished that he could pray facing the Ka`bah (at Makkah). The first prayer which he offered (facing the Ka`bah) was the `Asr (Afternoon) prayer in the company of some people. Then one of those who had offered that prayer with him, went out and passed by some people in a mosque who were in the bowing position (in Ruku`) during their prayers (facing Jerusalem). He addressed them saying, `By Allah, I bear witness that I have offered prayer with the Prophet facing Makkah (Ka`bah).' Hearing that, those people immediately changed their direction towards the House (Ka`bah) while still as they were (i.e., in the same bowing position). Some Muslims who offered prayer towards the previous Qiblah (Jerusalem) before it was changed towards the House (the Ka`bah in Makkah) had died or had been martyred, and we did not know what to say about them (regarding their prayers towards Jerusalem). Allah then revealed:

(And Allah would never make your faith (prayers) to be lost (i.e., the prayers of those Muslims were valid)) (2:143)."

Al-Bukhari collected this narration, while Muslim collected it using another chain of narrators. Muhammad bin Ishaq reported that Al-Bara' narrated: Allah's Messenger used to offer prayers towards Bayt Al-Maqdis (in Jerusalem), but would keep looking at the sky awaiting Allah's command (to change the Qiblah). Then Allah revealed:

(Verily, We have seen the turning of your (Muhammad's) face towards the heaven. Surely, We shall turn you to a Qiblah (prayer direction) that shall please you, so turn your face in the direction of Al-Masjid Al-Haram (at Makkah).) (2:144)

A man from among the Muslims then said, "We wish we could know about those among us who died before the Qiblah was changed (i.e., towards Makkah) and also about our own prayers, that we had performed towards Bayt Al-Maqdis." Allah then revealed:

(And Allah would never make your faith (prayers) to be lost.) (2:143)

The fools among the people, meaning the People of the Scripture (Jews and Christians), said, "What made them change the former Qiblah that they used to face" Allah then revealed:

(The fools (idolators, hypocrites, and Jews) among the people will say...)

until the end of the Ayah.

`Ali bin Abu Talhah related that Ibn `Abbas said: When Allah's Messenger migrated to Al-Madinah, Allah commanded him to face Bayt Al-Maqdis (Jerusalem). The Jews were delighted then. Allah's Messenger faced Jerusalem for over ten months. However, he liked (to offer prayer in the direction of) Prophet Ibrahim's Qiblah (the Ka`bah in Makkah) and used to supplicate to Allah and kept looking up to the sky (awaiting Allah's command in this regard). Allah then revealed:

(turn your faces (in prayer) in that direction.) meaning, its direction. The Jews did not like this change and said, "What made them change the Qiblah that they used to face (meaning Jerusalem)" Allah revealed:

(Say (O Muhammad ): "To Allah belong both, east and the west. He guides whom He wills to the straight way.")

There are several other Ahadith on this subject. In summary, Allah's Messenger was commanded to face Bayt Al-Maqdis (during the prayer) and he used to offer prayer towards it in Makkah between the two corners (of Ka`bah), so that the Ka`bah would be between him and Bayt Al-Maqdis8. When the Prophet migrated to Al-Madinah, this practice was no longer possible; then Allah commanded him to offer prayer towards Bayt Al-Maqdis, as Ibn Abbas and the majority of the scholars have stated.

Al-Bukhari reported in his Sahih that the news (of the change of Qiblah) was conveyed to some of the Ansar while they were performing the `Asr (Afternoon) prayer towards Bayt Al-Maqdis, upon hearing that, they immediately changed their direction and faced the Ka`bah.

It is reported in the Sahihayn (Al-Bukhari Muslim) that Ibn `Umar narrated: While the people were in Quba' (Mosque) performing the Fajr (Dawn) prayer, a man came and said, "A (part of the) Qur'an was revealed tonight to Allah's Messenger and he was commanded to face the Ka`bah. Therefore, face the Ka`bah. They were facing Ash-Sham, so they turned towards the Ka`bah.

These Hadiths prove that the Nasikh (a Text that abrogates a previous Text) only applies after one acquires knowledge of it, even if the Nasikh had already been revealed and announced. This is why the Companions mentioned above were not commanded to repeat the previous `Asr, Maghrib and `Isha' prayers (although they had prayed them towards Jerusalem after Allah had changed the Qiblah). Allah knows best.

When the change of Qiblah (to Ka`bah in Makkah) occurred, those inflicted with hypocrisy and mistrust, and the disbelieving Jews, both were led astray from the right guidance and fell into confusion. They said:

(What has turned them (Muslims) from their Qiblah to which they used to face in prayer.)

They asked, "What is the matter with these people (Muslims) who one time face this direction (Jerusalem), and then face that direction (Makkah)" Allah answered their questions when He stated:

(Say (O Muhammad ): "To Allah belong both, east and the west.) meaning, the command, the decision and the authority are for Allah Alone. Hence:

(...so wherever you turn (yourselves or your faces) there is the Face of Allah (and He is High above, over His Throne).) (2:115),

and:

( It is not Al-Birr (piety, righteousness) that you turn your faces towards east and (or) west (in prayers); but Al-Birr is the one who believes in Allah.) (2:177) This statement means, the best act is to adhere to Allah's commands. Hence, wherever He commands us to face, we should face. Also, since obedience requires implementing Allah's commands, if He commands us every day to face different places, we are His servants and under His disposal, and we face whatever He orders us to face. Certainly, Allah's care and kindness towards His servant and Messenger, Muhammad , and certainly, his Ummah (Muslim nation) is profoundly great. Allah has guided them to the Qiblah of (Prophet) Ibrahim -- Allah's Khalil (intimate friend). He has commanded them to face the Ka`bah, the most honorable house (of worship) on the face of the earth, which was built by Ibrahim Al-Khalil in the Name of Allah, the One without a partner. This is why Allah said afterwards:

(Say (O Muhammad ): "To Allah belong both, east and the west. He guides whom He wills to the straight way.")

Imam Ahmad reported that `A'ishah (the Prophet's wife) said that Allah's Messenger said about the People of the Scripture (Jews and Christians):

«إِنَّهُم لَا يَحْسِدُونَنَا عَلَى شَيْءٍ كَمَا يَحْسِدُونَنَا عَلَى يَوْمِ الْجُمُعَةِ الَّتِي هَدَانَا اللهُ لَهَا وَضَلُّوا عَنْهَا وَعَلَى الْقِبْلَةِ الَّتِي هَدَانَا اللهُ لَهَا وَضَلُّوا عَنْهَا وَعَلَى قَوْلِنَا خَلْفَ الْإِمَامِ: آمِين»

(They do not envy us for a matter more than they envy us for Jumu`ah (Friday) to which Allah has guided us and from which they were led astray; for the (true) Qiblah to which Allah has directed us and from which they were led astray; and for our saying `Amin' behind the Imam (leader of the prayer).)

## The Virtues of Muhammad's Nation

Allah said:

(Thus We have made you )true Muslims(, a Wasat (just) (and the best) nation, that you be witnesses over mankind and the Messenger (Muhammad ) be a witness over you.)

Allah stated that He has changed our Qiblah to the Qiblah of Ibrahim and chose it for us so that He makes us the best nation ever. Hence, we will be the witnesses over the nations on the Day of Resurrection, for all of them will then agree concerning our virtue. The word Wasat in the Ayah means the best and the most honored. Therefore, saying that (the Prophet's tribe) Quraysh is in the Wasat regarding Arab tribes and their areas, means the best. Similarly, saying that Allah's Messenger was in the Wasat of his people, means he was from the best subtribe. Also, `Asr, the prayer that is described as `Wusta' (a variation of the word Wasat), means the best prayer, as the authentic collections of Ahadith reported. Since Allah made this Ummah (Muslim nation) the Wasat, He has endowed her with the most complete legislation, the best Manhaj (way, method, etc.,) and the clearest Madhhab (methodology, mannerism, etc). Allah said:

(He has chosen you (to convey His Message of Islamic Monotheism to mankind), and has not laid upon you in religion any hardship: it is the religion of your father Ibrahim. It is He (Allah) Who has named you Muslims both before and in this (the Qur'an), that the Messenger (Muhammad ) may be a witness over you and you be witnesses over mankind!) (22:78)

Moreover, Imam Ahmad reported that Abu Sa`id narrated: Allah's Messenger said:

«قَالَ: وَالْوَسَطُ الْعَدْلُ، فَتُدْعَوْنَ فَتَشْهَدُونَ لَهُ بِالْبَلَاغِ ثُمَّ أَشْهَدُ عَلَيْكُم»

(Nuh will be called on the Day of Resurrection and will be asked, `Have you conveyed (the Message)' He will say, `Yes.' His people will be summoned and asked, `Has Nuh conveyed (the Message) to you' They will say, `No warner came to us and no one (Prophet) was sent to us.' Nuh will be asked, `Who testifies for you' He will say, `Muhammad and his Ummah.')

This is why Allah said:

(Thus We have made you a Wasat nation.)

The Prophet said; (The Wasat means the `Adl (just). You will be summoned to testify that Nuh has conveyed (his Message), and I will attest to your testimony.)

It was also recorded by Al-Bukhari, At-Tirmidhi, An-Nasa'i and Ibn Majah.

Imam Ahmad also reported that Abu Sa`id Khudri narrated: Allah's Messenger said:

«يَجِيءُ النَّبِيُّ يَوْمَ الْقِيَامَةِ وَمَعَهُ الرَّجُلَانِ وَأَكْثَرُ مِنْ ذلِكَ، فَيُدْعَى قَوْمُهُ، فَيُقَالُ: هَلْ بَلَّغَكُمْ هَذَا؟ فَيَقُولُونَ: لَا فَيُقَالُ لَهُ: هَلْ بَلَّغْتَ قَوْمَكَ؟ فَيَقُولُ: نَعَمْ، فَيُقَالُ: مَنْ يَشْهَدُ لَكَ؟ فَيَقُولُ: مُحَمَّدٌ وَأُمَّتُهُ، فَيُدْعَى مُحَمَّدٌ وَأُمَّتُهُ، فَيُقَالُ لَهُمْ: هَلْ بَلَّغَ هَذَا قَوْمَهُ؟ فَيَقُولُونَ: نَعَمْ، فَيُقَالُ: وَمَا عِلْمُكُمْ؟ فَيَقُولُونَ: جَاءَنَا نَبِيُّنَا صلى الله عليه وسلم فأخبَرَنَا أَنَّ الرُّسُلَ قَدْ بَلَّغُوا،

(The Prophet would come on the Day of Resurrection with two or more people (his only following!), and his people would also be summoned and asked, `Has he (their Prophet) conveyed (the Message) to you' They would say, `No.' He would be asked, `Have you conveyed (the Message) to your people' He would say, `Yes.' He would be asked, `Who testifies for you' He would say, `Muhammad and his Ummah.' Muhammad and his Ummah would then be summoned and asked, `Has he conveyed (the Message) to his people' They would say, `Yes.' They would be asked, `Who told you that' They would say, `Our Prophet (Muhammad) came to us and told us that the Messengers have conveyed (their Messages). ')

Hence Allah's statement:

فَذلِكَ قَوْلُهُ عَزَّ وَجَلَّ:

[وَكَذَلِكَ جَعَلْنَكُمْ أُمَّةً وَسَطًا]

(Thus We have made you a Wasat nation.)

He said, "(meaning) the `Adl,' (he then continued reciting the Ayah):

(Thus We have made you, a just (and the best) nation, that you be witnesses over mankind and the Messenger (Muhammad ) be a witness over you.)"

Furthermore, Imam Ahmad reported that Abul-Aswad narrated: I came to Al-Madinah and found that an epidemic had broken out that caused many fatalities. I sat next to `Umar bin Al-Khattab once when a funeral procession started and the people praised the dead person. `Umar said, "Wajabat (it will be recorded as such), Wajabat!" Then another funeral was brought forth and the people criticized the dead person. Again, `Umar said, "Wajabat." Abul-Aswad asked, "What is Wajabat, O Leader of the faithful" He said, "I said just like Allah's Messenger had said:

《أَيُّمَا مُسْلِمٍ شَهِدَ لَهُ أَرْبَعَةٌ بِخَيْرٍ أَدْخَلَهُ اللهُ الْجَنَّةَ》

(Any Muslim for whom four testify that he was righteous, then Allah will enter him into Paradise.'

We said, `What about three' He said,

《وَثَلَاثَةٌ》

`And three.'

We said, `And two' He said,

《وَاثْنَانِ》

`And two.'

We did not ask him about (the testimony) of one (believing) person.)"

This was also recorded by Al-Bukhari, At-Tirmidhi, and An-Nasa'i.

### The Wisdom behind changing the Qiblah

Allah then said:

(And We made the Qiblah (prayer direction towards Jerusalem) which you used to face, only to test those who followed the Messenger (Muhammad ) from those who would turn on their heels (i.e., disobey the Messenger). Indeed it was great (heavy, difficult) except for those whom Allah guided.)

Allah states thus: We have legislated for you, O Muhammad, facing Bayt Al-Maqdis at first and then changed it to the Ka`bah so as to find who will follow and obey you and thus face whatever you face.

(...from those who would turn on their heels.) meaning, reverts from his religion. )Allah then said:(

(Indeed it was great (heavy, difficult))

The Ayah indicates that changing the Qiblah from Bayt Al-Maqdis to the Ka`bah is heavy on the heart, except for whomever Allah has rightly guided their hearts, who believe in the truth of the Messenger with certainty and that whatever he was sent with is the truth without doubt. It is they who believe that Allah does what He wills, decides what He wills, commands His servants with what He wills, abrogates any of His commands that He wills, and that He has the perfect wisdom and the unequivocal proof in all this. (The attitude of the believers in this respect is) unlike those who have a disease in their hearts, to whom whenever a matter occurs, it causes doubts, just as this same matter adds faith and certainty to the believers. Similarly, Allah said:

(And whenever there comes down a Surah (chapter from the Qur'an), some of them (hypocrites) say: "Which of you has had his faith increased by it" As for those who believe, it has increased their faith, and they rejoice. But as for those in whose hearts is a disease (of doubt, disbelief and hypocrisy), it will add doubt and disbelief to their doubt and disbelief; and they die while they are disbelievers.) (9:124, 125)

and:

(And We send down of the Qur'an that which is a healing and a mercy to those who believe, and it increases the wrongdoers in nothing but loss.) (17:82)

Certainly, those who remained faithful to the Messenger , obeyed him and faced whatever Allah commanded them, without doubt or hesitation, were the leaders of the Companions. Some scholars stated that the Early Migrants (who migrated with the Prophet from Makkah to Al-Madinah) and Ansar (the residents of Al-Madinah who gave aid and refuge to both the Prophet and the Migrants) were those who offered prayers towards the two Qiblah (Bayt Al-Maqdis and then the Ka`bah). Al-Bukhari reported in the explanation of the Ayah (2:143) that Ibn `Umar narrated: While the people were performing the Fajr (Dawn) prayer in the Quba' Mosque, a man came and said, "Qur'an was revealed to the Prophet and he was ordered to face the Ka`bah. Therefore, face the Ka`bah." They then faced the Ka`bah. Muslim also recorded it.

At-Tirmidhi added that they were performing Ruku` (bowing down in prayer), and then changed the direction (of the Qiblah) to the Ka`bah while still bowing down. Muslim reported this last narration from Anas. These Hadiths all indicate the perfect obedience the Companions had for Allah and His Messenger and their compliance with Allah's commandments, may Allah be pleased with them all.

Allah said:

# Chapter 2: Al-Baqarah (The Cow), Verses 142-252

(And Allah would never make your faith (prayers) to be lost.) meaning, the reward of your prayers towards Bayt Al-Maqdis before would not be lost with Allah. It is reported in Sahih that Abu Ishaq As-Sabi`y related that Bara' narrated: "The people asked about the matter of those who offered prayers towards Bayt Al-Maqdis and died (before the Qiblah was changed to Ka`bah). Allah revealed:

(And Allah would never make your faith (prayers) to be lost.)"

It was also recorded by At-Tirmidhi from Ibn `Abbas, and At-Tirmidhi graded it Sahih.

Ibn Ishaq reported that Ibn `Abbas narrated:

(And Allah would never make your faith to be lost.) entails: Your (prayer towards) the first Qiblah and your believing your Prophet and obeying him by facing the second Qiblah; He will grant you the rewards for all these acts. Indeed,

(Truly, Allah is full of kindness, the Most Merciful towards mankind.)"

Furthermore, it is reported in the Sahih that Allah's Messenger saw a woman among the captives who was separated from her child. Whenever she found a boy (infant) among the captives, she would hold him close to her chest, as she was looking for her boy. When she found her child, she embraced him and gave him her breast to nurse. Allah's Messenger said:

«أَتَرَوْنَ هذِهِ طَارِحَةً وَلَدَهَا فِي النَّارِ وَهِيَ تَقْدِرُ عَلَى أَنْ لَا تَطْرَحَهُ»

(Do you think that this woman would willingly throw her son in the fire)

They said, "No, O Messenger of Allah!" He said,

«فَوَاللهِ للهُ أَرْحَمُ بِعِبَادِهِ مِنْ هذِهِ بِوَلَدِهَا»

(By Allah! Allah is more merciful with His servants than this woman with her son.)

### Surah: 2 Ayah: 144

﴿ قَدْ نَرَىٰ تَقَلُّبَ وَجْهِكَ فِي ٱلسَّمَآءِ ۖ فَلَنُوَلِّيَنَّكَ قِبْلَةً تَرْضَىٰهَا ۚ فَوَلِّ وَجْهَكَ شَطْرَ ٱلْمَسْجِدِ ٱلْحَرَامِ ۚ وَحَيْثُ مَا كُنتُمْ فَوَلُّواْ وُجُوهَكُمْ

شَطْرَهُ ۚ وَإِنَّ ٱلَّذِينَ أُوتُوا۟ ٱلْكِتَٰبَ لَيَعْلَمُونَ أَنَّهُ ٱلْحَقُّ مِن رَّبِّهِمْ ۗ وَمَا ٱللَّهُ بِغَٰفِلٍ عَمَّا يَعْمَلُونَ ﴿١٤٤﴾

144. Verily! We have seen the turning of your (Muhammad's (peace be upon him)) face towards the heaven. Surely, We shall turn you to a Qiblah (prayer direction) that shall please you, so turn your face in the direction of Al-Masjid- al-Harâm (at Makkah). And wheresoever you people are, turn your faces (in prayer) in that direction. Certainly, the people who were given the Scripture (i.e. Jews and the Christians) know well that, that (your turning towards the direction of the Ka'bah at Makkah in prayers) is the truth from their Lord. And Allâh is not unaware of what they do.

### Transliteration

144. Qad nara taqalluba wajhika fee alssama-i falanuwalliyannaka qiblatan tardaha fawalli wajhaka shatra almasjidi alharami wahaythu ma kuntum fawalloo wujoohakum shatrahu wa-inna allatheena ootoo alkitaba layaAAlamoona annahu alhaqqu min rabbihim wama Allahu bighafilin AAamma yaAAmaloona

### Tafsir Ibn Kathir

### The First Abrogation in the Qur'an was about the Qiblah

`Ali bin Abu Talhah related that Ibn `Abbas narrated: The first abrogated part in the Qur'an was about the Qiblah. When Allah's Messenger migrated to Al-Madinah, the majority of its people were Jews, and Allah commanded him to face Bayt Al-Maqdis. The Jews were delighted then. Allah's Messenger faced it for ten and some months, but he liked to face the Qiblah of Ibrahim (Ka`bah in Makkah). He used to supplicate to Allah and look up to the sky (awaiting Allah's command). Allah then revealed:

(Verily, We have seen the turning of your (Muhammad's) face towards the heaven), until,

(turn your faces (in prayer) in that direction.)

The Jews did not like this ruling and said:

("What has turned them (Muslims) from their Qiblah (prayer direction) to which they used to face in prayer." Say (O Muhammad), "To Allah belong both, east and the west.") (2:142)

Allah said:

(. ..so wherever you turn (yourselves or your faces) there is the Face of Allah) (2:115), and:

(And We made the Qiblah (prayer direction towards Jerusalem) which you used to face, only to test those who followed the Messenger (Muhammad ) from those who would turn on their heels (i.e., disobey the Messenger).) (2:143)

### Is the Qiblah the Ka`bah itself or its General Direction

Al-Hakim related that `Ali bin Abu Talib said:

(...so turn your face in the direction of Al-Masjid Al-Haram (at Makkah).) means its direction."

Al-Hakim then commented that the chain of this narration is authentic and that they (i.e., Al-Bukhari and Muslim) did not include it in their collections.

This ruling concerning the Qiblah is also the opinion of Abu Al-`Aliyah, Mujahid, `Ikrimah, Sa`id bin Jubayr, Qatadah, Ar-Rabi` bin Anas and others. Allah's Statement:

(And wheresoever you people are, turn your faces (in prayer) in that direction) is a command from Allah to face the Ka`bah from wherever one is on the earth: the east, west, north or south. The exception is of the voluntary prayer (Nafl) while one is traveling, for one is allowed to offer it in any direction his body is facing, while his heart is intending the Ka`bah. Also, when the battle is raging, one is allowed to offer prayer, however he is able. Also, included are those who are not sure of the direction and offer prayer in the wrong direction, thinking that it is the direction of the Qiblah, because Allah does not burden a soul beyond what it can bear.

### The Jews had Knowledge that the (Muslim) Qiblah would later be changed

Allah stated that:

(Certainly, the people who were given the Scripture (i.e., Jews and the Christians) know well that, that (your turning towards the direction of the Ka`bah at Makkah in prayers) is the truth from their Lord.)

This Ayah means: The Jews, who did not like that you change your Qiblah from Bayt Al-Maqdis, already knew that Allah will command you (O Muhammad) to face the Ka`bah. The Jews read in their Books their Prophets' description of Allah's Messenger and his Ummah, and that Allah has endowed and honored him with the complete and honorable legislation. Yet, the People of the Book deny these facts because of their envy, disbelief and rebellion. This is why Allah threatened them when He said:

(And Allah is not unaware of what they do.)

### Surah: 2 Ayah: 145

﴿ وَلَئِنْ أَتَيْتَ ٱلَّذِينَ أُوتُواْ ٱلْكِتَـٰبَ بِكُلِّ ءَايَةٍ مَّا تَبِعُواْ قِبْلَتَكَ وَمَآ أَنتَ بِتَابِعٍ قِبْلَتَهُمْ وَمَا بَعْضُهُم بِتَابِعٍ قِبْلَةَ بَعْضٍ وَلَئِنِ ٱتَّبَعْتَ أَهْوَآءَهُم مِّنۢ بَعْدِ مَا جَآءَكَ مِنَ ٱلْعِلْمِ إِنَّكَ إِذًا لَّمِنَ ٱلظَّـٰلِمِينَ ﴾

145. And even if you were to bring to the people of the Scripture (Jews and Christians) all the Ayât (proofs, evidences, verses, lessons, signs, revelations, etc.), they would not follow your Qiblah (prayer direction), nor are you going to follow their Qiblah (prayer direction). And they will not follow each other's Qiblah (prayer direction). Verily, if you follow their desires after that which you have received of knowledge (from Allâh), then indeed you will be one of the Zâlimûn (polytheists, wrong-doers, etc.).

### Transliteration

145. Wala-in atayta allatheena ootoo alkitaba bikulli ayatin ma tabiAAoo qiblataka wama anta bitabiAAin qiblatahum wama baAAduhum bitabiAAin qiblata baAAdin wala-ini ittabaAAta ahwaahum min baAAdi ma jaaka mina alAAilmi innaka ithan lamina al*thth*alimeena

### Tafsir Ibn Kathir

**The Stubbornness and Disbelief of the Jews**

Allah describes the Jews' disbelief, stubbornness and defiance of what they know of the truth of Allah's Messenger , that if the Prophet brought forward every proof to the truth of what he was sent with, they will never obey him or abandon following their desires. In another instance, Allah said:

(Truly, those, against whom the Word (wrath) of your Lord has been justified, will not believe. Even if every sign should come to them, until they see the painful torment.) (10:96, 97)

This is why Allah said here:

(And even if you were to bring to the People of the Scripture (Jews and Christians) all the Ayat (proofs, evidences, verses, lessons, signs, revelations, etc.), they would not follow your Qiblah (prayer direction)).

Allah's statement:

(...nor are you going to follow their Qiblah ), indicates the vigor with which Allah's Messenger implements what Allah commanded him. Allah's statement also indicates that as much as the Jews adhere to their opinions and desires, the Prophet adheres by Allah's commands, obeying Him and following what

# Chapter 2: Al-Baqarah (The Cow), Verses 142-252

pleases Him, and that he would never adhere to their desires in any case. Hence, praying towards Bayt Al-Maqdis was not because it was the Qiblah of the Jews, but because Allah had commanded it. Allah then warns those who knowingly defy the truth, because the proof against those who know is stronger than against other people. This is why Allah said to His Messenger and his Ummah:

(Verily, if you follow their desires after that which you have received of knowledge (from Allah), then indeed you will be one of the wrongdoers.)

## Surah: 2 Ayah: 146 & Ayah: 147

﴿ ٱلَّذِينَ ءَاتَيْنَٰهُمُ ٱلْكِتَٰبَ يَعْرِفُونَهُۥ كَمَا يَعْرِفُونَ أَبْنَآءَهُمْ وَإِنَّ فَرِيقًا مِّنْهُمْ لَيَكْتُمُونَ ٱلْحَقَّ وَهُمْ يَعْلَمُونَ ﴾

146. Those to whom We gave the Scripture (Jews and Christians) recognize him (Muhammad (peace be upon him) or the Ka'bah at Makkah) as they recognize their sons. But verily, a party of them conceal the truth while they know it - (i.e. the qualities of Muhammad (peace be upon him) which are written in the Taurât (Torah) and the Injeel (Gospel))

﴿ ٱلْحَقُّ مِن رَّبِّكَ فَلَا تَكُونَنَّ مِنَ ٱلْمُمْتَرِينَ ﴾

147. (This is) the truth from your Lord. So be you not one of those who doubt.

### Transliteration

146. Allatheena ataynahumu alkitaba yaAArifoonahu kama yaAArifoona abnaahum wa-inna fareeqan minhum layaktumoona alhaqqa wahum yaAAlamoona 147. Alhaqqu min rabbika fala takoonanna mina almumtareena

### Tafsir Ibn Kathir

#### The Jews know that the Prophet is True, but they hide the Truth

Allah states that the scholars of the People of the Scripture know the truth of what Allah's Messenger was sent with, just as one of them knows his own child, which is a parable that the Arabs use to describe what is very apparent. Similarly, in a Hadith, Allah's Messenger said to a man who had a youngster with him:

«ابْنُكَ هَذَا»

(Is this your son)

He said, "Yes, O Messenger of Allah! I testify to this fact." Allah's Messenger said:

»أَمَا إِنَّهُ لَا يَجْنِي عَلَيْكَ وَلَا تَجْنِي عَلَيْهِ«

(Well, you would not transgress against him nor would he transgress against you.)

According to Al-Qurtubi, it was narrated that `Umar said to `Abdullah bin Salam (an Israelite scholar who became a Muslim), "Do you recognize Muhammad as you recognize your own son" He replied, "Yes, and even more. The Honest One descended from heaven on the Honest One on the earth with his (i.e., Muhammad's) description and I recognized him, although I do not know anything about his mother's story."

Allah states next that although they had knowledge and certainty in the Prophet , they still:

(conceal the truth.)

The Ayah indicates that they hide the truth from the people, about the Prophet , that they find in their Books,

(while they know it. ) Allah then strengthens the resolve of His Prophet and the believers and affirms that what the Prophet came with is the truth without doubt, saying:

((This is) the truth from your Lord. So be you not one of those who doubt.)

### Surah: 2 Ayah: 148

﴿ وَلِكُلٍّ وِجْهَةٌ هُوَ مُوَلِّيهَا ۖ فَٱسْتَبِقُوا۟ ٱلْخَيْرَٰتِ ۚ أَيْنَ مَا تَكُونُوا۟ يَأْتِ بِكُمُ ٱللَّهُ جَمِيعًا ۚ إِنَّ ٱللَّهَ عَلَىٰ كُلِّ شَىْءٍ قَدِيرٌ ﴾

148. For every nation there is a direction to which they face (in their prayers). So hasten towards all that is good. Wheresoever you may be, Allâh will bring you together (on the Day of Resurrection). Truly, Allâh is Able to do all things.

### Transliteration

148. Walikullin wijhatun huwa muwalleeha faistabiqoo alkhayrati aynama takoonoo ya/ti bikumu Allahu jameeAAan inna Allaha AAala kulli shay-in qadeerun

### Tafsir Ibn Kathir

**Every Nation has a Qiblah**

Al-`Awfi reported that Ibn `Abbas said:

Chapter 2: Al-Baqarah (The Cow), Verses 142-252        33

(For every nation there is a direction to which they face (in their prayers))

"This talks about followers of the various religions. Hence, every nation and tribe has its own Qiblah that they choose, while Allah's appointed Qiblah is what the believers face."

Abul-`Aliyah said, "The Jew has a direction to which he faces (in the prayer). The Christian has a direction to which he faces. Allah has guided you, O (Muslim) Ummah, to a Qiblah which is the true Qiblah." This statement was also related to Mujahid, `Ata' Ad-Dahhak, Ar-Rabi` bin Anas, As-Suddi, and others.

This last Ayah is similar to what Allah said:

(To each among you, We have prescribed a law and a clear way. If Allah had willed, He would have made you one nation, but that (He) may test you in what He has given you; so compete in good deeds. The return of you (all) is to Allah.) (5:48)

In the Ayah (2:148), Allah said:

(Wheresoever you may be, Allah will bring you together (on the Day of Resurrection). Truly, Allah is able to do all things.) meaning: He is able to gather you from the earth even if your bodies and flesh disintegrated and scattered.

### Surah: 2 Ayah: 149 & Ayah: 150

﴿ وَمِنْ حَيْثُ خَرَجْتَ فَوَلِّ وَجْهَكَ شَطْرَ ٱلْمَسْجِدِ ٱلْحَرَامِ ۖ وَإِنَّهُ لَلْحَقُّ مِن رَّبِّكَ ۗ وَمَا ٱللَّهُ بِغَـٰفِلٍ عَمَّا تَعْمَلُونَ ۝ ﴾

149. And from wheresoever you start forth (for prayers), turn your face in the direction of Al-Masjid-al-Harâm (at Makkah), that is indeed the truth from your Lord. And Allâh is not unaware of what you do.

﴿ وَمِنْ حَيْثُ خَرَجْتَ فَوَلِّ وَجْهَكَ شَطْرَ ٱلْمَسْجِدِ ٱلْحَرَامِ ۚ وَحَيْثُ مَا كُنتُمْ فَوَلُّواْ وُجُوهَكُمْ شَطْرَهُۥ لِئَلَّا يَكُونَ لِلنَّاسِ عَلَيْكُمْ حُجَّةٌ إِلَّا ٱلَّذِينَ ظَلَمُواْ مِنْهُمْ فَلَا تَخْشَوْهُمْ وَٱخْشَوْنِى وَلِأُتِمَّ نِعْمَتِى عَلَيْكُمْ وَلَعَلَّكُمْ تَهْتَدُونَ ۝ ﴾

150. And from wheresoever you start forth (for prayers), turn your face in the direction of Al-Masjid-al-Harâm (at Makkah), and wheresoever you are, turn your faces towards, it (when you pray) so that men may have no

argument against you except those of them that are wrong-doers, so fear them not, but fear Me! - And so that I may complete My Blessings on you and that you may be guided.

### Transliteration

149. Wamin haythu kharajta fawalli wajhaka shatra almasjidi alharami wa-innahu lalhaqqu min rabbika wama Allahu bighafilin AAamma taAAmaloona
150. Wamin haythu kharajta fawalli wajhaka shatra almasjidi alharami wahaythu ma kuntum fawalloo wujoohakum shatrahu li-alla yakoona lilnnasi AAalaykum hujjatun illa allatheena thalamoo minhum fala takhshawhum waikhshawnee wali-otimma niAAmatee AAalaykum walaAAallakum tahtadoona

### Tafsir Ibn Kathir

### Why was changing the Qiblah mentioned thrice

This is a third command from Allah to face Al-Masjid Al-Haram (the Sacred Mosque) from every part of the world (during prayer). It was said that Allah mentioned this ruling again here because it is connected to whatever is before and whatever is after it. Hence, Allah first said:

(Verily, We have seen the turning of your (Muhammad's) face towards the heaven. Surely, We shall turn you to a Qiblah (prayer direction) that shall please you) (2:144), until:

(Certainly, the people who were given the Scripture (i.e., Jews and the Christians) know well that, that (your turning towards the direction of the Ka`bah at Makkah in prayers) is the truth from their Lord. And Allah is not unaware of what they do.) (2:144)

Allah mentioned in these Ayat His fulfillment of the Prophet's wish and ordered him to face the Qiblah that he liked and is pleased with. In the second command, Allah said:

(And from wheresoever you start forth (for prayers), turn your face in the direction of Al-Masid Al-Haram that is indeed the truth from your Lord. And Allah is not unaware of what you do.)

Therefore, Allah states here that changing the Qiblah is also the truth from Him, thus upgrading the subject more than in the first Ayah, in which Allah agreed to what His Prophet had wished for. Thus Allah states that this is also the truth from Him that He likes and is pleased with. In the third command, Allah refutes the Jewish assertion that the Prophet faced their Qiblah, as they knew in their Books that the Prophet will later on be commanded to face the Qiblah of Ibrahim, the Ka`bah. The Arab disbelievers had no more argument concerning the Prophet's Qiblah after Allah commanded the Prophet to face the Qiblah of Ibrahim, which is more respected and honored, rather than the Qiblah of the Jews. The Arabs used to honor the Ka`bah and liked the fact that the Messenger was commanded to face it.

## The Wisdom behind abrogating the Previous Qiblah

Allah said:

(...so that men may have no argument against you)

Therefore, the People of the Book knew from the description of the Muslim Ummah that they would be ordered to face the Ka`bah. If the Muslims did not fit this description, the Jews would have used this fact against the Muslims. If the Muslims had remained on the Qiblah of Bayt Al-Maqdis, which was also the Qiblah of the Jews, this fact could have been used as the basis of argument by the Jews against other people.

Allah's Statement:

(...except those of them that are wrongdoers,) indicates the Mushrikin (polytheists) of Quraysh. The reasoning of these unjust persons was the unsound statement: "This man (Muhammad) claims that he follows the religion of Ibrahim! Hence, if his facing Bayt Al-Maqdis was a part of the religion of Ibrahim, why did he change it" The answer to this question is that Allah has chosen His Prophet to face Bayt Al-Maqdis first for certain wisdom, and he obeyed Allah regarding this command. Then, Allah changed the Qiblah to the Qiblah of Ibrahim, which is the Ka`bah, and he also obeyed Allah in this command. He, obeys Allah in all cases and never engages in the defiance of Allah even for an instant, and his Ummah imitates him in this.

Allah said:

(...so fear them not, but fear Me!) meaning: `Do not fear the doubts that the unjust, stubborn persons raise and fear Me Alone.' Indeed, Allah Alone deserves to be feared.

Allah said:

(...so that I may complete My blessings on you.)

This Ayah relates to Allah's statement:

(...so that men may have no argument against you), meaning: I will perfect My bounty on you by legislating for you to face the Ka`bah, so that the (Islamic) Shari`ah (law) is complete in every respect. Allah said:

(...that you may be guided.), meaning: `To be directed and guided to what the nations have been led astray from, We have guided you to it and preferred you with it.' This is why this Ummah is the best and most honored nation ever.

## Surah: 2 Ayah: 151 & Ayah: 152

﴿ كَمَآ أَرْسَلْنَا فِيكُمْ رَسُولاً مِّنكُمْ يَتْلُواْ عَلَيْكُمْ ءَايَـٰتِنَا وَيُزَكِّيكُمْ وَيُعَلِّمُكُمُ ٱلْكِتَـٰبَ وَٱلْحِكْمَةَ وَيُعَلِّمُكُم مَّا لَمْ تَكُونُواْ تَعْلَمُونَ ۝ ﴾

151. Similarly (to complete My Blessings on you), We have sent among you a Messenger (Muhammad (peace be upon him)) of your own, reciting to you Our Verses (the Qur'ân) and purifying you, and teaching you the Book (the Qur'ân) and the Hikmah (i.e. Sunnah, Islâmic laws and Fiqh - jurisprudence), and teaching you that which you used not to know.

﴿ فَٱذْكُرُونِىٓ أَذْكُرْكُمْ وَٱشْكُرُواْ لِى وَلَا تَكْفُرُونِ ۝ ﴾

152. Therefore remember Me (by praying, glorifying), I will remember you, and be grateful to Me (for My countless Favors on you) and never be ungrateful to Me.

### Transliteration

151. Kama arsalna feekum rasoolan minkum yatloo AAalaykum ayatina wayuzakkeekum wayuAAallimukumu alkitaba waalhikmata wayuAAallimukum ma lam takoonoo taAAlamoona  152. Faothkuroonee athkurkum waoshkuroo lee wala takfurooni

### Tafsir Ibn Kathir

#### Muhammad's Prophecy is a Great Bounty from Allah

Allah reminds His believing servants with what He has endowed them with by sending Muhammad as a Messenger to them, reciting to them Allah's clear Ayat and purifying and cleansing them from the worst types of behavior, the ills of the souls and the acts of Jahiliyyah (pre-Islamic era). The Messenger also takes them away from the darkness (of disbelief) to the light (of faith) and teaches them the Book, the Qur'an, and the Hikmah (i.e., the wisdom), which is his Sunnah. He also teaches them what they knew not. During the time of Jahiliyyah, they used to utter foolish statements. Later on, and with the blessing of the Prophet's Message and the goodness of his prophecy, they were elevated to the status of the Awliya' (loyal friends of Allah) and the rank of the scholars. Hence, they acquired the deepest knowledge among the people, the most pious hearts, and the most truthful tongues. Allah said:

(Indeed, Allah conferred a great favor on the believers when He sent among them a Messenger (Muhammad ) from among themselves, reciting unto them His verses (the Qur'an), and purifying them (from sins).) (3:164)

Allah also criticized those who did not give this bounty its due consideration, when He said:

(Have you not seen those who have changed the favors of Allah into disbelief (by denying Prophet Muhammad ) and his Message of Islam), and caused their people to dwell in the house of destruction) (14:28)

Ibn `Abbas commented, "Allah's favor means Muhammad." Therefore, Allah has commanded the believers to affirm this favor and to appreciate it by thanking and remembering Him:

(Therefore, remember Me. I will remember you, and be grateful to Me, and never be ungrateful to Me.)

Mujahid said that Allah's statement:

(Similarly (to complete My favor on you), We have sent among you a Messenger (Muhammad ) of your own,)

means: Therefore, remember Me in gratitude to My favor.

Al-Hasan Al-Basri commented about Allah's statement:

(Therefore remember Me. I will remember you), "Remember Me regarding what I have commanded you and I will remember you regarding what I have compelled Myself to do for your benefit (i.e., His rewards and forgiveness)."

An authentic Hadith states:

«يَقُولُ اللهُ تَعَالَى: مَنْ ذَكَرَنِي فِي نَفْسِهِ ذَكَرْتُهُ فِي نَفْسِي وَمَنْ ذَكَرَنِي فِي مَلَإٍ ذَكَرْتُهُ فِي مَلَإٍ خَيْرٍ مِنْه»

(Allah the Exalted said, `Whoever mentions Me to himself, then I will mention him to Myself; and whoever mentions Me in a gathering, I will mention him in a better gathering.)'

Imam Ahmad reported that Anas narrated that Allah's Messenger said:

«قَالَ اللهُ عَزَّ وَجَلَّ: يَا ابْنَ آدَمَ، إِنْ ذَكَرْتَنِي فِي نَفْسِكَ ذَكَرْتُكَ فِي نَفْسِي، إِنْ ذَكَرْتَنِي فِي مَلَإٍ ذَكَرْتُكَ فِي مَلَإٍ مِنَ الْمَلَائِكَةِ أَوْ قَالَ: فِي مَلَإٍ خَيْرٍ مِنْهُ وَإِنْ دَنَوْتَ مِنِّي شِبْرًا دَنَوْتُ مِنْكَ ذِرَاعًا، وَإِنْ دَنَوْتَ مِنِّي ذِرَاعًا دَنَوْتُ مِنْكَ بَاعًا، وَإِنْ أَتَيْتَنِي تَمْشِي أَتَيْتُكَ هَرْوَلَة»

(Allah the Exalted said, `O son of Adam! If you mention Me to yourself, I will mention you to Myself. If you mention Me in a gathering, I will mention you in a gathering of the angels (or said in a better gathering). If you draw closer to Me by a hand span, I will draw closer to you by forearm's length. If you draw closer to Me by a forearm's length, I will draw closer to you by an arm's length. And if you come to Me walking, I will come to you running).

Its chain is Sahih, it was recorded by Al-Bukhari. Allah said:

(...and be grateful to Me (for My countless favors on you) and never be ungrateful to Me.)

In this Ayah, Allah commands that He be thanked and appreciated, and promises even more rewards for thanking Him. Allah said in another Ayah:

(And (remember) when your Lord proclaimed: "If you give thanks (by accepting faith and worshipping none but Allah), I will give you more (of My blessings); but if you are thankless (i.e., disbelievers), verily, My punishment is indeed severe.)

Abu Raja' Al-`Utaridi said: `Imran bin Husayn came by us once wearing a nice silken garment that we never saw him wear before or afterwards. He said, "Allah's Messenger said:

«مَنْ أَنْعَمَ اللهُ عَلَيْهِ نِعْمَةً فَإِنَّ اللهَ يُحِبُّ أَنْ يَرَى أَثَرَ نِعْمَتِهِ عَلَى خَلْقِهِ»

(Those whom Allah has favored with a bounty, then Allah likes to see the effect of His bounty on His creation),

or he said,

«عَلَى عَبْدِهِ»

"on His servant" - according to Ruh (one of the narrators of the Hadith).

### Surah: 2 Ayah: 153 & Ayah: 154

﴿ يَٰٓأَيُّهَا ٱلَّذِينَ ءَامَنُواْ ٱسْتَعِينُواْ بِٱلصَّبْرِ وَٱلصَّلَوٰةِ ۚ إِنَّ ٱللَّهَ مَعَ ٱلصَّٰبِرِينَ ﴾ ۝

153. O you who believe! Seek help in patience and As-Salât (the prayer). Truly! Allâh is with As-Sâbirûn (the patient).

# Chapter 2: Al-Baqarah (The Cow), Verses 142-252

﴿ وَلَا تَقُولُواْ لِمَن يُقْتَلُ فِى سَبِيلِ ٱللَّهِ أَمْوَٰتٌ ۚ بَلْ أَحْيَآءٌ وَلَـٰكِن لَّا تَشْعُرُونَ ﴾

154. And say not of those who are killed in the Way of Allâh, "They are dead." Nay, they are living, but you perceive (it) not.

### Transliteration

153. Ya ayyuha allatheena amanoo istaAAeenoo bialssabri waalssalati inna Allaha maAAa alssabireena 154. Wala taqooloo liman yuqtalu fee sabeeli Allahi amwatun bal ahyaon walakin la tashAAuroona

### Tafsir Ibn Kathir

#### The Virtue of Patience and Prayer

After Allah commanded that He be appreciated, He ordained patience and prayer. It is a fact that the servant is either enjoying a bounty that he should be thankful for, or suffering a calamity that he should meet with patience. A Hadith states:

«عَجَبًا لِلْمُؤْمِنِ لَا يَقْضِي اللهُ لَهُ قَضَاءً إِلَّا كَانَ خَيْرًا لَهُ: إِنْ أَصَابَتْهُ سَرَّاءُ فَشَكَرَ كَانَ خَيْرًا لَهُ وَإِنْ أَصَابَتْهُ ضَرَّاءُ فَصَبَرَ كَانَ خَيْرًا لَهُ»

(Amazing is the believer, for whatever Allah decrees for him, it is better for him! If he is tested with a bounty, he is grateful for it and this is better for him; and if he is afflicted with a hardship, he is patient with it and this is better for him.)

Allah has stated that the best tools to help ease the effects of the afflictions are patience and prayer. Earlier we mentioned Allah's statement:

(And seek help in patience and As-Salah (the prayer) and truly, it is extremely heavy and hard except for Al-Khashi`in )i.e., the true believers in Allah() (2:45)

There are several types of Sabr - patience: one for avoiding the prohibitions and sins, one for acts of worship and obedience. The second type carries more rewards than the first type. There is a third type of patience required in the face of the afflictions and hardships, which is mandatory, like repentance.

`Abdur-Rahman bin Zayd bin Aslam said, "Sabr has two parts: patience for the sake of Allah concerning what He is pleased with (i.e., acts of worship and obedience), even if it is hard on the heart and the body, and patience when avoiding what He dislikes, even if it is desired. Those who acquire these qualities will be among the patient persons whom Allah shall greet (when they meet Him in the Hereafter; refer to Surat Al-Ahzab 33:44), Allah willing."

**The Life enjoyed by Martyrs**

Allah's statement:

(And say not of those who are killed in the way of Allah, "They are dead." Nay, they are living,) indicates that the martyrs are alive and receiving their sustenance.

Muslim reported in his Sahih:

«أَنَّ أَرْوَاحَ الشُّهَدَاءِ فِي حَوَاصِلِ طَيْرٍ خُضْرٍ، تَسْرَحُ فِي الْجَنَّةِ حَيْثُ شَاءَتْ، ثُمَّ تَأْوِي إِلَى قَنَادِيلَ مُعَلَّقَةٍ تَحْتَ الْعَرْشِ، فَاطَّلَعَ عَلَيْهِمْ رَبُّكَ اطِّلَاعَةً، فَقَالَ: مَاذَا تَبْغُونَ؟ فَقَالُوا: يَا رَبَّنَا وَأَيَّ شَيْءٍ نَبْغِي، وَقَدْ أَعْطَيْتَنَا مَا لَمْ تُعْطِ أَحَدًا مِنْ خَلْقِكَ؟ ثُمَّ عَادَ إِلَيْهِمْ بِمِثْلِ هذَا، فَلَمَّا رَأَوْا أَنَّهُمْ لَا يُتْرَكُونَ مِنْ أَنْ يُسْأَلُوا، قَالُوا: نُرِيدُ أَنْ تَرُدَّنَا إِلَى الدَّارِ الدُّنْيَا فَنُقَاتِلَ فِي سَبِيلِكَ حَتَّى نُقْتَلَ فِيكَ مَرَّةً أُخْرَى لِمَا يَرَوْنَ مِنْ ثَوَابِ الشَّهَادَةِ فَيَقُولُ الرَّبُّ جَلَّ جَلَالُهُ: إِنِّي كَتَبْتُ أَنَّهُمْ إِلَيْهَا لَا يَرْجِعُونَ»

(The souls of the martyrs are inside green birds and move about in Paradise wherever they wish. Then, they take refuge in lamps that are hanging under the Throne (of Allah). Your Lord looked at them and asked them, `What do you wish for' They said, `What more could we wish for while You have favored us with what You have not favored any other of your creation' He repeated the question again. When they realize that they will be asked (until they answer), they said, `We wish that You send us back to the earthly life, so that we fight in Your cause until we are killed in Your cause again,' (because of what they enjoy of the rewards of martyrdom). The Lord then said, `I have written that they will not be returned to it (earthly life) again.)

Imam Ahmad reported that `Abdur-Rahman bin Ka`b bin Malik narrated from his father that Allah's Messenger said:

«نَسَمَةُ الْمُؤْمِنِ طَائِرٌ تَعْلَقُ فِي شَجَرِ الْجَنَّةِ حَتَّى يَرْجِعَهُ اللهُ إِلَى جَسَدِهِ

$$\text{«يَوْمَ يَبْعَثُهُ»}$$

(The believer's soul is a bird that feeds on the trees of Paradise until Allah sends it back to its body when the person is resurrected.)

This Hadith includes all the believers in its general meaning. Thus, the fact that the Qur'an mentions the martyrs in particular in the above Ayah serves to honor, glorify and favor them (although the other believers share the rewards they enjoy).

### Surah: 2 Ayah: 155, Ayah: 156 & Ayah: 157

$$\text{﴿ وَلَنَبْلُوَنَّكُم بِشَيْءٍ مِّنَ ٱلْخَوْفِ وَٱلْجُوعِ وَنَقْصٍ مِّنَ ٱلْأَمْوَالِ وَٱلْأَنفُسِ وَٱلثَّمَرَاتِ وَبَشِّرِ ٱلصَّابِرِينَ ﴾}$$

155. And certainly, We shall test you with something of fear, hunger, loss of wealth, lives and fruits, but give glad tidings to As-Sâbirûn (the patient).

$$\text{﴿ ٱلَّذِينَ إِذَآ أَصَابَتْهُم مُّصِيبَةٌ قَالُوٓاْ إِنَّا لِلَّهِ وَإِنَّآ إِلَيْهِ رَاجِعُونَ ﴾}$$

156. Who, when afflicted with calamity, say: "Truly! To Allâh we belong and truly, to Him we shall return."

$$\text{﴿ أُوْلَٰٓئِكَ عَلَيْهِمْ صَلَوَاتٌ مِّن رَّبِّهِمْ وَرَحْمَةٌ وَأُوْلَٰٓئِكَ هُمُ ٱلْمُهْتَدُونَ ﴾}$$

157. They are those on whom are the Salawât (i.e. who are blessed and will be forgiven) from their Lord, and (they are those who) receive His Mercy, and it is they who are the guided ones.

### Transliteration

155. Walanabluwannakum bishay-in mina alkhawfi waaljooAAi wanaqsin mina al-amwali waal-anfusi waaththamarati wabashshiri alssabireena 156. Allatheena itha asabat-hum museebatun qaloo inna lillahi wa-inna ilayhi rajiAAoona 157. Ola-ika AAalayhim salawatun min rabbihim warahmatun waola-ika humu almuhtadoona

### Tafsir Ibn Kathir

**The Believer is Patient with the Affliction and thus gains a Reward**

Allah informs us that He tests and tries His servants, just as He said in another Ayah:

(And surely, We shall try you till We test those who strive hard (for the cause of Allah) and As-Sabirin (the patient), and We shall test your facts (i.e., the one who is a liar, and the one who is truthful).) (47:31)

Hence, He tests them with the bounty sometimes and sometimes with the afflictions of fear and hunger. Allah said in another Ayah:

(So Allah made it taste extreme of hunger (famine) and fear.) (16:112)

The frightened and the hungry persons show the effects of the affliction outwardly and this is why Allah has used here the word `Libas' (cover or clothes) of fear and hunger. In the Ayat above, Allah used the words:

(with something of fear, hunger,) meaning, a little of each. Then (Allah said),

(loss of wealth,) meaning, some of the wealth will be destroyed,

(lives) meaning, losing friends, relatives and loved ones to death,

(and fruits,) meaning, the gardens and the farms will not produce the usual or expected amounts. This is why Allah said next:

(but give glad tidings to As-Sabirin (the patient).)

He then explained whom He meant by `the patient' whom He praised:

(Who, when afflicted with calamity, say: "Truly, to Allah we belong and truly, to Him we shall return.") meaning, those who recite this statement to comfort themselves in the face of their loss, know that they belong to Allah and that He does what He wills with His servants. They also know that nothing and no deed, even if it was the weight of an atom, will be lost with Allah on the Day of Resurrection. These facts thus compel them to admit that they are Allah's servants and that their return will be to Him in the Hereafter.

This is why Allah said:

(They are those on whom are the Salawat (i. e., who are blessed and will be forgiven) from their Lord, and (they are those who) receive His mercy,) meaning, Allah's praise and mercy will be with them. Sa`id bin Jubayr added, "Meaning, safety from the torment."

(and it is they who are the guided ones.) `Umar bin Al-Khattab commented: "What righteous things, and what a great heights.

(They are those on whom are the Salawat from their Lord, and (they are those who) receive His mercy) are the two righteous things.

(and it is they who are the guided ones) are the heights."

# Chapter 2: Al-Baqarah (The Cow), Verses 142-252

The heights means more rewards, and these people will be awarded their rewards and more.

## The Virtue of asserting that We all belong to Allah, during Afflictions

There are several Ahadith that mention the rewards of admitting that the return is to Allah by saying:

("Truly, to Allah we belong and truly, to Him we shall return.") when afflictions strike. For instance, Imam Ahmad reported that Umm Salamah narrated: Once, Abu Salamah came back after he was with Allah's Messenger and said: I heard Allah's Messenger recite a statement that made me delighted. He said:

«لَا يُصِيبُ أَحَدًا مِنَ الْمُسْلِمِينَ مُصِيبَةٌ فَيَسْتَرْجِعُ عِنْدَ مُصِيبَتِهِ ثُمَّ يَقُولُ: اللَّهُمَّ أْجُرْنِي فِي مُصِيبَتِي وَأَخْلِفْ لِي خَيْرًا مِنْهَا، إِلَّا فَعَلَ ذَلِكَ بِهِ»

(No Muslim is struck with an affliction and then says Istirja` when the affliction strikes, and then says: `O Allah! Reward me for my loss and give me what is better than it,' but Allah will do just that.) Umm Salamah said: So I memorized these words. When Abu Salamah died I said Istirja` and said: "O Allah! Compensate me for my loss and give me what is better than it." I then thought about it and said, "Who is better than Abu Salamah" When my `Iddah (the period of time before the widow or divorced woman can remarry) finished, Allah's Messenger asked for permission to see me while I was dyeing a skin that I had. I washed my hands, gave him permission to enter and handed him a pillow, and he sat on it. He then asked me for marriage and when he finished his speech, I said, "O Messenger of Allah! It is not because I do not want you, but I am very jealous and I fear that you might experience some wrong mannerism from me for which Allah would punish me. I am old and have children." He said:

«أَمَّا مَا ذَكَرْتِ مِنَ الْغَيْرَةِ فَسَوْفَ يُذْهِبُهَا اللهُ عَزَّ وَجَلَّ عَنْكِ، وَأَمَّا مَا ذَكَرْتِ مِنَ السِّنِّ فَقَدْ أَصَابَنِي مِثْلُ الَّذِي أَصَابَكِ، وَأَمَّا مَا ذَكَرْتِ مِنَ الْعِيَالِ فَإِنَّمَا عِيَالُكِ عِيَالِي»

(As for the jealousy that you mentioned, Allah the Exalted will remove it from you. As for your being old as you mentioned, I have suffered what you have suffered. And for your having children, they are my children too.) She said, "I have surrendered to Allah's Messenger." Allah's Messenger married her and

Umm Salamah said later, "Allah compensated me with who is better than Abu Salamah: Allah's Messenger ." Muslim reported a shorter version of this Hadith.

## Surah: 2 Ayah: 158

﴿ ۞ إِنَّ ٱلصَّفَا وَٱلْمَرْوَةَ مِن شَعَآئِرِ ٱللَّهِ ۖ فَمَنْ حَجَّ ٱلْبَيْتَ أَوِ ٱعْتَمَرَ فَلَا جُنَاحَ عَلَيْهِ أَن يَطَّوَّفَ بِهِمَا ۚ وَمَن تَطَوَّعَ خَيْرًا فَإِنَّ ٱللَّهَ شَاكِرٌ عَلِيمٌ ۝ ﴾

158. Verily! As-Safâ and Al-Marwah (two mountains in Makkah) are of the Symbols of Allâh. So it is not a sin on him who performs Hajj or 'Umrah (pilgrimage) of the House (the Ka'bah at Makkah) to perform the going (Tawâf) between them (As-Safâ and Al-Marwah). And whoever does good voluntarily, then verily, Allâh is All-Recogniser, All-Knower.

### Transliteration

158. Inna alssafa waalmarwata min shaAAa-iri Allahi faman hajja albayta awi iAAtamara fala junaha AAalayhi an yattawwafa bihima waman tatawwaAAa khayran fa-inna Allaha shakirun AAaleemun

### Tafsir Ibn Kathir

#### The Meaning of "it is not a sin" in the Ayah

Imam Ahmad reported that `Urwah said that he asked `A'ishah about what Allah stated:

(Verily, As-Safa and Al-Marwah (two mountains in Makkah) are of the symbols of Allah. So it is not a sin on him who performs Hajj or `Umrah (pilgrimage) of the House (the Ka`bah at Makkah) to perform the going (Tawaf) between them (As-Safa and Al-Marwah).) "By Allah! It is not a sin if someone did not perform Tawaf around them." `A'ishah said, "Worst is that which you said, O my nephew! If this is the meaning of it, it should have read, `It is not a sin if one did not perform Tawaf around them.' Rather, the Ayah was revealed regarding the Ansar, who before Islam, used to assume Ihlal (or Ihram for Hajj) in the area of Mushallal for their idol Manat that they used to worship. Those who assumed Ihlal for Manat, used to hesitate to perform Tawaf (going) between Mounts As-Safa and Al-Marwah. So they (during the Islamic era) asked Allah's Messenger about it, saying, `O Messenger of Allah! During the time of Jahiliyyah, we used to hesitate to perform Tawaf between As-Safa and Al-Marwah.' Allah then revealed:

(Verily, As-Safa and Al-Marwah are of the symbols of Allah. So it is not a sin on him who performs Hajj or `Umrah of the House to perform the going (Tawaf) between them.)" `A'ishah then said, " Allah's Messenger has made it the Sunnah to perform Tawaf between them (As-Safa and Al-Marwah), and thus, no one should abandon performing Tawaf between them." This Hadith is reported in the Sahihayn.

In another narration, Imam Az-Zuhri reported that `Urwah said: Later on I (`Urwah) told Abu Bakr bin `Abdur-Rahman bin Al-Harith bin Hisham (of `A'ishah's statement) and he said, "I have not heard of such information. However, I heard learned men saying that all the people, except those whom `A'ishah mentioned, said, `Our Tawaf between these two hills is a practice of Jahiliyyah. ' Some others among the Ansar said, `We were commanded to perform Tawaf of the Ka`bah, but not between As-Safa and Al-Marwah.' So Allah revealed:

(Verily, As-Safa and Al-Marwah are of the symbols of Allah.)" Abu Bakr bin `Abdur-Rahman then said, "It seems that this verse was revealed concerning the two groups." Al-Bukhari collected a similar narration by Anas.

Ash-Sha`bi said, "Isaf (an idol) was on As-Safa while Na'ilah (an idol) was on Al-Marwah, and they used to touch (or kiss) them. After Islam came, they were hesitant about performing Tawaf between them. Thereafter, the Ayah (2:158 above) was revealed."

### The Wisdom behind legislating Sa`i between As-Safa and Al-Marwah

Muslim recorded a long Hadith in his Sahih from Jabir, in which Allah's Messenger finished the Tawaf around the House, and then went back to the Rukn (pillar, i.e., the Black Stone) and kissed it. He then went out from the door near As-Safa while reciting:

(Verily, As-Safa and Al-Marwah are of the symbols of Allah.) The Prophet then said, (I start with what Allah has commanded me to start with )meaning start the Sa`i (i.e., fast walking) from the As-Safa(). In another narration of An-Nasa'i, the Prophet said, (Start with what Allah has started with (i.e., As-Safa).)

Imam Ahmad reported that Habibah bint Abu Tajrah said, "I saw Allah's Messenger performing Tawaf between As-Safa and Al-Marwah, while the people were in front of him and he was behind them walking in Sa`i. I saw his garment twisted around his knees because of the fast walking in Sa`i (he was performing) and he was reciting:

«اسْعَوْا فَإِنَّ اللهَ كَتَبَ عَلَيْكُمُ السَّعْيَ».

(Perform Sa`i, for Allah has prescribed Sa`i on you.)"'

This Hadith was used as a proof for the fact that Sa`i is a Rukn of Hajj. It was also said that Sa`i is Wajib, and not a Rukn of Hajj and that if one does not perform it by mistake or by intention, he could expiate the shortcoming with Damm. Allah has stated that Tawaf between As-Safa and Al-Marwah is among the symbols of Allah, meaning, among the acts that Allah legislated during the Hajj for Prophet Ibrahim.

Earlier we mentioned the Hadith by Ibn `Abbas that the origin of Tawaf comes from the Tawaf of Hajar (Prophet Ibrahim's wife), between As-Safa and Al-Marwah seeking water for her son (Isma`il) Ibrahim had left them in Makkah, where there was no habitation for her. When Hajar feared that her son would die, she stood up and begged Allah for His help and kept going back and forth in that blessed area between As-Safa and Al-Marwah. She was humble, fearful, frightened and meek before Allah. Allah answered her prayers, relieved her of her loneliness, ended her dilemma and made the well of Zamzam bring forth its water for her, which is:

《طَعَامُ طُعْمٍ، وَشِفَاءُ سُقْمٍ》

(A tasty (or nutritional) food and a remedy for the illness.)

Therefore, whoever performs Sa`i between As-Safa and Al-Marwah should remember his meekness, humbleness and need for Allah to guide his heart, lead his affairs to success and forgive his sins. He should also want Allah to eliminate his shortcomings and errors and to guide him to the straight path. He should ask Allah to keep him firm on this path until he meets death, and to change his situation from that of sin and errors to that of perfection and being forgiven, --- the same providence which was provided to Hajar.

Allah then states:

(And whoever does good voluntarily.)

It was said that the Ayah describes performing Tawaf more than seven times, it was also said that it refers to voluntary `Umrah or Hajj. It was also said that it means volunteering to do good works in general, as Ar-Razi has stated. The third opinion was attributed to Al-Hasan Al-Basri. Allah knows best.

Allah states:

(...then verily, Allah is All-Recognizer, All-Knower.) meaning, Allah's reward is immense for the little deed, and He knows about the sufficiency of the reward. Hence, He will not award insufficient rewards to anyone. Indeed:

(Surely, Allah wrongs not even of the weight of an atom, but if there is any good (done), He doubles it, and gives from Him a great reward.) (4:40)

### Surah: 2 Ayah: 159, Ayah: 160, Ayah: 161 & Ayah: 162

﴿ إِنَّ ٱلَّذِينَ يَكْتُمُونَ مَآ أَنزَلْنَا مِنَ ٱلْبَيِّنَٰتِ وَٱلْهُدَىٰ مِنۢ بَعْدِ مَا بَيَّنَّٰهُ لِلنَّاسِ فِى ٱلْكِتَٰبِ أُو۟لَٰٓئِكَ يَلْعَنُهُمُ ٱللَّهُ وَيَلْعَنُهُمُ ٱللَّٰعِنُونَ ﴾

159. Verily, those who conceal the clear proofs, evidences and the guidance, which We have sent down, after We have made it clear for the people in the Book, they are the ones cursed by Allâh and cursed by the cursers.

﴿ إِلَّا ٱلَّذِينَ تَابُوا۟ وَأَصْلَحُوا۟ وَبَيَّنُوا۟ فَأُو۟لَـٰٓئِكَ أَتُوبُ عَلَيْهِمْ ۚ وَأَنَا ٱلتَّوَّابُ ٱلرَّحِيمُ ﴿١٦٠﴾ ﴾

160. Except those who repent and do righteous deeds, and openly declare (the truth which they concealed). These, I will accept their repentance. And I am the One Who accepts repentance, the Most Merciful.

﴿ إِنَّ ٱلَّذِينَ كَفَرُوا۟ وَمَاتُوا۟ وَهُمْ كُفَّارٌ أُو۟لَـٰٓئِكَ عَلَيْهِمْ لَعْنَةُ ٱللَّهِ وَٱلْمَلَـٰٓئِكَةِ وَٱلنَّاسِ أَجْمَعِينَ ﴿١٦١﴾ ﴾

161. Verily, those who disbelieve, and die while they are disbelievers, it is they on whom is the Curse of Allâh and of the angels and of mankind, combined.

﴿ خَـٰلِدِينَ فِيهَا ۖ لَا يُخَفَّفُ عَنْهُمُ ٱلْعَذَابُ وَلَا هُمْ يُنظَرُونَ ﴿١٦٢﴾ ﴾

162. They will abide therein (under the curse in Hell), their punishment will neither be lightened, nor will they be reprieved.

### Transliteration

159. Inna allatheena yaktumoona ma anzalna mina albayyinati waalhuda min baAAdi ma bayyannahu lilnnasi fee alkitabi ola-ika yalAAanuhumu Allahu wayalAAanuhumu allaAAinoona   160. Illa allatheena taboo waaslahoo wabayyanoo faola-ika atoobu AAalayhim waana alttawwabu alrraheemu   161. Inna allatheena kafaroo wamatoo wahum kuffarun ola-ika AAalayhim laAAnatu Allahi waalmalaikati waalnnasi ajmaAAeena   162. Khalideena feeha la yukhaffafu AAanhumu alAAathabu wala hum yun*th*aroona

### Tafsir Ibn Kathir

### The Eternal Curse for Those Who hide Religious Commandments

These Ayat sternly warn against those who hide the clear signs that the Messengers were sent with which guide to the correct path and beneficial guidance for the hearts, after Allah has made such aspects clear for His servants through the Books that He revealed to His Messengers. Abu Al-`Aliyah said that these Ayat, "were revealed about the People of the Scripture who hid the description of Muhammad ." Allah then states that everything curses such people for this evil act. Certainly, just as everything asks for forgiveness for the scholar, even the fish in the sea and the bird in the air, then those who hide knowledge are cursed by Allah and by the cursers. A Hadith in the Musnad, narrated through several chains of narrators, that strengthens the overall judgment of the Hadith, states that Abu Hurayrah narrated that Allah's Messenger said:

«مَنْ سُئِلَ عَنْ عِلْمٍ فَكَتَمَهُ، أُلْجِمَ يَوْمَ الْقِيَامَةِ بِلِجَامٍ مِنْ نَارٍ»

(Whoever was asked about knowledge that one has, but he hid it, then a bridle made of fire will be tied around his mouth on the Day of Resurrection.)

It is also recorded by Al-Bukhari that Abu Hurayrah said, "If it was not for an Ayah in Allah's Book, I would not have narrated a Hadith for anyone:

(Verily, those who conceal the clear proofs, evidences and the guidance, which We have sent down,)"

Mujahid said, "When the earth is struck by drought, the animals say, `This is because of the sinners among the Children of Adam. May Allah curse the sinners among the Children of Adam.'"

Abu Al-`Aliyah, Ar-Rabi` bin Anas and Qatadah said that

(and cursed by the cursers) means that the angels and the believers will curse them. Moreover, a Hadith states that everything, including the fish in the sea, asks for forgiveness for the scholars. The Ayah (2:159 above) states that those who hide the knowledge will be cursed, (in this life and) on the Day of Resurrection, by Allah, the angels, all humanity, and those who curse (including the animals) each in its own distinct way. Allah knows best.

From this punishment, Allah excluded all who repent to Him:

(Except those who repent and do righteous deeds, and openly declare (the truth which they concealed).)

This Ayah refers to those who regret what they have been doing and correct their behavior and, thus, explain to the people what they have been hiding.

(These, I will accept their repentance. And I am the One Who accepts repentance, the Most Merciful.)

This Ayah also indicates that those who used to call to innovation, or even disbelief, and repent to Allah, then Allah will forgive them. Allah afterwards states that those who disbelieve in Him and remain in this state until they die, then:

(it is they on whom is the curse of Allah and of the angels and of mankind, combined. They will abide therein (under the curse in Hell).)

Therefore, they will suffer the eternal curse until the Day of Resurrection and after that in the fire of Jahannam, where,

(their punishment will neither be lightened)

Hence, the torment will not be decreased for them,

(nor will they be reprieved.)

The torment will not be changed or tempered for even an hour. Rather, it is continuous and eternal. We seek refuge with Allah from this evil end.

### Cursing the Disbelievers is allowed

There is no disagreement that it is lawful to curse the disbelievers. `Umar bin Al-Khattab and the Imams after him used to curse the disbelievers in their Qunut (a type of supplication) during the prayer and otherwise. As for cursing a specific disbeliever, some scholars stated that it is not allowed to curse him, because we do not know how Allah will make his end. Others said that it is allowed to curse individual disbelievers. For proof, they mention the story about the man who was brought to be punished repeatedly for drinking (alcohol), a man said, "May Allah curse him! He is being brought repeatedly (to be flogged for drinking)." Allah's Messenger said:

«لَا تَلْعَنْهُ فَإِنَّهُ يُحِبُّ اللهَ وَرَسُولَه»

(Do not curse him, for he loves Allah and His Messenger).

This Hadith indicates that it is allowed to curse those who do not love Allah and His Messenger . Allah knows best.

### Surah: 2 Ayah: 163 & Ayah: 164

﴿ وَإِلَٰهُكُمْ إِلَٰهٌ وَٰحِدٌ ۖ لَّآ إِلَٰهَ إِلَّا هُوَ ٱلرَّحْمَٰنُ ٱلرَّحِيمُ ۝ ﴾

163. And your Ilâh (God) is One Ilâh (God - Allâh), Lâ ilâha illa Huwa (there is none who has the right to be worshipped but He), the Most Gracious, the Most Merciful.

﴿ إِنَّ فِى خَلْقِ ٱلسَّمَٰوَٰتِ وَٱلْأَرْضِ وَٱخْتِلَٰفِ ٱلَّيْلِ وَٱلنَّهَارِ وَٱلْفُلْكِ ٱلَّتِى تَجْرِى فِى ٱلْبَحْرِ بِمَا يَنفَعُ ٱلنَّاسَ وَمَآ أَنزَلَ ٱللَّهُ مِنَ ٱلسَّمَآءِ مِن مَّآءٍ فَأَحْيَا بِهِ ٱلْأَرْضَ بَعْدَ مَوْتِهَا وَبَثَّ فِيهَا مِن كُلِّ دَآبَّةٍ وَتَصْرِيفِ ٱلرِّيَٰحِ وَٱلسَّحَابِ ٱلْمُسَخَّرِ بَيْنَ ٱلسَّمَآءِ وَٱلْأَرْضِ لَءَايَٰتٍ لِّقَوْمٍ يَعْقِلُونَ ۝ ﴾

164. Verily! In the creation of the heavens and the earth, and in the alternation of night and day, and the ships which sail through the sea with that which is of use to mankind, and the water (rain) which Allâh sends down from the sky and makes the earth alive therewith after its death, and the moving (living) creatures of all kinds that He has scattered therein, and in the veering of winds and clouds which are held between the sky and the earth, are indeed Ayât (proofs, evidences, signs, etc.) for people of understanding.

### Transliteration

163. Wa-ilahukum ilahun wahidun la ilaha illa huwa alrrahmanu alrraheemu
164. Inna fee khalqi alssamawati waal-ardi waikhtilafi allayli waalnnahari waalfulki allatee tajree fee albahri bima yanfaAAu alnnasa wama anzala Allahu mina alssama-i min ma-in faahya bihi al-arda baAAda mawtiha wabaththa feeha min kulli dabbatin watasreefi alrriyahi waalssahabi almusakhkhari bayna alssama-i waal-ardi laayatin liqawmin yaAAqiloona

### Tafsir Ibn Kathir

In this Ayah, Allah mentions that He is the only deity, and that He has no partners or equals. He is Allah, the One and Only, the Sustainer, and there is no deity worthy of worship except Him. He is the Most Gracious - Ar-Rahman, the Most Merciful - Ar-Rahim. We explained the meanings of these two Names in the beginning of Surat Al-Fatihah. Shahr bin Hawshab reported that Asma' bint Yazid bin As-Sakan narrated that Allah's Messenger said:

《اسْمُ اللهِ الْأَعْظَمُ فِي هَاتَيْنِ الآيَتَيْنِ》

(Allah's Greatest Name is contained in these two Ayat):

(And your Ilah (God) is One Ilah (God - Allah), La ilaha illa Huwa (there is none who has the right to be worshipped but He), the Most Gracious, the Most Merciful.) and:

(Alif-Lam-Mim. Allah! La ilaha illa Huwa (none has the right to be worshipped but He), Al-Haiyul-Qaiyum (the Ever Living, the One Who sustains and protects all that exists).) (3:1, 2)"

Then Allah mentions some of the proof that He is alone as the deity, that He is the One who created the heavens and the earth and all of the various creatures between them, all of which testify to His Oneness:

### The Proofs for Tawhid

Allah said:

(Verily, in the creation of the heavens and the earth...)

Therefore, the sky, with its height, intricate design, vastness, the heavenly objects in orbit, and this earth, with its density, its lowlands, mountains, seas, deserts, valleys, and other structures, and beneficial things that it has. Allah continues:

(...and in the alternation of night and day.)

This (the night) comes and then goes followed by the other (the day) which does not delay for even an instant, just as Allah said:

(It is not for the sun to overtake the moon, nor does the night outstrip the day. They all float, each in an orbit.) (36:40)

Sometimes, the day grows shorter and the night longer, and sometimes vice versa, one takes from the length of the other. Similarly Allah said:

(Allah merges the night into the day, and He merges the day into the night) (57:6) meaning, He extends the length of one from the other and vice versa. Allah then continues:

(...and the ships which sail through the sea with that which is of use to mankind,)

Shaping the sea in this manner, so that it is able to carry ships from one shore to another, so people benefit from what the other region has, and export what they have to them and vice versa.

Allah then continues:

(...and the water (rain) which Allah sends down from the sky and makes the earth alive therewith after its death), which is similar to Allah's statement:

(And a sign for them is the dead land. We give it life, and We bring forth from it grains, so that they eat thereof.) (36:33), until:

(which they know not.) (36:36)

Allah continues:

(and the moving (living) creatures of all kinds that He has scattered therein,) meaning, in various shapes, colors, uses and sizes, whether small or large. Allah knows all that, sustains it, and nothing is concealed from Him. Similarly, Allah said:

(And no moving (living) creature is there on earth but its provision is due from Allah. And He knows its dwelling place and its deposit (in the uterus or grave). All is in a Clear Book (Al-Lawh Al-Mahfuz - the Book of Decrees with Allah).) (11:6)

(...and in the veering of winds...)

Sometimes, the wind brings mercy and sometimes torment. Sometimes it brings the good news of the clouds that follow it, sometimes it leads the clouds, herding them, scattering them or directing them. Sometimes, the wind comes from the north (the northern wind), and sometimes from the south, sometimes from the east, and striking the front of the Ka`bah, sometimes from the west, striking its back. There are many books about the wind rain, stars and the regulations related to them, but here is not the place to elaborate on that, and Allah knows best.

Allah continues:

(...and clouds which are held between the sky and the earth,)

The clouds run between the sky and the earth to wherever Allah wills of lands and areas.

Allah said next:

(...are indeed Ayat for people of understanding,) meaning, all these things are clear signs that testify to Allah's Oneness. Similarly, Allah said:

(Verily, in the creation of the heavens and the earth, and in the alternation of night and day, there are indeed signs for men of understanding. Those who remember Allah (always, and in prayers) standing, sitting, and lying down on their sides, and think deeply about the creation of the heavens and the earth, (saying): "Our Lord! You have not created (all) this without purpose, glory to You! (Exalted are You above all that they associate with You as partners). Give us salvation from the torment of the Fire.") (3:190, 191)

### Surah: 2 Ayah: 165, Ayah: 166 & Ayah: 167

﴿ وَمِنَ ٱلنَّاسِ مَن يَتَّخِذُ مِن دُونِ ٱللَّهِ أَندَادًا يُحِبُّونَهُمْ كَحُبِّ ٱللَّهِ وَٱلَّذِينَ ءَامَنُوٓاْ أَشَدُّ حُبًّا لِّلَّهِ ۗ وَلَوْ يَرَى ٱلَّذِينَ ظَلَمُوٓاْ إِذْ يَرَوْنَ ٱلْعَذَابَ أَنَّ ٱلْقُوَّةَ لِلَّهِ جَمِيعًا وَأَنَّ ٱللَّهَ شَدِيدُ ٱلْعَذَابِ ﴾

165. And of mankind are some who take (for worship) others besides Allâh as rivals (to Allâh). They love them as they love Allâh. But those who believe, love Allâh more (than anything else). If only, those who do wrong could see, when they will see the torment, that all power belongs to Allâh and that Allâh is Severe in punishment.

﴿ إِذْ تَبَرَّأَ ٱلَّذِينَ ٱتُّبِعُواْ مِنَ ٱلَّذِينَ ٱتَّبَعُواْ وَرَأَوُاْ ٱلْعَذَابَ وَتَقَطَّعَتْ بِهِمُ ٱلْأَسْبَابُ ﴾

166. When those who were followed, disown (declare themselves innocent of) those who followed (them), and they see the torment, then all their relations will be cut off from them.

﴿ وَقَالَ ٱلَّذِينَ ٱتَّبَعُوا۟ لَوْ أَنَّ لَنَا كَرَّةً فَنَتَبَرَّأَ مِنْهُمْ كَمَا تَبَرَّءُوا۟ مِنَّا ۗ كَذَٰلِكَ يُرِيهِمُ ٱللَّهُ أَعْمَٰلَهُمْ حَسَرَٰتٍ عَلَيْهِمْ ۖ وَمَا هُم بِخَٰرِجِينَ مِنَ ٱلنَّارِ ۝ ﴾

167. And those who followed will say: "If only we had one more chance to return (to the worldly life), we would disown (declare ourselves as innocent from) them as they have disowned (declared themselves as innocent from) us." Thus Allâh will show them their deeds as regrets for them. And they will never get out of the Fire.

## Transliteration

165. Wamina alnnasi man yattakhithu min dooni Allahi andadan yuhibboonahum kahubbi Allahi waallatheena amanoo ashaddu hubban lillahi walaw yara allatheena *th*alamoo ith yarawna alAAathaba anna alquwwata lillahi jameeAAan waanna Allaha shadeedu alAAathabi 166. Ith tabarraa allatheena ittubiAAoo mina allatheena ittabaAAoo waraawoo alAAathaba wataqattaAAat bihimu al-asbabu 167. Waqala allatheena ittabaAAoo law anna lana karratan fanatabarraa minhum kama tabarraoo minna kathalika yureehimu Allahu aAAmalahum hasaratin AAalayhim wama hum bikharijeena mina alnnari

## Tafsir Ibn Kathir

### The Condition of the Polytheists in this Life and the Hereafter

In these Ayat, Allah mentions the condition of the polytheists in this life and their destination in the Hereafter. They appointed equals and rivals with Allah, worshipping them along with Allah and loving them, just as they love Allah. However, Allah is the only deity worthy of worship, Who has neither rival nor opponent nor partner. It is reported in the Sahihayn that `Abdullah bin Mas`ud said: I said, "O Messenger of Allah! What is the greatest sin" He said:

«أَنْ تَجْعَلَ لِلَّهِ نِدًّا وَهُوَ خَلَقَكَ»

(To appoint a rival to Allah while He Alone has created you.)

Allah said:

(But those who believe, love Allah more (than anything else))

Because these believers love Allah, know His greatness, revere Him, believe in His Oneness, then they do not associate anything or anyone with Him in the worship. Rather, they worship Him Alone, depend on Him and they seek help from Him for each and every need.

Then, Allah warns those who commit Shirk,

(If only, those who do wrong could see, when they will see the torment, that all power belongs to Allah.) if these people knew what they will face and the terrible punishment they are to suffer because of their disbelief and Shirk (polytheism), then they would shun the deviation that they live by.

Allah mentions their false beliefs in their idols, and that those they followed will declare their innocence of them. Allah said:

(When those who were followed disown (declare themselves innocent of) those who followed (them).) the angels, whom they used to claim that they worshipped, declare their innocence of them in the Hereafter, saying:

(We declare our innocence (from them) before You. It was not us they worshipped.) (28:63), and:

("Glorified be You! You are our Wali (Lord) instead of them. Nay, but they used to worship the Jinn; most of them were believers in them.") (34:4)

The Jinn will also disown the disbelievers who worshipped them, and they will reject that worship. Allah said:

(And who is more astray than one who calls on (invokes) besides Allah, such as will not answer him till the Day of Resurrection, and who are (even) unaware of their calls (invocations) to them And when mankind are gathered (on the Day of Resurrection), they (false deities) will become their enemies and will deny their worshipping.) (46:5, 6) Allah said:

(And they have taken (for worship) alihah (gods) besides Allah, that they might give them honor, power and glory (and also protect them from Allah' punishment). Nay, but they (the so-called gods) will deny their worship of them, and become opponents to them (on the Day of Resurrection).) (19:81, 82) Prophet Ibrahim said to his people:

(You have taken (for worship) idols instead of Allah. The love between you is only in the life of this world, but on the Day of Resurrection, you shall disown each other, and curse each other, and your abode will be the Fire, and you shall have no helper.) (29:25) Allah said:

(But if you could see when the Zalimun (polytheists and wrongdoers) will be made to stand before their Lord, how they will cast the (blaming) word one to another! Those who were deemed weak will say to those who were arrogant: "Had it not been for you, we should certainly have been believers!" And those who were arrogant will say to those who were deemed weak: "Did we keep you back from guidance after it had come to you Nay, but you were Mujrimin (polytheists, sinners, disbelievers, criminals)." Those who were deemed weak will say to those who were arrogant: "Nay, but it was your plotting by night and day, when you ordered us to disbelieve in Allah and set up rivals to Him!"

And each of them (parties) will conceal their own regrets (for disobeying Allah during this worldly life), when they behold the torment. And We shall put iron collars round the necks of those who disbelieved. Are they requited aught except what they used to do) (34:31-33) Allah said:

(And Shaytan (Satan) will say when the matter has been decided: "Verily, Allah promised you a promise of truth. And I too promised you, but I betrayed you. I had no authority over you except that I called you, and you responded to me. So blame me not, but blame yourselves. I cannot help you, nor can you help me. I deny your former act in associating me (Satan) as a partner with Allah (by obeying me in the life of the world). Verily, there is a painful torment for the Zalimin (polytheists and wrongdoers).) (14:22)

Allah then said:

(...and they see the torment, then all their relations will be cut off from them.) meaning, when they see Allah's torment, their power and means of salvation are all cut off, and they will have no way of making amends, nor will they find a way of escape from the Fire. `Ata' reported that Ibn `Abbas said about:

(then all their relations will be cut off from them.) "meaning the friendship." Mujahid reported a similar statement in another narration by Ibn Abu Najih.

Allah said:

(And those who followed will say: "If only we had one more chance to return (to the worldly life), we would disown (declare ourselves as innocent from) them as they have disowned (declared themselves as innocent from) us.")

This Ayah means: `If we only had a chance to go back to the life so that we could disown them (their idols, leaders, etc.) shun their worship, ignore them and worship Allah Alone instead.' But they utter a lie in this regard, because if they were given the chance to go back, they would only return to what they were prohibited from doing, just as Allah said. This is why Allah said:

(Thus Allah will show them their deeds as regrets for them.) meaning, their works will vanish and disappear. Similarly, Allah said:

(And We shall turn to whatever deeds they (disbelievers, polytheists, sinners) did, and We shall make such deeds as scattered floating particles of dust.) (25:23)

Allah also said:

(The parable of those who disbelieved in their Lord is that their works are as ashes, on which the wind blows furiously on a stormy day.) (14:18), and:

(As for those who disbelieved, their deeds are like a mirage in a desert. The thirsty one thinks it to be water.) (24:39)

This is why Allah said - at the end of the Ayah 2:167 above

(And they will never get out of the Fire.)

### Surah: 2 Ayah: 168 & 169

﴿ يَـٰٓأَيُّهَا ٱلنَّاسُ كُلُوا۟ مِمَّا فِى ٱلْأَرْضِ حَلَـٰلًا طَيِّبًا وَلَا تَتَّبِعُوا۟ خُطُوَٰتِ ٱلشَّيْطَـٰنِ إِنَّهُۥ لَكُمْ عَدُوٌّ مُّبِينٌ ۝ ﴾

168. O mankind! Eat of that which is lawful and good on the earth, and follow not the footsteps of Shaitân (Satan). Verily, he is to you an open enemy.

﴿ إِنَّمَا يَأْمُرُكُم بِٱلسُّوٓءِ وَٱلْفَحْشَآءِ وَأَن تَقُولُوا۟ عَلَى ٱللَّهِ مَا لَا تَعْلَمُونَ ۝ ﴾

169. He (Shaitân (Satan)) commands you only what is evil and Fahshâ (sinful), and that you should say against Allâh what you know not.

### Transliteration

168. Ya ayyuha alnnasu kuloo mimma fee al-ardi halalan tayyiban wala tattabiAAoo khutuwati alshshaytani innahu lakum AAaduwwun mubeenun 169. Innama ya/murukum bialssoo-i waalfahsha-i waan taqooloo AAala Allahi ma la taAAlamoona

### Tafsir Ibn Kathir

#### The Order to eat the Lawful Things, and the Prohibition of following the Footsteps of Shaytan

After Allah stated that there is no deity worthy of worship except Him and that He Alone created the creation, He stated that He is the Sustainer for all His creation, and He mentioned a favor that He granted them; He has allowed them to eat any of the pure lawful things on the earth that do not cause harm to the body or the mind. He also forbade them from following the footsteps of Shaytan, meaning his ways and methods with which he misguides his followers, like prohibiting the Bahirah (a she-camel whose milk was spared for the idols and nobody was allowed to milk it), or Sa'ibah (a she-camel let loose for free pasture for the idols and nothing was allowed to be carried on it), or a Wasilah (a she-camel set free for idols because it has given birth to a she-camel at its first delivery and then again gives birth to a she-camel at its second delivery), and all of the other things that Shaytan made attractive to them during the time of Jahiliyyah. Muslim recorded `Iyad bin Himar saying that Allah's Messenger said that Allah the Exalted says,

## Chapter 2: Al-Baqarah (The Cow), Verses 142-252

يَقُولُ اللهُ تَعَالَى: «إِنَّ كُلَّ مَالٍ مَنَحْتُهُ عِبَادِي فَهُوَ لَهُمْ حَلَالٌ، وَفِيهِ وَإِنِّي خَلَقْتُ عِبَادِي حُنَفَاءَ، فَجَاءَتْهُمُ الشَّيَاطِينُ فَاجْتَالَتْهُمْ عَنْ دِينِهِمْ، وَحَرَّمَتْ عَلَيْهِمْ مَا أَحْلَلْتُ لَهُمْ»

(`Every type of wealth I have endowed My servants is allowed for them...' (until), `I have created My servants Hunafa' (pure or upright), but the devils came to them and led them astray from their (true) religion and prohibited them from what I allowed for them. ')

Allah said:

(...he is to you an open enemy.)

warning against Satan. Allah said in another instance:

(Surely, Shaytan is an enemy to you, so take (treat) him as an enemy. He only invites his Hizb (followers) that they may become the dwellers of the blazing Fire.) (35:6), and:

(Will you then take him (Iblis) and his offspring as protectors and helpers rather than Me while they are enemies to you What an evil is the exchange for the Zalimin (polytheists, and wrongdoers, etc).) (18:50)

Qatadah and As-Suddi commented on what Allah said:

(...and follow not the footsteps of Shaytan (Satan)):

Every act of disobedience to Allah is among the footsteps of Satan.

`Abd bin Humayd reported that Ibn `Abbas said: "Any vow or oath that one makes while angry, is among the footsteps of Shaytan and its expiation is that of the vow. " Allah's statement:

(He (Satan) commands you only what is evil and Fahsha (sinful), and that you should say about Allah what you know not.)

The verse means: `Your enemy, Satan, commands you to commit evil acts and what is worse than that, such as adultery and so forth. He commands you to commit what is even worse, that is, saying about Allah without knowledge.' So this includes every innovator and disbeliever.

### Surah: 2 Ayah: 170 & Ayah: 171

﴿ وَإِذَا قِيلَ لَهُمُ ٱتَّبِعُواْ مَآ أَنزَلَ ٱللَّهُ قَالُواْ بَلْ نَتَّبِعُ مَآ أَلْفَيْنَا عَلَيْهِ ءَابَآءَنَآ أَوَلَوْ كَانَ ءَابَآؤُهُمْ لَا يَعْقِلُونَ شَيْـًٔا وَلَا يَهْتَدُونَ ﴾

170. When it is said to them: "Follow what Allâh has sent down." They say: "Nay! We shall follow what we found our fathers following." (Would they do that!) even though their fathers did not understand anything nor were they guided?

﴿ وَمَثَلُ ٱلَّذِينَ كَفَرُواْ كَمَثَلِ ٱلَّذِى يَنْعِقُ بِمَا لَا يَسْمَعُ إِلَّا دُعَآءً وَنِدَآءً صُمٌّ بُكْمٌ عُمْىٌ فَهُمْ لَا يَعْقِلُونَ ﴾

171. And the example of those who disbelieve is as that of him who shouts to the (flock of sheep) that hears nothing but calls and cries. (They are) deaf, dumb and blind. So they do not understand. (Tafsir Al-Qurtubî)

### Transliteration

170. Wa-itha qeela lahumu ittabiAAoo ma anzala Allahu qaloo bal nattabiAAu ma alfayna AAalayhi abaana awa law kana abaohum la yaAAqiloona shay-an wala yahtadoona 171. Wamathalu allatheena kafaroo kamathali allathee yanAAiqu bima la yasmaAAu illa duAAaan wanidaan summun bukmun AAumyun fahum la yaAAqiloona

### Tafsir Ibn Kathir

#### The Polytheist imitates Other Polytheists

Allah states that if the disbelievers and polytheists are called to follow what Allah has revealed to His Messenger and abandon the practices of misguidance and ignorance that they indulge in, they will say, "Rather. We shall follow what we found our fathers following," meaning, worshipping the idols and the false deities. Allah criticized their reasoning:

((Would they do that!) even though their fathers), meaning, those whom they follow and whose practices they imitate, and:

(...did not understand anything nor were they guided) meaning, they had no sound understanding or guidance. Ibn Ishaq reported that Ibn `Abbas said that this was revealed about a group of Jews whom Allah's Messenger called to Islam, but they refused, saying, "Rather, we shall follow what we found our forefathers following." So Allah revealed this Ayah (2:170) above."

#### The Disbeliever is just like an Animal

Allah then made a parable of the disbelievers, just as He said in another Ayah:

# Chapter 2: Al-Baqarah (The Cow), Verses 142-252

(For those who believe not in the Hereafter is an evil description.) (16:60)

Similarly, Allah said here (2:171 above)

(And the example of those who disbelieve...) meaning, in their injustice, misguidance and ignorance, they are just like wandering animals, not understanding what they are told; if the shepherd heralds them or calls them to what benefits them, they would not understand what is actually being said to them, for they only hear unintelligible sounds. This is what is reported from Ibn `Abbas, Abu Al-`Aliyah, Mujahid, `Ikrimah, `Ata', Al-Hasan, Qatadah, `Ata' Al-Khurasani and Ar-Rabi` bin Anas.

(They are deaf, dumb, and blind.) means, they are deaf, as they do not hear the truth; mute, as they do not utter it; and blind, as they do not see or recognize its path and way.

(So they do not understand.) means, they do not comprehend or understand anything.

## Surah: 2 Ayah: 172 & Ayah: 173

﴿ يَٰٓأَيُّهَا ٱلَّذِينَ ءَامَنُوا۟ كُلُوا۟ مِن طَيِّبَٰتِ مَا رَزَقْنَٰكُمْ وَٱشْكُرُوا۟ لِلَّهِ إِن كُنتُمْ إِيَّاهُ تَعْبُدُونَ ۝ ﴾

172. O you who believe (in the Oneness of Allâh - Islâmic Monotheism)! Eat of the lawful things that We have provided you with, and be grateful to Allâh, if it is indeed He Whom you worship.

﴿ إِنَّمَا حَرَّمَ عَلَيْكُمُ ٱلْمَيْتَةَ وَٱلدَّمَ وَلَحْمَ ٱلْخِنزِيرِ وَمَآ أُهِلَّ بِهِۦ لِغَيْرِ ٱللَّهِ فَمَنِ ٱضْطُرَّ غَيْرَ بَاغٍ وَلَا عَادٍ فَلَآ إِثْمَ عَلَيْهِ إِنَّ ٱللَّهَ غَفُورٌ رَّحِيمٌ ۝ ﴾

173. He has forbidden you only the Maitah (dead animals), and blood, and the flesh of swine, and that which is slaughtered as a sacrifice for others than Allâh (or has been slaughtered for idols, on which Allâh's Name has not been mentioned while slaughtering). But if one is forced by necessity without wilful disobedience nor transgressing due limits, then there is no sin on him. Truly, Allâh is Oft-Forgiving, Most Merciful.

### Transliteration

172. Ya ayyuha allatheena amanoo kuloo min tayyibati ma razaqnakum waoshkuroo lillahi in kuntum iyyahu taAAbudoona  173. Innama harrama AAalaykumu almaytata waalddama walahma alkhinzeeri wama ohilla bihi lighayri Allahi famani idturra ghayra baghin wala AAadin fala ithma AAalayhi inna Allaha ghafoorun raheemun

## Tafsir Ibn Kathir

### The Command to eat Pure Things and the Explanation of the Prohibited Things

Allah commands His believing servants to eat from the pure things that He has created for them and to thank Him for it, if they are truly His servants. Eating from pure sources is a cause for the acceptance of supplications and acts of worship, just as eating from impure sources prevents the acceptance of supplications and acts of worship, as mentioned in a Hadith recorded by Imam Ahmad, that Abu Hurayrah said that Allah's Messenger said:

«أَيُّهَا النَّاسُ إِنَّ اللهَ طَيِّبٌ، لَا يَقْبَلُ إِلَّا طَيِّبًا، وَإِنَّ اللهَ أَمَرَ الْمُؤْمِنِينَ بِمَا أَمَرَ بِهِ الْمُرْسَلِينَ، فَقَالَ:

[يأَيُّهَا الرُّسُلُ كُلُوا مِنَ الطَّيِّبَاتِ وَاعْمَلُوا صَلِحاً إِنِّى بِمَا تَعْمَلُونَ عَلِيمٌ]

، وَقَالَ:

[يأَيُّهَا الَّذِينَ ءَامَنُوا كُلُوا مِن طَيِّبَاتِ مَا رَزَقْنَكُمْ]

ثُمَّ ذَكَرَ الرَّجُلَ يُطِيلُ السَّفَرَ أَشْعَثَ أَغْبَرَ يَمُدُّ يَدَيْهِ إِلَى السَّمَاءِ: يَا رَبِّ يَا رَبِّ، وَمَطْعَمُهُ حَرَامٌ، وَمَشْرَبُهُ حَرَامٌ، وَمَلْبَسُهُ حَرَامٌ، وَغُذِّيَ بِالْحَرَامِ فَأَنَّى يُسْتَجَابُ لِذلِكَ؟»

(O people! Allah is Tayyib (Pure and Good) and only accepts that which is Tayyib. Allah has indeed commanded the believers with what He has commanded the Messengers, for He said: (O (you) Messengers! Eat of the Tayyibat and do righteous deeds. Verily, I am well-acquainted with what you do) (23:51), and: (O you who believe! Eat of the lawful things that We have provided you with) He then mentioned a man, (who is engaged in a long journey, whose hair is untidy and who is covered in dust, he raises his hands to the sky, and says, `O Lord! O Lord!' Yet, his food is from the unlawful, his drink is from the unlawful, his clothes are from the unlawful, and he was nourished by the unlawful, so how can it (his supplication) be accepted") It was also recorded by Muslim and At-Tirmidhi

## Chapter 2: Al-Baqarah (The Cow), Verses 142-252

After Allah mentioned how He has blessed His creatures by providing them with provisions, and after commanding them to eat from the pure things that He has provided them, He then stated that He has not prohibited anything for them, except dead animals. Dead animals are those that die before being slaughtered; whether they die by strangling, a violent blow, a headlong fall, the goring of horns or by being partly eaten by a wild animal. Dead animals of the sea are excluded from this ruling, as is explained later, Allah willing, as Allah said:

﴿أُحِلَّ لَكُمْ صَيْدُ الْبَحْرِ وَطَعَامُهُ﴾

(Lawful to you is (the pursuit of) watergame and its use for food) (5:96), and because of the Hadith about the whale recorded in the Sahih. The Musnad, Al-Muwatta' and the Sunan recorded the Prophet saying about the sea:

«هُوَ الطَّهُورُ مَاؤُهُ والْحِلُّ مَيْتَتُهُ»

(Its water is pure and its dead are permissible.)

Ash-Shafi`i, Ahmad, Ibn Majah, and Ad-Daraqutni reported that Ibn `Umar said that the Prophet said:

«أُحِلَّ لَنَا مَيْتَتَانِ وَدَمَانِ، السَّمَكُ وَالْجَرَادُ وَالْكَبِدُ وَالطِّحَال»

(We have been allowed two dead things and two bloody things: fish and locusts; and liver and spleen).

We will mention this subject again in Surat Al-Ma'idah (chapter 5 in the Qur'an), In sha' Allah (if Allah wills).

Issue: According to Ash-Shafi`i and other scholars, milk and eggs that are inside dead unslaughtered animals are not pure, because they are part of the dead animal. In one narration from him, Malik said that they are pure themselves, but become impure because of their location. Similarly, there is a difference of opinion over the cheeses (made with the milk) of dead animals. The popular view of the scholars is that it is impure, although they mentioned the fact that the Companions ate from the cheeses made by the Magians (fire worshippers). Hence, Al-Qurtubi commented: "Since only a small part of the dead animal is mixed with it, then it is permissible, because a minute amount of impurity does not matter if it is mixed with a large amount of liquid." Ibn Majah reported that Salman said that Allah's Messenger was asked about butter, cheese and fur. He said:

»الْحَلَالُ مَا أَحَلَّ اللهُ فِي كِتَابِهِ، وَالْحَرَامُ مَا حَرَّمَ اللهُ فِي كِتَابِهِ، وَمَا سَكَتَ عَنْهُ فَهُوَ مِمَّا عَفَا عَنْهُ«

(The allowed is what Allah has allowed in His Book and the prohibited is what Allah has prohibited in His Book. What He has not mentioned is a part of what He has pardoned.)

Allah has prohibited eating the meat of swine, whether slaughtered or not, and this includes its fat, either because it is implied, or because the term Lahm includes that, or by analogy. Similarly prohibited are offerings to other than Allah, that is what was slaughtered in a name other than His, be it for monuments, idols, divination, or the other practices of the time of Jahiliyyah. Al-Qurtubi mentioned that `A'ishah was asked about what non-Muslims slaughter for their feasts and then offer some of it as gifts for Muslims. She said, "Do not eat from what has been slaughtered for that day, (or feast) but eat from their vegetables."

### The Prohibited is Allowed in Cases of Emergency

Then Allah permitted eating these things when needed for survival or when there are no permissible types of food available. Allah said:

(But if one is forced by necessity without willful disobedience nor transgressing due limits), meaning, without transgression or overstepping the limits,

(...then there is no sin on him.) meaning, if one eats such items, for,

(Truly, Allah is Oft-Forgiving, Most Merciful.)

Mujahid said, "If one is forced by necessity without willful disobedience nor transgressing the set limits. For example, if he didn't, then he would have to resort to highway robbery, rising against the rulers, or some other kinds of disobedience to Allah, then the permission applies to him. If one does so transgressing the limits, or continually, or out of disobedience to Allah, then the permission does not apply to him even if he is in dire need." The same was reported from Sa`id bin Jubayr. Sa`id and Muqatil bin Hayyan are reported to have said that without willful disobedience means, "Without believing that it is permissible." It was reported that Ibn `Abbas commented on the Ayah:

(...without willful disobedience nor transgressing) saying, "Without willful disobedience means eating the dead animal and not continuing to do so. Qatadah said:

(without willful disobedience) "Without transgressing by eating from the dead animals, that is when the lawful is available."

Issue: When one in dire straits finds both - dead animals, and foods belong to other people which he could get without risking the loss of his hands or causing harm, then it is not allowed for him to eat the dead animals. Ibn Majah reported that `Abbad bin Shurahbil Al-Ghubari said, "One year we suffered from famine. I came to Al-Madinah and entered a garden. I took some grain that I cleaned, and ate, then I left some of it in my garment. The owner of the garden came, roughed me up and took possession of my garment. I then went to Allah's Messenger and told him what had happened. He said to the man:

《مَا أَطْعَمْتَهُ إِذْ كَانَ جَائِعًا أَوْ سَاغِبًا وَلَا عَلَّمْتَهُ إِذْ كَانَ جَاهِلًا》

(You have not fed him when he was hungry - or he said starving - nor have you taught him if he was ignorant.)

The Prophet commanded him to return `Abbad's garment to him, and to offer him a Wasq (around 180 kilograms) - or a half Wasq - of food

This has a sufficiently strong chain of narrators and there are many other witnessing narrations to support it, such as the Hadith that `Amr bin Shu`ayb narrated from his father that his grandfather said: Allah's Messenger was asked about the hanging clusters of dates. He said:

《مَنْ أَصَابَ مِنْهُ مِنْ ذِي حَاجَةٍ بِفِيهِ غَيْرَ مُتَّخِذٍ خُبْنَةً، فَلَا شَيْءَ عَلَيْهِ》

(There is no harm for whoever takes some of it in his mouth for a necessity without putting it in his garment.)

Muqatil bin Hayyan commented on:

(...then there is no sin on him. Truly, Allah is Oft-Forgiving, Most Merciful.) "For what is eaten out of necessity." Sa`id bin Jubayr said, "Allah is pardoning for what has been eaten of the unlawful, and Merciful' in that He allowed the prohibited during times of necessity." Masruq said, "Whoever is in dire need, but does not eat or drink until he dies, he will enter the Fire." This indicates that eating dead animals for those who are in need of it for survival is not only permissible but required.

### Surah: 2 Ayah: 174, 2 Ayah: 175 & 2 Ayah: 176

﴿ إِنَّ ٱلَّذِينَ يَكْتُمُونَ مَا أَنزَلَ ٱللَّهُ مِنَ ٱلْكِتَٰبِ وَيَشْتَرُونَ بِهِۦ ثَمَنًا قَلِيلًا أُو۟لَٰٓئِكَ مَا يَأْكُلُونَ فِى بُطُونِهِمْ إِلَّا ٱلنَّارَ وَلَا يُكَلِّمُهُمُ ٱللَّهُ يَوْمَ ٱلْقِيَٰمَةِ وَلَا يُزَكِّيهِمْ وَلَهُمْ عَذَابٌ أَلِيمٌ ﴾

174. Verily, those who conceal what Allâh has sent down of the Book, and purchase a small gain therewith (of worldly things), they eat into their bellies nothing but fire. Allâh will not speak to them on the Day of Resurrection, nor purify them, and theirs will be a painful torment.

﴿ أُوْلَـٰٓئِكَ ٱلَّذِينَ ٱشْتَرَوُاْ ٱلضَّلَـٰلَةَ بِٱلْهُدَىٰ وَٱلْعَذَابَ بِٱلْمَغْفِرَةِ ۚ فَمَآ أَصْبَرَهُمْ عَلَى ٱلنَّارِ ﴿١٧٥﴾ ﴾

175. Those are they who have purchased error at the price of Guidance, and torment at the price of Forgiveness. So how bold they are (for evil deeds which will push them) to the Fire.

﴿ ذَٰلِكَ بِأَنَّ ٱللَّهَ نَزَّلَ ٱلْكِتَـٰبَ بِٱلْحَقِّ ۗ وَإِنَّ ٱلَّذِينَ ٱخْتَلَفُواْ فِى ٱلْكِتَـٰبِ لَفِى شِقَاقٍ بَعِيدٍ ﴿١٧٦﴾ ﴾

176. That is because Allâh has sent down the Book (the Qur'ân) in truth. And verily, those who disputed as regards the Book are far away in opposition.

### Transliteration

174. Inna allatheena yaktumoona ma anzala Allahu mina alkitabi wayashtaroona bihi thamanan qaleelan ola-ika ma ya/kuloona fee butoonihim illa alnnara wala yukallimuhumu Allahu yawma alqiyamati wala yuzakkeehim walahum AAathabun aleemun 175. Ola-ika allatheena ishtarawoo alddalalata bialhuda waalAAathaba bialmaghfirati fama asbarahum AAala alnnari 176. Thalika bi-anna Allaha nazzala alkitaba bialhaqqi wa-inna allatheena ikhtalafoo fee alkitabi lafee shiqaqin baAAeedin

### Tafsir Ibn Kathir

#### Criticizing the Jews for concealing what Allah revealed

Allah said:

(Verily, those who conceal what Allah has sent down of the Book.) Meaning the Jews who concealed their Book's descriptions of Muhammad, all of which testify to his truth as a Messenger and a Prophet. They concealed this information so that they would not lose authority and the position that they had with the Arabs, where they would bring them gifts, and honor them. The cursed Jews feared that if they announced what they know about Muhammad, then the people would abandon them and follow him. So they hid the truth so that they may retain the little that they were getting, and they sold their souls for this little profit. They preferred the little that they gained over guidance and following the truth, believing in the Messenger and having faith in what Allah was sent him with. Therefore, they have profited failure and loss in this life and the Hereafter.

Chapter 2: Al-Baqarah (The Cow), Verses 142-252 65

As for this world, Allah made the truth about His Messenger known anyway, by the clear signs and the unequivocal proofs. Thereafter, those whom the Jews feared would follow the Prophet , believed in him and followed him anyway, and so they became his supporters against them. Thus, the Jews earned anger on top of the wrath that they already had earned before, and Allah criticized them again many times in His Book. For instance, Allah said in this Ayah (2:174 above):

(Verily, those who conceal what Allah has sent down of the Book, and purchase a small gain therewith (of worldly things).) meaning, the joys and delights of this earthly life. Allah said:

(...they eat into their bellies nothing but fire,) meaning, whatever they eat in return for hiding the truth, will turn into a raging fire in their stomachs on the Day of Resurrection.

Similarly, Allah said:

(Verily, those who unjustly eat up the property of orphans, they eat up only fire into their bellies, and they will be burnt in the blazing Fire!) (4:10)

Also, reported in an authentic Hadith is that Allah's Messenger said:

»الَّذِي يَأْكُلُ أَوْ يَشْرَبُ فِي آنِيةِ الذَّهَبِ وَالْفِضَّةِ إِنَّمَا يُجَرْجِرُ فِي بَطْنِهِ نَارَ جَهَنَّم«

(Those who eat or drink in golden or silver plates are filling their stomachs with the fire of Jahannam (Hell).)

Allah said:

(Allah will not speak to them on the Day of Resurrection, nor purify them, and theirs will be a painful torment.)

This is because Allah is furious with them for concealing the truth. They thus deserve Allah's anger, so Allah will not look at them or purify them, meaning that He will not praise them but will cause them to taste a severe torment. Then, Allah said about them:

(Those are they who have purchased error for guidance.)

Hence, they opposed the guidance, that is, not announcing the Prophet's description they find in their Books, the news about his prophecy and the good news of his coming which the previous Prophets proclaimed, as well as following and believing in him. Instead, they preferred misguidance by denying him, rejecting him and concealing his descriptions that were mentioned in their Books. Allah said:

(...and torment at the price of forgiveness,) meaning, they preferred torment over forgiveness due to the sins they have committed. Allah then said:

(So how bold they are (for evil deeds which will push them) to the Fire.)

Allah states that they will suffer such severe, painful torment that those who see them will be amazed at how they could bear the tremendous punishment, torture and pain that they will suffer. We seek refuge with Allah from this evil end. RAllah's Statement:

(That is because Allah has sent down the Book (the Qur'an) in truth. ) means, they deserve this painful torment because Allah has revealed Books to His Messenger Muhammad , and the Prophets before him, and these revelations bring about truth and expose falsehood. Yet, they took Allah's signs for mockery. Their Books ordered them to announce the truth and to spread the knowledge, but instead, they defied the knowledge and rejected it. This Final Messenger - Muhammad - called them to Allah, commanded them to work righteousness and forbade them from committing evil. Yet, they rejected, denied and defied him and hid the truth that they knew about him. They, thus, mocked the Ayat that Allah revealed to His Messengers, and this is why they deserved the torment and the punishment. This is why Allah said here (2:176):

(That is because Allah has sent down the Book (the Qur'an) in truth. And verily, those who disputed about the Book are far away in opposition.)

### Surah: 2 Ayah: 177

﴿ ۞ لَّيْسَ ٱلْبِرَّ أَن تُوَلُّواْ وُجُوهَكُمْ قِبَلَ ٱلْمَشْرِقِ وَٱلْمَغْرِبِ وَلَٰكِنَّ ٱلْبِرَّ مَنْ ءَامَنَ بِٱللَّهِ وَٱلْيَوْمِ ٱلْءَاخِرِ وَٱلْمَلَٰٓئِكَةِ وَٱلْكِتَٰبِ وَٱلنَّبِيِّۦنَ وَءَاتَى ٱلْمَالَ عَلَىٰ حُبِّهِۦ ذَوِى ٱلْقُرْبَىٰ وَٱلْيَتَٰمَىٰ وَٱلْمَسَٰكِينَ وَٱبْنَ ٱلسَّبِيلِ وَٱلسَّآئِلِينَ وَفِى ٱلرِّقَابِ وَأَقَامَ ٱلصَّلَوٰةَ وَءَاتَى ٱلزَّكَوٰةَ وَٱلْمُوفُونَ بِعَهْدِهِمْ إِذَا عَٰهَدُواْ ۖ وَٱلصَّٰبِرِينَ فِى ٱلْبَأْسَآءِ وَٱلضَّرَّآءِ وَحِينَ ٱلْبَأْسِ ۗ أُوْلَٰٓئِكَ ٱلَّذِينَ صَدَقُواْ ۖ وَأُوْلَٰٓئِكَ هُمُ ٱلْمُتَّقُونَ ﴾

177. It is not Al-Birr (piety, righteousness, and each and every act of obedience to Allâh, etc.) that you turn your faces towards east and (or) west (in prayers); but Al-Birr is (the quality of) the one who believes in Allâh, the Last Day, the Angels, the Book, the Prophets and gives his wealth, in spite of love for it, to the kinsfolk, to the orphans, and to Al-Masâkin (the poor),

and to the wayfarer, and to those who ask, and to set slaves free, performs As-Salât (Iqâmat-as-Salât), and gives the Zakât, and who fulfill their covenant when they make it, and who are patient in extreme poverty and ailment (disease) and at the time of fighting (during the battles). Such are the people of the truth and they are Al-Muttaqûn (the pious - see V.2:2).

## Transliteration

177. Laysa albirra an tuwalloo wujoohakum qibala almashriqi waalmaghribi walakinna albirra man amana biAllahi waalyawmi al-akhiri waalmala-ikati waalkitabi waalnnabiyyeena waata almala AAala hubbihi thawee alqurba waalyatama waalmasakeena waibna alssabeeli waalssa-ileena wafee alrriqabi waaqama alssalata waata alzzakata waalmoofoona biAAahdihim itha AAahadoo waalssabireena fee alba/sa-i waaldarra-i waheena alba/si ola-ika allatheena sadaqoo waola-ika humu almuttaqoona

## Tafsir Ibn Kathir

### Al-Birr (Piety, Righteousness)

This Ayah contains many great wisdoms, encompassing rulings and correct beliefs.

As for the explanation of this Ayah, Allah first commanded the believers to face Bayt Al-Maqdis, and then to face the Ka`bah during the prayer. This change was difficult for some of the People of the Book, and even for some Muslims. Then Allah sent revelation which clarified the wisdom behind this command, that is, obedience to Allah, adhering to His commands, facing wherever He commands facing, and implementing whatever He legislates, that is the objective. This is Birr, Taqwa and complete faith. Facing the east or the west does not necessitate righteousness or obedience, unless it is legislated by Allah. This is why Allah said:

(It is not Birr that you turn your faces towards east and (or) west (in prayers); but Birr is the one who believes in Allah and the Last Day,)

Similarly, Allah said about the sacrifices:

(It is neither their meat nor their blood that reaches Allah, but it is the piety from you that reaches Him.) (22:37)

Abu Al-`Aliyah said, "The Jews used to face the west for their Qiblah, while the Christians used to face the east for their Qiblah. So Allah said:

(It is not Birr that you turn your faces towards east and (or) west (in prayers)) (2: 177) meaning, "this is faith, and its essence requires implementation." Similar was reported from Al-Hasan and Ar-Rabi` bin Anas. Ath-Thawri recited:

(but Birr is the one who believes in Allah,) and said that what follows are the types of Birr. He has said the truth. Certainly, those who acquire the qualities mentioned in the Ayah will have indeed embraced all aspects of Islam and implemented all types of righteousness; believing in Allah, that He is the only God worthy of worship, and believing in the angels the emissaries between Allah and His Messengers.

The `Books' are the Divinely revealed Books from Allah to the Prophets, which were finalized by the most honorable Book (the Qur'an). The Qur'an supercedes all previous Books, it mentions all types of righteousness, and the way to happiness in this life and the Hereafter. The Qur'an abrogates all previous Books and testfies to all of Allah's Prophets, from the first Prophet to the Final Prophet, Muhammad, may Allah's peace and blessings be upon them all.

Allah's statement:

(...and gives his wealth, in spite of love for it,) refers to those who give money away while desiring it and loving it. It is recorded in the Sahihayn that Abu Hurayrah narrated that the Prophet said:

«أَفْضَلُ الصَّدَقةِ أَنْ تَصَدَّقَ وَأَنْتَ صَحِيحٌ شَحِيحٌ، تَأْمُلُ الْغِنَى وتَخْشَى الْفقْرَ»

(The best charity is when you give it away while still healthy and thrifty, hoping to get rich and fearing poverty.)

Allah said:

(And they give food, inspite of their love for it, to the Miskin (the poor), the orphan, and the captive (saying): "We feed you seeking Allah's Face only. We wish for no reward, nor thanks from you.") (76:8, 9)

and:

(By no means shall you attain Birr unless you spend of that which you love.) (3:92) Allah's statement:

(...and give them preference over themselves even though they were in need of that) (59:9) refers to a higher category and status, as the people mentioned here give away what they need, while those mentioned in the previous Ayat give away what they covet (but not necessarily need).

Allah's statement:

(the kinsfolk) refers to man's relatives, who have more rights than anyone else to one's charity, as the Hadith supports:

«الصَّدَقَةُ عَلَى الْمَسَاكِينِ صَدَقَةٌ، وعَلَى ذِي الرَّحِمِ اثْنَتَانِ: صَدَقَةٌ وَصِلَةٌ، فَهُمْ أَوْلَى النَّاسِ بِكَ وَبِبِرِّكَ وَإِعْطَائِكَ»

(Sadaqah (i. e., charity) given to the poor is a charity, while the Sadaqah given to the relatives is both Sadaqah and Silah (nurturing relations), for they are the most deserving of you and your kindness and charity).

Allah has commanded kindness to the relatives in many places in the Qur'an.

(to the orphans) The orphans are children who have none to look after them, having lost their fathers while they are still young, weak and unable to find their own sustenance since they have not reached the age of work and adolescence. `Abdur-Razzaq reported that `Ali said that the Prophet said:

(and to Al-Masakin) The Miskin is the person who does not have enough food, clothing, or he has no dwelling. So the Miskin should be granted the provisions to sustain him enough so that he can acquire his needs. In the Sahihayn it is recorded that Abu Hurayrah said that Allah's Messenger said:

«لَيْسَ الْمِسْكِينُ بِهَذَا الطَّوَّافِ الَّذِي تَرُدُّهُ التَّمْرَةُ والتَّمْرَتَانِ، واللُّقْمَةُ واللُّقْمَتَانِ، وَلَكِنِ الْمِسْكِينُ الَّذِي لَا يَجِدُ غِنًى يُغْنِيهِ وَلَا يُفْطَنُ لَهُ فَيُتَصَدَّقَ عَلَيْهِ»

(The Miskin is not the person who roams around, and whose need is met by one or two dates or one or two bites. Rather, the Miskin is he who does not have what is sufficient, and to whom the people do not pay attention and, thus, do not give him from the charity.)

(and to the wayfarer) is the needy traveler who runs out of money and should, thus, be granted whatever amount that helps him to go back to his land. Such is the case with whoever intends to go on a permissible journey, he is given what he needs for his journey and back. The guests are included in this category. `Ali bin Abu Talhah reported that Ibn `Abbas said, "Ibn As-Sabil (wayfarer) is the guest who is hosted by Muslims." Furthermore, Mujahid, Sa`id bin Jubayr, Abu Ja`far Al-Baqir, Al-Hasan, Qatadah, Ad-Dahhak, Az-Zuhri, Ar-Rabi` bin Anas and Muqatil bin Hayyan said similarly.

(and to those who ask) refers to those who beg people and are thus given a part of the Zakah and general charity.

(and to set servants free) These are the servants who seek to free themselves, but cannot find enough money to buy their freedom. We will mention several of these categories and types under the Tafsir of the Ayah on Sadaqah in Surat Bara'ah )chapter 9 in the Qur'an(, In sha' Allah.

Allah's statement:

(performs As-Salah (Iqamat-As-Salah)) means those who pray on time and give the prayer its due right; the bowing, prostration, and the necessary attention and humbleness required by Allah. Allah's statement:

(and gives the Zakah) means the required charity (Zakah) due on one's money, as Sa`id bin Jubayr and Muqatil bin Hayyan have stated.

Allah's statement:

(and who fulfill their covenant when they make it,)

is similar to:

(Those who fulfill the covenant of Allah and break not the Mithaq (bond, treaty, covenant).) (13:20)

The opposite of this characteristic is hypocrisy. As found in a Hadith:

«آيَةُ الْمُنَافِقِ ثَلَاثٌ: إِذَا حَدَّثَ كَذَبَ، وَإِذَا وَعَدَ أَخْلَفَ، وَإِذَا اؤْتُمِنَ خَانَ»

(The signs of a hypocrite are three: if he speaks, he lies; if he promises, he breaks his promise; and if he is entrusted, he breaches the trust.)

In another version:

«إِذَا حَدَّثَ كَذَبَ، وَإِذَا عَاهَدَ غَدَرَ، وَإِذَا خَاصَمَ فَجَرَ»

(If he speaks, he lies; if he vows, he breaks his vow; and if he disputes, he is lewd.)

Allah's statement:

(...and who are patient in extreme poverty and ailment (disease) and at the time of fighting (during the battles).) means, during the time of meekness and ailment.

(...and at the time of fighting (during the battles).) means on the battlefield while facing the enemy, as Ibn Mas`ud, Ibn `Abbas, Abu Al-`Aliyah, Murrah Al-Hamdani, Mujahid, Sa`id bin Jubayr, Al-Hasan, Qatadah, Ar-Rabi` bin Anas, As-Suddi, Muqatil bin Hayyan, Abu Malik, Ad-Dahhak and others have stated.

And calling them the patient here, is a form of praise, because of the importance of patience in these circumstances, and the suffering and difficulties that accompany them. And Allah knows best, it is He Whom help is sought from, and upon Him we rely.

Allah's statement:

(Such are the people of the truth) means, whoever acquires these qualities, these are truthful in their faith. This is because they have achieved faith in the heart and realized it in deed and upon the tongue. So they are the truthful,

(and they are Al-Muttaqun (the pious).) because they avoided the prohibitions and performed the acts of obedience.

### Surah: 2 Ayah: 178 & Ayah: 179

﴿ يَٰٓأَيُّهَا ٱلَّذِينَ ءَامَنُوا۟ كُتِبَ عَلَيْكُمُ ٱلْقِصَاصُ فِى ٱلْقَتْلَى ۖ ٱلْحُرُّ بِٱلْحُرِّ وَٱلْعَبْدُ بِٱلْعَبْدِ وَٱلْأُنثَىٰ بِٱلْأُنثَىٰ ۚ فَمَنْ عُفِىَ لَهُۥ مِنْ أَخِيهِ شَىْءٌ فَٱتِّبَاعٌۢ بِٱلْمَعْرُوفِ وَأَدَآءٌ إِلَيْهِ بِإِحْسَٰنٍ ۗ ذَٰلِكَ تَخْفِيفٌ مِّن رَّبِّكُمْ وَرَحْمَةٌ ۗ فَمَنِ ٱعْتَدَىٰ بَعْدَ ذَٰلِكَ فَلَهُۥ عَذَابٌ أَلِيمٌ ﴾

178. O you who believe! Al-Qisâs (the Law of Equality in punishment) is prescribed for you in case of murder: the free for the free, the slave for the slave, and the female for the female. But if the killer is forgiven by the brother (or the relatives, etc.) of the killed against blood-money, then adhering to it with fairness and payment of the blood-money, to the heir should be made in fairness. This is an alleviation and a mercy from your Lord. So after this whoever transgresses the limits (i.e. kills the killer after taking the blood-money), he shall have a painful torment.

﴿ وَلَكُمْ فِى ٱلْقِصَاصِ حَيَوٰةٌ يَٰٓأُو۟لِى ٱلْأَلْبَٰبِ لَعَلَّكُمْ تَتَّقُونَ ﴾

179. And there is (a saving of) life for you in Al-Qisâs (the Law of Equality in punishment), O men of understanding, that you may become Al-Muttaqûn (the pious - see V.2:2).

## Transliteration

178. Ya ayyuha allatheena amanoo kutiba AAalaykumu alqisasu fee alqatla alhurru bialhurri waalAAabdu bialAAabdi waalontha bialontha faman AAufiya lahu min akheehi shay-on faittibaAAun bialmaAAroofi waadaon ilayhi bi-ihsanin thalika takhfeefun min rabbikum warahmatun famani iAAtada baAAda thalika falahu AAathabun aleemun  179. Walakum fee alqisasi hayatun ya olee al-albabi laAAallakum tattaqoona

## Tafsir Ibn Kathir

### The Command and the Wisdom behind the Law of Equality

Allah states: O believers! The Law of equality has been ordained on you (for cases of murder), the free for the free, the slave for the slave and the female for the female. Therefore, do not transgress the set limits, as others before you transgressed them, and thus changed what Allah has ordained for them. The reason behind this statement is that (the Jewish tribe of) Banu An-Nadir invaded Qurayzah (another Jewish tribe) during the time of Jahiliyyah (before Islam) and defeated them. Hence, (they made it a law that) when a person from Nadir kills a person from Quraizah, he is not killed in retaliation, but only pays a hundred Wasq of dates. However, when a person from Quraizah kills a Nadir man, he would be killed for him. If Nadir wanted (to forfeit the execution of the murderer and instead require him) to pay a ransom, the Quraizah man pays two hundred Wasq of dates )double the amount Nadir pays in Diyah (blood money)(. So Allah commanded that justice be observed regarding the penal code, and that the path of the misguided and mischievous persons be avoided, who in disbelief and transgression, defy and alter what Allah has commanded them. Allah said:

(Al-Qisas (the Law of equality in punishment) is prescribed for you in case of murder: the free for the free, the slave for the slave, and the female for the female.)

Allah's statement:

(the free for the free, the slave for the slave, and the female for the female.) was abrogated by the statement life for life (5:45). However, the majority of scholars agree that the Muslim is not killed for a disbeliever whom he kills. Al-Bukhari reported that `Ali narrated that Allah's Messenger said:

»وَلَا يُقْتَلُ مُسْلِمٌ بِكَافِرٍ«

(The Muslim is not killed for the disbeliever (whom he kills).)

No opinion that opposes this ruling could stand correct, nor is there an authentic Hadith to contradict it. However, Abu Hanifah thought that the

## Chapter 2: Al-Baqarah (The Cow), Verses 142-252

Muslim could be killed for a disbeliever, following the general meaning of the Ayah (5:45) in Surat Al-Ma'idah (chapter 5 in the Qur'an).

The Four Imams (Abu Hanifah, Malik, Shafi`i and Ahmad) and the majority of scholars stated that the group is killed for one person whom they murder. `Umar said, about a boy who was killed by seven men, "If all the residents of San`a' (capital of Yemen today) collaborated on killing him, I would kill them all." No opposing opinion was known by the Companions during that time which constitutes a near Ijma` (consensus). There is an opinion attributed to Imam Ahmad that a group of people is not killed for one person whom they kill, and that only one person is killed for one person. Ibn Al-Mundhir also attributed this opinion to Mu`adh, Ibn Az-Zubayr, `Abdul-Malik bin Marwan, Az-Zuhri, Ibn Sirin and Habib bin Abu Thabit. Allah's statement:

(But if the killer is forgiven by the brother (or the relatives) of the killed (against blood money), then it should be sought in a good manner, and paid to him respectfully.) refers to accepting blood money (by the relatives of the victim in return for pardoning the killer) in cases of intentional murder. This opinion is attributed to Abu Al-`Aliyah, Abu Sha`tha', Mujahid, Sa`id bin Jubayr, `Ata' Al-Hasan, Qatadah and Muqatil bin Hayyan. Ad-Dahhak said that Ibn `Abbas said:

(But if the killer is forgiven by the brother (or the relatives) of the killed (against blood money)) means the killer is pardoned by his brother (i.e., the relative of the victim) and accepting the Diyah after capital punishment becomes due (against the killer), this is the `Afw (pardon mentioned in the Ayah)." Allah's statement:

(...then it should be sought in a good manner,) means, when the relative agrees to take the blood money, he should collect his rightful dues with kindness:

( and paid to him respectfully.) means, the killer should accept the terms of settlement without causing further harm or resisting the payment.

Allah's statement:

(This is an alleviation and a mercy from your Lord.) means the legislation that allows you to accept the blood money for intentional murder is an alleviation and a mercy from your Lord. It lightens what was required from those who were before you, either applying capital punishment or forgiving.

Sa`id bin Mansur reported that Ibn `Abbas said, "The Children of Israel were required to apply the Law of equality in murder cases and were not allowed to offer pardons (in return for blood money). Allah said to this Ummah (the Muslim nation):

(The Law of equality in punishment is prescribed for you in case of murder: the free for the free, the servant for the servant, and the female for the female.

But if the killer is forgiven by the brother (or the relatives) of the killed (against blood money),)

Hence, `pardoning' or `forgiving' means accepting blood money in intentional murder cases." Ibn Hibban also recorded this in his Sahih. Qatadah said:

(This is an alleviation from your Lord)

Allah had mercy on this Ummah by giving them the Diyah which was not allowed for any nation before it. The People of the Torah (Jews) were allowed to either apply the penal code (for murder, i.e., execution) or to pardon the killer, but they were not allowed to take blood money. The People of the Injil (the Gospel - the Christians) were required to pardon (the killer, but no Diyah was legislated). This Ummah (Muslims) is allowed to apply the penal code (execution) or to pardon and accept the blood money." Similar was reported from Sa`id bin Jubayr, Muqatil bin Hayyan and Ar-Rabi` bin Anas.

Allah's statement:

(So after this whoever transgresses the limits, he shall have a painful torment.) means, those who kill in retaliation after taking the Diyah or accepting it, they will suffer a painful and severe torment from Allah. The same was reported from Ibn `Abbas, Mujahid, `Ata' `Ikrimah, Al-Hasan, Qatadah, Ar-Rabi` bin Anas, As-Suddi and Muqatil bin Hayyan.

## The Benefits and Wisdom of the Law of Equality

Allah's statement:

(And there is life for you in Al-Qisas) legislating the Law of equality, i.e., killing the murderer, carries great benefits for you. This way, the sanctity of life will be preserved because the killer will refrain from killing, as he will be certain that if he kills, he would be killed. Hence life will be preserved. In previous Books, there is a statement that killing stops further killing! This meaning came in much clearer and eloquent terms in the Qur'an:

(And there is (a saving of) life for you in Al-Qisas (the Law of equality in punishment).)

Abu Al-`Aliyah said, "Allah made the Law of equality a `life'. Hence, how many a man who thought about killing, but this Law prevented him from killing for fear that he will be killed in turn." Similar statements were reported from Mujahid, Sa`id bin Jubayr, Abu Malik, Al-Hasan, Qatadah, Ar-Rabi` bin Anas and Muqatil bin Hayyan. Allah's statement:

(O men of understanding, that you may acquire Taqwa.) means, `O you who have sound minds, comprehension and understanding! Perhaps by this you will be compelled to refrain from transgressing the prohibitions of Allah and what

He considers sinful. ' Taqwa (mentioned in the Ayah) is a word that means doing all acts of obedience and refraining from all prohibitions.

## Surah: 2 Ayah: 180, Ayah: 181 & Ayah: 182

﴿ كُتِبَ عَلَيْكُمْ إِذَا حَضَرَ أَحَدَكُمُ ٱلْمَوْتُ إِن تَرَكَ خَيْرًا ٱلْوَصِيَّةُ لِلْوَٰلِدَيْنِ وَٱلْأَقْرَبِينَ بِٱلْمَعْرُوفِ حَقًّا عَلَى ٱلْمُتَّقِينَ ﴾

180. It is prescribed for you, when death approaches any of you, if he leaves wealth, that he make a bequest to parents and next of kin, according to reasonable manners. (This is) a duty upon Al-Muttaqûn (the pious - see V.2:2).

﴿ فَمَنۢ بَدَّلَهُۥ بَعْدَمَا سَمِعَهُۥ فَإِنَّمَآ إِثْمُهُۥ عَلَى ٱلَّذِينَ يُبَدِّلُونَهُۥٓ إِنَّ ٱللَّهَ سَمِيعٌ عَلِيمٌ ﴾

181. Then whoever changes the bequest after hearing it, the sin shall be on those who make the change. Truly, Allâh is All-Hearer, All-Knower.

﴿ فَمَنْ خَافَ مِن مُّوصٍ جَنَفًا أَوْ إِثْمًا فَأَصْلَحَ بَيْنَهُمْ فَلَآ إِثْمَ عَلَيْهِ إِنَّ ٱللَّهَ غَفُورٌ رَّحِيمٌ ﴾

182. But he who fears from a testator some unjust act or wrong-doing, and thereupon he makes peace between the parties concerned, there shall be no sin on him. Certainly, Allâh is Oft-Forgiving, Most Merciful.

### Transliteration

180. Kutiba AAalaykum itha hadara ahadakumu almawtu in taraka khayran alwasiyyatu lilwalidayni waal-aqrabeena bialmaAAroofi haqqan AAala almuttaqeena 181. Faman baddalahu baAAda ma samiAAahu fa-innama ithmuhu AAala allatheena yubaddiloonahu inna Allaha sameeAAun AAaleemun 182. Faman khafa min moosin janafan aw ithman faaslaha baynahum fala ithma AAalayhi inna Allaha ghafoorun raheemun

### Tafsir Ibn Kathir

**Including Parents and Relatives in the Will was later abrogated**

This Ayah contains the command to include parents and relatives in the will, which was obligatory, according to the most correct view, before the Ayah about inheritance was revealed. When the Ayah of inheritance was revealed, this Ayah was abrogated, so fixed shares of the inheritance for deserving recipients were legislated by Allah. Therefore, deserving inheritors take their fixed inheritance without the need to be included in the will or to be reminded of the favor of the inherited person. For this reason we see the Hadith narrated in the Sunan and other books that `Amr bin Kharijah said: I heard Allah's Messenger saying in a speech:

$$\text{«إِنَّ اللَّهَ قَدْ أَعْطَى كُلَّ ذِي حَقٍّ حَقَّهُ، فَلَا وَصِيَّةَ لِوَارِثٍ»}$$

(Allah has given each heir his fixed share. So there is no will for a deserving heir.)

Imam Ahmad recorded that Muhammad bin Sirin said: Ibn `Abbas recited Surat Al-Baqarah (chapter 2 in the Qur'an) until he reached the Ayah:

(...if he leaves wealth, that he makes a bequest to parents and next of kin.)

He then said, "This Ayah was abrogated." This was recorded by Sa`id bin Mansur and Al-Hakim in his Mustadrak Al-Hakim Said, "It is Sahih according to their criteria (Al-Bukhari and Muslim)". Ibn Abu Hatim reported that Ibn `Abbas said that Allah's statement:

(a bequest to parents and next of kin)

was abrogated by the Ayah:

(There is a share for men and a share for women from what is left by parents and those nearest related, whether the property be small or large - a legal share.) (4:7)

Ibn Abu Hatim then said, "It was reported from Ibn `Umar, Abu Musa, Sa`id bin Musayyib, Al-Hasan, Mujahid, `Ata' Sa`id bin Jubayr, Muhammad bin Sirin, `Ikrimah, Zayd bin Aslam and Ar-Rabi` bin Anas. Qatadah, As-Suddi, Muqatil bin Hayyan, Tawus, Ibrahim An-Nakha`i, Shurayh, Ad-Dahhak and Az-Zuhri said that this Ayah (2:180 above) was abrogated by the Ayah about the inheritors (4:7)."

## The Will for the Relatives that do not qualify as Inheritors

It is recommended that the remaining relatives who do not have a designated fixed share of the inheritance, be willed up to a third, due to the general meaning of the Ayah about the will. It is recorded in the Sahihayn that Ibn `Umar said that Allah's Messenger said:

$$\text{«مَا حَقُّ امْرِئٍ مُسْلِمٍ لَهُ شَيْءٌ يُوصِي فِيهِ يَبِيتُ لَيْلَتَيْنِ إِلَّا وَوَصِيَّتُهُ مَكْتُوبَةٌ عِنْدَه»}$$

(It is not permissible for any Muslim who has something to will to stay for two nights without having his last will and testament written and kept ready with him.)

Ibn `Umar commented, "Ever since I heard this statement from Allah's Messenger , no night has passed, but my will is kept ready with me." There are many other Ayat and Ahadith ordering kindness and generosity to one's relatives.

### The Will should observe Justice

The will should be fair, in that one designates a part of the inheritance to his relatives without committing injustice against his qualified inheritors and without extravagance or stinginess. It is recorded in the Sahihayn that Sa`d bin Abu Waqqas said, "O Allah's Messenger! I have some money and only a daughter inherits from me, should I will all my remaining property (to others)" He said, "No." Sa`d said, "Then may I will half of it" He said, "No." Sa`d said, "One-third" He said, "Yes, one-third, yet even one-third is too much. It is better for you to leave your inheritors wealthy than to leave them poor, begging from others." Al-Bukhari mentioned in his Sahih that Ibn `Abbas said, "I recommend that people reduce the proportion of what they bequeath by will to a fourth (of the whole legacy) rather than a third, for Allah's Messenger said:

》الثُّلُثُ وَالثُّلُثُ كَثِيرٌ《

(One-third, yet even one-third is too much.)"

Allah's statement:

(Then whoever changes it after hearing it, the sin shall be on those who make the change. Truly, Allah is All-Hearer, All-Knower.) means, whoever changed the will and testament or altered it by addition or deletion, including hiding the will as is obvious, then

(the sin shall be on those who make the change. )

Ibn `Abbas and others said, "The dead person's reward will be preserved for him by Allah, while the sin is acquired by those who change the will."

(Truly, Allah is All-Hearer, All-Knower.) means, Allah knows what the dead person has bequeathed and what the beneficiaries (or others) have changed in the will.

Allah's statement:

(But he who fears from a testator some unjust act or wrongdoing,)

Ibn `Abbas, Abu Al-`Aliyah, Mujahid, Ad-Dahhak, Ar-Rabi` bin Anas and As-Suddi said, "Error." These errors include such cases as when the inheritor indirectly acquires more than his fair share, such as by being allocated that a certain item mentioned in the legacy be sold to him. Or, the testator might include his daughter's son in the legacy to increase his daughter's share in the inheritance, and so forth. Such errors might occur out of the kindness of the heart without thinking about the consequences of these actions, or by sinful intention. In such cases, the executive of the will and testament is allowed to correct the errors and to replace the unjust items in the will with a better solution, so that both the Islamic law and what the dead person had wished for are respected and observed. This act would not constitute an alteration in the will and this is why Allah mentioned it specifically, so that it is excluded from the prohibition (that prohibits altering the will and testament) mentioned in the previous Ayah. And Allah knows best.

### The Virtue of Fairness in the Will

`Abdur-Razzaq reported that Abu Hurayrah said that Allah's Messenger said:

«إِنَّ الرَّجُلَ لَيَعْمَلُ بِعَمَلِ أَهْلِ الْخَيْرِ سَبْعِينَ سَنَةً، فَإِذَا أَوْصَى حَافَ فِي وَصِيَّتِهِ، فَيُخْتَمُ لَهُ بِشَرِّ عَمَلِهِ، فَيَدْخُلُ النَّارَ. وَإِنَّ الرَّجُلَ لَيَعْمَلُ بِعَمَلِ أَهْلِ الشَّرِّ سَبْعِينَ سَنَةً، فَيَعْدِلُ فِي وَصِيَّتِهِ، فَيُخْتَمُ لَهُ بِخَيْرِ عَمَلِهِ، فَيَدْخُلُ الْجَنَّةَ»

(A man might perform the works of righteous people for seventy years, but when he dictates his will, he commits injustice and thus his works end with the worst of his deeds and he enters the Fire. A man might perform the works of evil people for seventy years, but then dictates a just will and thus ends with the best of his deeds and then enters Paradise.)

Abu Hurayrah then said, "Read if you wish:

(These are the limits ordained by Allah, so do not transgress them.)" (2:229)

### Surah: 2 Ayah: 183 & Ayah: 184

﴿يَـٰٓأَيُّهَا ٱلَّذِينَ ءَامَنُواْ كُتِبَ عَلَيۡكُمُ ٱلصِّيَامُ كَمَا كُتِبَ عَلَى ٱلَّذِينَ مِن قَبۡلِكُمۡ لَعَلَّكُمۡ تَتَّقُونَ ۞﴾

183. O you who believe! Observing As-Saum (the fasting) is prescribed for you as it was prescribed for those before you, that you may become Al-Muttaqûn (the pious - see V.2:2).

### Chapter 2: Al-Baqarah (The Cow), Verses 142-252

﴿ أَيَّامًا مَّعْدُودَاتٍ ۚ فَمَن كَانَ مِنكُم مَّرِيضًا أَوْ عَلَىٰ سَفَرٍ فَعِدَّةٌ مِّنْ أَيَّامٍ أُخَرَ ۚ وَعَلَى ٱلَّذِينَ يُطِيقُونَهُۥ فِدْيَةٌ طَعَامُ مِسْكِينٍ ۖ فَمَن تَطَوَّعَ خَيْرًا فَهُوَ خَيْرٌ لَّهُۥ ۚ وَأَن تَصُومُوا۟ خَيْرٌ لَّكُمْ ۖ إِن كُنتُمْ تَعْلَمُونَ ﴿١٨٤﴾

184. Observing Saum (fasts)) for a fixed number of days, but if any of you is ill or on a journey, the same number (should be made up) from other days. And as for those who can fast with difficulty, (e.g. an old man, etc.), they have (a choice either to fast or) to feed a Miskîn (poor person) (for every day). But whoever does good of his own accord, it is better for him. And that you fast, it is better for you if only you know.

### Transliteration

183. Ya ayyuha allatheena amanoo kutiba AAalaykumu alssiyamu kama kutiba AAala allatheena min qablikum laAAallakum tattaqoona  184. Ayyaman maAAdoodatin faman kana minkum mareedan aw AAala safarin faAAiddatun min ayyamin okhara waAAala allatheena yuteeqoonahu fidyatun taAAamu miskeenin faman tatawwaAAa khayran fahuwa khayrun lahu waan tasoomoo khayrun lakum in kuntum taAAlamoona

### Tafsir Ibn Kathir

#### The Order to Fast

In an address to the believers of this Ummah, Allah ordered them to fast, that is, to abstain from food, drink and sexual activity with the intention of doing so sincerely for Allah the Exalted alone. This is because fasting purifies the souls and cleanses them from the evil that might mix with them and their ill behavior. Allah mentioned that He has ordained fasting for Muslims just as He ordained it for those before them, they being an example for them in that, so they should vigorously perform this obligation more obediently than the previous nations. Similarly, Allah said:

(To each among you, We have prescribed a law and a clear way. If Allah had willed, He would have made you one nation, but that (He) may test you in what He has given you; so compete in good deeds.) (5:48)

Allah said in this Ayah:

(O you who believe! Fasting is prescribed for you as it was prescribed for those before you, that you may have Taqwa).) since the fast cleanses the body and narrows the paths of Shaytan. In the Sahihayn the following Hadith was recorded:

«يَا مَعْشَرَ الشَّبَابِ مَنِ اسْتَطَاعَ مِنْكُمُ الْبَاءَةَ فَلْيَتَزَوَّجْ وَمَنْ لَمْ يَسْتَطِعْ

$$\text{«فَعَلَيْهِ بِالصَّوْمِ فَإِنَّهُ لَهُ وِجَاءٌ»}$$

.(O young people! Whoever amongst you can afford marriage, let him marry. Whoever cannot afford it, let him fast, for it will be a shield for him.)

Allah then states that the fast occurs during a fixed number of days, so that it does not become hard on the hearts, thereby weakening their resolve and endurance.)

### The various Stages of Fasting

Al-Bukhari and Muslim recorded that `A'ishah said, "(The day of) `Ashura' was a day of fasting. When the obligation to fast Ramadan was revealed, those who wished fasted, and those who wished did not." Al-Bukhari recorded the same from Ibn `Umar and Ibn Mas`ud.

Allah said:

(...those who can fast with difficulty, (e.g., an old man), they have (a choice either to fast or) to feed a Miskin (poor person) (for every day).)

Mu`adh commented, "In the beginning, those who wished, fasted and those who wished, did not fast and fed a poor person for each day." Al- Bukhari recorded Salamah bin Al-Akwa` saying that when the Ayah:

(...those who can fast with difficulty, (e.g., an old man), they have (a choice either to fast or) to feed a Miskin (poor person) (for every day).) was revealed, those who did not wish to fast, used to pay the Fidyah (feeding a poor person for each day they did not fast) until the following Ayah (2:185) was revealed abrogating the previous Ayah. It was also reported from `Ubaydullah from Nafi` that Ibn `Umar said; "It was abrogated." As-Suddi reported that Murrah narrated that `Abdullah said about this Ayah:

(those who can fast with difficulty, (e.g., an old man), they have (a choice either to fast or) to feed a Miskin (poor person) (for every day).) "It means `those who find it difficult (to fast).' Formerly, those who wished, fasted and those who wished, did not but fed a poor person instead." Allah then said:

(But whoever does good of his own accord) meaning whoever fed an extra poor person,

(it is better for him. And that you fast is better for you) Later the Ayah:

(So whoever of you sights (the crescent on the first night of) the month (of Ramadan, i.e., is present at his home), he must observe Sawm (fasting) that month) (2:185) was revealed and this abrogated the previous Ayah (2:184).

## The Fidyah (Expiation) for breaking the Fast is for the Old and the Ailing

Al-Bukhari reported that `Ata heard Ibn `Abbas recite:

(And as for those who can fast with difficulty, (e.g., an old man), they have (a choice either to fast or) to feed a Miskin (poor person) (for every day).)

Ibn `Abbas then commented, "(This Ayah) was not abrogated, it is for the old man and the old woman who are able to fast with difficulty, but choose instead to feed a poor person for every day (they do not fast)." Others reported that Sa`id bin Jubayr mentioned this from Ibn `Abbas. So the abrogation here applies to the healthy person, who is not traveling and who has to fast, as Allah said:

(So whoever of you sights (the crescent on the first night of) the month (of Ramadan, i.e., is present at his home), he must observe Sawm (fasting) that month.) (2:185)

As for the old man (and woman) who cannot fast, he is allowed to abstain from fasting and does not have to fast another day instead, because he is not likely to improve and be able to fast other days. So he is required to pay a Fidyah for every day missed. This is the opinion of Ibn `Abbas and several others among the Salaf who read the Ayah:

(And as for those who can fast with difficulty, (e.g., an old man)) to mean those who find it difficult to fast as Ibn Mas`ud stated. This is also the opinion of Al-Bukhari who said, "As for the old man (person) who cannot fast, (he should do like) Anas who, for one or two years after he became old fed some bread and meat to a poor person for each day he did not fast."

This point, which Al-Bukhari attributed to Anas without a chain of narrators, was collected with a continuous chain of narrators by Abu Ya`la Mawsuli in his Musnad, that Ayyub bin Abu Tamimah said; "Anas could no longer fast. So he made a plate of Tharid (broth, bread and meat) and invited thirty poor persons and fed them." The same ruling applies for the pregnant and breast-feeding women if they fear for themselves or their children or fetuses. In this case, they pay the Fidyah and do not have to fast other days in place of the days that they missed.

### Surah: 2 Ayah: 185

﴿ شَهْرُ رَمَضَانَ ٱلَّذِىٓ أُنزِلَ فِيهِ ٱلْقُرْءَانُ هُدًى لِّلنَّاسِ وَبَيِّنَٰتٍ مِّنَ ٱلْهُدَىٰ وَٱلْفُرْقَانِ ۚ فَمَن شَهِدَ مِنكُمُ ٱلشَّهْرَ فَلْيَصُمْهُ ۖ وَمَن كَانَ مَرِيضًا أَوْ عَلَىٰ سَفَرٍ فَعِدَّةٌ مِّنْ أَيَّامٍ أُخَرَ ۗ يُرِيدُ ٱللَّهُ بِكُمُ ٱلْيُسْرَ وَلَا يُرِيدُ بِكُمُ

ٱلْعُسْرَ وَلِتُكْمِلُواْ ٱلْعِدَّةَ وَلِتُكَبِّرُواْ ٱللَّهَ عَلَىٰ مَا هَدَىٰكُمْ وَلَعَلَّكُمْ تَشْكُرُونَ ﴿١٨٥﴾

185. The month of Ramadân in which was revealed the Qur'ân, a guidance for mankind and clear proofs for the guidance and the criterion (between right and wrong). So whoever of you sights (the crescent on the first night of) the month (of Ramadân i.e. is present at his home), he must observe Saum (fasts) that month, and whoever is ill or on a journey, the same number (of days which one did not observe Saum (fasts) must be made up) from other days. Allâh intends for you ease, and He does not want to make things difficult for you. (He wants that you) must complete the same number (of days), and that you must magnify Allâh (i.e. to say Takbîr (Allâhu Akbar; Allâh is the Most Great) for having guided you so that you may be grateful to Him.

### Transliteration

185. **Shahru ramadana** allathee onzila feehi alqur-anu hudan lilnnasi wabayyinatin mina alhuda waalfurqani faman shahida minkumu alshshahra falyasumhu waman kana mareedan aw AAala safarin faAAiddatun min ayyamin okhara yureedu Allahu bikumu alyusra wala yureedu bikumu alAAusra walitukmiloo alAAiddata walitukabbiroo Allaha AAala ma hadakum walaAAallakum tashkuroona

### Tafsir Ibn Kathir

#### The Virtue of Ramadan and the Revelation of the Qur'an in it.

Allah praised the month of Ramadan out of the other months by choosing it to send down the Glorious Qur'an, just as He did for all of the Divine Books He revealed to the Prophets. Imam Ahmad reported Wathilah bin Al-Asqa` that Allah's Messenger said:

«أُنْزِلَتْ صُحُفُ إِبْرَاهِيمَ فِي أَوَّلِ لَيْلَةٍ مِنْ رَمَضَانَ، وَأُنْزِلَتِ التَّوْرَاةُ لِسِتَّ مَضَيْنَ مِنْ رَمَضَانَ، وَالْإِنْجِيلُ لِثَلَاثَ عَشَرَةَ خَلَتْ مِنْ رَمَضَانَ، وَأَنْزَلَ اللهُ الْقُرْآنَ لِأَرْبَعٍ وَعِشْرِينَ خَلَتْ مِنْ رَمَضَانَ»

(The Suhuf (Pages) of Ibrahim were revealed during the first night of Ramadan. The Torah was revealed during the sixth night of Ramadan. The Injil was revealed during the thirteenth night of Ramadan. Allah revealed the Qur'an on the twenty-fourth night of Ramadan.)

#### The Virtues of the Qur'an

Allah said:

(...a guidance for mankind and clear proofs for the guidance and the criterion (between right and wrong).)

Here Allah praised the Qur'an, which He revealed as guidance for the hearts of those who believe in it and adhere to its commands. Allah said:

(and clear proofs) meaning, as clear and unambiguous signs and unequivocal proof for those who understand them. These proofs testify to the truth of the Qur'an, its guidance, the opposite of misguidance, and how it guides to the straight path, the opposite of the wrong path, and the distinction between the truth and falsehood, and the permissible and the prohibited.

## The Obligation of Fasting Ramadan

Allah said:

(So whoever of you sights (the crescent on the first night of) the month (of Ramadan, i.e., is present at his home), he must observe Sawm (fasting) that month.)

This Ayah requires the healthy persons who witness the beginning of the month, while residing in their land, to fast the month. This Ayah abrogated the Ayah that allows a choice of fasting or paying the Fidyah. When Allah ordered fasting, He again mentioned the permission for the ill person and the traveler to break the fast and to fast other days instead as compensation. Allah said:

(...and whoever is ill or on a journey, the same number )of days which one did not observe Sawm (fasting) must be made up( from other days.)

This Ayah indicates that ill persons who are unable to fast or fear harm by fasting, and the traveler, are all allowed to break the fast. When one does not fast in this case, he is obliged to fast other days instead. Allah said:

(Allah intends for you ease, and He does not want to make things difficult for you.)

This Ayah indicates that Allah allowed such persons, out of His mercy and to make matters easy for them, to break the fast when they are ill or traveling, while the fast is still obligatory on the healthy persons who are not traveling.

## Several Rulings concerning the Fast

The authentic Sunnah states that Allah's Messenger traveled during the month of Ramadan for the battle for Makkah. The Prophet marched until he reached the area of Kadid and then broke his fast and ordered those who were with him to do likewise. This was recorded in the Two Sahihs. Breaking the fast mentioned in this Hadith was not required, for the Companions used to go out with Allah's Messenger during the month of Ramadan, then, some of them would fast while some of them would not fast and neither category would criticize the others. If the command mentioned in the Hadith required breaking the fast, the Prophet would have criticized those who fasted. Allah's Messenger himself sometimes fasted while traveling. For instance, it is reported in the Two Sahihs that Abu Ad-Darda' said, "We once went with Allah's Messenger during Ramadan while the heat was intense. One of us would place his hand on his head because of the intense heat. Only Allah's Messenger and `Abdullah bin Rawahah were fasting at that time."

We should state that observing the permission to break the fast while traveling is better, as Allah's Messenger said about fasting while traveling:

»مَنْ أَفْطَرَ فَحَسَنٌ، وَمَنْ صَامَ فَلَا جُنَاحَ عَلَيْهِ«

(Those who did not fast have done good, and there is no harm for those who fasted.)

In another Hadith, the Prophet said:

»عَلَيْكُمْ بِرُخْصَةِ اللهِ الَّتِي رُخِّصَ لَكُمْ«

(Hold to Allah's permission that He has granted you.)

Some scholars say that the two actions are the same, as `A'ishah narrated that Hamzah bin `Amr Al-Aslami said, "O Messenger of Allah! I fast a lot, should I fast while traveling" The Prophet said:

»إِنْ شِئْتَ فَصُمْ، وَإِنْ شِئْتَ فَأَفْطِرْ«

(Fast if you wish or do not fast if you wish.)

This Hadith is in the Two Sahihs. It was reported that if the fast becomes difficult (while traveling), then breaking the fast is better. Jabir said that Allah's Messenger saw a man who was being shaded (by other people while traveling). The Prophet asked about him and he was told that man was fasting. The Prophet said:

»لَيْسَ مِنَ الْبِرِّ الصِّيَامُ فِي السَّفَرِ«

(It is not a part of Birr (piety) to fast while traveling.) This was recorded by Al-Bukhari and Muslim.

As for those who ignore the Sunnah and believe in their hearts that breaking the fast while traveling is disliked, they are required to break the fast and are not allowed to fast.

As for making up for missed fasting days, it is not required to be consecutive. One may do so consecutively or not consecutively. There are ample proofs to this fact. We should mention that fasting consecutive days is only required exclusively during Ramadan. After the month of Ramadan, what is required then is to merely make up for missed days. This is why Allah said:

(...the same number (should be made up) from other days.)

**Ease and not Hardship**

Allah then said:

(Allah intends for you ease, and He does not want to make things difficult for you.)

Imam Ahmad recorded Anas bin Malik saying that Allah's Messenger said:

«يَسِّرُوا وَلَا تُعَسِّرُوا وَسَكِّنُوا وَلَا تُنَفِّرُوا»

(Treat the people with ease and don't be hard on them; give them glad tidings and don't fill them with aversion.)

This Hadith was also collected in the Two Sahihs. It is reported in the Sahihayn that Allah's Messenger said to Mu`adh and Abu Musa when he sent them to Yemen:

«بَشِّرَا وَلَا تُنَفِّرَا، وَيَسِّرَا وَلَا تُعَسِّرَا، وَتَطَاوَعَا وَلَا تَخْتَلِفَا»

(Treat the people with ease and don't be hard on them; give them glad tidings and don't fill them with aversion; and love each other, and don't differ.)

The Sunan and the Musnad compilers recorded that Allah's Messenger said:

«بُعِثْتُ بِالْحَنِيفِيَّةِ السَّمْحَةِ»

(I was sent with the easy Hanifiyyah (Islamic Monotheism).)

Allah's statement:

(Allah intends for you ease, and He does not want to make things difficult for you. (He wants that you) must complete the same number (of days)) means: You were allowed to break the fast while ill, while traveling, and so forth, because Allah wanted to make matters easy for you. He only commanded you to make up for missed days so that you complete the days of one month.

## Remembering Allah upon performing the Acts of Worship

Allah's statement:

(...and that you must magnify Allah )i.e., to say Takbir (Allahu Akbar: Allah is the Most Great)( for having guided you) means: So that you remember Allah upon finishing the act of worship. This is similar to Allah's statement:

(So when you have accomplished your Manasik, (rituals) remember Allah as you remember your forefathers or with far more remembrance.) (2:200) and:

(...Then when the (Jumu`ah) Salah (prayer) is ended, you may disperse through the land, and seek the bounty of Allah (by working), and remember Allah much, that you may be successful.) (62:10) and:

(...and glorify the praises of your Lord, before the rising of the sun and before (its) setting. And during a part of the night, glorify His praises, and after the prayers.) (50:39, 40)

This is why the Sunnah encouraged Tasbih (saying Subhan Allah, i.e., all praise is due to Allah), Tahmid (saying Al-Hamdu Lillah, i.e., all the thanks are due to Allah) and Takbir (saying Allahu Akbar, i.e., Allah is the Most Great) after the compulsory prayers. Ibn `Abbas said, "We used to know that Allah's Messenger has finished the prayer by the Takbir." Similarly, several scholars have stated that reciting Takbir the during `Id-ul-Fitr was specified by the Ayah that states:

((He wants that you) must complete the same number (of days), and that you must magnify Allah )i.e., to say Takbir (Allahu Akbar: Allah is the Most Great)( for having guided you...) Allah's statement:

(...so that you may be grateful to Him.) means: If you adhere to what Allah commanded you, obeying Him by performing the obligations, abandoning the prohibitions and abiding by the set limits, then perhaps you will be among the grateful.

### Surah: 2 Ayah: 186

﴿ وَإِذَا سَأَلَكَ عِبَادِى عَنِّى فَإِنِّى قَرِيبٌ أُجِيبُ دَعْوَةَ ٱلدَّاعِ إِذَا دَعَانِ فَلْيَسْتَجِيبُوا۟ لِى وَلْيُؤْمِنُوا۟ بِى لَعَلَّهُمْ يَرْشُدُونَ ۝ ﴾

186. And when My slaves ask you (O Muhammad (peace be upon him)) concerning Me, then (answer them), I am indeed near (to them by My Knowledge). I respond to the invocations of the supplicant when he calls on Me (without any mediator or intercessor). So let them obey Me and believe in Me, so that they may be led aright.

### Transliteration

186. Wa-itha saalaka AAibadee AAannee fa-innee qareebun ojeebu daAAwata alddaAAi itha daAAani falyastajeeboo lee walyu/minoo bee laAAallahum yarshudoona

### Tafsir Ibn Kathir

### Allah hears the Servant's Supplication

Imam Ahmad reported that Abu Musa Al-Ash`ari said, "We were in the company of Allah's Messenger during a battle. Whenever we climbed a high place, went up a hill or went down a valley, we used to say, `Allah is the Most Great,' raising our voices. The Prophet came by us and said:

«يَا أَيُّهَا النَّاسُ، ارْبَعُوا عَلَى أَنْفُسِكُمْ، فَإِنَّكُمْ لَا تَدْعُونَ أَصَمَّ وَلَا غَائِبًا، إِنَّمَا تَدْعُونَ سَمِيعًا بَصِيرًا، إِنَّ الَّذِي تَدْعُونَ أَقْرَبُ إِلَى أَحَدِكُمْ مِنْ عُنُقِ رَاحِلَتِهِ، يَا عَبْدَاللهِ بْنَ قَيْسٍ، أَلَا أُعَلِّمُكَ كَلِمَةً مِنْ كُنُوزِ الْجَنَّةِ؟ لَا حَوْلَ وَلَا قُوَّةَ إِلَّا بِاللهِ»

(O people! Be merciful to yourselves (i.e., don't raise your voices), for you are not calling a deaf or an absent one, but One Who is All-Hearer, All-Seer. The One Whom you call is closer to one of you than the neck of his animal. O `Abdullah bin Qais (Abu Musa's name) should I teach you a statement that is a treasure of Paradise: `La hawla wa la quwwata illa billah (there is no power or strength except from Allah).')

This Hadith was also recorded in the Two Sahihs, and Abu Dawud, An-Nasa'i, At-Tirmidhi and Ibn Majah recorded similar wordings. Furthermore, Imam Ahmad recorded that Anas said that the Prophet said:

«يَقُولُ اللهُ تَعَالَى أَنَا عِنْدَ ظَنِّ عَبْدِي بِي وَأَنَا مَعَهُ إِذَا دَعَانِي»

("Allah the Exalted said, `I am as My servant thinks of Me, and I am with him whenever he invokes Me.') Allah accepts the Invocation

Imam Ahmad also recorded Abu Sa`id saying that the Prophet said:

«مَا مِنْ مُسْلِمٍ يَدْعُو اللهَ عَزَّ وَجَلَّ بِدَعْوَةٍ لَيْسَ فِيهَا إِثْمٌ وَلَا قَطِيعَةُ رَحِمٍ،

«إِلَّا أَعْطَاهُ اللَّهُ بِهَا إِحْدَى ثَلَاثِ خِصَالٍ: إِمَّا أَنْ يُعَجِّلَ لَهُ دَعْوَتَهُ، وَإِمَّا أَنْ يَدَّخِرَهَا لَهُ فِي الْأُخْرَى، وَإِمَّا أَنْ يَصْرِفَ عَنْهُ مِنَ السُّوءِ مِثْلَهَا»

(No Muslim supplicates to Allah with a Du`a that does not involve sin or cutting the relations of the womb, but Allah will grant him one of the three things. He will either hasten the response to his supplication, save it for him until the Hereafter, or would turn an equivalent amount of evil away from him.") They said, "What if we were to recite more (Du`a)." He said,

«اللَّهُ أَكْثَرُ»

(There is more with Allah.)

`Abdullah the son of Imam Ahmad recorded `Ubadah bin As-Samit saying that the Prophet said:

«مَا عَلَى ظَهْرِ الْأَرْضِ مِنْ رَجُلٍ مُسْلِمٍ يَدْعُو اللَّهَ عَزَّ وَجَلَّ بِدَعْوَةٍ إِلَّا آتَاهُ اللَّهُ إِيَّاهَا، أَوْ كَفَّ عَنْهُ مِنَ السُّوءِ مِثْلَهَا مَا لَمْ يَدْعُ بِإِثْمٍ أَوْ قَطِيعَةِ رَحِمٍ»

(There is no Muslim man on the face of the earth who supplicates to Allah but Allah would either grant it to him, or avert a harm from him of equal proportions, as long as his supplication does not involve sin or cutting the relations of the womb.) At-Tirmidhi recorded this Hadith.

Imam Malik recorded that Abu Hurayrah narrated that Allah's Messenger said:

«يُسْتَجَابُ لِأَحَدِكُمْ مَا لَمْ يَعْجَلْ، يَقُولُ: دَعَوْتُ فَلَمْ يُسْتَجَبْ لِي»

(One's supplication will be accepted as long as he does become get hasty and say, `I have supplicated but it has not been accepted from me.'")

### Allah accepts the Invocation

Imam Ahmad also recorded Abu Sa`id saying that the Prophet said:

«مَا مِنْ مُسْلِمٍ يَدْعُو اللَّهَ عَزَّ وَجَلَّ بِدَعْوَةٍ لَيْسَ فِيهَا إِثْمٌ وَلَا قَطِيعَةُ رَحِمٍ،

## Chapter 2: Al-Baqarah (The Cow), Verses 142-252

»إِلَّا أَعْطَاهُ اللهُ بِهَا إِحْدَى ثَلَاثِ خِصَالٍ: إِمَّا أَنْ يُعَجِّلَ لَهُ دَعْوَتَهُ، وَإِمَّا أَنْ يَدَّخِرَهَا لَهُ فِي الْأُخْرَى، وَإِمَّا أَنْ يَصْرِفَ عَنْهُ مِنَ السُّوءِ مِثْلَهَا«

(No Muslim supplicates to Allah with a Du`a that does not involve sin or cutting the relations of the womb, but Allah will grant him one of the three things. He will either hasten the response to his supplication, save it for him until the Hereafter, or would turn an equivalent amount of evil away from him.") They said, "What if we were to recite more (Du`a)." He said,

»اللهُ أَكْثَرُ«

(There is more with Allah.)

`Abdullah the son of Imam Ahmad recorded `Ubadah bin As-Samit saying that the Prophet said:

»مَا عَلَى ظَهْرِ الْأَرْضِ مِنْ رَجُلٍ مُسْلِمٍ يَدْعُو اللهَ عَزَّ وَجَلَّ بِدَعْوَةٍ إِلَّا آتَاهُ اللهُ إِيَّاهَا، أَوْ كَفَّ عَنْهُ مِنَ السُّوءِ مِثْلَهَا مَا لَمْ يَدْعُ بِإِثْمٍ أَوْ قَطِيعَةِ رَحِمٍ«

(There is no Muslim man on the face of the earth who supplicates to Allah but Allah would either grant it to him, or avert a harm from him of equal proportions, as long as his supplication does not involve sin or cutting the relations of the womb.) At-Tirmidhi recorded this Hadith.

Imam Malik recorded that Abu Hurayrah narrated that Allah's Messenger said:

»يُسْتَجَابُ لِأَحَدِكُمْ مَا لَمْ يَعْجَلْ، يَقُولُ: دَعَوْتُ فَلَمْ يُسْتَجَبْ لِي«

(One's supplication will be accepted as long as he does become get hasty and say, `I have supplicated but it has not been accepted from me.")

This Hadith is recorded in the Two Sahihs from Malik, and this is the wording of Al-Bukhari.

Muslim recorded that the Prophet said:

«لَا يَزَالُ يُسْتَجَابُ لِلْعَبْدِ مَا لَمْ يَدْعُ بِإِثْمٍ أَوْ قَطِيعَةِ رَحِمٍ مَا لَمْ يَسْتَعْجِلْ»

قِيلَ: يَا رَسُولَ اللهِ، وَمَا الِاسْتِعْجَالُ؟ قَالَ:

«يَقُولُ: قَدْ دَعَوْتُ وقَدْ دَعَوْتُ، فَلَمْ أَرَ يُسْتَجَابُ لِي، فَيَسْتَحْسِرُ عِنْدَ ذَلِكَ وَيَدَعُ الدُّعَاءَ»

(The supplication of the servant will be accepted as long as he does not supplicate for what includes sin, or cutting the relations of the womb, and as long as he does not become hasty.) He was asked, "O Messenger of Allah! How does one become hasty" He said, (He says, `I supplicated and supplicated, but I do not see that my supplication is being accepted from me.' He thus looses interest and abandons supplicating (to Allah).)

### Three Persons Whose Supplication will not be rejected

In the Musnad of Imam Ahmad and the Sunans of At-Tirmidhi, An-Nasa'i and Ibn Majah it is recorded that Abu Hurayrah narrated that Allah's Messenger said:

«ثَلَاثَةٌ لَا تُرَدُّ دَعْوَتُهُمْ: الْإِمَامُ الْعَادِلُ، وَالصَّائِمُ حَتَّى يُفْطِرَ، وَدَعْوَةُ الْمَظْلُومِ، يَرْفَعُهَا اللهُ دُونَ الْغَمَامِ يَوْمَ الْقِيَامَةِ، وَتُفْتَحُ لَهَا أَبْوَابُ السَّمَاءِ، يَقُولُ: بِعِزَّتِي لَأَنْصُرَنَّكَ وَلَوْ بَعْدَ حِينٍ»

(Three persons will not have their supplication rejected: the just ruler, the fasting person until breaking the fast, and the supplication of the oppressed person, for Allah raises it above the clouds on the Day of Resurrection, and the doors of heaven will be opened for it, and Allah says, `By My grace! I will certainly grant it for you, even if after a while.')

### Surah: 2 Ayah: 187

﴿أُحِلَّ لَكُمْ لَيْلَةَ ٱلصِّيَامِ ٱلرَّفَثُ إِلَىٰ نِسَآئِكُمْ ۚ هُنَّ لِبَاسٌ لَّكُمْ وَأَنتُمْ لِبَاسٌ لَّهُنَّ ۗ عَلِمَ ٱللَّهُ أَنَّكُمْ كُنتُمْ تَخْتَانُونَ أَنفُسَكُمْ فَتَابَ عَلَيْكُمْ

# Chapter 2: Al-Baqarah (The Cow), Verses 142-252

وَعَفَا عَنكُمْ ۖ فَٱلْـَٰٔنَ بَـٰشِرُوهُنَّ وَٱبْتَغُوا۟ مَا كَتَبَ ٱللَّهُ لَكُمْ ۚ وَكُلُوا۟ وَٱشْرَبُوا۟ حَتَّىٰ يَتَبَيَّنَ لَكُمُ ٱلْخَيْطُ ٱلْأَبْيَضُ مِنَ ٱلْخَيْطِ ٱلْأَسْوَدِ مِنَ ٱلْفَجْرِ ۖ ثُمَّ أَتِمُّوا۟ ٱلصِّيَامَ إِلَى ٱلَّيْلِ ۚ وَلَا تُبَـٰشِرُوهُنَّ وَأَنتُمْ عَـٰكِفُونَ فِى ٱلْمَسَـٰجِدِ ۗ تِلْكَ حُدُودُ ٱللَّهِ فَلَا تَقْرَبُوهَا ۗ كَذَٰلِكَ يُبَيِّنُ ٱللَّهُ ءَايَـٰتِهِۦ لِلنَّاسِ لَعَلَّهُمْ يَتَّقُونَ ۝١٨٧

187. It is made lawful for you to have sexual relations with your wives on the night of As-Saum (the fasts). They are Lîbas (i.e. body cover, or screen, or Sakan, (i.e. you enjoy the pleasure of living with them - as in Verse 7:189) Tafsir At-Tabarî), for you and you are the same for them. Allâh knows that you used to deceive yourselves, so He turned to you (accepted your repentance) and forgave you. So now have sexual relations with them and seek that which Allâh has ordained for you (offspring), and eat and drink until the white thread (light) of dawn appears to you distinct from the black thread (darkness of night), then complete your Saum (fast) till the nightfall. And do not have sexual relations with them (your wives) while you are in I'tikâf (i.e. confining oneself in a mosque for prayers and invocations leaving the worldly activities) in the mosques. These are the limits (set) by Allâh, so approach them not. Thus does Allâh make clear His Ayât (proofs, evidences, lessons, signs, revelations, verses, laws, legal and illegal things, Allâh's set limits, orders) to mankind that they may become Al-Muttaqûn (the pious - see V.2:2).

## Transliteration

187. Ohilla lakum laylata alssiyami alrrafathu ila nisa-ikum hunna libasun lakum waantum libasun lahunna AAalima Allahu annakum kuntum takhtanoona anfusakum fataba AAalaykum waAAafa AAankum faal-ana bashiroohunna waibtaghoo ma kataba Allahu lakum wakuloo waishraboo hatta yatabayyana lakumu alkhaytu al-abyadu mina alkhayti al-aswadi mina alfajri thumma atimmoo alssiyama ila allayli wala tubashiroohunna waantum AAakifoona fee almasajidi tilka hudoodu Allahi fala taqrabooha kathalika yubayyinu Allahu ayatihi lilnnasi laAAallahum yattaqoona

## Tafsir Ibn Kathir

### Eating, Drinking and Sexual Intercourse are allowed during the Nights of Ramadan

These Ayat contain a relief from Allah for the Muslims by ending the practice that was observed in the early years of Islam. At that time, Muslims were allowed to eat, drink and have sexual intercourse only until the `Isha' (Night) prayer, unless one sleeps before the `Isha' prayer. Those who slept before `Isha' or offered the `Isha' prayer, were not allowed to drink, eat or sexual intervourse sex until the next night. The Muslims found that to be difficult for them.

The Ayat used the word `Rafath' to indicate sexual intercourse, according to Ibn `Abbas, `Ata' and Mujahid. Similar Tafsir was offered by Sa`id bin Jubayr, Tawus, Salim bin `Abdullah, `Amr bin Dinar, Al-Hasan, Qatadah, Az-Zuhri, Ad-Dahhak, Ibrahim An-Nakha`i, As-Suddi, `Ata' Al-Khurasani and Muqatil bin Hayyan.

Allah said:

(They are Libas )i.e., body-cover, or screen( for you and you are Libas for them.)

Ibn `Abbas, Mujahid, Sa`id bin Jubayr, Al-Hasan, Qatadah, As-Suddi and Muqatil bin Hayyan said that this Ayah means, "Your wives are a resort for you and you for them." Ar-Rabi` bin Anas said, "They are your cover and you are their cover." In short, the wife and the husband are intimate and have sexual intercourse with each other, and this is why they were permitted to have sexual activity during the nights of Ramadan, so that matters are made easier for them.

Abu Ishaq reported that Al-Bara' bin `Azib said, "When the Companions of Allah's Messenger observed fast but would sleep before breaking their fast, they would continue fasting until the following night. Qays bin Sirmah Al-Ansari was fasting one day and was working in his land. When the time to break the fast came, he went to his wife and said, `Do you have food' She said, `No. But I could try to get you some.' His eyes then were overcome by sleep and when his wife came back, she found him asleep. She said, `Woe unto you! Did you sleep' In the middle of the next day, he lost consciousness and mentioned what had happened to the Prophet . Then, this Ayah was revealed: r

(It is made lawful for you to have sexual relations with your wives on the night of As-Siyam (fasting)) until...

(and eat and drink until the white thread (light) of dawn appears to you distinct from the black thread (darkness of night), then complete your fast till the nightfall. ) Consequently, they were very delighted." Al-Bukhari reported this Hadith by Abu Ishaq who related that he heard Al-Bara' say, "When fasting Ramadan was ordained, Muslims used to refrain from sleeping with their wives the entire month, but some men used to deceive themselves. Allah revealed:

(Allah knows that you used to deceive yourselves, so He turned to you (accepted your repentance) and forgave you.)

`Ali bin Abu Talhah narrated that Ibn `Abbas said, "During the month of Ramadan, after Muslims would pray `Isha', they would not touch their women and food until the next night. Then some Muslims, including `Umar bin Al-Khattab, touched (had sex with) their wives and had some food during

Ramadan after `Isha'. They complained to Allah's Messenger . Then Allah sent down:

(Allah knows that you used to deceive yourselves, so He turned to you (accepted your repentance) and forgave you. So now have sexual relations with them)" This is the same narration that Al-`Awfi related from Ibn `Abbas.

Allah said:

(. ..and seek that which Allah has ordained for you (offspring),)

Abu Hurayrah, Ibn `Abbas, Anas, Shurayh Al-Qadi, Mujahid, `Ikrimah, Sa`id bin Jubayr, `Ata', Ar-Rabi` bin Anas, As-Suddi, Zayd bin Aslam, Hakam bin `Utbah, Muqatil bin Hayyan, Al-Hasan Al-Basri, Ad-Dahhak, Qatadah, and others said that this Ayah refers to having offspring. Qatadah said that the Ayah means, "Seek the permission that Allah has allowed for you." Sa`id narrated that Qatadah said,

(and seek that which Allah has ordained for you,)

## Time for Suhur

Allah said:

(...and eat and drink until the white thread (light) of dawn appears to you distinct from the black thread (darkness of night), then complete your fast till the nightfall.)

Allah has allowed eating and drinking, along with having sexual intercourse, as we have stated, during any part of the night until the light of dawn is distinguished from the darkness of the night. Allah has described that time as `distinguishing the white thread from the black thread.' He then made it clearer when He said:

(of dawn.)

As stated in a Hadith that Imam Abu `Abdullah Al-Bukhari recorded, Sahl bin Sa`d said, "When the following verse was revealed:

(Eat and drink until the white thread appears to you, distinct from the black thread) and (of dawn) was not revealed, some people who intended to fast, tied black and white threads to their legs and went on eating till they differentiated between the two. Allah then revealed the words, (of dawn), and it became clear to them that it meant (the darkness of) night and (the light of) day."

Al-Bukhari recorded that Ash-Sha`bi said that `Adi said, "I took two strings, one black and the other white and kept them under my pillow and went on looking at them throughout the night, but could not make any distinction between the two. So, the next morning I went to Allah's Messenger and told him the whole story. He said:

«إِنَّ وِسَادَكَ إِذًا لَعَرِيضٌ، أَنْ كَانَ الْخَيْطُ الْأَبْيَضُ وَالْأَسْوَدُ تَحْتَ وِسَادَتِكَ»

(Your pillow is very wide if the white and black threads are under it!) Some wordings for this Hadith read,

«إِنَّكَ لَعَرِيضُ الْقَفَا»

(Your Qafa (back side of your neck) is wide!)

Some people said that these words meant that `Adi was not smart. This is a weak opinion. The narration that Al-Bukhari collected explains this part of the Hadith. Al-Bukhari recorded that `Adi bin Hatim narrated: I said, "O Messenger of Allah! What is the white thread from the black thread Are they actual threads" He said:

«إِنَّكَ لَعَرِيضُ الْقَفَا أَنْ أَبْصَرْتَ الْخَيْطَيْنِ، ثُمَّ قَالَ: لَا بَلْ هُوَ سَوَادُ اللَّيْلِ وَبَيَاضُ النَّهَارِ»

(Your Qafa is wide if you see the two threads. Rather, they are the blackness of the night and the whiteness of the daylight.)

**Suhur is recommended**

Allah allowed eating and drinking until dawn, it represents proof that Suhur is encouraged, since it is a Rukhsah (concession or allowance) and Allah likes that the Rukhsah is accepted and implemented. The authentic Sunnah indicates that eating the Suhur is encouraged. It is reported in the Two Sahihs that Anas narrated that Allah's Messenger said:

«تَسَحَّرُوا فَإِنَّ فِي السَّحُورِ بَرَكَةً»

(Eat the Suhur, for there is a blessing in Suhur.)

Muslim reported that `Amr bin Al-`As narrated that Allah's Messenger said:

## Chapter 2: Al-Baqarah (The Cow), Verses 142-252

«إِنَّ فَصْلَ مَا بَيْنَ صِيَامِنَا وصِيَامِ أَهْلِ الْكِتَابِ أَكْلَةُ السَّحَرِ»

(The distinction between our fast and the fast of the People of the Book is the meal of Suhur.)

Imam Ahmad reported that Abu Sa`id narrated that Allah's Messenger said:

«السُّحُورُ أَكْلُهُ بَرَكَةٌ فَلَا تَدَعُوهُ، وَلَوْ أَنَّ أَحَدَكُمْ يَجْرَعُ جُرْعَةَ مَاءٍ، فَإِنَّ اللهَ وَمَلَائِكَتَهُ يُصَلُّونَ عَلَى الْمُتَسَحِّرِينَ»

(Suhur is a blessed meal. Hence, do not abandon it, even if one just takes a sip of water. Indeed, Allah and His angels send Salah (blessings) upon those who eat Suhur.)

There are several other Hadiths that encourage taking the Suhur, even if it only consists of a sip of water.

It is preferred that Suhur be delayed until the time of dawn. It is recorded in the Two Sahihs that Anas bin Malik narrated that Zayd bin Thabit said, "We had Suhur with Allah's Messenger and then went on to pray." Anas asked, "How much time was there between the Adhan (call to prayer) and the Suhur" He said, "The time that fifty Ayat take (to recite)."

Imam Ahmad recorded Abu Dharr saying that Allah's Messenger said:

«لَا تَزَالُ أُمَّتِي بِخَيْرٍ مَا عَجَّلُوا الْإِفْطَارَ وَأَخَّرُوا السُّحُورَ»

(My Ummah will always retain goodness as long as they hasten in breaking the fast and delay the Suhur.)

There are several Hadiths that narrate that the Prophet called Suhur "the blessed meal."

There are narrations from several of the Salaf that they allowed the Suhur to be eaten later until close to Fajr. This is is reported from Abu Bakr, `Umar, `Ali, Ibn Mas`ud, Hudhayfah, Abu Hurayrah, Ibn `Umar, Ibn `Abbas and Zayd bin Thabit. It is also reported from many of the Tabi`in, such as Muhammad bin `Ali bin Husayn, Abu Mijlaz, Ibrahim An-Nakha`i, Abu Ad-Duha, Abu Wa'il and other companions of Ibn Mas`ud. This is also the opinion of `Ata', Al-Hasan, Hakam bin `Uyainah, Mujahid, `Urwah bin Az-Zubayr, Abu Sha`tha' Jabir bin Zayd, Al- A`mash and Ma`mar bin Rashid. We have mentioned the chains of narrations for their statements in our (Ibn Kathir's) book about Siyam (Fasting), and all praise is due to Allah.

It is also recorded in the Two Sahihs that Al-Qasim said that `A'ishah narrated that Allah's Messenger said:

«لَا يَمْنَعُكُمْ أَذَانُ بِلَالٍ عَنْ سَحُورِكُمْ، فَإِنَّهُ يُنَادِي بِلَيْلٍ، فَكُلُوا وَاشْرَبُوا حَتَّى تَسْمَعُوا أَذَانَ ابْنِ أُمِّ مَكْتُومٍ، فَإِنَّهُ لَا يُؤَذِّنُ حَتَّى يَطْلُعَ الْفَجْرُ»

(The Adhan pronounced by Bilal should not stop you from taking Suhur, for he pronounces the Adhan at night. Hence, eat and drink until you hear the Adhan by Ibn Umm Maktum, for he does not call the Adhan until dawn.)

This is the wording collected by Al-Bukhari.

Imam Ahmad reported that Qays bin Talq quoted from his father that Allah's Messenger said:

«لَيْسَ الْفَجْرُ الْمُسْتَطِيلَ فِي الْأُفُقِ وَلَكِنِ الْمُعْتَرِضُ الْأَحْمَرُ»

(Dawn is not the (ascending) glow of white light of the horizon. Rather, it is the red (radiating) light.)

Abu Dawud and At-Tirmidhi also recorded this Hadith, but their wording is:

«كُلُوا واشْرَبُوا، وَلَا يَهِيدَنَّكُمُ السَّاطِعُ الْمُصْعِدُ، فَكُلُوا واشْرَبُوا حَتَّى يَعْتَرِضَ لَكُمُ الْأَحْمَرُ»

(Eat and drink and do not be rushed by the ascending (white) light. Eat and drink until the redness (of the dawn) appears.)

Ibn Jarir (At-Tabari) recorded that Samurah bin Jundub narrated that Allah's Messenger said:

«لَا يَغُرَّنَّكُمْ أَذَانُ بِلَالٍ وَلَا هَذَا الْبَيَاضُ لِعَمُودِ الصُّبْحِ حَتَّى يَسْتَطِيرَ»

(Do not be stopped by Bilal's Adhan or the (ascending) whiteness, until it spreads.) Muslim also recorded this Hadith.

### There is no Harm in beginning the Fast while Junub (a state of major ritual impurity)

Issue: Among the benefits of allowing sexual activity, eating and drinking until dawn for those who are fasting, is that it is allowed to start the fast while

Junub (in the state of impurity after sexual discharge), and there is no harm in this case if one takes a bath any time in the morning after waking up, and completes the fast. This is the opinion of the Four Imams and the majority of the scholars. Al-Bukhari and Muslim recorded that `A'ishah and Umm Salamah said that Allah's Messenger used to wake up while Junub from sexual intercourse, not wet dreams, and he would take a bath and fast. Umm Salamah added that he would not break his fast or make up for that day.

Muslim recorded that `A'ishah said that a man asked:

"O Messenger of Allah! The (Dawn) prayer time starts while I am Junub, should I fast" Allah's Messenger replied,

»وَأَنَا تُدْرِكُنِي الصَّلَاةُ وَأَنَا جُنُبٌ فَأَصُومُ«

(And I. The prayer time starts while I am Junub and I fast.)

He said, "You are not like us, O Messenger of Allah! Allah has forgiven your previous and latter sins." Allah's Messenger said:

»وَاللهِ إِنِّي لَأَرْجُو أَنْ أَكُونَ أَخْشَاكُمْ لِلهِ وَأَعْلَمَكُمْ بِمَا أَتَّقِي«

(By Allah! I hope that I have the most fear from Allah among you and the best knowledge of what Taqwa is.)

**Fasting ends at Sunset**

Allah said:

(...then complete your fast till the nightfall.)

This Ayah orders breaking the fast at sunset. It is recorded in the Two Sahihs that `Umar bin Al-Khattab said that Allah's Messenger said:

»إِذَا أَقْبَلَ اللَّيْلُ مِنْ هٰهُنَا، وَأَدْبَرَ النَّهَارُ مِنْ هٰهُنَا فَقَدْ أَفْطَرَ الصَّائِمُ«

(If the night comes from this direction (the east), and the day departs from that direction (the west), then the fasting person breaks his fast.)

It is reported that Sahl bin Sa`d As-Sa`idi narrated that Allah's Messenger said:

»لَا يَزَالُ النَّاسُ بِخَيْرٍ مَا عَجَّلُوا الْفِطْرَ«

(The people will retain goodness as long as they hasten in breaking the fast.)

Imam Ahmad recorded that Abu Hurayrah narrated that the Prophet said:

«يَقُولُ اللهُ عَزَّ وَجَلَّ: إِنَّ أَحَبَّ عِبَادِي إِلَيَّ أَعْجَلُهُمْ فِطْرًا»

(Allah the Exalted said, 'The dearest among My servants to Me are those who hasten in breaking the fast the most.')

At-Tirmidhi recorded this Hadith and said that this Hadith is Hasan Gharib.

### Prohibition of Uninterrupted Fasting (Wisal)

There are several authentic Hadiths that prohibit Al-Wisal, which means continuing the fast through the night to the next night, without eating. Imam Ahmad recorded Abu Hurayrah saying that Allah's Messenger said:

«لَا تُوَاصِلُوا»

(Do not practice Al-Wisal in fasting.) So, they said to him, "But you practice Al-Wisal, O Allah's Messenger!" The Prophet replied,

«فَإِنِّي لَسْتُ مِثْلَكُمْ إِنِّي أَبِيتُ يُطْعِمُنِي رَبِّي وَيَسْقِينِي»

"(I am not like you, I am given food and drink during my sleep by my Lord.) So, when the people refused to stop Al-Wisal, the Prophet fasted two days and two nights (along with those who practiced Wisal) and then they saw the crescent moon (of the month of Shawwal). The Prophet said to them (angrily):

«لَوْ تَأَخَّرَ الْهِلَالُ لَزِدْتُكُمْ»

(If the crescent had not appeared, I would have made you fast for a longer period.)

That was as a punishment for them (when they refused to stop practicing Al-Wisal). This Hadith is also recorded in the Sahihayn.

The prohibition of Al-Wisal was also mentioned in a number of other narrations. It is a fact that practicing Al-Wisal was one of the special qualities of the Prophet , for he was capable and assisted in his practice of it. It is obvious that the food and drink that the Prophet used to get while practicing Al-Wisal was spiritual and not material, otherwise he would not be practicing Al-Wisal. We should mention that it is allowed to refrain from breaking the fast from sunset until before dawn (Suhur). A Hadith narrated by Abu Sa`id Khudri states that Allah's Messenger said:

»لَا تُوَاصِلُوا فَأَيُّكُمْ أَرَادَ أَنْ يُوَاصِلَ فَلْيُوَاصِلْ إِلَى السَّحَرِ«

(Do not practice Al-Wisal, but whoever wishes is allowed to practice it until the Suhur.)

They said, "You practice Al-Wisal, O Messenger of Allah!" He said:

»إِنِّي لَسْتُ كَهَيْئَتِكُمْ، إِنِّي أَبِيتُ لِي مُطْعِمٌ يُطْعِمُنِي وَسَاقٍ يَسْقِينِي«

(I am not similar to you, for I have One Who makes me eat and drink during the night.) This Hadith is also collected in the Two Sahihs.

### The Rulings of I`tikaf

Allah said:

(And do not have sexual relations with them (your wives) while you are in I`tikaf in the Masjids.)

`Ali bin Abu Talhah reported that Ibn `Abbas said, "This Ayah is about the man who stays in I`tikaf at the mosque during Ramadan or other months, Allah prohibited him from touching (having sexual intercourse with) women, during the night or day, until he finishes his I`tikaf." Ad-Dahhak said, "Formerly, the man who practiced I`tikaf would go out of the mosque and, if he wished, would have sexual intercourse (with his wife). Allah then said:

(And do not have sexual relations with them (your wives) while you are in I`tikaf in the Masjids.) meaning, `Do not touch your wives as long as you are in I`tikaf, whether you were in the mosque or outside of it'." It is also the opinion of Mujahid, Qatadah and several other scholars, that the Muslims used to have sexual intercourse with the wife while in I`tikaf if they departed the mosque until the Ayah was revealed. Ibn Abu Hatim commented, "It was reported that Ibn Mas`ud, Muhammad bin Ka`b, Mujahid, `Ata' Al-Hasan, Qatadah, Ad-Dahhak, As-Suddi, Ar-Rabi` bin Anas and Muqatil said that the Ayah means, `Do not touch the wife while in I`tikaf.'"

What Ibn Abu Hatim reported from these people is the agreed upon practice among the scholars. Those who are in I`tikaf are not allowed to have sexual intercourse as long as they are still in I`tikaf in the mosque. If one has to leave the mosque to attend to a need, such as to relieve the call of nature or to eat, he is not allowed to kiss or embrace his wife or to busy himself with other than his I`tikaf. He is not even allowed to visit ailing persons, but he can merely ask about their condition while passing by. I`tikaf has several other rulings that are explained in the books (of Fiqh), and we have mentioned several of these rulings at the end of our book on Siyam (Fasting), all praise is due to Allah. Furthermore, the scholars of Fiqh used to follow their explanation of the rules for fasting with the explanation of the rules for I`tikaf, as this is the way these acts of worship were mentioned in the Qur'an.

By mentioning I`tikaf after fasting, Allah draws attention to practicing I`tikaf during the month of the fast, especially the last part of the month. The Sunnah of Allah's Messenger is that he used to perform I`tikaf during the last ten nights of the month of Ramadan until he died. Afterwards, the Prophet's wives used to perform I`tikaf as the Two Sahihs recorded from `A'ishah the Mother of the believers. It is reported in the Two Sahihs that Safiyyah, the daughter of Huyai, went to Allah's Messenger to visit him in the mosque while he was in I`tikaf. She had a talk with him for a while, then she got up in order to return home. The Prophet accompanied her back home, as it was night. Her house was at Usamah bin Zayd's house on the edge of Al-Madinah. While they were walking, two Ansari men met them and passed by them in a hurry, for they were shy to bother the Prophet while he was walking with his wife. He told them:

«عَلَى رِسْلِكُمَا، إِنَّهَا صَفِيَّةُ بِنْتُ حُيَي»

(Do not run away! She is (my wife) Safiyyah bint Huyai.) Both of them said, "All praise is due to Allah, (How dare we think of any evil) O Allah's Messenger!" The Prophet said (to them):

«إِنَّ الشَّيْطَانَ يَجْرِي مِنِ ابْنِ آدَمَ مَجْرَى الدَّمِ، وَإِنِّي خَشِيتُ أَنْ يَقْذِفَ فِي قُلُوبِكُمَا شَيْئًا، أَوْ قَالَ: شَرًّا»

(Shaytan reaches everywhere in the human body, that the blood reaches. I was afraid lest Shaytan might suggest an evil thought in your minds.)

Imam Ash-Shafi`i commented, "Allah's Messenger sought to teach his Ummah to instantly eliminate any evil thought, so that they do not fall into the prohibited. They (the two Ansari men) had more fear of Allah than to think evil of the Prophet. Allah knows best."

The Ayah (2:187) prohibits sexual intercourse and anything like kissing or embracing that might lead to it during I`tikaf. As for having the wife helping the husband, it is allowed. It is reported in the Two Sahihs that `A'ishah said, "Allah's Messenger would bring his head near me (in her room) and I would comb his hair, while I was on my menses. He would enter the room only to attend to what a man needs."

Allah's statement:

(These are the limits (set) by Allah) means, `This is what We have explained, ordained, specified, allowed and prohibited for fasting. We also mentioned the fast's objectives, what is permitted during it, and what is required of it. These are the set limits that Allah has legislated and explained, so do not come near them or transgress them.' `Abdur-Rahman bin Zayd bin Aslam said, "(Allah's set limits mentioned in the Ayah) mean these four limits (and he then recited):

(It is made lawful for you to have sexual relations with your wives on the night of As-Siyam (fasting).) and he recited up to:

(then complete your Sawm (fast) till the nightfall.) My father and other's used to say similarly and recite the same Ayah to us."

Allah said:

(Thus does Allah make clear His Ayat to mankind) meaning, `Just as He explains the fast and its rulings, He also explains the other rulings by the words of His servant and Messenger, Muhammad .' Allah continues:

(to mankind that they may attain Taqwa.) meaning, `So that they know how to acquire the true guidance and how to worship (Allah).' Similarly, Allah said:

(It is He Who sends down manifest Ayat to His servant (Muhammad ) that He may bring you out from (types of) darkness into the light. And verily, Allah is to you full of kindness, Most Merciful.) (57:9)

### Surah: 2 Ayah: 188

﴿ وَلَا تَأْكُلُوٓاْ أَمْوَٰلَكُم بَيْنَكُم بِٱلْبَٰطِلِ وَتُدْلُواْ بِهَآ إِلَى ٱلْحُكَّامِ لِتَأْكُلُواْ فَرِيقًا مِّنْ أَمْوَٰلِ ٱلنَّاسِ بِٱلْإِثْمِ وَأَنتُمْ تَعْلَمُونَ ﴿١٨٨﴾ ﴾

188. And eat up not one another's property unjustly (in any illegal way e.g. stealing, robbing, deceiving, etc.), nor give bribery to the rulers (judges before presenting your cases) that you may knowingly eat up a part of the property of others sinfully.

### Transliteration

188. Wala ta/kuloo amwalakum baynakum bialbatili watudloo biha ila alhukkami lita/kuloo fareeqan min amwali alnnasi bial-ithmi waantum taAAlamoona

### Tafsir Ibn Kathir

#### Bribery is prohibited and is a Sin

`Ali bin Abu Talhah reported that Ibn `Abbas said, "This (Ayah 2:188) is about the indebted person when there is no evidence of the loan. So he denies taking the loan and the case goes to the authorities, even though he knows that it is not his money and that he is a sinner, consuming what is not allowed for him."

This opinion was also reported from Mujahid, Sa`id bin Jubayr, `Ikrimah, Al-Hasan, Qatadah, As-Suddi, Muqatil bin Hayan and `Abdur-Rahman bin Zayd bin Aslam. They all stated, "Do not dispute when you know that you are being unjust."

## The Judge's Ruling does not allow the Prohibited or prohibit the Lawful

It is reported in the Two Sahihs that Umm Salamah narrated that Allah's Messenger said:

«أَلَا إِنَّمَا أَنَا بَشَرٌ، وَإِنَّمَا يَأْتِينِي الْخَصْمُ، فَلَعَلَّ بَعْضَكُمْ أَنْ يَكُونَ أَلْحَنَ بِحُجَّتِهِ مِنْ بَعْضٍ فَأَقْضِيَ لَهُ، فَمَنْ قَضَيْتُ لَهُ بِحَقِّ مُسْلِمٍ فَإِنَّمَا هِيَ قِطْعَةٌ مِنْ نَارٍ، فَلْيَحْمِلْهَا أَوْ لِيَذَرْهَا»

(I am only human! You people present your cases to me, and as some of you may be more eloquent and persuasive in presenting his argument, I might issue a judgment in his benefit. So, if I give a Muslim's right to another, I am really giving him a piece of fire; so he should not take it.)

The Ayah and the Hadith prove that the judgment of the authorities in any case does not change the reality of the truth. Hence, the ruling does not allow what is in fact prohibited or prohibit what is in fact allowed. It is only applicable in that case. So if the ruling agrees with the truth, then there is no harm in this case. Otherwise, the judge will acquire his reward, while the cheater will acquire the evil burden.

This is why Allah said:

(And eat up not one another's property unjustly, nor give bribery to the rulers (judges before presenting your cases) that you may knowingly eat up a part of the property of others sinfully.) meaning, `While you know the falsehood of what you claim.' Qatadah said, "O son of Adam! Know that the judge's ruling does not allow you what is prohibited or prohibit you from what is allowed. The judge only rules according to his best judgment and according to the testimony of the witnesses. The judge is only human and is bound to make mistakes. Know that if the judge erroneously rules in some one's favor, then that person will still encounter the dispute when the disputing parties meet Allah on the Day of Resurrection. Then, the unjust person will be judged swiftly and precisely with that which will surpass whatever he acquired by the erroneous judgment he received in the life of this world."

# Chapter 2: Al-Baqarah (The Cow), Verses 142-252

**Surah: 2 Ayah: 189**

﴿ ۞ يَسْـَٔلُونَكَ عَنِ ٱلْأَهِلَّةِ ۖ قُلْ هِيَ مَوَٰقِيتُ لِلنَّاسِ وَٱلْحَجِّ ۗ وَلَيْسَ ٱلْبِرُّ بِأَن تَأْتُوا۟ ٱلْبُيُوتَ مِن ظُهُورِهَا وَلَٰكِنَّ ٱلْبِرَّ مَنِ ٱتَّقَىٰ ۗ وَأْتُوا۟ ٱلْبُيُوتَ مِنْ أَبْوَٰبِهَا ۚ وَٱتَّقُوا۟ ٱللَّهَ لَعَلَّكُمْ تُفْلِحُونَ ﴾ ﴿١٨٩﴾

189. They ask you (O Muhammad (peace be upon him)) about the new moons. Say: These are signs to mark fixed periods of time for mankind and for the pilgrimage. It is not Al-Birr (piety, righteousness) that you enter the houses from the back but Al-Birr (is the quality of the one) who fears Allâh. So enter houses through their proper doors, and fear Allâh that you may be successful.

### Transliteration

189. Yas-aloonaka AAani al-ahillati qul hiya mawaqeetu lilnnasi waalhajji walaysa albirru bi-an ta/too albuyoota min thuhooriha walakinna albirra mani ittaqa wa/too albuyoota min abwabiha waittaqoo Allaha laAAallakum tuflihoona

### Tafsir Ibn Kathir

**The Crescent Moons**

Al-`Awfi related that Ibn `Abbas said, "The people asked Allah's Messenger about the crescent moons. Thereafter, this Ayah was revealed:

(They ask you (O Muhammad) about the crescents. Say, "These are signs to mark fixed periods of time for mankind...) so that they mark their acts of worship, the `Iddah (the period of time a divorced woman or a widow is required to wait before remarrying) of their women and the time of their Hajj (pilgrimage to Makkah)." `Abdur-Razzaq reported that Ibn `Umar narrated that Allah's Messenger said:

«جَعَلَ اللهُ الْأَهِلَّةَ مَوَاقِيتَ لِلنَّاسِ، فَصُومُوا لِرُؤْيَتِهِ، وَأَفْطِرُوا لِرُؤْيَتِهِ، فَإِنْ غُمَّ عَلَيْكُمْ فَعُدُّوا ثَلَاثِينَ يَوْمًا»

(Allah has made the crescents signs to mark fixed periods of time for mankind. Hence, fast on seeing it (the crescent for Ramadan) and break the fast on seeing it (the crescent for Shawwal). If it (the crescent) was obscure to you then count thirty days (mark that month as thirty days).) WThis Hadith was also collected by Al-Hakim in his Mustadrak, and he said, "The chain is Sahih, and they (Al-Bukhari and Muslim) did not recorded it."

## Righteousness comes from Taqwa

Allah said:

(It is not Al-Birr (piety, righteousness, etc.) that you enter the houses from the back, but Al-Birr is from Taqwa. So enter houses through their proper doors.)

Al-Bukhari recorded that Al-Bara' said, "During the time of Jahiliyyah, they used to enter the house from the back upon assuming the Ihram. Thereafter, Allah revealed (the following Ayah):

(It is not Al-Birr (piety, righteousness, etc.) that you enter the houses from the back but Al-Birr is from Taqwa. So enter houses through their proper doors.)

Abu Dawud At-Tayalisi recorded the same Hadith from Al-Bara' but with the wording; "The Ansar used to enter their houses from the back when returning from a journey. Thereafter, this Ayah (2:189 above) was revealed..."

Al-Hasan said, "When some people during the time of Jahiliyyah would leave home to travel, and then decide not to travel, they would not enter the house from its door. Rather, they would climb over the back wall. Allah the Exalted said:

(It is not Al-Birr (piety, righteousness) that you enter the houses from the back,)."

Allah's statement:

(...and have Taqwa of Allah that you may be successful.) Have Taqwa of Allah, means to do what He has commanded you and refrain from what He has forbidden for you,

(that you may be successful.) tomorrow when you stand before Him and He thus rewards you perfectly.

### Surah: 2 Ayah: 190, Ayah: 191, Ayah: 192 & Ayah: 193

﴿ وَقَاتِلُوا۟ فِى سَبِيلِ ٱللَّهِ ٱلَّذِينَ يُقَاتِلُونَكُمْ وَلَا تَعْتَدُوٓا۟ إِنَّ ٱللَّهَ لَا يُحِبُّ ٱلْمُعْتَدِينَ ۝ ﴾

190. And fight in the Way of Allâh those who fight you, but transgress not the limits. Truly, Allâh likes not the transgressors. (This Verse is the first one that was revealed in connection with Jihâd, but it was supplemented by another ).

﴿ وَٱقْتُلُوهُمْ حَيْثُ ثَقِفْتُمُوهُمْ وَأَخْرِجُوهُم مِّنْ حَيْثُ أَخْرَجُوكُمْ وَٱلْفِتْنَةُ أَشَدُّ مِنَ ٱلْقَتْلِ وَلَا تُقَـٰتِلُوهُمْ عِندَ ٱلْمَسْجِدِ ٱلْحَرَامِ حَتَّىٰ يُقَـٰتِلُوكُمْ فِيهِ فَإِن قَـٰتَلُوكُمْ فَٱقْتُلُوهُمْ كَذَٰلِكَ جَزَآءُ ٱلْكَـٰفِرِينَ ﴿١٩١﴾ ﴾

191. And kill them wherever you find them, and turn them out from where they have turned you out. And Al-Fitnah is worse than killing. And fight not with them at Al-Masjid-al-Harâm (the sanctuary at Makkah), unless they (first) fight you there. But if they attack you, then kill them. Such is the recompense of the disbelievers.

﴿ فَإِنِ ٱنتَهَوْاْ فَإِنَّ ٱللَّهَ غَفُورٌ رَّحِيمٌ ﴿١٩٢﴾ ﴾

192. But if they cease, then Allâh is Oft-Forgiving, Most Merciful.

﴿ وَقَـٰتِلُوهُمْ حَتَّىٰ لَا تَكُونَ فِتْنَةٌ وَيَكُونَ ٱلدِّينُ لِلَّهِ فَإِنِ ٱنتَهَوْاْ فَلَا عُدْوَٰنَ إِلَّا عَلَى ٱلظَّـٰلِمِينَ ﴿١٩٣﴾ ﴾

193. And fight them until there is no more Fitnah (disbelief and worshipping of others along with Allâh) and (all and every kind of) worship is for Allâh (Alone). But if they cease, let there be no transgression except against Az-Zâlimûn (the polytheists, and wrong-doers)

### Transliteration

190. Waqatiloo fee sabeeli Allahi allatheena yuqatiloonakum wala taAAtadoo inna Allaha la yuhibbu almuAAtadeena  191. Waoqtuloohum haythu thaqiftumoohum waakhrijoohum min haythu akhrajookum waalfitnatu ashaddu mina alqatli wala tuqatiloohum AAinda almasjidi alharami hatta yuqatilookum feehi fa-in qatalookum faoqtuloohum kathalika jazao alkafireena  192. Fa-ini intahaw fa-inna Allaha ghafoorun raheemun  193. Waqatiloohum hatta la takoona fitnatun wayakoona alddeenu lillahi fa-ini intahaw fala AAudwana illa AAala al*th*alimeena

### Tafsir Ibn Kathir

### The Command to fight Those Who fight Muslims and killing Them wherever They are found

Abu Ja`far Ar-Razi said that Ar-Rabi` bin Anas said that Abu Al-`Aliyah commented on what Allah said:

(And fight in the way of Allah those who fight you,)

Abu Al-`Aliyah said, "This was the first Ayah about fighting that was revealed in Al-Madinah. Ever since it was revealed, Allah's Messenger used to fight only those who fought him and avoid non-combatants. Later, Surat Bara'ah (chapter 9 in the Qur'an) was revealed." `Abdur-Rahman bin Zayd bin Aslam said similarly, then he said that this was later abrogated by the Ayah:

(then kill them wherever you find them) (9:5).

However, this statement is not plausible, because Allah's statement:

(...those who fight you) applies only to fighting the enemies who are engaged in fighting Islam and its people. So the Ayah means, `Fight those who fight you', just as Allah said (in another Ayah):

(...and fight against the Mushrikin collectively as they fight against you collectively.) (9:36)

This is why Allah said later in the Ayah:

(And kill them wherever you find them, and turn them out from where they have turned you out.) meaning, `Your energy should be spent on fighting them, just as their energy is spent on fighting you, and on expelling them from the areas from which they have expelled you, as a law of equality in punishment.'

### The Prohibition of mutilating the Dead and stealing from the captured Goods

Allah said:

(but transgress not the limits. Truly, Allah likes not the transgressors.)

This Ayah means, `Fight for the sake of Allah and do not be transgressors,' such as, by committing prohibitions. Al-Hasan Al-Basri stated that transgression (indicated by the Ayah), "includes mutilating the dead, theft (from the captured goods), killing women, children and old people who do not participate in warfare, killing priests and residents of houses of worship, burning down trees and killing animals without real benefit." This is also the opinion of Ibn `Abbas, `Umar bin `Abdul-`Aziz, Muqatil bin Hayyan and others. Muslim recorded in his Sahih that Buraydah narrated that Allah's Messenger said:

«اغْزُوا فِي سَبِيلِ اللهِ، قَاتِلُوا مَنْ كَفَرَ بِاللهِ، اغْزُوا وَلَا تَغُلُّوا وَلَا تَغْدِرُوا وَلَا تَمْثُلُوا وَلَا تَقْتُلُوا وَلِيدًا وَلَا أَصْحَابَ الصَّوَامِعِ»

(Fight for the sake of Allah and fight those who disbelieve in Allah. Fight, but do not steal (from the captured goods), commit treachery, mutilate (the dead), or kill a child, or those who reside in houses of worship.)

It is reported in the Two Sahihs that Ibn `Umar said, "A woman was found dead during one of the Prophet's battles and the Prophet then forbade killing women and children." There are many other Hadiths on this subject.

## Shirk is worse than Killing

Since Jihad involves killing and shedding the blood of men, Allah indicated that these men are committing disbelief in Allah, associating with Him (in the worship) and hindering from His path, and this is a much greater evil and more disastrous than killing. Abu Malik commented about what Allah said:

(And Al-Fitnah is worse than killing.) Meaning what you (disbelievers) are committing is much worse than killing." Abu Al-`Aliyah, Mujahid, Sa`id bin Jubayr, `Ikrimah, Al-Hasan, Qatadah, Ad-Dahhak and Ar-Rabi` bin Anas said that what Allah said:

(And Al-Fitnah is worse than killing.) "Shirk (polytheism) is worse than killing."

## Fighting in the Sacred Area is prohibited, except in Self-Defense

Allah said:

(And fight not with them at Al-Masjid Al-Haram (the sanctuary at Makkah))

It is reported in the Two Sahihs that the Prophet said:

«إِنَّ هَذَا الْبَلَدَ حَرَّمَهُ اللهُ يَوْمَ خَلَقَ السَّمَوَاتِ وَالْأَرْضَ، فَهُوَ حَرَامٌ بِحُرْمَةِ اللهِ إِلَى يَوْمِ الْقِيَامَةِ، وَلَمْ يَحِلَّ لِي إِلَّا سَاعَةً مِنْ نَهَارٍ، وَإِنَّهَا سَاعَتِي هَذِهِ حَرَامٌ بِحُرْمَةِ اللهِ إِلَى يَوْمِ الْقِيَامَةِ، لَا يُعْضَدُ شَجَرُهُ، وَلَا يُخْتَلَى خَلَاهُ، فَإِنْ أَحَدٌ تَرَخَّصَ بِقِتَالِ رَسُولِ اللهِ صلى الله عليه وسلّم، فَقُولُوا: إِنَّ اللهَ أَذِنَ لِرَسُولِهِ وَلَمْ يَأْذَنْ لَكُم»

(Allah has made this city a sanctuary since the day He created the heavens and the earth. So, it is a sanctuary by Allah's decree till the Day of Resurrection. Fighting in it was made legal for me only for an hour in the daytime. So, it (i.e., Makkah) is a sanctuary, by Allah's decree, from now on until the Day of Resurrection. Its trees should not be cut, and its grass should not be uprooted. If anyone mentions the fighting in it that occurred by Allah's Messenger, then say that Allah allowed His Messenger, but did not allow you.)

In this Hadith, Allah's Messenger mentions fighting the people of Makkah when he conquered it by force, leading to some deaths among the polytheists in the area of the Khandamah. This occurred after the Prophet proclaimed:

«مَنْ أَغْلَقَ بَابَهُ فَهُوَ آمِنٌ، وَمَنْ دَخَلَ الْمَسْجِدَ فَهُوَ آمِنٌ، وَمَنْ دَخَلَ دَارَ أَبِي سُفْيَانَ فَهُوَ آمِنٌ»

(Whoever closed his door is safe. Whoever entered the (Sacred) Mosque is safe. Whoever entered the house of Abu Sufyan is also safe.)

Allah said:

(...unless they (first) fight you there. But if they attack you, then kill them. Such is the recompense of the disbelievers.)

Allah states: `Do not fight them in the area of the Sacred Mosque unless they start fighting you in it. In this case, you are allowed to fight them and kill them to stop their aggression.' Hence, Allah's Messenger took the pledge from his Companions under the tree (in the area of Al-Hudaybiyyah) to fight (the polytheists), after the tribes of Quraysh and their allies, Thaqif and other groups, collaborated against the Muslims (to stop them from entering Makkah to visit the Sacred House). Then, Allah stopped the fighting before it started between them and said:

(And He it is Who has withheld their hands from you and your hands from them in the midst of Makkah, after He had made you victors over them.) (48:24) and:

(Had there not been believing men and believing women whom you did not know, that you may kill them and on whose account a sin would have been committed by you without (your) knowledge, that Allah might bring into His mercy whom He wills - if they (the believers and the disbelievers) had been apart, We verily, would have punished those of them who disbelieved with painful torment.) (48:25)

Allah's statement:

(But if they cease, then Allah is Oft-Forgiving, Most Merciful.) which means, `If they (polytheists) cease fighting you in the Sacred Area, and come to Islam and repent, then Allah will forgive them their sins, even if they had before killed Muslims in Allah's Sacred Area.' Indeed, Allah's forgiveness encompasses every sin, whatever its enormity, when the sinner repents it.

### The Order to fight until there is no more Fitnah

Allah then commanded fighting the disbelievers when He said:

# Chapter 2: Al-Baqarah (The Cow), Verses 142-252

(...until there is no more Fitnah) meaning, Shirk. This is the opinion of Ibn `Abbas, Abu Al-`Aliyah, Mujahid, Al-Hasan, Qatadah, Ar-Rabi`, Muqatil bin Hayyan, As-Suddi and Zayd bin Aslam.

Allah's statement:

(...and the religion (all and every kind of worship) is for Allah (Alone).) means, `So that the religion of Allah becomes dominant above all other religions.' It is reported in the Two Sahihs that Abu Musa Al-Ash`ari said: "The Prophet was asked, `O Allah's Messenger! A man fights out of bravery, and another fights to show off, which of them fights in the cause of Allah' The Prophet said:

《مَنْ قَاتَلَ لِتَكُونَ كَلِمَةُ اللهِ هِيَ الْعُلْيَا فَهُوَ فِي سَبِيلِ اللهِ》

(He who fights so that Allah's Word is superior, then he fights in Allah's cause.) In addition, it is reported in the Two Sahihs:

《أُمِرْتُ أَنْ أُقَاتِلَ النَّاسَ حَتَّى يَقُولُوا لَا إِلَهَ إِلَّا اللهُ، فَإِذَا قَالُوهَا عَصَمُوا مِنِّي دِمَاءَهُم وَأَمْوَالَهُمْ إِلَّا بِحَقِّهَا وَحِسَابُهُمْ عَلَى اللهِ》

(I have been ordered (by Allah) to fight the people until they proclaim, `None has the right to be worshipped but Allah'. Whoever said it, then he will save his life and property from me, except for cases of the law, and their account will be with Allah.)

Allah's statement:

(But if they cease, let there be no transgression except against the wrongdoers.) indicates that, `If they stop their Shirk and fighting the believers, then cease warfare against them. Whoever fights them afterwards will be committing an injustice. Verily aggression can only be started against the unjust.' This is the meaning of Mujahid's statement that only combatants should be fought. Or, the meaning of the Ayah indicates that, `If they abandon their injustice, which is Shirk in this case, then do not start aggression against them afterwards.' The aggression here means retaliating and fighting them, just as Allah said:

(Then whoever transgresses against you, you transgress likewise against him.) (2:194)

Similarly, Allah said:

(The recompense for an evil is an evil like thereof.) (42:40), and:

(And if you punish them, then punish them with the like of that with which you were afflicted. ) (16:126)

`Ikrimah and Qatadah stated, "The unjust person is he who refuses to proclaim, `There is no God worthy of worship except Allah'."

Under Allah's statement:

(And fight them until there is no more Fitnah) Al-Bukhari recorded that Nafi` said that two men came to Ibn `Umar during the conflict of Ibn Az-Zubayr and said to him, "The people have fallen into shortcomings and you are the son of `Umar and the Prophet's Companion. Hence, what prevents you from going out" He said, "What prevents me is that Allah has for bidden shedding the blood of my (Muslim) brother." They said, "Did not Allah say:

(And fight them until there is no more Fitnah (disbelief and worshipping of others along with Allah))" He said, "We did fight until there was no more Fitnah and the religion became for Allah Alone. You want to fight until there is Fitnah and the religion becomes for other than Allah!"

`Uthman bin Salih added that a man came to Ibn `Umar and asked him, "O Abu `Abdur-Rahman! What made you perform Hajj one year and `Umrah another year and abandon Jihad in the cause of Allah, although you know how much He has encouraged performing it" He said, "O my nephew! Islam is built on five (pillars): believing in Allah and His Messenger, the five daily prayers, fasting Ramadan, paying the Zakah and performing Hajj (pilgrimage) to the House." They said, "O Abu `Abdur-Rahman! Did you not hear what Allah said in His Book:

(And if two parties (or groups) among the believers fall to fighting, then make peace between them both. But if one of them outrages against the other, then fight you (all) against the one that which outrages till it complies with the command of Allah.) (49:9) and:

(And fight them until there is no more Fitnah (disbelief))

He said, "That we did during the time of Allah's Messenger when Islam was still weak and (the Muslim) man used to face trials in his religion, such as killing or torture. When Islam became stronger (and apparent), there was no more Fitnah." He asked, "What do you say about `Ali and `Uthman" He said, "As for `Uthman, Allah has forgiven him. However, you hated the fact that Allah had forgiven him! As for `Ali, he is the cousin of Allah's Messenger and his son-in-law." He then pointed with his hand, saying, "This is where his house is located (meaning, `so close to the Prophet's house just as `Ali was so close to the Prophet himself')."

## Surah: 2 Ayah: 194

﴿ ٱلشَّهْرُ ٱلْحَرَامُ بِٱلشَّهْرِ ٱلْحَرَامِ وَٱلْحُرُمَـٰتُ قِصَاصٌ ۚ فَمَنِ ٱعْتَدَىٰ عَلَيْكُمْ فَٱعْتَدُواْ عَلَيْهِ بِمِثْلِ مَا ٱعْتَدَىٰ عَلَيْكُمْ ۚ وَٱتَّقُواْ ٱللَّهَ وَٱعْلَمُوٓاْ أَنَّ ٱللَّهَ مَعَ ٱلْمُتَّقِينَ ﴾

194. The sacred month is for the sacred month, and for the prohibited things, there is the Law of Equality (Qisâs). Then whoever transgresses the prohibition against you, you transgress likewise against him. And fear Allâh, and know that Allâh is with Al-Muttaqûn (the pious - see V.2:2).

### Transliteration

194. Alshshahru alharamu bialshshahri alharami waalhurumatu qisasun famani iAAtada AAalaykum faiAAtadoo AAalayhi bimithli ma iAAtada AAalaykum waittaqoo Allaha waiAAlamoo anna Allaha maAAa almuttaqeena

### Tafsir Ibn Kathir

### Fighting during the Sacred Months is prohibited, except in Self-Defense

Ibn `Abbas, Ad-Dahhak, As-Suddi, Qatadah, Miqsam, Ar-Rabi` bin Anas and `Ata said, "Allah's Messenger went for `Umrah on the sixth year of Hijrah. Then, the idolators prevented him from entering the Sacred House (the Ka`bah in Makkah) along with the Muslims who came with him. This incident occurred during the sacred month of Dhul-Qa`dah. The idolators agreed to allow them to enter the House the next year. Hence, the Prophet entered the House the following year, along with the Muslims who accompanied him, and Allah permitted him to avenge the idolators' treatment of him, when He said:

(The sacred month is for the sacred month, and for the prohibited things, there is the Law of equality (Qisas).)

Imam Ahmad recorded that Jabir bin `Abdullah said, "Allah's Messenger would not engage in warfare during the Sacred Month unless he was first attacked, then he would march forth. He would otherwise remain idle until the end of the Sacred Months." This Hadith has an authentic chain of narrators.

Hence, when the Prophet was told that `Uthman was killed (in Makkah) when he was camped at the area of Al-Hudaybiyyah, after he had sent `Uthman as his emissary to the polytheists, he accepted the pledge from his Companions under the tree to fight the polytheists. They were one thousand and four hundred then. When the Prophet was informed that `Uthman was not killed, he abandoned the fight and reverted to peace.

When the Prophet finished fighting with (the tribes of) Hawazin during the battle of Hunayn and Hawazin took refuge in (the city of) At-Ta'if, he laid siege to that city. Then, the (sacred) month of Dhul-Qa`dah started, while At-Ta'if was still under siege. The siege went on for the rest of the forty days (rather, from the day the battle of Hunayn started until the Prophet went back to Al-Madinah from Al-Ji`ranah, were forty days), as reported in the Two Sahihs and narrated by Anas. When the Companions suffered mounting casualties (during the siege), the Prophet ended the siege before conquering At-Ta'if. He then went back to Makkah, performed `Umrah from Al-Ji`ranah, where he divided the war booty of Hunayn. This `Umrah occurred during Dhul-Qa`dah of the eighth year of Al-Hijrah.

Allah's statement:

(...whoever transgresses against you, you transgress likewise against him.) ordains justice even with the polytheists. Allah also said in another Ayah:

(And if you punish, then punish them with the like of that with which you were afflicted.) (16:126)

Allah's statement:

(And fear Allah, and know that Allah is with Al-Muttaqin (the pious)) (2:194) commands that Allah be obeyed and feared out of Taqwa. The Ayah informs us that Allah is with those who have Taqwa by His aid and support in this life and the Hereafter.

### Surah: 2 Ayah: 195

﴿ وَأَنفِقُواْ فِى سَبِيلِ ٱللَّهِ وَلَا تُلْقُواْ بِأَيْدِيكُمْ إِلَى ٱلتَّهْلُكَةِ ۛ وَأَحْسِنُوٓاْ ۛ إِنَّ ٱللَّهَ يُحِبُّ ٱلْمُحْسِنِينَ ﴾

195. And spend in the Cause of Allâh (i.e. Jihâd of all kinds) and do not throw yourselves into destruction (by not spending your wealth in the Cause of Allâh), and do good. Truly, Allâh loves Al-Muhsinûn (the good-doers).

### Transliteration

195. Waanfiqoo fee sabeeli Allahi wala tulqoo bi-aydeekum ila alttahlukati waahsinoo inna Allaha yuhibbu almuhsineena

### Tafsir Ibn Kathir

#### The Command to spend in the Cause of Allah

Al-Bukhari recorded that Hudhayfah said:

(And spend in the cause of Allah and do not throw yourselves into destruction.) "It was revealed about spending." Ibn Abu Hatim reported him saying similarly.

He then commented, "Similar is reported from Ibn `Abbas, Mujahid, `Ikrimah, Sa`id bin Jubayr, `Ata', Ad-Dahhak, Al-Hasan, Qatadah, As-Suddi and Muqatil bin Hayyan."

Aslam Abu `Imran said, "A man from among the Ansar broke enemy (Byzantine) lines in Constantinople (Istanbul). Abu Ayyub Al-Ansari was with us then. So some people said, `He is throwing himself to destruction.' Abu Ayyub said, `We know this Ayah (2:195) better, for it was revealed about us, the Companions of Allah's Messenger who participated in Jihad with him and aided and supported him. When Islam became strong, we, the Ansar, met and said to each other, `Allah has honored us by being the Companions of His Prophet and in supporting him until Islam became victorious and its following increased. We had before ignored the needs of our families, estates and children. Warfare has ceased, so let us go back to our families and children and attend to them.' So this Ayah was revealed about us:

(And spend in the cause of Allah and do not throw yourselves into destruction.) the destruction refers to staying with our families and estates and abandoning Jihad'." This was recorded by Abu Dawud, At-Tirmidhi, An-Nasa'i, `Abd bin Humayd in his Tafsir, Ibn Abu Hatim, Ibn Jarir, Ibn Marduwyah, Al-Hafiz Abu Ya`la in his Musnad, Ibn Hibban and Al-Hakim. At-Tirmidhi said; "Hasan, Sahih, Gharib" Al-Hakim said, "It meets the criteria of the Two Shaykhs (Al-Bukhari and Muslim) but they did not record it."

Abu Dawud's version mentions that Aslam Abu `Imran said, "We were at (the siege of) Constantinople. Then, `Uqbah bin `Amr was leading the Egyptian forces, while the Syrian forces were led by Fadalah bin `Ubayd. Later on, a huge column of Roman (Byzantine) soldiers departed the city, and we stood in lines against them. A Muslim man raided the Roman lines until he broke through them and came back to us. The people shouted, `All praise is due to Allah! He is sending himself to certain demise.' Abu Ayyub said, `O people! You explain this Ayah the wrong way. It was revealed about us, the Ansar when Allah gave victory to His religion and its following increased. We said to each other, `It would be better for us now if we return to our estates and attend to them.' Then Allah revealed this Ayah (2:195)'."

Abu Bakr bin `Aiyash reported that Abu Ishaq As-Subai`y related that a man said to Al-Bara' bin `Azib, "If I raided the enemy lines alone and they kill me, would I be throwing myself to certain demise" He said, "No. Allah said to His Messenger :

(Then fight (O Muhammad ) in the cause of Allah, you are not tasked (held responsible) except for yourself.) (4:84) That Ayah (2:195) is about (refraining from) spending." Ibn Marduwyah reported this Hadith, as well as Al-Hakim in his Mustadrak who said; "It meets the criteria of the Two Shaykhs (Al-Bukhari and Muslim) but they did not record it." Ath-Thawri and Qays bin Ar-Rabi` related it from Al-Bara'. but added:

(You are not tasked (held responsible) except for yourself.) (4:84) "Destruction refers to the man who sins and refrains from repenting, thus throwing himself to destruction."

Ibn `Abbas said:

(And spend in the cause of Allah and do not throw yourselves into destruction) "This is not about fighting. But about refraining from spending for the sake of Allah, in which case, one will be throwing his self into destruction."

The Ayah (2:195) includes the order to spend in Allah's cause, in the various areas and ways that involve obedience and drawing closer to Allah. It especially applies to spending in fighting the enemies and on what strengthens the Muslims against the enemy. Allah states that those who refrain from spending in this regard will face utter and certain demise and destruction, meaning those who acquire this habit. Allah commands that one should acquire Ihsan (excellence in the religion), as it is the highest part of the acts of obedience. Allah said:

(and do good. Truly, Allah loves Al-Muhsinin (those who do good).)

### Surah: 2 Ayah: 196

﴿ وَأَتِمُّواْ ٱلْحَجَّ وَٱلْعُمْرَةَ لِلَّهِ ۚ فَإِنْ أُحْصِرْتُمْ فَمَا ٱسْتَيْسَرَ مِنَ ٱلْهَدْىِ ۖ وَلَا تَحْلِقُواْ رُءُوسَكُمْ حَتَّىٰ يَبْلُغَ ٱلْهَدْىُ مَحِلَّهُۥ ۚ فَمَن كَانَ مِنكُم مَّرِيضًا أَوْ بِهِۦٓ أَذًى مِّن رَّأْسِهِۦ فَفِدْيَةٌ مِّن صِيَامٍ أَوْ صَدَقَةٍ أَوْ نُسُكٍ ۚ فَإِذَآ أَمِنتُمْ فَمَن تَمَتَّعَ بِٱلْعُمْرَةِ إِلَى ٱلْحَجِّ فَمَا ٱسْتَيْسَرَ مِنَ ٱلْهَدْىِ ۚ فَمَن لَّمْ يَجِدْ فَصِيَامُ ثَلَـٰثَةِ أَيَّامٍ فِى ٱلْحَجِّ وَسَبْعَةٍ إِذَا رَجَعْتُمْ ۗ تِلْكَ عَشَرَةٌ كَامِلَةٌ ۗ ذَٰلِكَ لِمَن لَّمْ يَكُنْ أَهْلُهُۥ حَاضِرِى ٱلْمَسْجِدِ ٱلْحَرَامِ ۚ وَٱتَّقُواْ ٱللَّهَ وَٱعْلَمُوٓاْ أَنَّ ٱللَّهَ شَدِيدُ ٱلْعِقَابِ

196. And perform properly (i.e. all the ceremonies according to the ways of Prophet Muhammad (peace be upon him)) the Hajj and 'Umrah (i.e. the pilgrimage to Makkah) for Allâh. But if you are prevented (from completing them), sacrifice a Hady (animal, i.e. a sheep, a cow, or a camel) such as you can afford, and do not shave your heads until the Hady reaches the place of sacrifice. And whosoever of you is ill or has an ailment in his scalp (necessitating shaving), he must pay a Fidyah (ransom) of either observing Saum (fasts) (three days) or giving Sadaqah (charity - feeding six poor persons) or offering sacrifice (one sheep). Then if you are in safety and whosoever performs the 'Umrah in the months of Hajj, before

(performing) the Hajj, (i.e. Hajj-at-Tamattu' and Al-Qirân), he must slaughter a Hady such as he can afford, but if he cannot afford it, he should observe Saum (fasts) three days during the Hajj and seven days after his return (to his home), making ten days in all. This is for him whose family is not present at Al-Masjid-al-Harâm (i.e. non-resident of Makkah). And fear Allâh much and know that Allâh is Severe in punishment.

## Transliteration

196. Waatimmoo alhajja waalAAumrata lillahi fa-in ohsirtum fama istaysara mina alhadyi wala tahliqoo ruoosakum hatta yablugha alhadyu mahillahu faman kana minkum mareedan aw bihi athan min ra/sihi fafidyatun min siyamin aw sadaqatin aw nusukin fa-itha amintum faman tamattaAAa bialAAumrati ila alhajji fama istaysara mina alhadyi faman lam yajid fasiyamu thalathati ayyamin fee alhajji wasabAAatin itha rajaAAtum tilka AAasharatun kamilatun thalika liman lam yakun ahluhu hadiree almasjidi alharami waittaqoo Allaha waiAAlamoo anna Allaha shadeedu alAAiqabi

## Tafsir Ibn Kathir

### The Command to complete Hajj and `Umrah

After Allah mentioned the rulings for fasting and Jihad, he explained the rituals by commanding the Muslims to complete Hajj and `Umrah, meaning, to finish the rituals of Hajj and `Umrah after one starts them. This is why Allah said afterwards:

(But if you are prevented) meaning, if your way to the House is obstructed, and you are prevented from finishing it. This is why the scholars agree that starting the acts of Hajj and `Umrah requires one to finish them. As for Makhul, he said, "Complete, means to start them from the Miqat (areas the Prophet designated to assume Ihram from)." `Abdur-Razzaq said that Az-Zuhri said: "We were told that `Umar commented on:

(And complete Hajj and `Umrah for Allah.) "Complete Hajj and `Umrah means performing each of them separately, and to perform `Umrah outside of the months of Hajj, for Allah the Exalted says:

(The Hajj (pilgrimage) is (in) the well-known (lunar year) months. )"

As-Suddi said,

(And complete Hajj and `Umrah for Allah.) means, "Maintain the performance of Hajj and `Umrah." Ibn `Abbas was reported to have said, "Hajj is `Arafat, while `Umrah is Tawaf." Al-A`mash related that Ibrahim said that `Alqamah commented on Allah's statement:

(And complete Hajj and `Umrah for Allah.) "Abdullah (Ibn Mas`ud) recited it this way: `Complete Hajj and `Umrah to the House, so that one does not exceed the area of the House during the `Umrah'." Ibrahim then said, "I mentioned this statement to Sa`id bin Jubayr and he said; `Ibn `Abbas also said that.'" Sufyan reported that Ibrahim said that `Alqamah said (regarding the Ayah 2:196), "Perform the Hajj and `Umrah to the House." Ath-Thawri reported that Ibrahim read (the Ayah), "Perform the Hajj and `Umrah to the House."

## If One is prevented while in Route, He slaughters the Sacrifice, shaves his Head and ends Ihram

Allah's statement:

(But if you are prevented, sacrifice a Hady (animals for sacriface) such as you can afford,) was revealed in the sixth year of Hijrah, the year of the treaty of Al-Hudaybiyyah when the polytheists prevented Allah's Messenger from reaching the House. Allah revealed Surat Al-Fath (chapter 48 in the Qur'an) then, and allowed the Muslims to slaughter any Hady (animals for sacrifice) they had. They had seventy camels with them for that purpose. They were also permitted to shave their heads and end their Ihram. When the Prophet commanded them to shave their heads and end the state of Ihram, they did not obey him, as they were awaiting that order to be abrogated. When they saw that the Prophet went out after shaving his head, they imitated him. Some of them did not shave, but only shortened their hair. This is why the Prophet said:

«رَحِمَ اللهُ الْمُحَلِّقِينَ»

(May Allah award His mercy to those who shaved.)

They said, "What about those who shortened the hair" He said in the third time, "And to those who shortened." Every seven among them shared one camel for their sacrifice. They were one thousand and four hundred Companions and were camping in the area of Al-Hudaybiyyah, outside the Sacred Area. It was also reported that they were within the boundaries of the Sacred Area. Allah knows best.

Being prevented from the House (Hasr) includes more than just being sick, fearing an enemy or getting lost on the way to Makkah. Imam Ahmad reported that Al-Hajjaj bin `Amr Al-Ansari said that he heard Allah's Messenger saying:

«مَنْ كُسِرَ أَوْ عَرِجَ فَقَدْ حَلَّ وَعَلَيْهِ حَجَّةٌ أُخْرَى»

(Whoever suffered a broken bone or a limb, will have ended his Ihram and has to perform Hajj again.) He said, "I mentioned that to Ibn `Abbas and Abu Hurayrah and they both said, `He (Al-Hajjaj) has said the truth'." This Hadith is also reported in the Four Collections. In the version of Abu Dawud and Ibn

Majah, the Prophet said, "Whoever limped, had a broken bone or became ill..." Ibn Abu Hatim also recorded it and said, "It was reported that Ibn Mas`ud, Ibn Az-Zubayr, `Alqamah, Sa`id bin Musayyib, `Urwah bin Az-Zubayr, Mujahid, An-Nakha`i, `Ata' and Muqatil bin Hayyan said that being prevented (Hasr) entails an enemy, an illness or a fracture." Ath-Thawri also said, "Being prevented entails everything that harms the person."

It is reported in the Two Sahihs that `A'ishah said that Allah's Messenger went to Duba`ah bint Az-Zubayr bin `Abdul-Muttalib who said, "O Messenger of Allah! I intend to perform Hajj but I am ill." He said, "Perform Hajj and make the condition: `My place is where You prevent (or halt) me." Muslim recorded similarly from Ibn `Abbas. So saying such a condition for Hajj is allowed is based on this Hadith.

Allah's statement:

(...sacrifice a Hady such as you can afford) includes a sheep also, as Imam Malik reported that `Ali bin Abu Talib used to say. Ibn `Abbas said, "The Hady includes eight types of animals: camels, cows, goats and sheep." `Abdur-Razzaq reported that Ibn `Abbas said about what Allah said:

(...sacrifice a Hady such as you can afford)

"As much as one could afford." Al-`Awfi said that Ibn `Abbas said, "If one can afford it, then camels, otherwise cows, or sheep." Hisham bin `Urwah quoted his father:

(...sacrifice a Hady (animal, i.e., a sheep, a cow, or a camel) such as you can afford) `Depending on the price.'

The proof that sacrificing only a sheep is allowed in the case of being prevented from continuing the rites, is that Allah has required sacrificing whatever is available as a Hady, and the Hady is any type of cattle; be it camels, cows or sheep. This is the opinion of Ibn `Abbas the cousin of Allah's Messenger and the scholar of Tafsir. It is reported in the Two Sahihs that `A'ishah, the Mother of the believers, said, "The Prophet once offered some sheep as Hady."

Allah's statement:

(...and do not shave your heads until the Hady reaches the place of sacrifice.) is a continuation of His statement:

(And complete, the Hajj and `Umrah for Allah.) and is not dependent upon:

(But if you are prevented, then sacrifice a Hady) as Ibn Jarir has erroneously claimed. When the Prophet and his Companions were prevented from entering the Sacred House during the Al-Hudaybiyyah year by the polytheists from Quraysh, they shaved their heads and sacrificed their Hady outside the Haram

(Sacred) area. In normal circumstances, and when one can safely reach the House, he is not allowed to shave his head until:

(.. .and do not shave your heads until the Hady reaches the place of sacrifice.) and then he ends the rituals of Hajj or `Umrah, or both if he had assumed Ihram for both. It is recorded in the Two Sahihs that Hafsah said, "O Allah's Messenger! What is wrong with the people, they have finished their Ihram for `Umrah but you have not" The Prophet said,

«إِنِّي لَبَّدْتُ رَأْسِي وَقَلَّدْتُ هَدْيِي، فَلَا أَحِلُّ حَتَّى أَنْحَر»

(I matted my hair and I have garlanded my Hady (animals for sacrifice), so I will not finish my Ihram till I offer the sacrifice.)

### Whoever shaved his Head during Ihram, will have to pay the Fidyah

Allah said:

(And whosoever of you is ill or has an ailment on his scalp (necessitating shaving), he must pay a Fidyah.)

Al-Bukhari reported that `Abdur-Rahman bin Asbahani said that he heard `Abdullah bin Ma`qil saying that he sat with Ka`b bin `Ujrah in the mosque of Kufah (in Iraq). He then asked him about the Fidyah of the fasting. Ka`b said, "This was revealed concerning my case especially, but it is also for you in general. I was carried to Allah's Messenger and the lice were falling in great numbers on my face. The Prophet said:

«مَا كُنْتُ أُرَى أَنَّ الْجُهْدَ بَلَغَ بِكَ هَذَا، أَمَا تَجِدُ شَاةً»

(I never thought that your ailment (or struggle) had reached to such an extent as I see. Can you afford a sheep (for sacrifice)' I replied in the negative.) He then said:

«صُمْ ثَلَاثَةَ أَيَّامٍ أَوْ أَطْعِمْ سِتَّةَ مَسَاكِينَ، لِكُلِّ مِسْكِينٍ نِصْفُ صَاعٍ مِنْ طَعَامٍ، وَاحْلِقْ رَأْسَكَ»

(Fast for three days or feed six poor persons, each with half a Sa` of food (1 Sa` = 3 kilograms approx.) and shave your head.)

So this is a general judgement derived from a specific case.

# Chapter 2: Al-Baqarah (The Cow), Verses 142-252

Imam Ahmad recorded that Ka`b bin `Ujrah said, "Allah's Messenger came by while I was igniting the fire under a pot and while the lice were falling down my head or my eyelids. He said:

«يُؤْذِيكَ هَوَامُّ رَأْسِك»

(Do these lice in your head bother you) I said, `Yes.' He said:

«فَاحْلِقْهُ، وَصُمْ ثَلاَثَةَ أَيَّامٍ، أَوْ أَطْعِمْ سِتَّةَ مَسَاكِينَ، أَوِ انْسُكْ نَسِيكَة»

(Shave it, then fast three days, or feed six poor people, or sacrifice an animal.)

Ayyub (one of the narrators of the Hadith) commented, "I do not know which alternative was stated first." The wording of the Qur'an begins with the easiest then the more difficult options: "Pay a Fidyah of fasting (three days), feeding (six poor persons) or sacrificing (an animal)." Meanwhile, the Prophet advised Ka`b with the more rewarding option first, that is, sacrificing a sheep, then feeding six poor persons, then fasting three days. Each Text is suitable in its place and context, all the thanks and praises are due to Allah.

## Tamattu` during Hajj

Allah said:

(Then if you are in safety and whosoever performs the `Umrah (in the months of Hajj), before (performing) the Hajj, he must slaughter a Hady such as he can afford,)

That is, when you are able to complete the rites, so whoever among you connects his `Umrah with Hajj having the same Ihram for both, or, first assuming Ihram for `Umrah, and then assuming Ihram for Hajj when finished the `Umrah, this is the more specific type of Tamattu` which is well-known among the discussion of the scholars whereas in general there are two types of Tamattu`, as the authentic Hadiths prove, since among the narrators are those who said, "Allah's Messenger performed Tamattu`, and others who said, "Qarin" but there is no difference between them over the Hady.

So Allah said,

(Then if you are in safety and whosoever performs the `Umrah (in the months of Hajj), before (performing) the Hajj (i.e., Hajj At-Tamattu` and Al-Qiran), he must slaughter a Hady such as he can afford,) means let him sacrifice whatever Hady is available to him, the least of which is a sheep. One is also allowed to sacrifice a cow because the Prophet slaughtered cows on behalf of his wives. Al-Awza`i reported that Abu Hurayrah narrated that Allah's

Messenger slaughtered cows on behalf of his wives when they were performing Tamattu`. This was reported by Abu Bakr bin Marduwyah.

This last Hadith proves that Tamattu` is legislated. It is reported in the Two Sahihs that `Imran bin Husayn said, "We performed Hajj At-Tamattu` in the lifetime of Allah's Messenger and then the Qur'an was revealed (regarding Hajj At-Tamattu`). Nothing was revealed to forbid it, nor did he (the Prophet ) forbid it until he died. And somebody said what he wished (regarding Hajj At-Tamattu`) according to his own opinion." Al-Bukhari said that `Imran was talking about `Umar. It is reported in an authentic narration that `Umar used to discourage the people from performing Tamattu`. He used to say, "If we refer to Allah's Book, we should complete it," meaning:

(...whosoever performs the `Umrah (in the months of Hajj), before (performing) the Hajj, he must slaughter a Hady such as he can afford,)

However `Umar did not say that Tamattu` is unlawful. He only prevented them so that the people would increase their trips to the House for Hajj (during the months of Hajj) and `Umrah (throughout the year), as he himself has stated.

### Whoever performs Tamattu` should fast Ten Days if He does not have a Hady

Allah said:

(...but if he cannot (afford it), he should fast three days during the Hajj and seven days after his return (to his home), making ten days in all.)

This Ayah means: "Those who do not find a Hady, let them fast three days during the Hajj season." Al-`Awfi said that Ibn `Abbas said, "If one does not have a Hady, he should fast three days during Hajj, before `Arafah day. If the day of `Arafah was the third day, then his fast is complete. He should also fast seven days when he gets back home." Abu Ishaq reported from Wabarah from Ibn `Umar who said, "One fasts one day before the day of Tarwiyah, the day of Tarwiyah (eighth day of Dhul-Hijjah) and then `Arafah day (the ninth day of the month of Dhul-Hijjah)." The same statement was reported by Ja`far bin Muhammad from his father from `Ali.

If one did not fast these three days or at least some of them before `Id day (the tenth day of Dhul-Hijjah), he is allowed to fast during the Tashriq days (11-12-13th day of Dhul-Hijjah). `A'ishah and Ibn `Umar said, "Fasting the days of Tashriq was only allowed for those who did not find the Hady," as Al-Bukhari has reported. Sufyan related that Ja`far bin Muhammad narrated that his father said that `Ali said, "Whoever did not fast the three days during the Hajj, should fast them during the days of Tashriq." This is also the position taken by `Ubayd bin `Umayr Al-Laythi, `Ikrimah, Al-Hasan Al-Basri and `Urwah bin Az-Zubayr, referring to the general meaning of Allah's statement:

(...fast three days during the Hajj...)

## Chapter 2: Al-Baqarah (The Cow), Verses 142-252

As for what Muslim reported that Qutaybah Al-Hudhali said that Allah's Messenger said:

«أَيَّامُ التَّشْرِيقِ أَيَّامُ أَكْلٍ وَشُرْبٍ، وَذِكْرِ اللهِ عَزَّ وَجَلَّ»

(The days of Tashriq are days of eating and drinking and remembering Allah the Exalted.)

This narration is general in meaning while what `A'ishah and Ibn `Umar narrated is specific.

Allah said:

(...and seven days after his return.)

There are two opinions regarding the meaning of this Ayah. First, it means 'when you return to the camping areas'. The second, upon going back home. `Abdur-Razzaq reported that Salim narrated that he heard Ibn `Umar saying:

"(...but if he cannot (afford it), he should fast three days during the Hajj and seven days after his return,) means when he goes back to his family. " The same opinion was reported from Sa`id bin Jubayr, Abu Al-`Aliyah, Mujahid, `Ata', `Ikrimah, Al-Hasan, Qatadah, Imam Az-Zuhri and Ar-Rabi` bin Anas.

Al-Bukhari reported that Salim bin `Abdullah narrated that Ibn `Umar said, "During the Farewell Hajj of Allah's Messenger , he performed Tamattu` with `Umrah and Hajj. He drove a Hady along with him from Dhul-Hulayfah. Allah's Messenger started by assuming Ihram for `Umrah, and then for Hajj. And the people, too, performed the `Umrah and Hajj along with the Prophet . Some of them brought the Hady and drove it along with them, while the others did not. So, when the Prophet arrived at Makkah, he said to the people:

«مَنْ كَانَ مِنْكُم أَهْدَى فَإِنَّهُ لَا يَحِلُّ مِنْ شَيْءٍ حَرُمَ مِنْهُ حَتَّى يَقْضِيَ حَجَّهُ، وَمَنْ لَمْ يَكُنْ مِنْكُمْ أَهْدَى فَلْيَطُفْ بِالْبَيْتِ وبِالصَّفَا وَالْمَرْوَة وَلْيُقَصِّرْ وَلْيَحْلِلْ، ثُمَّ لْيُهِلَّ بِالْحَجِّ، فَمَنْ لَمْ يَجِدْ هَدْيًا فَلْيَصُمْ ثَلَاثَةَ أَيَّامٍ فِي الْحَجِّ، وَسَبْعَةً إِذَا رَجَعَ إِلَى أَهْلِهِ»

(Whoever among you has driven the Hady, should not finish his Ihram till he completes his Hajj. And whoever among you has not (driven) the Hady with him, he should perform Tawaf of the Ka`bah and between As-Safa and Al-Marwah. Then, he should shave or cut his hair short and finish his Ihram, and should later assume Ihram for Hajj; (but he must offer a Hady (sacrifice)). And if anyone cannot afford a Hady, he should fast for three days during the Hajj and seven days when he returns home.)

He then mentioned the rest of the Hadith, which is reported in the Two Sahihs.

Allah said:

(...making ten days in all.) to emphasize the ruling we mentioned above. This method is common in the Arabic language, for they would say, `I have seen with my eyes, heard with my ears and written with my hand,' to emphasize such facts. Similarly, Allah said:

(...nor a bird that flies with its two wings) (6:38) and:

(...nor did you write any book (whatsoever) with your right hand) (29:48) and:

(And We appointed for Musa thirty nights and added (to the period) ten (more), and he completed the term, appointed by his Lord, of forty nights.) (7:142)

It was also said that the meaning of "ten days in all" emphasizes the order to fast for ten days, not less than that.

### The Residents of Makkah do not perform Tamattu"

Allah said:

(This is for him whose family is not present at Al-Masjid Al-Haram (i.e., non-resident of Makkah).) This Ayah concerns the residents of the area of the Haram, for they do not perform Tamattu`. `Abdur-Razzaq reported that Tawus said, "Tamattu` is for the people, those whose families are not residing in the Haram area (Makkah), not for the residents of Makkah. Hence Allah's Statement:

(This is for him whose family is not present at Al-Masjid Al-Haram (i.e., non-resident of Makkah).)

`Abdur-Razzaq then said, "I was also told that Ibn `Abbas said similar to Tawus." Allah said:

(...and fear Allah) meaning, in what He has commanded you and what He prohibited for you. He then said:

(...and know that Allah is severe in punishment) for those who defy His command and commit what He has prohibited.

## Surah: 2 Ayah: 197

﴿ ٱلْحَجُّ أَشْهُرٌ مَّعْلُومَـٰتٌ ۚ فَمَن فَرَضَ فِيهِنَّ ٱلْحَجَّ فَلَا رَفَثَ وَلَا فُسُوقَ وَلَا جِدَالَ فِى ٱلْحَجِّ ۗ وَمَا تَفْعَلُوا۟ مِنْ خَيْرٍ يَعْلَمْهُ ٱللَّهُ ۗ وَتَزَوَّدُوا۟ فَإِنَّ خَيْرَ ٱلزَّادِ ٱلتَّقْوَىٰ ۚ وَٱتَّقُونِ يَـٰٓأُو۟لِى ٱلْأَلْبَـٰبِ ﴿١٩٧﴾ ﴾

197. The Hajj (pilgrimage) is (in) the well-known (lunar year) months (i.e. the 10th month, the 11th month and the first ten days of the 12th month of the Islâmic calendar, i.e. two months and ten days). So whosoever intends to perform Hajj therein (by assuming Ihrâm), then he should not have sexual relations (with his wife), nor commit sin, nor dispute unjustly during the Hajj. And whatever good you do, (be sure) Allâh knows it. And take a provision (with you) for the journey, but the best provision is At-Taqwa (piety, righteousness). So fear Me, O men of understanding!

### Transliteration

197. Alhajju ashhurun maAAloomatun faman farada feehinna alhajja fala rafatha wala fusooqa wala jidala fee alhajji wama tafAAaloo min khayrin yaAAlamhu Allahu watazawwadoo fa-inna khayra alzzadi alttaqwa waittaqooni ya olee al-albabi

### Tafsir Ibn Kathir

#### When does Ihram for Hajj start

Allah said:

(The Hajj is (in) the well-known months.)

This Ayah indicates that Ihram for Hajj only occurs during the months of Hajj. This was reported from Ibn `Abbas, Jabir, `Ata', Tawus and Mujahid. The proof for this is Allah's statement that Hajj occurs during known, specific months, which indicates that Hajj is not allowed before that, just as the prayer has a fixed time (before which one's prayer is not accepted).

Ash-Shafi`i recorded that Ibn `Abbas said, "No person should assume Ihram for Hajj before the months of the Hajj, for Allah said:

(The Hajj is (in) the well-known months.)

Ibn Khuzaymah reported that Ibn `Abbas said, "No Ihram for Hajj should be assumed, except during the months of Hajj, for among the Sunnah of Hajj is that one assume Ihram for it during the Hajj months." This is an authentic narration and the Companion's statement that such and such is among the Sunnah is considered as a Hadith of the Prophet, according to the majority of the scholars. This is especially the case when it is Ibn `Abbas who issued this statement, as he is the Tarjuman (translator, interpreter, explainer) of the Qur'an.

There is a Hadith about this subject too. Ibn Marduwyah related that Jabir narrated that the Prophet said:

«لَا يَنْبَغِي لِأَحَدٍ أَنْ يُحْرِمَ بِالْحَجِّ إِلَّا فِي أَشْهُرِ الْحَجِّ»

(No one should assume Ihram for Hajj, but during the months of Hajj.)

The chain of narrators for this Hadith is reasonable. Ash-Shafi`i and Al-Bayhaqi recorded this Hadith from Ibn Jurayj who related that Abu Az-Zubayr said that he heard Jabir bin `Abdullah being asked, "Does one assume Ihram for Hajj before the months of the Hajj" He said, "No." This narration is more reliable than the narration that we mentioned from the Prophet . In short, this statement is the opinion of the Companion, supported by Ibn `Abbas' statement that it is a part of the Sunnah not to assume Ihram for Hajj before the months of the Hajj. Allah knows best.

### The Months of Hajj

Allah said:

(...the well-known months.)

Al-Bukhari said that Ibn `Umar said that these are Shawwal, Dhul-Qa`dah and the first ten days of Dhul-Hijjah. This narration for which Al-Bukhari did not mention the chain of narrators, was collected by a continuous chain of narrators that Ibn Jarir rendered authentic, leading to Ibn `Umar, who said:

(The Hajj (pilgrimage) is (in) the well-known (lunar year) months.) "which are Shawwal, Dhul-Qa`dah and the (first) ten days of Dhul-Hijjah." Its chain is Sahih. Al-Hakim also recorded it in his Mustadrak, and he said,"It meets the criteria of the Two Shaykhs."

This statement is also reported from `Umar, `Ali, Ibn Mas`ud, `Abdullah bin Az-Zubayr, Ibn `Abbas, `Ata', Tawus, Mujahid, Ibrahim An-Nakha`i, Imam Ash-Sha`bi, Al-Hasan, Ibn Sirin, Makhul, Qatadah, Ad-Dahhak bin Muzahim, Ar-Rabi` bin Anas and Muqatil bin Hayyan. This opinion was preferred by Ibn Jarir who said, "It is a common practice to call two months and a part of the third month as `months'. This is similar to the Arab's saying, `I visited such and such person this year or this day.' He only visited him during a part of the year and a part of the day. Allah said:

(But whosoever hastens to leave in two days, there is no sin on him.)

In this case, one will only be hastening for one and a half days."

Allah then said:

(So whosoever intends (Farada) to perform Hajj therein (by assuming Ihram),) meaning that one's assuming the Ihram requires a Hajj, for the person is required to complete the rituals of Hajj after assuming Ihram. Ibn Jarir said that Al-`Awfi said, "The scholars agree that (Farada) `intends' mentioned in the Ayah means it is a requirement and an obligation." `Ali bin Abu Talhah said that Ibn `Abbas said: f

(So whosoever intends to perform Hajj therein (by assuming Ihram), ) refers to those who assume Ihram for Hajj and `Umrah". `Ata' said, "'Intends', means, assumes the Ihram." Similar statements were attributed to Ibrahim, Ad-Dahhak and others.

### Prohibition of Rafath (Sexual Intercourse) during Hajj

Allah said:

(He should not have Rafath)

This Ayah means that those who assume the Ihram for Hajj or `Umrah are required to avoid the Rafath, meaning, sexual intercourse. Allah's statement here is similar to His statement:

(It is made lawful for you to have Rafath (sexual relations) with your wives on the night of the fast.) (2:187)

Whatever might lead to sexual intercourse, such as embracing, kissing and talking to women about similar subjects, is not allowed. Ibn Jarir reported that Nafi` narrated that `Abdullah bin `Umar said, "Rafath means sexual intercourse or mentioning this subject with the tongue, by either men or women." `Ata' bin Abu Rabah said that Rafath means sexual intercourse and foul speech. This is also the opinion of `Amr bin Dinar. `Ata' also said that they used to even prevent talking (or hinting) about this subject. Tawus said that Rafath includes one's saying, "When I end the Ihram I will have sex with you." This is also the same explanation offered by Abu Al-`Aliyah regarding Rafath. `Ali bin Abu Talhah said that Ibn `Abbas said, "Rafath means having sex with the wife, kissing, fondling and saying foul words to her, and similar acts." Ibn `Abbas and Ibn `Umar said that Rafath means to have sex with women. This is also the opinion of Sa`id bin Jubayr, `Ikrimah, Mujahid, Ibrahim An-Nakha`i, Abu Al-`Aliyah who narrated it from `Ata' and Makhul, `Ata Al-Khurasani, `Ata' bin Yasar, `Atiyah, Ibrahim, Ar-Rabi`, Az-Zuhri, As-Suddi, Malik bin Anas, Muqatil bin Hayyan, `Abdul-Karim bin Malik, Al-Hasan, Qatadah and Ad-Dahhak, and others.

### The Prohibition of Fusuq during Hajj

Allah said:

(...nor commit sin) Miqsam and several other scholars related that Ibn `Abbas said, "It is disobedience." This is also the opinion of `Ata,' Mujahid, Tawus, `Ikrimah, Sa`id bin Jubayr, Muhammad bin Ka`b, Al-Hasan, Qatadah, Ibrahim An-Nakha`i, Az-Zuhri, Ar-Rabi` bin Anas, `Ata' bin Yasar, `Ata' Al-Khurasani and Muqatil bin Hayyan.

Ibn Wahb reported that Nafi` narrated that `Abdullah bin `Umar said, "Fusuq (or sin mentioned in the Ayah (2:197)) refers to committing what Allah has forbidden in the Sacred Area."

Several others said that Fusuq means cursing others, they based this on the authentic Hadith:

«سِبَابُ الْمُسْلِمِ فُسُوقٌ وَقِتَالُهُ كُفْرٌ»

(Cursing the Muslim is Fusuq, while fighting him is Kufr.)

`Abdur-Rahman bin Zayd bin Aslam said Fusuq here means slaughtering animals for the idols, as Allah said:

(...or impious (Fisq) meat (of an animal) which is slaughtered as a sacrifice for others than Allah.) (6: 145)

Ad-Dahhak said that Fusuq is insulting one another with bad nicknames.

Those who said that the Fusuq means all types of disobedience are correct. Allah has also prohibited committing injustice during the months of Hajj in specific, although injustice is prohibited throughout the year. This is why Allah said:

(...of them four are sacred. That is the right religion, so wrong not yourselves therein.) (9:36)

Allah said about the Sacred Area:

(...and whoever inclines to evil actions therein or to do wrong, him We shall cause to taste from a painful torment.) (22:25)

It is recorded in the Two Sahihs that Abu Hurayrah narrated that Allah's Messenger said:

«مَنْ حَجَّ هَذَا الْبَيْتَ، فَلَمْ يَرْفُثْ وَلَمْ يَفْسُقْ خَرَجَ مِنْ ذُنُوبِهِ كَيَوْمَ وَلَدَتْهُ أُمُّهُ»

(Whoever performed Hajj to this (Sacred) House and did not commit Rafath or Fusuq, will return sinless, just as the day his mother gave birth to him.)

### The Prohibition of arguing during Hajj

Allah said:

(nor should there be Jidal during Hajj) meaning, disputes and arguments. Ibn Jarir related that `Abdullah bin Mas`ud said that what Allah said:

(...nor dispute unjustly during the Hajj.) means to argue with your companion (or fellow) until you make him angry. This is similar to the the opinion that Miqsam and Ad-Dahhak related to Ibn `Abbas. This is also the same meaning reported from Abu Al-`Aliyah, `Ata', Mujahid, Sa`id bin Jubayr, `Ikrimah, Jabir bin Zayd, `Ata' Al-Khurasani, Makhul, As-Suddi, Muqatil bin Hayyan, `Amr bin Dinar, Ad-Dahhak, Ar-Rabi` bin Anas, Ibrahim An-Nakha`i, `Ata bin Yasar, Al-Hasan, Qatadah and Az-Zuhri.

### The Encouragement for Righteous Deeds and to bring Provisions for Hajj

Allah said:

(And whatever good you do, Allah knows it.)

After Allah prohibited evil in deed and tongue, He encouraged righteous, good deeds, stating that He is knowledgeable of the good that they do, and He will reward them with the best awards on the Day of Resurrection.

Allah said next:

(And take provisions (with you) for the journey, but the best provision is At-Taqwa (piety, righteousness).)

Al-Bukhari and Abu Dawud reported that Ibn `Abbas said, "The people of Yemen used to go to Hajj without taking enough supplies with them. They used to say, `We are those who have Tawakkul (reliance on Allah).' Allah revealed this Ayah:

(And take provisions (with you) for the journey, but the best provision is At-Taqwa (piety, righteousness).)

Ibn Jarir and Ibn Marduwyah narrated that Ibn `Umar said, "When people assumed Ihram, they would throw away whatever provisions they had and would acquire other types of provisions. Allah revealed:

(And take a provisions (with you) for the journey, but the best provision is At-Taqwa (piety, righteousness).) Allah forbade them from this practice and required them to take flour and Sawiq (a type of food usually eaten with dates) with them."

## The Provisions of the Hereafter

Allah said:

(...but the best provision is At-Taqwa (piety, righteousness).) When Allah required mankind to supply themselves with what sustains them for the journeys of this life, He directed them to the necessary provisions for the Hereafter: Taqwa. Allah said in another Ayah:

(...and as an adornment; and the raiment of Taqwa, that is better.) (7:26)

Allah mentioned the material covering and then He mentioned the spiritual covering, which includes humbleness, obedience and Taqwa. He also stated that the latter provision is better and more beneficial than the former.

(So fear Me, O men of understanding!) meaning: 'Fear My torment, punishment, and affliction for those who defy Me and do not adhere to My commands, O people of reason and understanding.'

### Surah: 2 Ayah: 198

﴿ لَيْسَ عَلَيْكُمْ جُنَاحٌ أَن تَبْتَغُواْ فَضْلاً مِّن رَّبِّكُمْ فَإِذَآ أَفَضْتُم مِّنْ عَرَفَٰتٍ فَٱذْكُرُواْ ٱللَّهَ عِندَ ٱلْمَشْعَرِ ٱلْحَرَامِ وَٱذْكُرُوهُ كَمَا هَدَىٰكُمْ وَإِن كُنتُم مِّن قَبْلِهِۦ لَمِنَ ٱلضَّآلِّينَ ﴾

198. There is no sin on you if you seek the Bounty of your Lord (during pilgrimage by trading). Then when you leave 'Arafât, remember Allâh (by glorifying His Praises, i.e. prayers and invocations) at the Mash'ar-il-Harâm. And remember Him (by invoking Allâh for all good.) as He has guided you, and verily, you were, before, of those who were astray.

### Transliteration

198. Laysa AAalaykum junahun an tabtaghoo fadlan min rabbikum fa-itha afadtum min AAarafatin faothkuroo Allaha AAinda almashAAari alharami waothkuroohu kama hadakum wa-in kuntum min qablihi lamina alddalleena

### Tafsir Ibn Kathir

#### Commercial Transactions during Hajj

Al-Bukhari reported that Ibn `Abbas said, "`Ukaz, Mijannah and Dhul-Majaz were trading posts during the time of Jahiliyyah. During that era, they did not like the idea of conducting business transactions during the Hajj season. Later, this Ayah was revealed:

(There is no sin on you if you seek the bounty of your Lord.) during the Hajj season."

Abu Dawud and others recorded that Ibn `Abbas said, "They used to avoid conducting business transactions during the Hajj season, saying that these are the days of Dhikr. Allah revealed:

(There is no sin on you if you seek the bounty of your Lord (during pilgrimage by trading).)

This is also the explanation of Mujahid, Sa`id bin Jubayr, `Ikrimah, Mansur bin Al-Mu`tamir, Qatadah, Ibrahim An-Nakha`i, Ar-Rabi` bin Anas and others. Ibn Jarir reported that Abu Umaymah said that when Ibn `Umar was asked about conducting trade during the Hajj, he recited the Ayah:

(There is no sin on you if you seek the bounty of your Lord (during pilgrimage by trading). )

This Hadith is related to Ibn `Umar with a strong chain of narrators. This Hadith is also related to the Prophet , as Ahmad reported that Abu Umamah At-Taymi said, "I asked Ibn `Umar, `We buy (and sell during the Hajj), so do we still have a valid Hajj' He said, `Do you not perform Tawaf around the House, stand at `Arafat, throw the pebbles and shave your heads' I said, `Yes.' Ibn `Umar said, `A man came to the Prophet and asked him about what you asked me, and the Prophet did not answer him until Jibril came down with this Ayah:

(There is no sin on you if you seek the bounty of your Lord (during pilgrimage by trading).) The Prophet summoned the man and said: (You are pilgrims)." Ibn Jarir narrated that Abu Salih said to `Umar, "`O Leader of the faithful! Did you conduct trade transactions during the Hajj" He said, "Was their livelihood except during Hajj"

### Standing at `Arafat

Allah said:

(Then when you leave `Arafat, remember Allah (by glorifying His praises, i.e., prayers and invocations) at the Mash`ar-il-Haram.)

`Arafat is the place where one stands during the Hajj and it is a pillar of the rituals of Hajj. Imam Ahmad and the Sunan compilers recorded that `Abdur-Rahman bin Ya`mar Ad-Diyli said that he heard Allah's Messenger saying:

»الْحَجُّ عَرَفَاتٌ ثَلَاثًا فَمَنْ أَدْرَكَ عَرَفَةَ قَبْلَ أَنْ يَطْلُعَ الْفَجْرُ فَقَدْ أَدْرَكَ، وَأَيَّامُ مِنًى ثَلَاثَةٌ، فَمَنْ تَعَجَّلَ فِي يَوْمَيْنِ فَلَا إِثْمَ عَلَيْهِ، وَمَنْ تَأَخَّرَ فَلَا إِثْمَ عَلَيه«

(Hajj is `Arafat, (thrice). Hence, those who have stood at `Arafat before dawn will have performed (the rituals of the Hajj). The days of Mina are three, and there is no sin for those who move on after two days, or for those who stay.)

The time to stand on `Arafat starts from noon on the day of `Arafah until dawn the next day, which is the day of the Sacrifice (the tenth day of Dhul-Hijjah). The Prophet stood at `Arafat during the Farewell Hajj, after he had offered the Zuhr (noon) prayer, until sunset. He said, "Learn your rituals from me." In this Hadith (i. e., in the previous paragraph) he said, "Whoever stood at `Arafat before dawn, will have performed (the rituals of Hajj)." `Urwah bin Mudarris bin Harithah bin Lam At-Ta'i said, "I came to Allah's Messenger at Al-Muzdalifah when it was time to pray. I said, `O Messenger of Allah! I came from the two mountains of Tayy', and my animal became tired and I became tired. I have not left any mountain, but stood on it. Do I have a valid Hajj' Allah's Messenger said:

»مَنْ شَهِدَ صَلَاتَنَا هذِهِ، فَوَقَفَ مَعَنَا حَتَّى نَدْفَعَ، وَقَدْ وَقَفَ بِعَرَفَةَ قَبْلَ ذلِكَ لَيْلًا أَوْ نَهَارًا فَقَدْ تَمَّ حَجُّهُ وَقَضَى تَفَثَه«

(Whoever performed this prayer with us, stood with us until we moved forth, and had stood at `Arafat before that, day or night, will have performed the Hajj and completed its rituals)."

This Hadith was collected by Imam Ahmad and the compilers of the Sunan, and At-Tirmidhi graded it Sahih. It was reported that the mount was called `Arafat because, as `Abdur-Razzaq reported that `Ali bin Abu Talib said, "Allah sent Jibril to Prophet Ibrahim and he performed Hajj for him (to teach him its rituals). When Ibrahim reached `Arafat he said, `I have `Araftu (I know this place).' He had come to that area before. Thereafter, it was called `Arafat." Ibn Al-Mubarak said that `Ata' said, "It was called `Arafat because Jibril used to teach Ibrahim the rituals of Hajj. Ibrahim would say, `I have `Araftu, I have `Araftu.' It was thereafter called `Arafat." Similar statements were attributed to Ibn `Abbas, Ibn `Umar and Abu Mijlaz. Allah knows best.

`Arafat is also called Al-Mash`ar Al-Haram, Al-Mash`ar Al-Aqsa and Ilal, while the mount that is in the middle of `Arafat is called Jabal Ar-Rahmah (Mount of Mercy).

### The Time to leave `Arafat and Al-Muzdalifah

Ibn Abu Hatim reported that Ibn `Abbas said, "During the time of Jahiliyyah, the people used to stand at `Arafat. When the sun would be on top of the mountains, just as the turban is on top of a man's head, they would move on. Allah's Messenger delayed moving from `Arafat until sunset." Ibn Marduwyah related this Hadith and added, "He then stood at Al-Muzdalifah and offered the Fajr (Dawn) prayer at an early time. When the light of dawn broke, he moved on." This Hadith has a Hasan chain of narrators. The long Hadith that Jabir bin `Abdullah narrated, which Muslim collected, stated, "The Prophet kept standing there (meaning at `Arafat) until sunset, when the yellow light had somewhat gone and the disc of the sun had disappeared. Then, the Prophet made Usamah sit behind him, and in order to keep her under control, pulled the nose string of Al-Qaswa' so hard, that its head touched the saddle. He gestured with his right hand and said, "Proceed calmly people, calmly!" Whenever he happened to pass over an elevated tract of sand, he lightly loosened the nose string of his camel till she climbed up and this is how they reached Al-Muzdalifah. There, he led the Maghrib (Evening) and `Isha' (Night) prayers with one Adhan and two Iqamah (which announces the imminent start of the acts of the prayer) and did not glorify Allah in between them (i.e., he did not perform voluntary Rak`ah). Allah's Messenger then laid down till dawn and offered the Fajr (Dawn) prayer with Adhan and Iqamah, when the morning light was clear. He again mounted Al-Qaswa', and when he came to Al-Mash`ar Al-Haram, he faced towards Qiblah, supplicated to Allah, glorifying Him and saying, La ilaha illallah, and he continued standing until the daylight was very clear. He then went quickly before the sun rose."

It is reported in the Two Sahihs that Usamah bin Zayd was asked, "How was the Prophet's pace when he moved" He said, "Slow, unless he found space, then he would go a little faster."

## Al-Mash`ar Al-Haram

`Abdur-Razzaq reported that Ibn `Umar said that all of Al-Muzdalifah is Al-Mash`ar Al-Haram. It was reported that Ibn `Umar was asked about Allah's statement:

(...remember Allah (by glorifying His praises, i.e., prayers and invocations) at the Mash`ar-il-Haram.) He said, "It is the Mount and the surrounding area." It was reported that Al-Mash`ar Al-Haram is what is between the two Mounts (refer to the following Hadith), as Ibn `Abbas, Sa`id bin Jubayr, `Ikrimah, Mujahid, As-Suddi, Ar-Rabi` bin Anas, Al-Hasan and Qatadah have stated.

Imam Ahmad recorded that Jubayr bin Mut`im narrated that the Prophet said:

«كُلُّ عَرَفَاتٍ مَوْقِفٌ، وَارْفَعُوا عَنْ عُرَنَةَ، وَكُلُّ مُزْدَلِفَةَ مَوْقِفٌ، وَارْفَعُوا عَنْ مُحَسِّرٍ، وَكُلُّ فِجَاجِ مَكَّةَ مَنْحَرٌ، وَكُلُّ أَيَّامِ التَّشْرِيقِ ذَبْحٌ»

(All of `Arafat is a place of standing, and keep away from `Uranah. All of Al-Muzdalifah is a place for standing, and keep away from the bottom of Muhassir. All of the areas of Makkah are a place for sacrifice, and all of the days of Tashriq are days of sacrifice.)

Allah then said:

(And remember Him (by invoking Allah for all good) as He has guided you.)

This Ayah reminds Muslims of Allah's bounty on them that He has directed and taught them the rituals of Hajj according to the guidance of Prophet Ibrahim Al-Khalil. This is why Allah said:

(...and verily, you were, before, of those who were astray.)

It was said that this Ayah refers to the condition before the guidance or the Qur'an or the Messenger, all of which are correct meanings.

## Surah: 2 Ayah: 199

﴿ ثُمَّ أَفِيضُواْ مِنْ حَيْثُ أَفَاضَ ٱلنَّاسُ وَٱسْتَغْفِرُواْ ٱللَّهَ إِنَّ ٱللَّهَ غَفُورٌ رَّحِيمٌ ﴿١٩٩﴾ ﴾

199. Then depart from the place whence all the people depart and ask Allâh for His Forgiveness. Truly, Allâh is Oft-Forgiving, Most-Merciful.

### Transliteration

199. Thumma afeedoo min haythu afada alnnasu waistaghfiroo Allaha inna Allaha ghafoorun raheemun

### Tafsir Ibn Kathir

#### The Order to stand on `Arafat and to depart from it

This Ayah contains Allah's order to those who stand at `Arafat to also move on to Al-Muzdalifah, so that they remember Allah at Al-Mash`ar Al-Haram. Allah commands the Muslim to stand with the rest of the pilgrims at `Arafat, unlike Quraysh who (before Islam) used to remain in the sanctuary, near Al-Muzdalifah, saying that they are the people of Allah's Town and the servants of His House. Al-Bukhari reported that `A'ishah said, "Quraysh and their allies, who used to be called Al-Hums, used to stay in Al-Muzdalifah while the rest of the Arabs would stand at `Arafat. When Islam came, Allah commanded His Prophet to stand at `Arafat and then proceed from there. Hence Allah's statement:

(...from the place whence all the people depart.)

This was also said by Ibn `Abbas, Mujahid, `Ata', Qatadah and As-Suddi and others. Ibn Jarir chose this opinion and said that there is Ijma` (a consensus among the scholars) for it.

Imam Ahmad reported that Jubayr bin Mut`im said, "My camel was lost and I went out in search of it on the day of `Arafah, and I saw the Prophet standing in `Arafat. I said to myself, `By Allah he is from the Hums. What has brought him here'" This Hadith is also reported in the Sahihayn. Al-Bukhari reported that Ibn `Abbas said that `depart' mentioned in the Ayah refers to proceeding from Al-Muzdalifah to Mina to stone the pillars. Allah knows best.

### Asking Allah for His Forgiveness

Allah said:

(...and ask Allah for His forgiveness. Truly, Allah is Oft-Forgiving, Most-Merciful.)

Allah frequently orders remembrance of Him after acts of worship are finished. Muslim reported that Allah's Messenger used to ask Allah for His forgiveness thrice after the prayer is finished. It is reported in the Two Sahihs that the Prophet encouraged Tasbih (saying Subhan Allah, i.e., Glorified is Allah), Tahmid (saying Al-Hamdu Lillah, i.e., praise be to Allah) and Takbir (saying Allahu Akbar, i.e., Allah is the Most Great) thirty-three times each (after prayer).

Ibn Marduwyah collected the Hadith that Al-Bukhari reported from Shaddad bin Aws, who stated that Allah's Messenger said:

«سَيِّدُ الِاسْتِغْفَارِ أَنْ يَقُولَ الْعَبْدُ: اللَّهُمَّ أَنْتَ رَبِّي، لَا إِلهَ إِلَّا أَنْتَ، خَلَقْتَنِي وَأَنَا عَبْدُكَ، وَأَنَا عَلَى عَهْدِكَ وَوَعْدِكَ مَا اسْتَطَعْتُ، أَعُوذُ بِكَ مِنْ شَرِّ مَا صَنَعْتُ، أَبُوءُ لَكَ بِنِعْمَتِكَ عَلَيَّ، وَأَبُوءُ بِذَنْبِي، فَاغْفِرْ لِي فَإِنَّهُ لَا يَغْفِرُ الذُّنُوبَ إِلَّا أَنْتَ، مَنْ قَالَهَا فِي لَيْلَةٍ فَمَاتَ فِي لَيْلَتِهِ دَخَلَ الْجَنَّةَ، وَمَنْ قَالَهَا فِي يَوْمِهِ فَمَاتَ دَخَلَ الْجَنَّةَ»

(The master of supplication for forgiveness, is for the servant to say: `O Allah! You are my Lord, there is no deity worthy of worship except You. You have created me and I am Your servant. I am on Your covenant, as much as I can be, and awaiting Your promise. I seek refuge with You from the evil that I have committed. I admit Your favor on me and admit my faults. So forgive me, for none except You forgives the sins.' Whoever said these words at night and died that same night will enter Paradise. Whoever said it during the day and died will enter Paradise.)

Furthermore, it is reported in the Two Sahihs that `Abdullah bin `Amr said that Abu Bakr said, "O Messenger of Allah! Teach me an invocation so that I may invoke (Allah) with it in my prayer. He told me to say:

«قُلْ: اللَّهُمَّ إِنِّي ظَلَمْتُ نَفْسِي ظُلْمًا كَثِيرًا وَلَا يَغْفِرُ الذُّنُوبَ إِلَّا أَنْتَ فَاغْفِرْ لِي مَغْفِرَةً مِنْ عِنْدِكَ، وَارْحَمْنِي إِنَّكَ أَنْتَ الْغَفُورُ الرَّحِيمُ»

(Allahumma inni zalamtu nafsi zulman kathiran, wa la yaghfirudh-dhunuba illa Anta faghfirli maghfiratan min `indika, war-hamni innaka Antal-Ghafur-ur-Rahim (O Allah! I have done great injustice to myself and none except You forgives sins, so please forgive me and be merciful to me as You are the Forgiver, the Merciful).)

There are many other Hadiths on this subject.

### Surah: 2 Ayah: 200, Ayah: 201 & Ayah: 202

﴿ فَإِذَا قَضَيْتُم مَّنَـٰسِكَكُمْ فَٱذْكُرُوا۟ ٱللَّهَ كَذِكْرِكُمْ ءَابَآءَكُمْ أَوْ أَشَدَّ ذِكْرًا ۗ فَمِنَ ٱلنَّاسِ مَن يَقُولُ رَبَّنَآ ءَاتِنَا فِى ٱلدُّنْيَا وَمَا لَهُۥ فِى ٱلْـَٔاخِرَةِ مِنْ خَلَـٰقٍ ﴾

200. So when you have accomplished your Manâsik, remember Allâh as you remember your forefathers or with a far more remembrance. But of mankind there are some who say: "Our Lord! Give us (Your Bounties) in this world!" and for such there will be no portion in the Hereafter.

﴿ وَمِنْهُم مَّن يَقُولُ رَبَّنَآ ءَاتِنَا فِى ٱلدُّنْيَا حَسَنَةً وَفِى ٱلْـَٔاخِرَةِ حَسَنَةً وَقِنَا عَذَابَ ٱلنَّارِ ﴾

201. And of them there are some who say: "Our Lord! Give us in this world that which is good and in the Hereafter that which is good, and save us from the torment of the Fire!"

﴿ أُو۟لَـٰٓئِكَ لَهُمْ نَصِيبٌ مِّمَّا كَسَبُوا۟ ۚ وَٱللَّهُ سَرِيعُ ٱلْحِسَابِ ﴾

202. For them there will be allotted a share for what they have earned. And Allâh is Swift at reckoning.

### Transliteration

200. Fa-itha qadaytum manasikakum faothkuroo Allaha kathikrikum abaakum aw ashadda thikran famina alnnasi man yaqoolu rabbana atina fee alddunya wama lahu fee al-akhirati min khalaqin  201. Waminhum man yaqoolu rabbana atina fee alddunya hasanatan wafee al-akhirati hasanatan waqina AAathaba

alnnari 202. Ola-ika lahum naseebun mimma kasaboo waAllahu sareeAAu alhisabi

### Tafsir Ibn Kathir

### The Order for Remembrance of Allah and seeking Good in this Life and the Hereafter upon completing the Rites of Hajj

Allah commands that He be remembered after the rituals are performed.

(...as you remember your forefathers)

Sa`id bin Jubayr said that Ibn `Abbas said, "During the time of Jahiliyyah, people used to stand during the (Hajj) season, and one of them would say, `My father used to feed (the poor), help others (end their disputes, with his money), pay the Diyah (i.e., blood money),' and so forth. The only Dhikr that they had was that they would remember the deeds of their fathers. Allah then revealed to Muhammad :

(Remember Allah as you remember your forefathers or with far more remembrance.)

Therefore, remembering Allah the Exalted and Ever High is always encouraged. We should mention that when Allah used "or" in the Ayah, He meant to encourage the people to remember Him more than they remember their forefathers, not that the word entails a doubt (as to which is larger or bigger). This statement is similar to the Ayat:

(...as stones or even worse in hardness) (2:74) and,

(...fear men as they fear Allah or even more) (4:77) and,

(And We sent him to a hundred thousand (people) or even more) (37:147) and,

(And was at a distance of two bows' length or (even) nearer.) (53:9)

Allah encourages calling Him in supplication after remembering Him, because this will make it more likely that the supplication will be accepted. Allah also criticizes those who only supplicate to Him about the affairs of this life, while ignoring the affairs of the Hereafter. Allah said:

(But of mankind there are some who say: "Our Lord! Give us (Your bounties) in this world!" and for such there will be no portion in the Hereafter.) qmeaning, they have no share in the Hereafter. This criticism serves to discourage other people from imitating those mentioned.

Sa`id bin Jubayr said that Ibn `Abbas said, "Some bedouins used to come to the standing area (`Arafat) and supplicate saying, `O Allah! Make it a rainy year, a fertile year and a year of good child bearing.' They would not mention any of the affairs of the Hereafter. Thus, Allah revealed about them:

(But of mankind there are some who say: "Our Lord! Give us (Your bounties) in this world!" and for such there will be no portion in the Hereafter.)

The believers who came after them used to say:

(Our Lord! Give us in this world that which is good and in the Hereafter that which is good, and save us from the torment of the Fire!")

Next, Allah revealed:

(For them there will be alloted a share for what they have earned. And Allah is swift at reckoning.)

Hence, Allah praised those who ask for the affairs of both this life and the Hereafter. He said:

(And of them there are some who say: "Our Lord! Give us in this world that which is good and in the Hereafter that which is good, and save us from the torment of the Fire!")

The supplication mentioned and praised in the Ayah includes all good aspects of this life and seeks refuge from all types of evil. The good of this life concerns every material request of well-being, spacious dwelling, pleasing mates, sufficient provision, beneficial knowledge, good profession or deeds, comfortable means of transportation and good praise, all of which the scholars of Tafsir have mentioned regarding this subject. All of these are but a part of the good that is sought in this life. As for the good of the Hereafter, the best of this includes acquiring Paradise, which also means acquiring safety from the greatest horror at the gathering place. It also refers to being questioned lightly and the other favors in the Hereafter.

As for acquiring safety from the Fire, it includes being directed to what leads to this good end in this world, such as avoiding the prohibitions, sins of all kinds and doubtful matters.

Al-Qasim bin `Abdur-Rahman said, "Whoever is gifted with a grateful heart, a remembering tongue and a patient body, will have been endowed with a good deed in this life, a good deed in the Hereafter and saved from the torment of the Fire."

This is why the Sunnah encourages reciting this Du`a' (i.e., in the Ayah about gaining a good deed in this life and the Hereafter). Al-Bukhari reported that Anas bin Malik narrated that the Prophet used to say:

»اللَّهُمَّ رَبَّنَا آتِنَا فِي الدُّنْيَا حَسَنَةً، وَفِي الآخِرَةِ حَسَنَةً، وَقِنَا عَذَابَ

النَّارِ»

(O Allah, our Lord! Give us that which is good in this life, that which is good in the Hereafter and save us from the torment of the Fire.)

Imam Ahmad reported that Anas said, "Allah's Messenger visited a Muslim man who had become as weak as a sick small bird. Allah's Messenger said to him, `Were you asking or supplicating to Allah about something' He said, `Yes. I used to say: O Allah! Whatever punishment you saved for me in the Hereafter, give it to me in this life.' Allah's Messenger said:

«سُبْحَانَ اللهِ لَا تُطِيقُهُ أَوْ لَا تَسْتَطِيعُهُ، فَهَلَّا قُلْتَ:

[رَبَّنَآ ءَاتِنَا فِى ٱلدُّنْيَا حَسَنَةً وَفِى ٱلْءَاخِرَةِ حَسَنَةً وَقِنَا عَذَابَ ٱلنَّارِ]

(All praise is due to Allah! You cannot bear it -or stand it-. You should have said: (Our Lord! Give us in this world that which is good and in the Hereafter that which is good, and save us from the torment of the Fire!))

The man began reciting this Du`a and he was cured." Muslim also recorded it.

Al-Hakim reported that Sa`id bin Jubayr said, "A man came to Ibn `Abbas and said, `I worked for some people and settled for a part of my compensation in return for their taking me to perform Hajj with them. Is this acceptable' Ibn `Abbas said, `You are among those whom Allah described:

(For them there will be alloted a share for what they have earned. And Allah is swift at reckoning.)

Al-Hakim then commented; "This Hadith is authentic according to the criteria of the Two Shaykhs (Al-Bukhari and Muslim) although they did not record it."

### Surah: 2 Ayah: 203

﴿ ۞ وَٱذْكُرُوا۟ ٱللَّهَ فِىٓ أَيَّامٍ مَّعْدُودَٰتٍ ۚ فَمَن تَعَجَّلَ فِى يَوْمَيْنِ فَلَآ إِثْمَ عَلَيْهِ وَمَن تَأَخَّرَ فَلَآ إِثْمَ عَلَيْهِ ۚ لِمَنِ ٱتَّقَىٰ ۗ وَٱتَّقُوا۟ ٱللَّهَ وَٱعْلَمُوٓا۟ أَنَّكُمْ إِلَيْهِ تُحْشَرُونَ ﴾ ۝

203. And remember Allâh during the appointed Days. But whosoever hastens to leave in two days, there is no sin on him and whosoever stays on, there is no sin on him, if his aim is to do good and obey Allâh (fear Him), and know that you will surely be gathered unto Him.

### Transliteration

203. Waothkuroo Allaha fee ayyamin maAAdoodatin faman taAAajjala fee yawmayni fala ithma AAalayhi waman taakhkhara fala ithma AAalayhi limani ittaqa waittaqoo Allaha waiAAlamoo annakum ilayhi tuhsharoona

### Tafsir Ibn Kathir

## Remembering Allah during the Days of Tashriq - Days of Eating and Drinking

Ibn `Abbas said, `The Appointed Days are the Days of Tashriq (11-12-13th of Dhul-Hijjah) while the Known Days are the (first) ten (days of Dhul-Hijjah)." `Ikrimah said that:

(And remember Allah during the Appointed Days.) means reciting the Takbir -- Allahu Akbar, Allahu Akbar, during the days of Tashriq after the compulsory prayers.

Imam Ahmad reported that `Uqbah bin `Amr said that Allah's Messenger said:

«يَوْمُ عَرَفَةَ، وَيَوْمُ النَّحْرِ، وَأَيَّامُ التَّشْرِيقِ، عِيدُنَا أَهْلَ الْإِسْلَامِ، وَهِيَ أَيَّامُ أَكْلٍ وَشُرْبٍ»

(The day of `Arafah (9th of Dhul-Hijjah), the day of the Sacrifice (10th) and the days of the Tashriq (11-12-13th) are our `Id (festival) for we people of Islam. These are days of eating and drinking.)

Imam Ahmad reported that Nubayshah Al-Hudhali said that Allah's Messenger said:

«أَيَّامُ التَّشْرِيقِ أَيَّامُ أَكْلٍ وشُرْبٍ وَذِكْرِ الله»

(The days of Tashriq are days of eating, drinking and Dhikr (remembering) of Allah.)

Muslim also recorded this Haith

We also mentioned the Hadith of Jubayr bin Mut`im:

«عَرَفَةُ كُلُّهَا مَوْقِفٌ، وَأَيَّامُ التَّشْرِيقِ كُلُّهَا ذَبْحٌ»

(All of `Arafat is a standing place and all of the days of Tashriq are days of Sacrifice. )

We also mentioned the Hadith by `Abdur-Rahman bin Ya`mar Ad-Diyli:

 «وَأَيَّامُ مِنىً ثَلَاثَةٌ فَمَنْ تَعَجَّلَ فِي يَوْمَيْنِ فَلَا إِثْمَ عَلَيْهِ وَمَنْ تَأَخَّرَ فَلَا إِثْمَ عَلَيْهِ»

(The days of Mina (Tashriq) are three. Those who hasten in two days then there is no sin in it, and those who delay (i.e., remain in Mina for a third day) then there is no sin in it.)

Ibn Jarir reported that Abu Hurayrah narrated that Allah's Messenger said:

«أَيَّامُ التَّشْرِيقِ أَيَّامُ طُعْمٍ وَذِكْرِ اللهِ»

(The days of Tashriq are days of eating and remembering Allah.)

Ibn Jarir reported that Abu Hurayrah narrated that Allah's Messenger sent `Abdullah bin Hudhafah to Mina proclaiming:

«لَا تَصُومُوا هَذِهِ الْأَيَّامَ، فَإِنَّهَا أَيَّامُ أَكْلٍ وَشُرْبٍ وَذِكْرِ اللهِ عَزَّ وَجَل»

(Do not fast these days (i.e., Tashriq days), for they are days of eating, drinking and remembering Allah the Exalted and Most Honored.))

## The Appointed Days

Miqsam said that Ibn `Abbas said that the Appointed Days are the days of Tashriq, four days: the day of the Sacrifice (10th of Dhul-Hijjah) and three days after that.

This opinion was also reported of Ibn `Umar, Ibn Az-Zubayr, Abu Musa, `Ata', Mujahid, `Ikrimah, Sa`id bin Jubayr, Abu Malik, Ibrahim An-Nakha`i, Yahya bin Abu Kathir, Al-Hasan, Qatadah, As-Suddi, Az-Zuhri, Ar-Rabi` bin Anas, Ad-Dahhak, Muqatil bin Hayyan, `Ata' Al-Khurasani, Malik bin Anas, and others. In addition, the apparent meaning of the following Ayah supports this opinion:

(But whosoever hastens to leave in two days, there is no sin on him and whosoever stays on, there is no sin on him.)

So the Ayah hints to the three days after the day of Sacrifice.

Allah's statement:

(And remember Allah during the Appointed Days) directs remembering Allah upon slaughtering the animals, after the prayers, and by Dhikr (supplication) in general. It also includes Takbir and remembering Allah while throwing the pebbles every day during the Tashriq days. A Hadith that Abu Dawud and several others collected states:

(Tawaf around the House, Sa`i between As-Safa and Al-Marwah and throwing the pebbles were legislated so that Allah is remembered in Dhikr.)

When mentioning the first procession (refer to 2:199) and the second procession of the people upon the end of the Hajj season, when they start to return to their areas, after they had gathered during the rituals and at the standing places, Allah said,

(and obey Allah (fear Him), and know that you will surely be gathered unto Him.)

Similarly, Allah said:

(And it is He Who has created you on the earth, and to Him you shall be gathered back.) (23:79)

## Surah: 2 Ayah: 204, Ayah: 205, Ayah: 206 & Ayah: 207

﴿ وَمِنَ ٱلنَّاسِ مَن يُعْجِبُكَ قَوْلُهُ فِى ٱلْحَيَوٰةِ ٱلدُّنْيَا وَيُشْهِدُ ٱللَّهَ عَلَىٰ مَا فِى قَلْبِهِۦ وَهُوَ أَلَدُّ ٱلْخِصَامِ ۝ ﴾

204. And of mankind there is he whose speech may please you (O Muhammad (peace be upon him)) in this worldly life, and he calls Allâh to witness as to that which is in his heart, yet he is the most quarrelsome of the opponents.

﴿ وَإِذَا تَوَلَّىٰ سَعَىٰ فِى ٱلْأَرْضِ لِيُفْسِدَ فِيهَا وَيُهْلِكَ ٱلْحَرْثَ وَٱلنَّسْلَ وَٱللَّهُ لَا يُحِبُّ ٱلْفَسَادَ ۝ ﴾

205. And when he turns away (from you "O Muhammad (peace be upon him)"), his effort in the land is to make mischief therein and to destroy the crops and the cattle, and Allâh likes not mischief.

﴿ وَإِذَا قِيلَ لَهُ ٱتَّقِ ٱللَّهَ أَخَذَتْهُ ٱلْعِزَّةُ بِٱلْإِثْمِ فَحَسْبُهُ جَهَنَّمُ وَلَبِئْسَ ٱلْمِهَادُ ۝ ﴾

206. And when it is said to him, "Fear Allâh", he is led by arrogance to (more) crime. So enough for him is Hell, and worst indeed is that place to rest!

﴿ وَمِنَ ٱلنَّاسِ مَن يَشْرِى نَفْسَهُ ٱبْتِغَآءَ مَرْضَاتِ ٱللَّهِ ۗ وَٱللَّهُ رَءُوفٌ بِٱلْعِبَادِ ﴾

207. And of mankind is he who would sell himself, seeking the Pleasure of Allâh. And Allâh is full of Kindness to (His) slaves.

### Transliteration

204. Wamina alnnasi man yuAAjibuka qawluhu fee alhayati alddunya wayushhidu Allaha AAala ma fee qalbihi wahuwa aladdu alkhisami  205. Wa-itha tawalla saAAa fee al-ardi liyufsida feeha wayuhlika alhartha waalnnasla waAllahu la yuhibbu alfasada  206. Wa-itha qeela lahu ittaqi Allaha akhathat-hu alAAizzatu bial-ithmi fahasbuhu jahannamu walabisa almihadu  207. Wamina alnnasi man yashree nafsahu ibtighaa mardati Allahi waAllahu raoofun bialAAibadi

### Tafsir Ibn Kathir

#### The Characteristics of the Hypocrites

As-Suddi said that these Ayat were revealed about Al-Akhnas bin Shariq Ath-Thaqafi who came to Allah's Messenger and announced his Islam although his heart concealed otherwise.

Ibn `Abbas narrated that these Ayat were revealed about some of the hypocrites who criticized Khubayb and his companions who were killed during the Raji` incident. Thereafter, Allah sent down His condemnation of the hypocrites and His praise for Khubayb and his companions:

(And of mankind is he who would sell himself, seeking the pleasure of Allah.)

It was also said that they refer to the hypocrites and the believers in general. This is the opinion of Qatadah, Mujahid, Ar-Rabi` bin Anas and several others, and it is correct.

Ibn Jarir related that Al-Qurazi said that Nawf Al-Bikali, who used to read (previous Divine) Books said, "I find the description of some members of this Ummah in the previously revealed Books of Allah: they (hypocrites) are people who use the religion to gain material benefit. Their tongues are sweeter than honey, but their hearts are more bitter than Sabir (a bitter plant, aloe). They show the people the appearance of sheep while their hearts hide the viciousness of wolves. Allah said, `They dare challenge Me, but they are deceived by Me. I swear by Myself that I will send a Fitnah (trial, calamity) on them that will make the wise man bewildered.' I contemplated about these statements and found them in the Qur'an describing the hypocrites:

(And of mankind there is he whose speech may please you (O Muhammad ), in this worldly life, and he calls Allah to witness as to that which is in his heart,)

This statement by Al-Qurazi is Hasan Sahih. Allah said:

(...and he calls Allah to witness as to that which is in his heart,)

This Ayah indicates that such people pretend to be Muslims, but defy Allah by the disbelief and hypocrisy that their hearts conceal. Similarly Allah said:

(They may hide (their crimes) from men, but they cannot hide (them) from Allah.) (4:108)

This Tafsir was reported from Ibn `Abbas by Ibn Ishaq. It was also said that the Ayah means that when such people announce their Islam, they swear by Allah that what is in their hearts is the same of what their tongues are pronouncing. This is also a correct meaning for the Ayah that was chosen by `Abdur-Rahman bin Zayd bin Aslam. It is also the choice of Ibn Jarir who related it to Ibn `Abbas and Mujahid. Allah knows best.

Allah said:

(Yet he is the most Aladd of the opponents.) (2:204) |The Ayah used the word Aladd here, which literally means `wicked' (here it means `quarrelsome'). A variation of the word Ludda was also used in another Ayah:

(So that you (Muhammad) warn with it (the Qur'an) a Ludda people.) (19:97)

Hence, a hypocrite lies, alters the truth when he quarrels and does not care for the truth. Rather, he deviates from the truth, deceives and becomes most quarrelsome. It is reported in Sahih that Allah's Messenger said:

《آيَةُ الْمُنَافِقِ ثَلَاثٌ: إِذَا حَدَّثَ كَذَبَ، وَإِذَا عَاهَدَ غَدَرَ، وَإِذَا خَاصَمَ فَجَرَ》

(The signs of a hypocrite are three: Whenever he speaks, he tells a lie. Whenever he promises, he always breaks it (his promise). If you have a dispute with him, he is most quarrelsome.)

Imam Bukhari reported that `A'ishah narrated that the Prophet said:

《إِنَّ أَبْغَضَ الرِّجَالِ إِلَى اللهِ الْأَلَدُّ الْخَصِمُ》

(The most hated person to Allah is he who is Aladd and Khasim (meaning most quarrelsome).)

Allah then said:

(And when he turns away (from you O Muhammad), he struggles in the land to make mischief therein and to destroy the crops and the cattle, and Allah likes not mischief.)

This Ayah indicates that such persons are deviant in the tongue, evil in the deeds, their words are fabricated, their belief is wicked and their works are immoral. The Ayah used the (Arabic word) Sa`a (literally, `tries' or `intends'). This word was also used to describe Pharaoh:

(Then he turned his back, Yas`a (striving hard against Allah). Then he gathered (his people) and cried aloud saying, `I am your lord, most high.' So Allah, seized him with a punishing example for his last and first transgression. Verily, in this is an instructive admonition for whosoever fears Allah.) (79:22-26)

(Sa`a was also used in the Ayah):

(O you who believe (Muslims)! When the call is proclaimed for the Salah (prayer) on the day of Friday (Jumu`ah prayer), As`aw come to the remembrance of Allah.) (62:9)

This Ayah means, `(when the call to the Friday prayer is announced) intend and then proceed to attend the Friday prayer.' We should mention that hastening to the mosque is condemned by the Sunnah (as this is another meaning for the word Sa`a):

»إِذَا أَتَيْتُمُ الصَّلَاةَ فَلَا تَأْتُوهَا وَأَنْتُمْ تَسْعَوْنَ، وَأْتُوهَا وَعَلَيْكُمُ السَّكِينَةُ وَالْوَقَارِ«

(When you come to attend the prayer, do not come in a Sa`i (haste). Rather, come to it while walking at ease and in peace (or grace).)

The hypocrite has no motive in this life but to cause mischief and to destroy the crops and the offspring, including what the animals produce and what the people depend on for their livelihood. Mujahid said, "If the hypocrite strives for mischief in the land, Allah prevents the rain from falling and thus the crops and the offspring perish." The Ayah continues:

(...and Allah likes not mischief.) that is, Allah does not like those who possess these characteristics, or those who act like this.

### Rejecting Advice is Characteristic of the Hypocrites

Allah said:

(And when it is said to him, "Fear Allah", he is led by arrogance to (more) crime.)

This Ayah indicates that when the hypocrite, who deviates in his speech and deeds, is advised and commanded to fear Allah, refrain from his evil deeds and adhere to the truth, he refuses and becomes angry and outraged, as he is used to doing evil. This Ayah is similar to what Allah said:

(And when Our clear verses are recited to them, you will notice a denial on the faces of the disbelievers! They are nearly ready to attack with violence those who recite Our verses to them. Say: "Shall I tell you of something worse than that The Fire (of Hell) which Allah has promised to those who disbelieved, and worst indeed is that destination!) (22:72)

This is why in this Ayah, Allah said:

(So enough for him is Hell, and worst indeed is that place to rest) meaning, the Fire is enough punishment for the hypocrite.

### The Sincere Believer prefers pleasing Allah

Allah said:

(And of mankind is he who would sell himself, seeking the pleasure of Allah.)

After Allah described the evil characteristics of the hypocrites, He mentioned the good qualities of the believers. Allah said:

(And of mankind is he who would sell himself, seeking the pleasure of Allah.)

Ibn `Abbas, Anas, Sa`id bin Musayyib, Abu `Uthman An-Nahdi, `Ikrimah and several other scholars said that this Ayah was revealed about Suhayb bin Sinan Ar-Rumi. When Suhayb became a Muslim in Makkah and intended to migrate (to Al-Madinah), the people (Quraysh) prevented him from migrating with his money. They said that if he forfeits his property, he is free to migrate. He abandoned his money and preferred to migrate, and Allah revealed this Ayah about him. `Umar bin Khattab and several other Companions met Suhayb close to the outskirts of Al-Madinah at Al-Harrah (flat lands with black stones). They said to him, "The trade has indeed been successful." He answered them, "You too, may Allah never allow your trade to fail. What is the matter" `Umar told him that Allah has revealed this Ayah (2:207) about him. It was also reported that Allah's Messenger said, "The trade has been successful, O Suhayb!"

The meaning of the Ayah (2:207) includes every Mujahid in the way of Allah. Allah said in another Ayah:

(Verily, Allah has purchased of the believers their lives and their properties for (the price) that theirs shall be the Paradise. They fight in Allah's cause, so they kill (others) and are killed. It is a promise in truth which is binding on Him in the Tawrah and the Injil and the Qur'an. And who is truer to his covenant than Allah Then rejoice in the bargain which you have concluded. That is the supreme success.) (9:111)

# Chapter 2: Al-Baqarah (The Cow), Verses 142-252

When Hisham bin `Amr penetrated the lines of the enemy, some people criticized him. `Umar bin Al-Khattab and Abu Hurayrah refuted them and recited this Ayah:

(And of mankind is he who would sell himself, seeking the pleasure of Allah. And Allah is full of kindness to (His) servants.)

## Surah: 2 Ayah: 208 & Ayah: 209

﴿ يَٰٓأَيُّهَا ٱلَّذِينَ ءَامَنُوا۟ ٱدْخُلُوا۟ فِى ٱلسِّلْمِ كَآفَّةً وَلَا تَتَّبِعُوا۟ خُطُوَٰتِ ٱلشَّيْطَٰنِ إِنَّهُۥ لَكُمْ عَدُوٌّ مُّبِينٌ ۝ ﴾

208. O you who believe! Enter perfectly in Islâm (by obeying all the rules and regulations of the Islâmic religion) and follow not the footsteps of Shaitân (Satan). Verily! He is to you a plain enemy.

﴿ فَإِن زَلَلْتُم مِّنۢ بَعْدِ مَا جَآءَتْكُمُ ٱلْبَيِّنَٰتُ فَٱعْلَمُوٓا۟ أَنَّ ٱللَّهَ عَزِيزٌ حَكِيمٌ ۝ ﴾

209. Then if you slide back after the clear signs (Prophet Muhammad (peace be upon him) and this Qur'ân, and Islâm) have come to you, then know that Allâh is All-Mighty, All-Wise.

### Transliteration

208. Ya ayyuha allatheena amanoo odkhuloo fee alssilmi kaffatan wala tattabiAAoo khutuwati alshshaytani innahu lakum AAaduwwun mubeenun 209. Fa-in zalaltum min baAAdi ma jaatkumu albayyinatu faiAAlamoo anna Allaha AAazeezun hakeemun

### Tafsir Ibn Kathir

**Entering Islam in its Entirety is obligated**

Allah commands His servants who believe in Him and have faith in His Messenger to implement all of Islam's legislation and law, to adhere to all of its commandments, as much as they can, and to refrain from all of its prohibitions. `Al-`Awfi said that Ibn `Abbas said, and also Mujahid, Tawus, Ad-Dahhak, `Ikrimah, Qatadah, As-Suddi and Ibn Zayd said that Allah's statement:

(Enter Silm) means Islam. Allah's statement:

(...perfectly) means, in its entirety. This is the Tafsir of Ibn `Abbas, Mujahid, Abu Al-`Aliyah, `Ikrimah, Ar-Rabi` bin Anas, As-Suddi, Muqatil bin Hayyan, Qatadah and Ad-Dahhak. Mujahid said that the Ayah means, `Perform all the good works and the various pious deeds, this is especially addressed to those from among the People of the Scripture who embraced the faith.'

Ibn Abu Hatim reported that Ibn `Abbas said that:

(O you who believe! Enter Silm perfectly) refers to the believers among the People of the Scripture. This is because they believed in Allah, some of them still followed some parts of the Tawrah and the previous revelations. So Allah said:

(Enter Islam perfectly.) Allah thus commanded them to embrace the legislation of the religion of Muhammad in its entirety and to avoid abandoning any part of it. They should no longer adhere to the Tawrah.

Allah then said:

(...and follow not the footsteps of Shaytan) meaning, perform the acts of worship and avoid what Satan commands you to do. This is because:

(He (Shaytan) commands you only what is evil and Fahsha' (sinful), and that you should say about Allah what you know not.) (2:169) and:

(He only invites his Hizb (followers) that they may become the dwellers of the blazing Fire.) (35:6) Hence, Allah said:

(Verily, he is to you an open enemy.)

Allah said:

(Then if you slide back after the clear signs have come to you) meaning, if you deviate from the Truth after clear proofs have been established against you,

(...then know that Allah is All-Mighty) in His punishment, and no one can escape His vengeance or defeat Him.

(All-Wise) in His decisions, actions and rulings. Hence Abu Al-`Aliyah, Qatadah and Ar-Rabi` bin Anas said, "He is Mighty in His vengeance, Wise in His decision."

## Surah: 2 Ayah: 210

﴿ هَلْ يَنظُرُونَ إِلَّا أَن يَأْتِيَهُمُ ٱللَّهُ فِى ظُلَلٍ مِّنَ ٱلْغَمَامِ وَٱلْمَلَـٰٓئِكَةُ وَقُضِىَ ٱلْأَمْرُ وَإِلَى ٱللَّهِ تُرْجَعُ ٱلْأُمُورُ ﴾

210. Do they then wait for anything other than that Allâh should come to them in the shadows of the clouds and the angels? (Then) the case would be already judged. And to Allâh return all matters (for decision).

## Transliteration

210. Hal yan*th*uroona illa an ya/tiyahumu Allahu fee *th*ulalin mina alghamami waalmala-ikatu waqudiya al-amru wa-ila Allahi turjaAAu al-omooru

## Tafsir Ibn Kathir

### Do not delay embracing the Faith

(Do they then wait for anything other than that Allah should come to them over the shadows of the clouds and the angels) on the Day of Resurrection to judge the early and the latter creations. Allah shall then reward each according to his or her deeds; and whoever does good shall see it, and whoever does evil shall see it. This is why Allah said:

((Then) the case would be already judged. And to Allah return all matters (for decision).)

Similarly, Allah said:

(Nay! When the earth is ground to powder. And your Lord comes with the angels in rows. And Hell will be brought near that Day. On that Day will man remember, but how will that remembrance (then) avail him) (89:21-23) and:

(Do they then wait for anything other than that the angels should come to them, or that your Lord (Allah) should come, or that some of the signs of your Lord should come (i. e., portents of the Hour, e.g., rising of the sun from the west)!) (6:158)

Abu Ja`far Razi reported that Abu Al-`Aliyah narrated that:

(Do they then wait for anything other than that Allah should come to them over the shadows of the clouds and the angels) means, the angels will descend on the shadows of clouds, while Allah comes as He wills. Some of the reciters read it,

Do they then wait for anything other than that Allah should come to them and also the angels over the shadows of the clouds. This is similar to Allah's other statement:

(And (remember) the Day when the heaven shall be rent asunder with clouds, and the angels will be sent down, with a grand descending.) (25:25)

### Surah: 2 Ayah: 211 & Ayah: 212

﴿ سَلْ بَنِى إِسْرَٰٓءِيلَ كَمْ ءَاتَيْنَٰهُم مِّنْ ءَايَةٍۭ بَيِّنَةٍ ۗ وَمَن يُبَدِّلْ نِعْمَةَ ٱللَّهِ مِنۢ بَعْدِ مَا جَآءَتْهُ فَإِنَّ ٱللَّهَ شَدِيدُ ٱلْعِقَابِ ۝ ﴾

211. Ask the Children of Israel how many clear Ayât (proofs, evidences, verses, lessons, signs, revelations, etc.) We gave them. And whoever changes Allâh's Favor after it had come to him, (e.g. renounces the Religion of Allâh (Islâm) and accepts Kufr (disbelief)) then surely, Allâh is Severe punishment.

﴿ زُيِّنَ لِلَّذِينَ كَفَرُواْ ٱلْحَيَوٰةُ ٱلدُّنْيَا وَيَسْخَرُونَ مِنَ ٱلَّذِينَ ءَامَنُواْ وَٱلَّذِينَ ٱتَّقَوْاْ فَوْقَهُمْ يَوْمَ ٱلْقِيَـٰمَةِ ۗ وَٱللَّهُ يَرْزُقُ مَن يَشَآءُ بِغَيْرِ حِسَابٍ ﴾

212. Beautified is the life of this world for those who disbelieve, and they mock at those who believe. But those who obey Allâh's Orders and keep away from what He has forbidden, will be above them on the Day of Resurrection. And Allâh gives (of His Bounty, Blessings, Favors, Honors on the Day of Resurrection) to whom He wills without limit.

### Transliteration

211. Sal banee isra-eela kam ataynahum min ayatin bayyinatin waman yubaddil niAAmata Allahi min baAAdi ma jaat-hu fa-inna Allaha shadeedu alAAiqabi 212. Zuyyina lillatheena kafaroo alhayatu alddunya wayaskharoona mina allatheena amanoo waallatheena ittaqaw fawqahum yawma alqiyamati waAllahu yarzuqu man yashao bighayri hisabin

### Tafsir Ibn Kathir

### The Punishment for changing Allah's Favor and mocking the Believers

Allah mentioned that the Children of Israel, were witnesses to many clear signs that attest to the truth of Moses regarding what he was sent with for them. They witnessed his hand (when it became lit with light), his parting the sea, his striking the rock (and water flowed from the rock), the clouds that shaded them during the intense heat, the manna and the quails, and so forth. These signs attested to the existence of the Creator and the truth of Moses by whose hand these signs appeared. Yet, so many among them changed Allah's favor, by preferring disbelief to faith and by ignoring Allah's favors,

(And whoever changes Allah's favor after it had come to him, then surely, Allah is severe in punishment.)

Similarly, Allah said about the disbelievers of Quraysh:

(Have you not seen those who have changed the blessings of Allah into disbelief, and caused their people to dwell in the house of destruction Hell, in which they will burn, - and what an evil place to settle in!) (14:28, 29)

Then Allah states that He has made the life of this world beautiful for the disbelievers who are satisfied with it, who collect wealth, but refrain from spending it on what they have been commanded, which could earn them

Allah's pleasure. Instead, they ridicule the believers who ignore this life and who spend whatever they earn on what pleases their Lord. The believers spend seeking Allah's Face, and this is why they have gained the ultimate happiness and the best share on the Day of the Return. Therefore, they will be exalted above the disbelievers at the Gathering Place, when they are gathered, during the resurrection and in their final destination. The believers will reside in the highest grades in the utmost highs, while the disbelievers will reside in the lowest of lows (in the Fire).

This is why Allah said:

(And Allah gives to whom He wills without limit.)

This Ayah indicates that Allah gives sustenance to whomever He wills of His servants without count or limit in this and the Hereafter. A Hadith has stated (that Allah said):

«ابْنَ آدَمَ أَنْفِقْ أُنْفِقْ عَلَيْكَ»

(O son of Adam! Spend (in Allah's cause) and I (Allah) will spend on you.) The Prophet said:

«أَنْفِقْ بِلَالُ وَلَا تَخْشَ مِنْ ذِي الْعَرْشِ إِقْلَالًا»

(O Bilal! Spend and do not fear deprivation from the Owner of the Throne.)

Allah said:

(...and whatsoever you spend of anything (in Allah's cause), He will replace it.) (34:39) In addition, it is reported in the Sahih (that the Prophet said):

«أَنَّ مَلَكَيْنِ يَنْزِلَانِ مِنَ السَّمَاءِ صَبِيحَةَ كُلِّ يَوْمٍ فَيَقُولُ أَحَدُهُمَا: اللَّهُمَّ أَعْطِ مُنْفِقًا خَلَفًا، وَيَقُولُ الْآخَرُ: اللَّهُمَّ أَعْطِ مُمْسِكًا تَلَفًا»

(Every day two angels come down from heavens and one of them says, `O Allah! Compensate every person who spends in Your cause,' and the other (angel) says, `O Allah! Destroy every miser.') Also in the Sahih:

«يَقُولُ ابْنُ آدَمَ: مَالِي مَالِي. وَهَلْ لَكَ مِنْ مَالِكَ إِلَّا مَا أَكَلْتَ فَأَفْنَيْتَ، وَمَا لَبِسْتَ فَأَبْلَيْتَ، وَمَا تَصَدَّقْتَ فَأَمْضَيْتَ، وَمَا سِوَى ذَلِكَ

»فَذَاهِبٌ وَتَارِكُهُ لِلنَّاسِ«

(The son of Adam says, `My money, my money!' Yet, what is your money except that which you eat and use up, wear and tear, and spend in charity and thus keep (in your record). Other than that, it will go away and will be left for the people (the inheritors).)

In addition, Imam Ahmad reported that the Prophet said:

»الدُّنْيَا دَارُ مَنْ لَا دَارَ لَهُ، وَمَالُ مَنْ لَا مَالَ لَهُ، وَلَهَا يَجْمَعُ مَنْ لَا عَقْلَ لَه«

(The Dunya (life of this world) is the residence of those who have no residence, the wealth of those who have no wealth, and it is harvested by those who have no sense of reason.)

### Surah: 2 Ayah: 213

﴿كَانَ ٱلنَّاسُ أُمَّةً وَٰحِدَةً فَبَعَثَ ٱللَّهُ ٱلنَّبِيِّـۧنَ مُبَشِّرِينَ وَمُنذِرِينَ وَأَنزَلَ مَعَهُمُ ٱلْكِتَٰبَ بِٱلْحَقِّ لِيَحْكُمَ بَيْنَ ٱلنَّاسِ فِيمَا ٱخْتَلَفُوا۟ فِيهِ ۚ وَمَا ٱخْتَلَفَ فِيهِ إِلَّا ٱلَّذِينَ أُوتُوهُ مِنۢ بَعْدِ مَا جَآءَتْهُمُ ٱلْبَيِّنَٰتُ بَغْيًۢا بَيْنَهُمْ ۖ فَهَدَى ٱللَّهُ ٱلَّذِينَ ءَامَنُوا۟ لِمَا ٱخْتَلَفُوا۟ فِيهِ مِنَ ٱلْحَقِّ بِإِذْنِهِۦ ۗ وَٱللَّهُ يَهْدِى مَن يَشَآءُ إِلَىٰ صِرَٰطٍ مُّسْتَقِيمٍ ۝٢١٣﴾

213. Mankind were one community and Allâh sent Prophets with glad tidings and warnings, and with them He sent down the Scripture in truth to judge between people in matters wherein they differed. And only those to whom (the Scripture) was given differed concerning it after clear proofs had come unto them through hatred, one to another. Then Allâh by His Leave guided those who believed to the truth of that wherein they differed. And Allâh guides whom He wills to the Straight Path.

### Transliteration

213. Kana alnnasu ommatan wahidatan fabaAAatha Allahu alnnabiyyeena mubashshireena wamunthireena waanzala maAAahumu alkitaba bialhaqqi liyahkuma bayna alnnasi feema ikhtalafoo feehi wama ikhtalafa feehi illa allatheena ootoohu min baAAdi ma jaat-humu albayyinatu baghyan baynahum fahada Allahu allatheena amanoo lima ikhtalafoo feehi mina alhaqqi bi-ithnihi waAllahu yahdee man yashao ila siratin mustaqeemin

## Tafsir Ibn Kathir

### Disputing, after the Clear Signs have come, indicates Deviation

Ibn Jarir reported that Ibn `Abbas said, "There were ten generations between Adam and Nuh, all of them on the religion of Truth. They later disputed so Allah sent the Prophets as warners and bringers of glad tidings." He then said that this is how `Abdullah read the Ayah:

The people were one Ummah and they then disputed.

Al-Hakim recorded this in his Mustadrak and said, "Its chain of narrators is Sahih, but they (Al-Bukhari and Muslim) did not record it." Abu Ja`far Razi reported that Abu Al-`Aliyah said that Ubayy bin Ka`b read the Ayah as:

The people were one Ummah and they then disputed and Allah sent the Prophets as warners and bringers of glad tidings.

`Abdur-Razzaq said that Ma`mar said that Qatadah said that Allah's statement:

(Mankind was one community) means; "They all had the guidance. Then:

They disputed and Allah sent Prophets.

The first to be sent was Nuh."

`Abdur-Razzaq reported that Abu Hurayrah commented on:

(Then Allah by His leave guided those who believed to the truth of that wherein they differed. ) saying that the Prophet said:

«نَحْنُ الْآخِرُونَ الْأَوَّلُونَ يَوْمَ الْقِيَامَةِ، نَحْنُ أَوَّلُ النَّاسِ دُخُولًا الْجَنَّةَ، بَيْدَ أَنَّهُمْ أُوتُوا الْكِتَابَ مِنْ قَبْلِنَا وَأُوتِينَاهُ مِنْ بَعْدِهِمْ، فَهَدَانَا اللهُ لِمَا اخْتَلَفُوا فِيهِ مِنَ الْحَقِّ بِإِذْنِهِ، فَهَذَا الْيَوْمُ الَّذِي اخْتَلَفُوا فِيهِ فَهَدَانَا اللهُ لَهُ، فَالنَّاسُ لَنَا فِيهِ تَبَعٌ، فَغَدًا لِلْيَهُودِ، وَبَعْدَ غَدٍ لِلنَّصَارَى»

(We are the last (nation), but the first (foremost) on the Day of Resurrection. We are the first people to enter Paradise, although they (Jews and Christians) have been given the Book before us and we after them. Allah has guided us to the truth wherever they disputed over it. This is the day (Friday) that they disputed about, Allah guided us to it. So, the people follow us, as tomorrow is for the Jews and the day after is for the Christians.)

Ibn Wahb related that `Abdur-Rahman bin Zayd bin Aslam said that his father said about the Ayah:

(Then Allah by His leave guided those who believed to the truth of that wherein they differed.)

They disputed about the day of Congregation (Friday). The Jews made it Saturday while the Christians chose Sunday. Allah guided the Ummah of Muhammad to Friday. They also disputed about the true Qiblah. The Christians faced the east while the Jews faced Bayt Al-Maqdis. Allah guided the Ummah of Muhammad to the true Qiblah (Ka`bah in Makkah). They also disputed about the prayer, as some of them bow down, but do not prostrate, while others prostrate, but do not bow down. Some of them pray while talking and some while walking. Allah guided the Ummah of Muhammad to the truth. They also disputed about the fast; some of them fast during a part of the day, while others fast from certain types of foods. Allah guided the Ummah of Muhammad to the truth. They also disputed about Ibrahim. The Jews said, `He was a Jew,' while the Christians considered him Christian. Allah has made him a Haniyfan Musliman. Allah has guided the Ummah of Muhammad to the truth.

They also disputed about `Isa. The Jews rejected him and accused his mother of a grave sin, while the Christians made him a god and the son of God. Allah made him by His Word and a spirit from (those He created) Him. Allah guided the Ummah of Muhammad to the truth."

Allah then said:

(...by His leave) meaning, `By His knowledge of them and by what He has directed and guided them to,' according to Ibn Jarir. Also:

(And Allah guides whom He wills) means from among His creation. (Allah said:)

(...to the straight way) meaning, He commands the decision and the clear proof. Al-Bukhari and Muslim reported that `A'ishah narrated that when Allah's Messenger used to wake up at night to pray, he would say:

(O Allah, the Lord of (angels) Jibril, Mika'il and Israfil, Creator of the heavens and earth and Knower of the seen and the unseen. You judge between Your servants regarding what they have disputed in, so guide me to what have been the subject of dispute of the truth by Your leave. Indeed, You guide whom You will to the straight path.(

A Du`a reads:

»اللَّهُمَّ أَرِنَا الْحَقَّ حَقًّا، وَارْزُقْنَا اتِّبَاعَهُ، وَأَرِنَا الْبَاطِلَ بَاطِلًا، وَارْزُقْنَا اجْتِنَابَهُ، وَلَا تَجْعَلْهُ مُلْتَبِسًا عَلَيْنَا فَنَضِلَّ، وَاجْعَلْنَا لِلْمُتَّقِينَ إِمَامًا«

(O Allah! Show us the truth as truth, and bestow adherence to it on us. Show us the evil as evil, and make us stay away from it, and do not confuse us regarding the reality of evil so that we will not be led astray by it, and make us leaders for the believers.)

### Surah: 2 Ayah: 214

﴿ أَمْ حَسِبْتُمْ أَن تَدْخُلُوا۟ ٱلْجَنَّةَ وَلَمَّا يَأْتِكُم مَّثَلُ ٱلَّذِينَ خَلَوْا۟ مِن قَبْلِكُم مَّسَّتْهُمُ ٱلْبَأْسَآءُ وَٱلضَّرَّآءُ وَزُلْزِلُوا۟ حَتَّىٰ يَقُولَ ٱلرَّسُولُ وَٱلَّذِينَ ءَامَنُوا۟ مَعَهُۥ مَتَىٰ نَصْرُ ٱللَّهِ أَلَآ إِنَّ نَصْرَ ٱللَّهِ قَرِيبٌ ﴾

214. Or think you that you will enter Paradise without such (trials) as came to those who passed away before you? They were afflicted with severe poverty and ailments and were so shaken that even the Messenger and those who believed along with him said, "When (will come) the Help of Allâh?" Yes! Certainly, the Help of Allâh is near!

### Transliteration

214. Am hasibtum an tadkhuloo aljannata walamma ya/tikum mathalu allatheena khalaw min qablikum massat-humu alba/sao waalddarrao wazulziloo hatta yaqoola alrrasoolu waallatheena amanoo maAAahu mata nasru Allahi ala inna nasra Allahi qareebun

### Tafsir Ibn Kathir

#### Victory only comes after succeeding in the Trials

Allah said:

(Or think you that you will enter Paradise) before you are tested and tried just like the nations that came before you This is why Allah said:

(...without such (trials) as came to those who passed away before you They were afflicted with severe poverty and ailments) meaning, illnesses, pain, disasters and hardships. Ibn Mas`ud, Ibn `Abbas, Abu Al-`Aliyah, Mujahid, Sa`id bin Jubayr, Murrah Al-Hamdani, Al-Hasan, Qatadah, Ad-Dahhak, Ar-Rabi`, As-Suddi and Muqatil bin Hayyan said that

(Al-Ba'sa') means poverty. Ibn `Abbas said that

(...and Ad-Darra') means ailments.

(and were so shaken) for fear of the enemy, and were tested, and put to a tremendous trial. An authentic Hadith narrated that Khabbab bin Al-Aratt said, "We said, `O Messenger of Allah! Why do you not invoke Allah to support us Why do you not supplicate to Allah for us' He said:

«إِنَّ مَنْ كَانَ قَبْلَكُمْ كَانَ أَحَدُهُمْ يُوضَعُ الْمِنْشَارُ عَلَى مَفْرِقِ رَأْسِهِ فَيَخْلُصُ إِلَى قَدَمَيْهِ لَا يَصْرِفُهُ ذَلِكَ عَنْ دِينِهِ، وَيُمْشَطُ بِأَمْشَاطِ الْحَدِيدِ مَا بَيْنَ لَحْمِهِ وَعَظْمِهِ، لَا يَصْرِفُهُ ذَلِكَ عَنْ دِينِهِ.»

(The saw would be placed on the middle of the head of one of those who were before you (believers) and he would be sawn until his feet, and he would be combed with iron combs between his skin and bones, yet that would not make him change his religion.)

He then said:

«وَاللهِ لَيُتِمَّنَّ اللهُ هَذَا الْأَمْرَ حَتَّى يَسِيرَ الرَّاكِبُ مِنْ صَنْعَاءَ إِلَى حَضْرَمَوْتَ، لَا يَخَافُ إِلَّا اللهَ وَالذِّئْبَ عَلَى غَنَمِهِ، وَلَكِنَّكُمْ قَوْمٌ تَسْتَعْجِلُونَ»

(By Allah! This matter (religion) will spread (or expand) by Allah until the traveler leaves San`a' to Hadramawt (both in Yemen, but at a great distance from each other) fearing only Allah and then the wolf for the sake of his sheep. You are just a hasty people.)

And Allah said:

(Alif-Lam-Mim. Do people think that they will be left alone because they say: "We believe," and will not be tested And We indeed tested those who were before them. And Allah will certainly make (it) known (the truth of) those who are true, and will certainly make (it) known (the falsehood of) those who are liars.) (29:1-3)

The Companions experienced tremendous trials during the battle of Al-Ahzab (the Confederates). Allah said:

(When they came upon you from above you and from below you, and when the eyes grew wild and the hearts reached to the throats, and you were harboring doubts about Allah. There, the believers were tried and shaken with a mighty shaking. And when the hypocrites and those in whose hearts is a disease (of doubts) said: "Allah and His Messenger promised us nothing but delusion!") (33:10-12)

When Heraclius asked Abu Sufyan, "Did you fight him (Prophet Muhammad)" He said, "Yes." Heraclius said, "What was the outcome of warfare between you" Abu Sufyan said, "Sometimes we lose and sometimes he loses." He said, "Such is the case with Prophets, they are tested, but the final victory is theirs."

Allah's statement:

(...without (such) (trials) as came to those who passed away before you) meaning, their way of life. Similarly, Allah said:

(Then We destroyed men stronger (in power) than these - and the example of the ancients has passed away (before them)) (43: 8) and:

(...were so shaken that even the Messenger and those who believed along with him said, "When (will come) the help of Allah.")

They pleaded (to Allah) for victory against their enemies and invoked Him for aid and deliverance from their hardships and trials. Allah said:

(Yes! Certainly, the help of Allah is near!)

Allah said:

(Verily, along with every hardship is relief. Verily, along with every hardship is relief.) (94:5, 6)

So just as there is hardship, its equal of relief will soon arrive. This is why Allah said:

(Yes! Certainly, the help of Allah is near!)

### Surah: 2 Ayah: 215

﴿ يَسْـَٔلُونَكَ مَاذَا يُنفِقُونَ ۖ قُلْ مَآ أَنفَقْتُم مِّنْ خَيْرٍ فَلِلْوَٰلِدَيْنِ وَٱلْأَقْرَبِينَ وَٱلْيَتَـٰمَىٰ وَٱلْمَسَـٰكِينِ وَٱبْنِ ٱلسَّبِيلِ ۗ وَمَا تَفْعَلُوا۟ مِنْ خَيْرٍ فَإِنَّ ٱللَّهَ بِهِۦ عَلِيمٌ

215. They ask you (O Muhammad (peace be upon him)) what they should spend. Say: Whatever you spend of good must be for parents and kindred and orphans and Al-Masâkin (the poor) and the wayfarers, and whatever you do of good deeds, truly, Allâh knows it well.

### Transliteration

215. Yas-aloonaka matha yunfiqoona qul ma anfaqtum min khayrin falilwalidayni waal-aqrabeena waalyatama waalmasakeeni waibni alssabeeli wama tafAAaloo min khayrin fa-inna Allaha bihi AAaleemun

### Translation

215. They ask you (O Muhammad SAW) what they should spend. Say: Whatever you spend of good must be for parents and kindred and orphans and *AlMasâkin* (the poor) and the wayfarers, and whatever you do of good deeds, truly, Allâh knows it well.

### Tafsir Ibn Kathir

#### Who deserves the Nafaqah (Spending or Charity)

Muqatil bin Hayyan said that this Ayah was revealed about the voluntary charity. The Ayah means, `They ask you (O Muhammad ) how they should spend,' as Ibn `Abbas and Mujahid have stated. So, Allah explained it for them, saying:

(Say: "Whatever you spend of good must be for parents and kindred and orphans and Al-Masakin and the wayfarer,") meaning, spend it on these categories or areas. Similarly, a Hadith states (that those who deserve one's generosity the most, are):

»أُمَّكَ وَأَبَاكَ وَأُخْتَكَ وَأَخَاكَ ثُمَّ أَدْنَاكَ أَدْنَاكَ«

(Your mother, father, sister, brother, the closest and then the farthest (relatives).)

Maymun bin Mihran once recited this Ayah (2:215) and commented, "These are the areas of spending. Allah did not mention among them the drums, pipe, wooden pictures, or the curtains that cover the walls."

Next, Allah said:

(...and whatever you do of good deeds, truly, Allah knows it well.) meaning, whatever you perform of good works, Allah knows them and He will reward you for them in the best manner, no one will be dealt with unjustly, even the weight of an atom.

### Surah: 2 Ayah: 216

﴿كُتِبَ عَلَيْكُمُ ٱلْقِتَالُ وَهُوَ كُرْهٌ لَّكُمْ ۖ وَعَسَىٰ أَن تَكْرَهُوا۟ شَيْـًٔا وَهُوَ خَيْرٌ لَّكُمْ ۖ وَعَسَىٰ أَن تُحِبُّوا۟ شَيْـًٔا وَهُوَ شَرٌّ لَّكُمْ ۗ وَٱللَّهُ يَعْلَمُ وَأَنتُمْ لَا تَعْلَمُونَ ﴾

216. Jihâd (holy fighting in Allâh's Cause) is ordained for you (Muslims) though you dislike it, and it may be that you dislike a thing which is good for you

and that you like a thing which is bad for you. Allâh knows but you do not know.

## Transliteration

216. Kutiba AAalaykumu alqitalu wahuwa kurhun lakum waAAasa an takrahoo shay-an wahuwa khayrun lakum waAAasa an tuhibboo shay-an wahuwa sharrun lakum waAllahu yaAAlamu waantum la taAAlamoona

## Tafsir Ibn Kathir

### Jihad is made Obligatory

In this Ayah, Allah made it obligatory for the Muslims to fight in Jihad against the evil of the enemy who transgress against Islam. Az-Zuhri said, "Jihad is required from every person, whether he actually joins the fighting or remains behind. Whoever remains behind is required to give support, if support is warranted; to provide aid, if aid is needed; and to march forth, if he is commanded to do so. If he is not needed, then he remains behind." It is reported in the Sahih:

«مَنْ مَاتَ وَلَمْ يَغْزُ وَلَمْ يُحَدِّثْ نَفْسَهُ بِالْغَزْوِ، مَاتَ مِيتَةً جَاهِلِيَّةً»

(Whoever dies but neither fought (i.e., in Allah's cause), nor sincerely considered fighting, will die a death of Jahiliyyah (pre-Islamic era of ignorance).)

On the day of Al-Fath (when he conquered Makkah), the Prophet said:

«لَا هِجْرَةَ بَعْدَ الْفَتْحِ وَلكِنْ جِهَادٌ وَنِيَّةٌ، وَإِذَا اسْتُنْفِرْتُمْ فَانْفِرُوا»

(There is no Hijrah (migration from Makkah to Al-Madinah) after the victory, but only Jihad and good intention. If you were required to march forth, then march forth.)

Allah's statement:

(...though you dislike it) means, `Fighting is difficult and heavy on your hearts.' Indeed, fighting is as the Ayah describes it, as it includes being killed, wounded, striving against the enemies and enduring the hardship of travel. Allah then said:

(...and it may be that you dislike a thing which is good for you) meaning, fighting is followed by victory, dominance over the enemy, taking over their lands, money and offspring. Allah continues:

(...and that you like a thing which is bad for you.)

This Ayah is general in meaning. Hence, one might covet something, yet in reality it is not good or beneficial for him, such as refraining from joining the Jihad, for it might lead to the enemy taking over the land and the government. Then, Allah said:

(Allah knows, but you do not know.) meaning, He has better knowledge than you of how things will turn out to be in the end, and of what benefits you in this earthly life and the Hereafter. Hence, obey Him and adhere to His commands, so that you may acquire the true guidance.

### Surah: 2 Ayah: 217 & Ayah: 218

﴿ يَسْـَٔلُونَكَ عَنِ ٱلشَّهْرِ ٱلْحَرَامِ قِتَالٍ فِيهِ ۖ قُلْ قِتَالٌ فِيهِ كَبِيرٌ ۖ وَصَدٌّ عَن سَبِيلِ ٱللَّهِ وَكُفْرٌ بِهِۦ وَٱلْمَسْجِدِ ٱلْحَرَامِ وَإِخْرَاجُ أَهْلِهِۦ مِنْهُ أَكْبَرُ عِندَ ٱللَّهِ ۚ وَٱلْفِتْنَةُ أَكْبَرُ مِنَ ٱلْقَتْلِ ۗ وَلَا يَزَالُونَ يُقَـٰتِلُونَكُمْ حَتَّىٰ يَرُدُّوكُمْ عَن دِينِكُمْ إِنِ ٱسْتَطَـٰعُوا۟ ۚ وَمَن يَرْتَدِدْ مِنكُمْ عَن دِينِهِۦ فَيَمُتْ وَهُوَ كَافِرٌ فَأُو۟لَـٰٓئِكَ حَبِطَتْ أَعْمَـٰلُهُمْ فِى ٱلدُّنْيَا وَٱلْـَٔاخِرَةِ ۖ وَأُو۟لَـٰٓئِكَ أَصْحَـٰبُ ٱلنَّارِ هُمْ فِيهَا خَـٰلِدُونَ ﴿٢١٧﴾

217. They ask you concerning fighting in the Sacred Months (i.e. 1st, 7th, 11th and 12th months of the Islâmic calendar). Say, "Fighting therein is a great (transgression) but a greater (transgression) with Allâh is to prevent mankind from following the Way of Allâh, to disbelieve in Him, to prevent access to Al-Masjid-al-Harâm (at Makkah), and to drive out its inhabitants, and Al-Fitnah is worse than killing. And they will never cease fighting you until they turn you back from your religion (Islâmic Monotheism) if they can. And whosoever of you turns back from his religion and dies as a disbeliever, then his deeds will be lost in this life and in the Hereafter, and they will be the dwellers of the Fire. They will abide therein forever."

﴿ إِنَّ ٱلَّذِينَ ءَامَنُوا۟ وَٱلَّذِينَ هَاجَرُوا۟ وَجَـٰهَدُوا۟ فِى سَبِيلِ ٱللَّهِ أُو۟لَـٰٓئِكَ يَرْجُونَ رَحْمَتَ ٱللَّهِ ۚ وَٱللَّهُ غَفُورٌ رَّحِيمٌ ﴿٢١٨﴾

218. Verily, those who have believed, and those who have emigrated (for Allâh's Religion) and have striven hard in the Way of Allâh, all these hope for Allâh's Mercy. And Allâh is Oft-Forgiving, Most-Merciful.

### Transliteration

217. Yas-aloonaka AAani alshshahri alharami qitalin feehi qul qitalun feehi kabeerun wasaddun AAan sabeeli Allahi wakufrun bihi waalmasjidi alharami

wa-ikhraju ahlihi minhu akbaru AAinda Allahi waalfitnatu akbaru mina alqatli wala yazaloona yuqatiloonakum hatta yaruddookum AAan deenikum ini istataAAoo waman yartadid minkum AAan deenihi fayamut wahuwa kafirun faola-ika habitat aAAmaluhum fee alddunya waal-akhirati waola-ika as-habu alnnari hum feeha khalidoona 218. Inna allatheena amanoo waallatheena hajaroo wajahadoo fee sabeeli Allahi ola-ika yarjoona rahmata Allahi waAllahu ghafoorun raheemun

### Tafsir Ibn Kathir

### The Nakhlah Military Maneuvers, and the Ruling on Fighting during the Sacred Months

Ibn Abu Hatim reported that Jundub bin `Abdullah said: Allah's Messenger assembled a group of men under the command of Abu `Ubaydah bin Jarrah. When he was about to march, he started crying for the thought of missing Allah's Messenger . Consequently, the Messenger relieved Abu `Ubaydah from command, appointed `Abdullah bin Jahsh instead, gave him some written instructions and commanded him not to read the instructions until he reached such and such area. He also said to `Abdullah:

«لَا تُكْرِهَنَّ أَحَدًا عَلَى السَّيْرِ مَعَكَ مِنْ أَصْحَابِكَ».

(Do not compel any of your men to continue marching with you thereafter.)

When `Abdullah read the instructions, he recited Istirja` (saying, `Truly! to Allah we belong and truly, to Him we shall return'; and refer to (2:156)) and said, "I hear and obey Allah and His Messenger." He then told his companions the story and read the instructions to them, and two men went back while the rest remained. Soon after, they found Ibn Hadrami (one of the disbelievers of Quraysh) and killed him not knowing that that day was in Rajab or Jumadi (where Rajab is the Sacred Month). The polytheists said to the Muslims, "You have committed murder in the Sacred Month." Allah then revealed:

(They ask you concerning fighting in the Sacred Months. Say, "Fighting therein is a great (transgression)...")

Abdul-Malik bin Hisham, who compiled the Sirah (life story of the Prophet ), related that Ziyad bin `Abdullah Bakka'i said that Muhammad bin Ishaq bin Yasar Al-Madani wrote in his book on the Sirah, "Allah's Messenger sent `Abdullah bin Jahsh bin Riyab Al-Asadi in Rajab, after he (the Prophet ) came back from the first battle of Badr. The Prophet sent eight people with him, all from among the Muhajirun and none from the Ansar. He also gave him some written instructions and ordered him not to read them until he marched for two days. `Abdullah should then read the instructions and march to implement them, but should not force any of those who were with him to accompany him.

The companions of `Abdullah bin Jahsh were all from the Muhajirun, from the tribe of Banu `Abd Shams bin `Abd Manaf, there was Abu Hudhayfah bin `Utbah bin Rabi`ah bin `Abd Shams bin `Abd Manaf. From their allies, there was `Abdullah bin Jahsh, who was the commander of the army unit, and `Ukkashah bin Mihsan from the tribe of Banu Asad bin Khuzaymah. From the tribe of Banu Nawfal bin `Abd Manaf, there was `Utbah bin Ghazwan bin Jabir, one of their allies. From the tribe of Banu Zuhrah bin Kilab, there was Sa`d bin Abu Waqqas. From Banu Ka`b, there were their allies: `Adi bin `Amr bin Ar-Rabi`ah not from the tribe of Ibn Wa'il; Waqid bin `Abdullah bin `Abd Manaf bin `Arin bin Tha`labah bin Yarbu` from Banu Tamim; and Khalid bin Bukair from the tribe of Banu Sa`d bin Layth, Suhayl bin Bayda' from Banu Al-Harith bin Fihr was also among them. When `Abdullah bin Jahsh marched for two days, he opened and read the (Prophet's) instructions, "When you read these instructions, march until you set camp at Nakhlah between Makkah and At-Ta'if. There, watch the movements of the caravan of Quraysh and collect news about them for us." When `Abdullah bin Jahsh read the document, he said, "I hear and obey." He then said to his companions, "Allah's Messenger has commanded me to march forth to Nakhlah to watch the movements of the caravan of Quraysh and to inform him about their news. He has prohibited me from forcing any of you (to go with me). So, those who seek martyrdom, they should march with me. Those who dislike the idea of martyrdom, let them turn back. Surely, I will implement the command of Allah's Messenger ." He and his companions continued without any of them turning back.

`Abdullah entered the Hijaz area (western Arabia) until he reached an area called Buhran, close to Furu`. There, Sa`d bin Abu Waqqas and `Utbah bin Ghazwan lost the camel that they were riding in turns, and they went back to search for it while `Abdullah bin Jahsh and the rest of his companions continued until they reached Nakhlah. Then, a caravan belonging to the Quraysh passed by carrying raisins, food stuff and some trade items for the Quraysh. `Amr bin Hadrami, whose name was `Abdullah bin `Abbad, was in the caravan, as well as `Uthman bin `Abdullah bin Al-Mughirah and his brother Nawfal bin `Abdullah from the tribe of Makhzum, and Al-Hakam bin Kaysan, a freed slave of Hisham bin Al-Mughirah. When they saw the Companions they were frightened, but when they saw `Ukkashah bin Mihsan their fears subsided, since his head was shaved. They said, "These people seek the `Umrah, so there is no need to fear them."

The Companions conferred among themselves. That day was the last day in the (sacred) month of Rajab. They said to each other, "By Allah! If you let them pass, they will soon enter the Sacred Area and take refuge in it from you. If you kill them, you will kill them during the Sacred Month." They at first hesitated and did not like to attack them. They then began encouraging themselves and decided to kill whomever they could among the disbelievers and to confiscate whatever they had. Hence, Waqid bin `Abdullah At-Tamimi shot an arrow at `Amr bin Al-Hadrami and killed him. `Uthman bin `Abdullah and Al-Hakam bin Kaysan gave themselves up, while Nawfal bin `Abdullah was able to outrun them in flight. Later on, `Abdullah bin Jahsh and his companions

Chapter 2: Al-Baqarah (The Cow), Verses 142-252

went back to Allah's Messenger in Al-Madinah with the caravan and the two prisoners. dIbn Ishaq went on: I was told that some members of the family of `Abdullah bin Jahsh said that `Abdullah said to his companions: "Allah's Messenger will have one-fifth of what we have confiscated." This occurred before Allah required one-fifth for His Messenger from the war booty. So, `Abdullah designated one-fifth of the caravan for Allah's Messenger and divided the rest among his companions. Ibn Ishaq also stated that at first, when the Sariyah came back to Allah's Messenger , he said to them:

《مَا أَمَرْتُكُمْ بِقِتَالٍ فِي الشَّهْرِ الْحَرَامِ》

(I have not commanded you to conduct warfare during the Sacred Month. )

He left the caravan and the two prisoners alone and did not take any share of the war booty.

When Allah's Messenger did that, the soldiers from the attack were concerned and felt that they were destroyed, and their Muslim brethren criticized them for what they did. The Quraysh said that Muhammad and his Companions violated the sanctity of the Sacred Month and shed blood, confiscated property and took prisoners during it. Those who refuted them among the Muslims who remained in Makkah replied that the Muslims had done that during the month of Sha`ban (which is not a sacred month). Meanwhile, the Jews were pleased about what happened to Allah's Messenger . They said, ` Amr bin Hadrami was killed by Waqid bin `Abdullah: `Amr, means the war has started, Hadrami means the war has come, as for Waqid (bin `Abdullah): the war has raged (using some of the literal meanings of these names to support their fortune-telling!)." But, Allah made all that turn against them.

The people continued talking about this matter, then Allah revealed to His Messenger :

(They ask you concerning fighting in the Sacred Months. Say, "Fighting therein is a great (transgression) but a greater (transgression) with Allah is to prevent mankind from following the way of Allah, to disbelieve in Him, to prevent access to Al-Masjid Al-Haram (at Makkah), and to drive out its inhabitants, and Al-Fitnah is worse than killing.)

This Ayah means, `If you had killed during the Sacred Month, they (disbelievers of Quraysh) have hindered you from the path of Allah and disbelieved in it. They also prevented you from entering the Sacred Mosque, and expelled you from it, while you are its people,

(...a greater (transgression) with Allah) than killing whom you killed among them. Also:

(...and Al-Fitnah is worse than killing.) means, trying to force the Muslims to revert from their religion and re-embrace Kufr after they had believed, is worse with Allah than killing.' Allah said:

(And they will never cease fighting you until they turn you back from your religion (Islamic Monotheism) if they can.)

So, they will go on fighting you with unrelenting viciousness.

Ibn Ishaq went on: When the Qur'an touched this subject and Allah brought relief to the Muslims instead of the sadness that had befallen them, Allah's Messenger took possession of the caravan and the two prisoners. The Quraysh offered to ransom the two prisoners, `Uthman bin `Abdullah and Hakam bin Kaysan. Allah's Messenger said:

«لَا نَفْدِيكُمُوهُمَا حَتَّى يَقْدَمَ صَاحِبَانَا»

(We will not accept your ransom until our two companions return safely. ) meaning Sa`d bin Abu Waqqas and `Utbah bin Ghazwan, "For we fear for their safety with you. If you kill them, we will kill your people." Later on, Sa`d and `Utbah returned safely and Allah's Messenger accepted the Quraysh's ransom for their prisoners. As for Al-Hakam bin Kaysan, he became Muslim and his Islam strengthened. He remained with Allah's Messenger until he was martyred during the incident at Bir Ma`unah (when the Prophet sent seventy Companions to Najd to teach them Islam, but Banu Sulaim killed them all except two). As for `Uthman bin `Abdullah, he went back to Makkah and died there as a disbeliever.

Ibn Ishaq went on: When `Abdullah bin Jahsh and his companions were relieved from their depressing thoughts after the Qur'an was revealed about this subject, they sought the reward of the fighters (in Allah's way). They said, "O Messenger of Allah! We wish that this incident be considered a battle for us, so that we gain the rewards of the Mujahidin." Then, Allah revealed:

(Verily, those who have believed, and those who have emigrated (for Allah's religion) and have striven hard in the way of Allah, all these hope for Allah's mercy. And Allah is Oft-Forgiving, Most Merciful.)

Hence, Allah has greatly elevated their hopes of gaining what they had wished for.

## Surah: 2 Ayah: 219 & Ayah: 220

﴿ ۞ يَسْـَٔلُونَكَ عَنِ ٱلْخَمْرِ وَٱلْمَيْسِرِ ۖ قُلْ فِيهِمَآ إِثْمٌ كَبِيرٌ وَمَنَـٰفِعُ لِلنَّاسِ وَإِثْمُهُمَآ أَكْبَرُ مِن نَّفْعِهِمَا ۗ وَيَسْـَٔلُونَكَ مَاذَا يُنفِقُونَ قُلِ ٱلْعَفْوَ ۗ كَذَٰلِكَ يُبَيِّنُ ٱللَّهُ لَكُمُ ٱلْـَٔايَـٰتِ لَعَلَّكُمْ تَتَفَكَّرُونَ ﴿٢١٩﴾ ﴾

219. They ask you (O Muhammad (peace be upon him)) concerning alcoholic drink and gambling. Say: "In them is a great sin, and (some) benefit for men, but the sin of them is greater than their benefit." And they ask you what they ought to spend. Say: "That which is beyond your needs." Thus Allâh makes clear to you His Laws in order that you may give thought."

﴿ فِى ٱلدُّنْيَا وَٱلْـَٔاخِرَةِ ۗ وَيَسْـَٔلُونَكَ عَنِ ٱلْيَتَـٰمَىٰ ۖ قُلْ إِصْلَاحٌ لَّهُمْ خَيْرٌ ۖ وَإِن تُخَالِطُوهُمْ فَإِخْوَٰنُكُمْ ۚ وَٱللَّهُ يَعْلَمُ ٱلْمُفْسِدَ مِنَ ٱلْمُصْلِحِ ۚ وَلَوْ شَآءَ ٱللَّهُ لَأَعْنَتَكُمْ ۚ إِنَّ ٱللَّهَ عَزِيزٌ حَكِيمٌ ﴿٢٢٠﴾ ﴾

220. In (to) this worldly life and in the Hereafter. And they ask you concerning orphans. Say: "The best thing is to work honestly in their property, and if you mix your affairs with theirs, then they are your brothers. And Allâh knows him who means mischief (e.g. to swallow their property) from him who means good (e.g. to save their property). And if Allâh had wished, He could have put you into difficulties. Truly, Allâh is All-Mighty, All-Wise."

### Transliteration

219. Yas-aloonaka AAani alkhamri waalmaysiri qul feehima ithmun kabeerun wamanafiAAu lilnnasi wa-ithmuhuma akbaru min nafAAihima wayas-aloonaka matha yunfiqoona quli alAAafwa kathalika yubayyinu Allahu lakumu al-ayati laAAallakum tatafakkaroona 220. Fee alddunya waal-akhirati wayas-aloonaka AAani alyatama qul islahun lahum khayrun wa-in tukhalitoohum fa-ikhwanukum waAllahu yaAAlamu almufsida mina almuslihi walaw shaa Allahu laAAnatakum inna Allaha AAazeezun hakeemun

### Tafsir Ibn Kathir

### The Gradual Prohibition of Khamr (Alchoholic Drink)

Imam Ahmad recorded that Abu Maysarah said that `Umar once said, "O Allah! Give us a clear ruling regarding Al-Khamr!" Allah sent down the Ayah of Surat Al-Baqarah:

(They ask you (O Muhammad ) concerning alcoholic drink and gambling. Say: "In them is a great sin...)

`Umar was then summoned and the Ayah was recited to him. Yet, he still said, "O Allah! Give us a clear ruling regarding Al-Khamr." Then, this Ayah that is in Surat An-Nisa' was revealed:

(O you who believe! Approach not As-Salah (the prayer) when you are in a drunken state.) (4:43)

Then, when the prayer was called for, a person used to herald on behalf of Allah's Messenger, "No drunk person should attend the prayer." `Umar was summoned again and the Ayah was recited to him. Yet, he still said, "O Allah! Give us a clear ruling regarding Al-Khamr." Then, the Ayah that is in Surat Al-Ma'idah was revealed, `Umar was again summoned and the Ayah was recited to him. When he reached:

(So, will you not then abstain) (5:91) he said, "We did abstain, we did abstain." This is also the narration that Abu Dawud, At-Tirmidhi and An-Nasai collected in their books. `Ali bin Al-Madini and At-Tirmidhi said that the chain of narrators for this Hadith is sound and authentic. We will mention this Hadith again along with what Imam Ahmad collected by Abu Hurayrah Allah's saying in Surat Al-Ma'idah:

(Intoxicants and gambling, and Al-Ansab, and Al-Azlam are an abomination of Satan's handiwork. So avoid (strictly all) that (abomination) in order that you may be successful.) (5:90)

Allah said:

(They ask you (O Muhammad ) concerning alcoholic drinks and gambling.)

As for Al-Khamr, `Umar bin Khattab, the Leader of the faithful, used to say, "It includes all what intoxicates the mind." We will also mention this statement in the explanation of Surat Al-Ma'idah, along with the topic of gambling.

Allah said:

(Say: In them is a great sin, and (some) benefits for men.)

As for the harm that the Khamr and gambling cause, it effects the religion. As for their benefit, it is material, including benefit for the body, digesting the food, getting rid of the excrements, sharpening the mind, bringing about a joyous sensation and financially benefiting from their sale. Also, (their benefit includes) earnings through gambling that one uses to spend on his family and on himself. Yet, these benefits are outweighed by the clear harm that they cause which affects the mind and the religion. This is why Allah said:

(...but the sin of them is greater than their benefit.)

This Ayah was the beginning of the process of prohibiting Khamr, not explicity, but it only implied this meaning. So when this Ayah was recited to `Umar, he still said, "O Allah! Give us a clear ruling regarding Al-Khamr." Soon after, Allah sent down a clear prohibition of Khamr in Surat Al-Ma'idah:

(O you who believe! Intoxicants (all kinds of alcoholic drinks), and gambling, and Al-Ansab, and Al-Azlam are an abomination of Shaytan's handiwork. So avoid (strictly all) that (abomination) in order that you may be successful. Shaytan wants only to excite enmity and hatred between you with intoxicants (alcoholic drinks) and gambling, and hinder you from the remembrance of Allah and from As-Salah (the prayer). So, will you not then abstain) (5:90, 91)

We will mention this subject, by the will of Allah, when we explain Surat Al-Ma'idah.

Ibn `Umar, Ash-Sha`bi, Mujahid, Qatadah, Ar-Rabi` bin Anas and `Abdur-Rahman bin Aslam stated that the first Ayah revealed about Khamr was:

(They ask you about Khamr and gambling. Say: "In them there is great sin.") (2:219)

Then, the Ayah in Surat An-Nisa' was revealed (on this subject) and then the Ayah in Surat Al-Ma'idah which prohibited Khamr.

### Spending whatever One could spare of his Money on Charity

Allah said:

(And they ask you what they ought to spend. Say: "That which is (spare) beyond your needs.")

Al-Hakam said that Miqsam said that Ibn `Abbas said that this Ayah means, whatever you can spare above the needs of your family. This is also the opinion of Ibn `Umar, Mujahid, `Ata', `Ikrimah, Sa`id bin Jubayr, Muhammad bin Ka`b, Al-Hasan, Qatadah, Al-Qasim, Salim, `Ata' Al-Khurasani and Ar-Rabi` bin Anas.

Ibn Jarir related that Abu Hurayrah said that a man said, "O Messenger of Allah! I have a Dinar (a currency)." The Prophet said:

«أَنْفِقْهُ عَلَى نَفْسِكَ»

(Spend it you on yourself.) He said, "I have another Dinar." He said:

«أَنْفِقْهُ عَلَى أَهْلِكَ»

(Spend it on your wife.) He said, "I have another Dinar." He said:

«أَنْفِقْهُ عَلَى وَلَدِكَ»

(Spend it on your offspring.) He said, "I have another Dinar." He said:

«فَأَنْتَ أَبْصَرُ»

(You have better knowledge (meaning how and where to spend it in charity).)

Muslim also recorded this Hadith in his Sahih.

Muslim recorded that Jabir said that Allah's Messenger said to a man:

«ابْدَأْ بِنَفْسِكَ فَتَصَدَّقْ عَلَيْهَا، فَإِنْ فَضَلَ شَيْءٌ فَلِأَهْلِكَ، فَإِنْ فَضَلَ شَيْءٌ عَنْ أَهْلِكَ فَلِذِي قَرَابَتِكَ، فَإِنْ فَضَلَ عَنْ ذِي قَرَابَتِكَ شَيْءٌ فَهكَذَا وَهكَذَا»

(Start with yourself and grant it some charity. If anything remains, then spend it on your family. If anything remains, then spend it on your relatives. If anything remains, then spend it like this and like that (i.e., on various charitable purposes).)

A Hadith states:

«ابْنَ آدَمَ إِنَّكَ أَنْ تَبْذُلَ الْفَضْلَ خَيْرٌ لَكَ، وَأَنْ تُمْسِكَهُ شَرٌّ لَكَ، وَلَا تُلَامُ عَلَى كَفَافٍ»

(O son of Adam! If you spend whatever you can spare, it would be better for you; but if you keep it, it would be worse for you. You shall not be blamed for whatever is barely sufficient.)

Allah said:

(Thus Allah makes clear to you His Ayat in order that you may give thought. In (to) this worldly life and in the Hereafter.) meaning, just as He stated and explained these commandments for you, He also explains the rest of His Ayat regarding the commandments and His promises and warnings, so that you might give thought in this life and the Hereafter. `Ali bin Abu Talhah said that Ibn `Abbas commented, "Meaning about the imminent demise and the brevity of this life, and the imminent commencement of the Hereafter and its continuity."

## Maintaining the Orphan's Property

Allah said:

(And they ask you concerning orphans. Say: "The best thing is to work honestly in their property, and if you mix your affairs with theirs, then they are your brothers. And Allah knows him who means mischief (e.g., to swallow their property) from him who means good (e.g., to save their property). And if Allah had wished, He could have put you into difficulties.)

Ibn Jarir reported that Ibn `Abbas said, "When the Ayat:

(And come not near to the orphan's property, except to improve it.) (6:152) and

(Verily, those who unjustly eat up the property of orphans, they eat up only fire into their bellies, and they will be burnt in the blazing Fire!) (4:10) were revealed, those who took care of some orphans, separated their food and drink from the orphans' food and drink. When some of the orphans' food and drink remained, they would keep it for them until they eat it or otherwise get spoiled. This situation was difficult for them and they mentioned this subject to Allah's Messenger .

(And they ask you concerning orphans. Say: "The best thing is to work honestly in their property, and if you mix your affairs with theirs, then they are your brothers.) Hence, they joined their food and drink with the food and drink of the orphans." This Hadith was also collected by Abu Dawud, An-Nasa'i and Al-Hakim in his Mustadrak. Several others said similarly about the circumstances surrounding the revelation of the Ayah (2:220), including Mujahid, `Ata', Ash-Sha`bi, Ibn Abu Layla, Qatadah and others among the Salaf and those after them.

Ibn Jarir reported that `A'ishah said, "I dislike that an orphan's money be under my care, unless I mix my food with his food and my drink with his drink."

Allah said:

(Say: The best thing is to work honestly in their property.) meaning, on the one hand (i.e., this is required in any case). Allah then said:

(...and if you mix your affairs with theirs, then they are your brothers.) meaning, there is no harm if you mix your food and drink with their food and drink, since they are your brothers in the religion. This is why Allah said afterwards:

(And Allah knows (the one) who means mischief (e.g., to swallow their property) from (the one) who means good (e.g., to save their property). ) meaning, He knows those whose intent is to cause mischief or righteousness. He also said:

(And if Allah had wished, He could have put you into difficulties. Truly, Allah is All-Mighty, All-Wise) meaning, if Allah wills, He will make this matter difficult for you. But, He made it easy for you, and allowed you to mix your affairs with the orphans' affairs in a way that is better. Similarly, Allah said:

(And come not near to the orphan's property, except to improve it.) (6:152)

Allah has thus allowed spending from the orphan's estate by its executor, in reasonable proportions, on the condition that he has the intention to compensate the orphan later on, when he can afford it. We will mention about it in detail in Surat An-Nisa' by Allah's will.

### Surah: 2 Ayah: 221

﴿ وَلَا تَنكِحُوا۟ ٱلْمُشْرِكَٰتِ حَتَّىٰ يُؤْمِنَّ ۚ وَلَأَمَةٌ مُّؤْمِنَةٌ خَيْرٌ مِّن مُّشْرِكَةٍ وَلَوْ أَعْجَبَتْكُمْ ۗ وَلَا تُنكِحُوا۟ ٱلْمُشْرِكِينَ حَتَّىٰ يُؤْمِنُوا۟ ۚ وَلَعَبْدٌ مُّؤْمِنٌ خَيْرٌ مِّن مُّشْرِكٍ وَلَوْ أَعْجَبَكُمْ ۗ أُو۟لَٰٓئِكَ يَدْعُونَ إِلَى ٱلنَّارِ ۖ وَٱللَّهُ يَدْعُوٓا۟ إِلَى ٱلْجَنَّةِ وَٱلْمَغْفِرَةِ بِإِذْنِهِۦ ۖ وَيُبَيِّنُ ءَايَٰتِهِۦ لِلنَّاسِ لَعَلَّهُمْ يَتَذَكَّرُونَ ﴾

221. And do not marry Al-Mushrikât (idolatresses) till they believe (worship Allâh Alone). And indeed a slave woman who believes is better than a (free) Mushrikah (idolatress), even though she pleases you. And give not (your daughters) in marriage to Al-Mushrikûn till they believe (in Allâh Alone) and verily, a believing slave is better than a (free) Mushrik (idolater), even though he pleases you. Those (Al-Mushrikûn) invite you to the Fire, but Allâh invites (you) to Paradise and Forgiveness by His Leave, and makes His Ayât (proofs, evidences, verses, lessons, signs, revelations) clear to mankind that they may remember.

### Transliteration

221. Wala tankihoo almushrikati hatta yu/minna walaamatun mu/minatun khayrun min mushrikatin walaw aAAjabatkum wala tunkihoo almushrikeena hatta yu/minoo walaAAabdun mu/minun khayrun min mushrikin walaw aAAjabakum ola-ika yadAAoona ila alnnari waAllahu yadAAoo ila aljannati waalmaghfirati bi-ithnihi wayubayyinu ayatihi lilnnasi laAAallahum yatathakkaroona

## Tafsir Ibn Kathir

### The Prohibition of marrying Mushrik Men and Women

Allah prohibited the believers from marrying Mushrik women who worship idols. Although the meaning is general and includes every Mushrik woman from among the idol worshippers and the People of the Scripture, Allah excluded the People of the Scripture from this ruling. Allah stated:

((Lawful to you in marriage) are chaste women from those who were given the Scripture (Jews and Christians) before your time when you have given their due dowry, desiring chastity (i.e., taking them in legal wedlock) not committing illegal sexual intercourse.) (5:5)

`Ali bin Abu Talhah said that Ibn `Abbas said about what Allah said:

(And do not marry Al-Mushrikat (female idolators) till they believe (worship Allah Alone).) "Allah has excluded the women of the People of the Scripture." This is also the explanation of Mujahid, `Ikrimah, Sa`id bin Jubayr, Makhul, Al-Hasan, Ad-Dahhak, Zayd bin Aslam and Ar-Rabi` bin Anas and others. Some scholars said that the Ayah is exclusively talking about idol worshippers and not the People of the Scripture, and this meaning is similar to the first meaning we mentioned. Allah knows best.

Abu Ja`far bin Jarir (At-Tabari) said, after mentioning that there is Ijma` that marrying women from the People of the Scripture is allowed, "`Umar disliked this practice so that the Muslims do not refrain from marrying Muslim women, or for similar reasons." An authentic chain of narrators stated that Shaqiq said: Once Hudhayfah married a Jewish woman and `Umar wrote to him, "Divorce her." He wrote back, "Do you claim that she is not allowed for me so that I divorce her" He said, "No. But, I fear that you might marry the whores from among them." Ibn Jarir related that Zayd bin Wahb said that `Umar bin Khattab said, "The Muslim man marries the Christian woman, but the Christian man does not marry the Muslim woman." This Hadith has a stronger, authentic chain of narrators than the previous Hadith.

Ibn Abu Hatim said that Ibn `Umar disliked marrying the women from the People of the Scripture. He relied on his own explanation for the Ayah:

(And do not marry Al-Mushrikat (female idolators) till they believe (worship Allah Alone).)

Al-Bukhari also reported that Ibn `Umar said, "I do not know of a bigger Shirk than her saying that Jesus is her Lord!"

Allah said:

(And indeed a slave woman who believes is better than a (free) Mushrikah (female idolators), even though she pleases you.)

It is recorded in the Two Sahihs that Abu Hurayrah narrated that the Prophet said:

«تُنْكَحُ الْمَرْأَةُ لِأَرْبَعٍ: لِمَالِهَا وَلِحَسَبِهَا وَلِجَمَالِهَا وَلِدِينِهَا، فَاظْفَرْ بِذَاتِ الدِّينِ، تَرِبَتْ يَدَاكَ»

(A woman is chosen for marriage for four reasons: her wealth, social status, beauty, and religion. So, marry the religious woman, may your hands be filled with sand (a statement of encouragement).)

Muslim reported this Hadith from Jabir. Muslim also reported that Ibn `Amr said that Allah's Messenger said:

«الدُّنْيَا مَتَاعٌ، وَخَيْرُ مَتَاعِ الدُّنْيَا الْمَرْأَةُ الصَّالِحَةُ»

(The life of this world is but a delight, and the best of the delights of this earthly life is the righteous wife.)

Allah then said:

(And give not (your daughters) in marriage to Al-Mushrikin till they believe (in Allah Alone).) meaning, do not marry Mushrik men to believing women. This statement is similar to Allah's statement:

(They are not lawful (wives) for them, nor are they lawful (husbands) for them.) (60:10)

Next, Allah said:

(. ..and verily, a believing servant is better than a (free) Mushrik (idolator), even though he pleases you.)

This Ayah indicates that a believing man, even an Abyssinian servant, is better than a Mushrik man, even if he was a rich master.

(Those (Al-Mushrikun) invite you to the Fire) meaning, associating and mingling with the disbelievers makes one love this life and prefer it over the Hereafter, leading to the severest repercussions. Allah said:

(...but Allah invites (you) to Paradise and forgiveness by His leave) meaning, by His Law, commandments and prohibitions. Allah said:

(...and makes His Ayat clear to mankind that they may remember.)

## Surah: 2 Ayah: 222 & Ayah: 223

﴿ وَيَسْـَٔلُونَكَ عَنِ ٱلْمَحِيضِ ۖ قُلْ هُوَ أَذًى فَٱعْتَزِلُوا۟ ٱلنِّسَآءَ فِى ٱلْمَحِيضِ ۖ وَلَا تَقْرَبُوهُنَّ حَتَّىٰ يَطْهُرْنَ ۖ فَإِذَا تَطَهَّرْنَ فَأْتُوهُنَّ مِنْ حَيْثُ أَمَرَكُمُ ٱللَّهُ ۚ إِنَّ ٱللَّهَ يُحِبُّ ٱلتَّوَّٰبِينَ وَيُحِبُّ ٱلْمُتَطَهِّرِينَ ﴿٢٢٢﴾ ﴾

222. They ask you concerning menstruation. Say: that is an Adha (a harmful thing for a husband to have a sexual intercourse with his wife while she is having her menses), therefore keep away from women during menses and go not unto them till they are purified (from menses and have taken a bath). And when they have purified themselves, then go in unto them as Allâh has ordained for you (go in unto them in any manner as long as it is in their vagina). Truly, Allâh loves those who turn unto Him in repentance and loves those who purify themselves (by taking a bath and cleaning and washing thoroughly their private parts, bodies, for their prayers).

﴿ نِسَآؤُكُمْ حَرْثٌ لَّكُمْ فَأْتُوا۟ حَرْثَكُمْ أَنَّىٰ شِئْتُمْ ۖ وَقَدِّمُوا۟ لِأَنفُسِكُمْ ۚ وَٱتَّقُوا۟ ٱللَّهَ وَٱعْلَمُوٓا۟ أَنَّكُم مُّلَـٰقُوهُ ۗ وَبَشِّرِ ٱلْمُؤْمِنِينَ ﴿٢٢٣﴾ ﴾

223. Your wives are a tilth for you, so go to your tilth, when or how you will, and send (good deeds, or ask Allâh to bestow upon you pious offspring) for your ownselves beforehand. And fear Allâh, and know that you are to meet Him (in the Hereafter), and give good tidings to the believers (O Muhammad (peace be upon him))

### Transliteration

222. Wayas-aloonaka AAani almaheedi qul huwa athan faiAAtaziloo alnnisaa fee almaheedi wala taqraboohunna hatta yathurna fa-itha tatahharna fa/toohunna min haythu amarakumu Allahu inna Allaha yuhibbu alttawwabeena wayuhibbu almutatahhireena 223. Nisaokum harthun lakum fa/too harthakum anna shi/tum waqaddimoo li-anfusikum waittaqoo Allaha waiAAlamoo annakum mulaqoohu wabashshiri almu/mineena

### Tafsir Ibn Kathir

### Sexual Intercourse with Menstruating Women is prohibited

Imam Ahmad recorded that Anas said that the Jews used to avoid their menstruating women, they would not eat, or even mingle with them in the house. The Companions of the Prophet asked about this matter and Allah revealed:

(They ask you concerning menstruation. Say: "That is an Adha, therefore, keep away from women during menses and go not in unto them till they are purified.)

Allah's Messenger said:

«اصْنَعُوا كُلَّ شَيْءٍ إِلَّا النِّكَاحَ»

(`Do everything you wish, except having sexual intercourse.)

When the Jews were told about the Prophet's statement, they said, "What is the matter with this man He would not hear of any of our practices, but would defy it." Then, Usayd bin Hudayr and `Abbad bin Bishr came and said, "O Messenger of Allah! The Jews said this and that, should we have sex with our women (meaning, during the menstruation period)" The face of Allah's Messenger changed color, until the Companions thought that he was angry with them. They left. Soon after, some milk was brought to Allah's Messenger as a gift, and he sent some of it for them to drink. They knew then that Allah's Messenger was not angry with them. Muslim also reported this Hadith. Allah said:

(. ..therefore, keep away from women during menses.) meaning, avoid the sexual organ. The Prophet said:

«اصْنَعُوا كُلَّ شَيْءٍ إِلَّا النِّكَاحَ»

(Do anything you wish except having sexual intercourse.)

This is why most of the scholars said that it is allowed to fondle the wife, except for having sexual intercourse (when she is having her menses). Abu Dawud reported that `Ikrimah related to one of the Prophet's wives that she said that whenever the Prophet wanted to fondle (one of his wives) during her menses, he would cover her sexual organ with something.

Abu Ja`far bin Jarir related that Masruq went to `A'ishah and greeted her, and `A'ishah greeted him in return. Masruq said, "I wish to ask you about a matter, but I am shy." She replied, "I am your mother and you are my son." He said, "What can the man enjoy of his wife when she is having her menses" She said, "Everything except her sexual organ." This is also the opinion of Ibn `Abbas, Mujahid, Al-Hasan and `Ikrimah.

One is allowed to sleep next to his wife and to eat with her (when she is having her menses). `A'ishah said, "Allah's Messenger used to ask me to wash his hair while I was having the menses. He would lay on my lap and read the Qur'an while I was having the period." It is also reported in the Sahih that `A'ishah said, "While having the menses, I used to eat from a piece of meat and give it to the Prophet who would eat from the same place I ate from. I used to have sips of a drink and would then give the cup to the Prophet who would place his mouth where I placed my mouth."

It is also reported in the Two Sahihs that Maymunah bint Al-Harith Al-Hilaliyah said, "Whenever the Prophet wanted to fondle any of his wives during the periods (menses), he used to ask her to wear an Izar (a sheet covering the lower-half of the body)." These are the wordings collected by Al-Bukhari. Similar was reported from `A'ishah. In addition, Imam Ahmad, Abu Dawud, At-Tirmidhi and Ibn Majah reported that `Abdullah bin Sa`d Al-Ansari asked Allah's Messenger , "What am I allowed of my wife while she is having her menses" He said, "What is above the Izar (a sheet covering the lower-half of the body)." Hence, Allah's statement: h

(...and go not in unto them till they are purified.) explains His statement:

(...therefore, keep away from women during menses.)

Allah prohibited having sexual intercourse with the wife during menstruation, indicating that sexual intercourse is allowed otherwise.

Allah's statement:

(And when they have purified themselves, then go in unto them as Allah has ordained for you.) indicates that men should have sexual intercourse with their wives after they take a bath. The scholars agree that the woman is obliged to take a bath, or to perform Tayammum with sand, if she is unable to use water, before she is allowed to have sexual intercourse with her husband, after the monthly period ends. Ibn `Abbas said:

"(till they are purified) means from blood, and,

(And when they have purified themselves) means with water." This is also the Tafsir of Mujahid, `Ikrimah, Al-Hasan, Muqatil bin Hayyan and Al-Layth bin Sa`d and others.

### Anal Sex is prohibited

Allah said:

(...as Allah has ordained for you.) this refers to Al-Farj (the vagina), as Ibn `Abbas, Mujahid and other scholars have stated. Therefore, anal sex is prohibited, as we will further emphasize afterwards, Allah willing. Abu Razin, `Ikrimah and Ad-Dahhak and others said that:

(...then go in unto them as Allah has ordained for you.) means when they are pure, and not during the menses. Allah said afterwards:

(Truly, Allah loves those who turn unto Him in repentance) from the sin even if it was repeated, (and loves those who purify themselves.) meaning, those who purify themselves from the impurity and the filth that include having sexual intercourse with the wife during the menses and anal sex.

## The Reason behind revealing Allah's Statement: "Your Wives are a Tilth for You.

Allah said:

(Your wives are a tilth for you,)

Ibn `Abbas commented, "Meaning the place of pregnancy." (Allah then said:)

(...so go to your tilth, when or how you will,) meaning, wherever you wish from the front or from behind, as long as sex takes place in one valve (the female sexual organ), as the authentic Hadiths have indicated.

For instance, Al-Bukhari recorded that Ibn Al-Munkadir said that he heard Jabir say that the Jews used to claim that if one has sex with his wife from behind (in the vagina) the offspring would become cross-eyed. Then, this Ayah was revealed:

(Your wives are a tilth for you, so go to your tilth, when or how you will,)

Muslim and Abu Dawud also reported this Hadith.

Ibn Abu Hatim said that Muhammad bin Al-Munkadir narrated that Jabir bin `Abdullah told him that the Jews claimed to the Muslims that if one has sex with their wife from behind (in the vagina) their offspring will become cross-eyed. Allah revealed afterwards:

(Your wives are a tilth for you, so go to your tilth, when or how you will,)

Ibn Jurayj (one of the reporters of the Hadith) said that Allah's Messenger said:

«مُقْبِلَةً وَمُدْبِرَةً إِذَا كَانَ ذَلِكَ فِي الْفَرْجِ»

(From the front or from behind, as long as that occurs in the Farj (vagina).)

Imam Ahmad recorded that Ibn `Abbas said, "The Ayah,

(Your wives are a tilth for you) was revealed about some people from the Ansar who came to the Prophet and asked him (about having sex with the wife from behind). He said to them:

«ائْتِهَا عَلَى كُلِّ حَالٍ إِذَا كَانَ فِي الْفَرْجِ»

## Chapter 2: Al-Baqarah (The Cow). Verses 142-252

(Have sex with her as you like as long as that occurs in the vagina.)

Imam Ahmad recorded that `Abdullah bin Sabit said: I went to Hafsah bint `Abdur-Rahman bin Abu Bakr and said, "I wish to ask you about something, but I am shy." She said, "Do not be shy, O my nephew." He said, "About having sex from behind with women." She said, "Umm Salamah told me that the Ansar used to refrain from having sex from behind (in the vagina). The Jews claimed that those who have sex with their women from behind would have offspring with crossed-eyes. When the Muhajirun came to Al-Madinah, they married Ansar women and had sex with them from behind. One of these women would not obey her husband and said, `You will not do that until I go to Allah's Messenger (and ask him about this matter). ' She went to Umm Salamah and told her the story. Umm Salamah said, `Wait until Allah's Messenger comes.' When Allah's Messenger came, the Ansari woman was shy to ask him about this matter, so she left. Umm Salamah told Allah's Messenger the story and he said:

«ادْعِي الْأَنْصَارِيَّة»

(Summon the Ansari woman.)"

She was summoned and he recited this Ayah to her:

(Your wives are a tilth for you, so go to your tilth, when or how you will.) He added:

«صِمَامًا وَاحِدًا»

(Only in one valve (the vagina).)"

This Hadith was also collected by At-Tirmidhi who said, "Hasan."

An-Nasa'i reported that Ka`b bin `Alqamah said that Abu An-Nadr said that he asked Nafi`, "The people are repeating the statement that you relate from Ibn `Umar that he allowed sex with women in their rear (anus)." He said, "They have said a lie about me. But let me tell you what really happened. Ibn `Umar was once reciting the Qur'an while I was with him and he reached the Ayah:

(Your wives are a tilth for you, so go to your tilth, when or how you will,) He then said, `O Nafi`! Do you know the story behind this Ayah' I said, `No.' He said, `We, the people of Quraysh, used to have sexual intercourse with our wives from the back (in the vagina). When we migrated to Al-Madinah and married some Ansari women, we wanted to do the same with them. They disliked it and made a big issue out of it. The Ansari women had followed the practice of the Jews who have sex with their women while they lay on their sides. Then, Allah revealed:

(Your wives are a tilth for you, so go to your tilth, when or how you will,)"

This has an authentic chain of narrators.

Imam Ahmad reported that Khuzaymah bin Thabit Al-Khatami narrated that Allah's Messenger said:

«لَا يَسْتَحْيِي اللهُ مِنَ الْحَقِّ ثَلَاثًا لَا تَأْتُوا النِّسَاءَ فِي أَعْجَازِهِنَّ»

(Allah does not shy from the truth - he said it thrice-, do not have anal sex with women.)

This Hadith was collected by An-Nasa'i and Ibn Majah.

Abu `Isa At-Tirmidhi and An-Nasa'i reported that Ibn `Abbas narrated that Allah's Messenger said:

«لَا يَنْظُرُ اللهُ إِلَى رَجُلٍ أَتَى رَجُلًا أَوِ امْرَأَةً فِي الدُّبُرِ»

(Allah does not look at a man who had anal sex with another man or a woman.)

At-Tirmidhi said, "Hasan Gharib." This is also the narration that Ibn Hibban collected in his Sahih, while Ibn Hazm stated that this is an authentic Hadith.

In addition, Imam Ahmad reported that `Ali bin Talaq said, "Allah's Messenger forbade anal sex with women, for Allah does not shy away from truth." Abu `Isa At-Tirmidhi also reported this Hadith and said, "Hasan".

Abu Muhammad `Abdullah bin `Abdur-Rahman Darimi reported in his Musnad that Sa`id bin Yasar Abu Hubab said: I said to Ibn `Umar, "What do you say about having sex with women in the rear" He said, "What does it mean" I said, "Anal sex." He said, "Does a Muslim do that" This Hadith has an authentic chain of narrators and is an explicit rejection of anal sex from Ibn `Umar.

Abu Bakr bin Ziyad Naysaburi reported that Isma`il bin Ruh said that he asked Malik bin Anas, "What do you say about having sex with women in the anus" He said, "You are not an Arab Does sex occur but in the place of pregnancy Do it only in the Farj (vagina)." I said, "O Abu `Abdullah! They say that you allow that practice." He said, "They utter a lie about me, they lie about me." This is Malik's firm stance on this subject. It is also the view of Sa`id bin Musayyib, Abu Salamah, `Ikrimah, Tawus, `Ata , Sa`id bin Jubayr, `Urwah bin Az-Zubayr, Mujahid bin Jabr, Al-Hasan and other scholars of the Salaf (the Companions and the following two generations after them). They all, along with the majority of the scholars, harshly rebuked the practice of anal sex and many of them called this practice a Kufr.

# Chapter 2: Al-Baqarah (The Cow), Verses 142-252

Allah said:

(...and send for your own selves beforehand.) meaning, by performing the acts of worship while refraining from whatever Allah has prohibited for you. This is why Allah said afterwards:

(And fear Allah, and know that you are to meet Him (in the Hereafter),)

meaning, He will hold you accountable for all of your deeds,

(...and give good tidings to the believers (O Muhammad ).) meaning, those who obey what Allah has commanded and refrain from what He has prohibited. Ibn Jarir reported that `Ata' said, or related it to Ibn `Abbas,

(...and send for your own selves beforehand.) means, mention Allah's Name, by saying, `Bismillah', before having sexual intercourse." Al-Bukhari also reported that Ibn `Abbas narrated that Allah's Messenger said:

«لَوْ أَنَّ أَحَدَكُمْ إِذَا أَرَادَ أَنْ يَأْتِيَ أَهْلَهُ قَالَ: بِاسْمِ اللهِ، اللَّهُمَّ جَنِّبْنَا الشَّيْطَانَ وَجَنِّبِ الشَّيْطَانَ مَا رَزَقْتَنَا، فَإِنَّهُ إِنْ يُقَدَّرْ بَيْنَهُمَا وَلَدٌ فِي ذَلِكَ، لَمْ يَضُرَّهُ الشَّيْطَانُ أَبَدًا»

(If anyone of you on having sexual relations with his wife said: `In the Name of Allah. O Allah! Protect us from Satan and also protect what you bestow upon us (i.e., the coming offspring) from Satan,' and if it is destined that they should have a child then, Satan will never be able to harm him.)

### Surah: 2 Ayah: 224 & Ayah: 225

﴿ وَلَا تَجْعَلُوا اللَّهَ عُرْضَةً لِأَيْمَانِكُمْ أَن تَبَرُّوا وَتَتَّقُوا وَتُصْلِحُوا بَيْنَ النَّاسِ ۗ وَاللَّهُ سَمِيعٌ عَلِيمٌ ﴾

224. And make not Allâh's (Name) an excuse in your oaths against your doing good and acting piously, and making peace among mankind. And Allâh is All-Hearer, All-Knower (i.e. do not swear much and if you have sworn against doing something good then give an expiation for the oath and do good).

﴿ لَّا يُؤَاخِذُكُمُ اللَّهُ بِاللَّغْوِ فِي أَيْمَانِكُمْ وَلَٰكِن يُؤَاخِذُكُم بِمَا كَسَبَتْ قُلُوبُكُمْ ۗ وَاللَّهُ غَفُورٌ حَلِيمٌ ﴾

225. Allâh will not call you to account for that which is unintentional in your oaths, but He will call you to account for that which your hearts have earned. And Allâh is Oft-Forgiving, Most-Forbearing.

### Transliteration

224. Wala tajAAaloo Allaha AAurdatan li-aymanikum an tabarroo watattaqoo watuslihoo bayna alnnasi waAllahu sameeAAun AAaleemun   225. La yu-akhithukumu Allahu biallaghwi fee aymanikum walakin yu-akhithukum bima kasabat quloobukum waAllahu ghafoorun haleemun

### Tafsir Ibn Kathir

### The Prohibition of swearing to abandon a Good Deed

Allah commands, 'You should not implement your vows in Allah's Name to refrain from pious acts and severing the relations with the relatives, if you swear to abandon such causes.' Allah said in another Ayah:

(And let not those among you who are blessed with graces and wealth swear not to give (any sort of help) to their kinsmen, Al-Masakin (the poor), and those who left their homes for Allah's cause. Let them pardon and forgive. Do you not love that Allah should forgive you) (24:22)

Continuity in a sinful vow is more sinful than breaking it by expiation. Allah's Messenger said:

«وَاللهِ لَأَنْ يَلَجَّ أَحَدُكُمْ بِيَمِينِهِ فِي أَهْلِهِ آثَمُ لَهُ عِنْدَ اللهِ مِنْ أَنْ يُعْطِيَ كَفَّارَتَهُ الَّتِي افْتَرَضَ اللهُ عَلَيْه»

(By Allah! It is more sinful to Allah that one of you implements his vow regarding (severing the relations with) his relatives than (breaking his promise and) paying the Kaffarah that Allah has required in such cases.)

This is how Muslim reported this Hadith and also Imam Ahmad.

'Ali bin Abu Talhah reported that Ibn 'Abbas said that what Allah said:

(And make not Allah's (Name) an excuse in your oaths) means, "Do not vow to refrain from doing good works. (If you make such vow then) break it, pay the Kaffarah and do the good work." This was also said by Masruq, Ash-Sha`bi, Ibrahim An-Nakha`i, Mujahid, Tawus, Sa`id bin Jubayr, `Ata', `Ikrimah, Makhul, Az-Zuhri, Al-Hasan, Qatadah, Muqatil bin Hayyan, Ar-Rabi` bin Anas, Ad-Dahhak, `Ata' Al-Khurasani and As-Suddi.

Suporting this view, which is the majority view, is what is reported in the Two Sahihs that Abu Musa Al-Ash`ari narrated that Allah's Messenger said:

»إِنِّي وَاللهِ إِنْ شَاءَ اللهُ، لَا أَحْلِفُ عَلَى يَمِينٍ فَأَرَى غَيْرَهَا خَيْرًا مِنْهَا إِلَّا أَتَيْتُ الَّذِي هُوَ خَيْرٌ وَتَحَلَّلْتُهَا«

(By Allah! Allah willing, I will not vow to do a thing and then see a better act, but I would do what is better and break my vow.) Muslim reported that Abu Hurayrah said that Allah's Messenger said:

»مَنْ حَلَفَ عَلَى يَمِينٍ فَرَأَى غَيْرَهَا مِنْهَا خَيْرًا فَلْيُكَفِّرْ عَنْ يَمِينِهِ، وَلْيَفْعَلِ الَّذِي هُوَ خَيْرٌ«

(Whoever makes a vow and then finds what is better than his vow (should break his vow,) pay the Kaffarah and perform the better deed.)

### The Laghw (Unintentional) Vows

Allah said:

(Allah will not call you to account for that which is unintentional in your oaths,)

This Ayah means, `Allah does not punish or hold you accountable for the Laghw (unintentional) vows that you make.' The Laghw vows are unintentional and are just like the habitual statements that the tongue repeats, without really intending them. For instance, it is reported in the Two Sahihs that Abu Hurayrah narrated that Allah's Messenger said:

»مَنْ حَلَفَ فَقَالَ فِي حَلِفِهِ بِاللَّاتِ وَالْعُزَّى، فَلْيَقُلْ لَا إِلَهَ إِلَّا اللهُ«

(Whoever swore and (unintentionally) mentioned Al-Lat and Al-`Uzza (two idols) in his vow, should then say, `There is no deity worthy of worship except Allah'.)

The Messenger said this statement to some new Muslims whose tongues were, before Islam, used to vowing by their idol Al-Lat. Therefore, the Prophet ordered them to intentionally recite the slogan of Ikhlas, just as they mentioned these words by mistake, so that it (the word of Ikhlas) may eradicate the word (of Shirk). This is why Allah said:

(...but He will call you to account for that which your hearts have earned.) and in another Ayah:

(...for your deliberate oaths) (5:89)

Abu Dawud reported under Chapter: `The Laghw Vows' that `Ata' said that `A'ishah said that Allah's Messenger said:

«اللَّغْوُ فِي الْيَمِينِ هُوَ كَلَامُ الرَّجُلِ فِي بَيْتِهِ: كَلَّا وَاللهِ، وَبَلَى وَاللهِ»

(The Laghw in the vows includes what the man says in his house, such as, `No, by Allah,' and, `Yes, by Allah'.)

Ibn Abu Hatim reported that Ibn `Abbas said, "The Laghw vow includes vowing while angry."

He also reported that Ibn `Abbas said, "The Laghw vow includes vowing to prohibit what Allah has allowed, and this type does not require a Kaffarah (expiation)." Similar was said by Sa`id bin Jubayr.

In addition, Abu Dawud related under Chapter: `Vowing while Angry' that Sa`id bin Musayyib said that two Ansari brothers both received inheritance and one of them asked that the inheritance be divided. His brother said, "If you ask me about dividing the inheritance again, then all of what I have will be spent on the Ka`bah's door." `Umar said to him, "The Ka`bah does not need your money. So break your vow, pay the Kaffarah and come to terms with your brother. I heard Allah's Messenger saying:

«لَا يَمِينَ عَلَيْكَ وَلَا نَذْرَ فِي مَعْصِيَةِ الرَّبِّ عَزَّ وَجَلَّ، وَفِي قَطِيعَةِ الرَّحِمِ، وَفِيمَا لَا تَمْلِكُ»

(Do not make a vow against yourself, nor to disobey the Lord, cut the relations of the womb or dispose of what you do not own.)"

Allah said:

(...but He will call you to account for that which your hearts have earned,)

Ibn `Abbas, Mujahid and several others said that this Ayah means swearing about a matter while knowing that he is lying. Mujahid and others said this Ayah is similar to what Allah said:

(...but He will punish you for your deliberate oaths.) (5:89) Allah said (2:225 above):

(And Allah is Oft-Forgiving, Most-Forbearing.) meaning, He is Oft-Forgiving to His servants and Most Forbearing with them.

## Surah: 2 Ayah: 226 & Ayah: 227

﴿ لِّلَّذِينَ يُؤْلُونَ مِن نِّسَآئِهِمْ تَرَبُّصُ أَرْبَعَةِ أَشْهُرٍ فَإِن فَآءُو فَإِنَّ ٱللَّهَ غَفُورٌ رَّحِيمٌ ﴾

226. Those who take an oath not to have sexual relation with their wives must wait four months, then if they return (change their idea in this period), verily, Allâh is Oft-Forgiving, Most Merciful.

﴿ وَإِنْ عَزَمُوا۟ ٱلطَّلَـٰقَ فَإِنَّ ٱللَّهَ سَمِيعٌ عَلِيمٌ ﴾

227. And if they decide upon divorce, then Allâh is All-Hearer, All-Knower.

### Transliteration

226. Lillatheena yu/loona min nisa-ihim tarabbusu arbaAAati ashhurin fa-in faoo fa-inna Allaha ghafoorun raheemun  227. Wa-in AAazamoo alttalaqa fa-inna Allaha sameeAAun AAaleemun

### Tafsir Ibn Kathir

#### The Ila' and its Rulings

Ila' is a type of vow where a man swears not to sleep with his wife for a certain period, whether less or more than four months. If the vow of Ila' was for less than four months, the man has to wait for the vow's period to end and then is allowed to have sexual intercourse with his wife. She has to be patient and she cannot ask her husband, in this case, to end his vow before the end of its term. It is reported in the Two Sahihs that `A'ishah said that Allah's Messenger swore he would stay away from with his wives for a month. He then came down after twenty-nine days saying:

«الشَّهْرُ تِسْعٌ وَعِشْرُونَ»

(The (lunar) month is twenty-nine days.)

Similar was narrated by `Umar bin Al-Khattab and reported in the Two Sahihs. If the period of Ila' is for more than four months, the wife is allowed in this case to ask her husband, upon the end of the four months, to end the Ila' and have sexual relations with her. Otherwise, he should divorce her, by being forced to do so by the authorities if necessary, so that the wife is not harmed. Allah said:

(Those who take an oath not to have sexual relations with their wives) meaning, swear not to have sexual relations with the wife. This Ayah indicates that the Ila' involves the wife and not a slave-women, as the majority of the scholars have agreed,

(...must wait for four months,) meaning, the husband waits for four months from the time of the vow and then ends the Ila' (if the vow was for four or more months) and is required to either return to his wife or divorce her. This is why Allah said next:

(...then if they return,) meaning, to a normal relationship, having sexual intercourse with the wife. This is the Tafsir of Ibn `Abbas, Masruq, Ash-Sha`bi, Sa`id bin Jubayr and Ibn Jarir.

(...verily, Allah is Oft-Forgiving, Most Merciful.) with any shortcomings that occurred in the rights of the wife because of the vow of Ila'.

Allah said:

(And if they decide upon divorce,) indicating that divorce does not occur by merely passing the four month mark (during the Ila'). Malik reported from Nafi` that `Abdullah bin `Umar said, "If the man swears to Ila' from his wife, then divorce does not occur automatically even after the four months have passed. When he stops at the four months mark, he should either divorce or return." Al-Bukhari also reported this Hadith. Ibn Jarir reported that Suhayl bin Abu Salih said that his father said, "I asked twelve Companions about the man who does Ila' with his wife. They all stated that he does not have to do anything until the four months have passed and then has to either retain or divorce her." Ad-Daraqutni also reported this from Suhayl.

It is also reported from `Umar, `Uthman, `Ali, Abu Ad-Darda', `A'ishah, Ibn `Umar and Ibn `Abbas. This is also the opinion of Sa`id bin Musayyib, `Umar bin `Abdul-`Aziz, Mujahid, Tawus, Muhammad bin Ka`b and Al-Qasim.

### Surah: 2 Ayah: 228

﴿ وَٱلْمُطَلَّقَٰتُ يَتَرَبَّصْنَ بِأَنفُسِهِنَّ ثَلَٰثَةَ قُرُوٓءٍ وَلَا يَحِلُّ لَهُنَّ أَن يَكْتُمْنَ مَا خَلَقَ ٱللَّهُ فِىٓ أَرْحَامِهِنَّ إِن كُنَّ يُؤْمِنَّ بِٱللَّهِ وَٱلْيَوْمِ ٱلْءَاخِرِ وَبُعُولَتُهُنَّ أَحَقُّ بِرَدِّهِنَّ فِى ذَٰلِكَ إِنْ أَرَادُوٓا۟ إِصْلَٰحًا وَلَهُنَّ مِثْلُ ٱلَّذِى عَلَيْهِنَّ بِٱلْمَعْرُوفِ وَلِلرِّجَالِ عَلَيْهِنَّ دَرَجَةٌ وَٱللَّهُ عَزِيزٌ حَكِيمٌ ۝ ﴾

228. And divorced women shall wait (as regards their marriage) for three menstrual periods, and it is not lawful for them to conceal what Allâh has created in their wombs, if they believe in Allâh and the Last Day. And their husbands have the better right to take them back in that period, if they wish for reconciliation. And they (women) have rights (over their husbands as regards living expenses) similar (to those of their husbands) over them (as regards obedience and respect) to what is reasonable, but

men have a degree (of responsibility) over them. And Allâh is All-Mighty, All-Wise.

## Transliteration

228. Waalmutallaqatu yatarabbasna bi-anfusihinna thalathata quroo-in wala yahillu lahunna an yaktumna ma khalaqa Allahu fee arhamihinna in kunna yu/minna biAllahi waalyawmi al-akhiri wabuAAoolatuhunna ahaqqu biraddihinna fee thalika in aradoo islahan walahunna mithlu allathee AAalayhinna bialmaAAroofi walilrrijali AAalayhinna darajatun waAllahu AAazeezun hakeemun

## Tafsir Ibn Kathir

### The `Iddah (Waiting Period) of the Divorced Woman

This Ayah contains a command from Allah that the divorced woman, whose marriage was consummated and who still has menstruation periods, should wait for three (menstrual) periods (Quru') after the divorce and then remarry if she wishes.

### The Meaning of Al-Quru

Ibn Jarir related that `Alqamah said: We were with `Umar bin Al-Khattab when a woman came and said, "My husband divorced me one or two periods ago. He then came back to me while I had prepared my water )for taking a bath(, took off my clothes and closed my door." `Umar asked `Abdullah bin Mas`ud, "What do you think" He said, "I think that she is still his wife, as long as she is not allowed to resume praying (i.e., until the third period ends before he takes her back)." `Umar said, "This is my opinion too." This is also the opinion of Abu Bakr As-Siddiq, `Umar, `Uthman, `Ali, Abu Ad-Darda', `Ubadah bin As-Samit, Anas bin Malik, Ibn Mas`ud, Mu`adh, Ubayy bin Ka`b, Abu Musa Al-Ash`ari and Ibn `Abbas. Furthermore, this is the opinion of Sa`id bin Musayyib, `Alqamah, Aswad, Ibrahim, Mujahid, `Ata', Tawus, Sa`id bin Jubayr, `Ikrimah, Muhammad bin Sirin, Al-Hasan, Qatadah, Ash-Sha`bi, Ar-Rabi`, Muqatil bin Hayyan, As-Suddi, Makhul, Ad-Dahhak and `Ata' Al-Khurasani. They all stated that the Quru' is the menstruation period. What testifies to this is the Hadith that Abu Dawud and An-Nasa'i reported that Fatimah bint Abu Hubaiysh said that Allah's Messenger said to her:

(Do not pray during your Aqra' (pl. for Quru', the menstruation period).)

If this Hadith was authentic, it would have been a clear proof that the Quru' is the menstruation period. However, one of the narrators of this Hadith, Al-Mundhir, is an unknown person (in Hadith terminology), as Abu Hatim has stated, although Ibn Hibban has mentioned Al-Mundhir in his book Ath-Thiqat.

### A Woman's Statement about Menses and Purity is to be accepted

Allah said:

(...and it is not lawful for them to conceal what Allah has created in their wombs,) meaning, of pregnancy or menstruation periods. This is the Tafsir of Ibn `Abbas, Ibn `Umar, Mujahid, Ash-Sha`bi, Al-Hakam bin `Utaybah, Ar-Rabi` bin Anas, Ad-Dahhak and others.

Allah then said:

(...if they believe in Allah and the Last Day.)

This Ayah warns women against hiding the truth (if they were pregnant or on their menses), indicating that they are the authority in such matters as they alone know such facts about themselves. Since verifying such matters is difficult, Allah left this decision with them. Yet, women were warned not to hide the truth in case they wish to end the `Iddah sooner, or later, according to their desires. Women were thus commanded to say the truth (if they were pregnant or on their menses), no more and no less.

## The Husband has the Right to take back his Divorced Wife during the `Iddah (Waiting Period)

Allah said:

(And their husbands have the better right to take them back in that period, if they wish for reconciliation.)

Hence, the husband who divorces his wife can take her back, providing she is still in her `Iddah (time spent before a divorced woman or a widow can remarry) and that his aim, by taking her back, is righteous and for the purpose of bringing things back to normal. However, this ruling applies where the husband is eligible to take his divorced wife back. We should mention that (when this Ayah 2:228 was revealed), the ruling that made the divorce thrice and specified when the husband is ineligible to take his divorced wife back, had not been revealed yet. Previously, the man used to divorce his wife and then take her back even if he had divorced her a hundred separate times. Thereafter, Allah revealed the following Ayah (2:229) that made the divorce only thrice. So there was now a reversible divorce and an irreversible final divorce.

## The Rights the Spouses have over Each Other

Allah said:

(And they (women) have rights (over their husbands as regards living expenses) similar (to those of their husbands) over them (as regards obedience and respect) to what is reasonable,)

This Ayah indicates that the wife has certain rights on her husband, just as he has certain rights on her, and each is obliged to give the other spouse his due rights. Muslim reported that Jabir said that Allah's Messenger said:

«فَاتَّقُوا اللهَ فِي النِّسَاءِ، فَإِنَّكُمْ أَخَذْتُمُوهُنَّ بِأَمَانَةِ اللهِ، وَاسْتَحْلَلْتُمْ فُرُوجَهُنَّ بِكَلِمَةِ اللهِ، وَلَكُمْ عَلَيْهِنَّ أَنْ لَا يُوطِئْنَ فُرُشَكُمْ أَحَدًا تَكْرَهُونَهُ، فَإِنْ فَعَلْنَ ذَلِكَ فَاضْرِبُوهُنَّ ضَرْبًا غَيْرَ مُبَرِّحٍ، وَلَهُنَّ رِزْقُهُنَّ وَكِسْوَتُهُنَّ بِالْمَعْرُوفِ»

(Fear Allah regarding your women, for you have taken them by Allah's covenant and were allowed to enjoy with them sexually by Allah's Words. You have the right on them that they do not allow anyone you dislike to sit on your mat. If they do that, then discipline them leniently. They have the right to be spent on and to be bought clothes in what is reasonable.)

Bahz bin Hakim said that Mu`awiyah bin Haydah Al-Qushayri related that his grandfather said, "O Messenger of Allah! What is the right the wife of one of us has" The Prophet said:

«أَنْ تُطْعِمَهَا إِذَا طَعِمْتَ، وتَكْسُوَهَا إِذَا اكْتَسَيْتَ، وَلَا تَضْرِبِ الْوَجْهَ، وَلَا تُقَبِّحْ، وَلَا تَهْجُرْ إِلَّا فِي الْبَيْتِ»

(To feed her when you eat, buy her clothes when you buy for yourself and to refrain from striking her on the face, cursing her or staying away from her except in the house.)

Waki` related that Ibn `Abbas said, "I like to take care of my appearance for my wife just as I like for her to take care of her appearance for me. This is because Allah says:

(And they (women) have rights similar (to those of their husbands) over them to what is reasonable.)" This statement is reported by Ibn Jarir and Ibn Abu Hatim.

### The Virtue Men have over Women

Allah said:

(but men have a degree (of responsibility) over them.)

This Ayah indicates that men are in a more advantageous position than women physically as well as in their mannerism, status, obedience (of women to them), spending, taking care of the affairs and in general, in this life and in the Hereafter. Allah said (in another Ayah):

(Men are the protectors and maintainers of women, because Allah has made one of them to excel the other, and because they spend (to support them) from their means.) (4:34)

Allah's statement:

(And Allah is All-Mighty, All-Wise) means, He is Mighty in His punishment of those who disobey and defy His commands. He is Wise in what He commands, destines and legislates.

## Surah: 2 Ayah: 229 & 2 Ayah: 230

﴿ ٱلطَّلَٰقُ مَرَّتَانِ ۖ فَإِمْسَاكٌۢ بِمَعْرُوفٍ أَوْ تَسْرِيحٌۢ بِإِحْسَٰنٍ ۗ وَلَا يَحِلُّ لَكُمْ أَن تَأْخُذُوا۟ مِمَّآ ءَاتَيْتُمُوهُنَّ شَيْـًٔا إِلَّآ أَن يَخَافَآ أَلَّا يُقِيمَا حُدُودَ ٱللَّهِ ۖ فَإِنْ خِفْتُمْ أَلَّا يُقِيمَا حُدُودَ ٱللَّهِ فَلَا جُنَاحَ عَلَيْهِمَا فِيمَا ٱفْتَدَتْ بِهِۦ ۗ تِلْكَ حُدُودُ ٱللَّهِ فَلَا تَعْتَدُوهَا ۚ وَمَن يَتَعَدَّ حُدُودَ ٱللَّهِ فَأُو۟لَٰٓئِكَ هُمُ ٱلظَّٰلِمُونَ ﴾

229. The divorce is twice, after that, either you retain her on reasonable terms or release her with kindness. And it is not lawful for you (men) to take back (from your wives) any of your Mahr (bridal-money given by the husband to his wife at the time of marriage) which you have given them, except when both parties fear that they would be unable to keep the limits ordained by Allâh (e.g. to deal with each other on a fair basis). Then if you fear that they would not be able to keep the limits ordained by Allâh, then there is no sin on either of them if she gives back (the Mahr or a part of it) for her Al-Khul' (divorce). These are the limits ordained by Allâh, so do not transgress them. And whoever transgresses the limits ordained by Allâh, then such are the Zâlimûn (wrong-doers).

﴿ فَإِن طَلَّقَهَا فَلَا تَحِلُّ لَهُۥ مِنۢ بَعْدُ حَتَّىٰ تَنكِحَ زَوْجًا غَيْرَهُۥ ۗ فَإِن طَلَّقَهَا فَلَا جُنَاحَ عَلَيْهِمَآ أَن يَتَرَاجَعَآ إِن ظَنَّآ أَن يُقِيمَا حُدُودَ ٱللَّهِ ۗ وَتِلْكَ حُدُودُ ٱللَّهِ يُبَيِّنُهَا لِقَوْمٍ يَعْلَمُونَ ﴾

230. And if he has divorced her (the third time), then she is not lawful unto him thereafter until she has married another husband. Then, if the other husband divorces her, it is no sin on both of them that they reunite, provided they feel that they can keep the limits ordained by Allâh. These are the limits of Allâh, which He makes plain for the people who have knowledge.

## Transliteration

229. Alttalaqu marratani fa-imsakun bimaAAroofin aw tasreehun bi-ihsanin wala yahillu lakum an ta/khuthoo mimma ataytumoohunna shay-an illa an yakhafa alla yuqeema hudooda Allahi fa-in khiftum alla yuqeema hudooda Allahi fala junaha AAalayhima feema iftadat bihi tilka hudoodu Allahi fala taAAtadooha waman yataAAadda hudooda Allahi faola-ika humu al*thth*alimoona 230. Fa-in tallaqaha fala tahillu lahu min baAAdu hatta tankiha zawjan ghayrahu fa-in tallaqaha fala junaha AAalayhima an yatarajaAAa in *th*anna an yuqeema hudooda Allahi watilka hudoodu Allahi yubayyinuha liqawmin yaAAlamoona

## Tafsir Ibn Kathir

### Divorce is Thrice

This honorable Ayah abrogated the previous practice in the beginning of Islam, when the man had the right to take back his divorced wife even if he had divorced her a hundred times, as long as she was still in her `Iddah (waiting period). This situation was harmful for the wife, and this is why Allah made the divorce thrice, where the husband is allowed to take back his wife after the first and the second divorce (as long as she is still in her `Iddah). The divorce becomes irrevocable after the third divorce, as Allah said:

(The divorce is twice, after that, either you retain her on reasonable terms or release her with kindness.)

In his Sunan, Abu Dawud reported in Chapter: "Taking the Wife back after the third (Divorce) is an abrogated practice," that Ibn `Abbas commented on the Ayah:

(And divorced women shall wait (as regards their marriage) for three menstrual periods, and it is not lawful for them to conceal what Allah has created in their wombs,) (2:228) The man used to have the right to take back his wife even if he had divorced her thrice. Allah abrogated this and said:

(The divorce is twice.)

This Hadith was also collected by An-Nasa'i. Ibn Abu Hatim reported that `Urwah said that a man said to his wife, "I will neither divorce you nor take you back." She said, "How" He said, "I will divorce you and when your term of `Iddah nears its end, I will take you back." She went to Allah's Messenger and told him what happened, and Allah revealed:

(The divorce is twice.)

Ibn Jarir (At-Tabari) also reported this Hadith in his Tafsir.

Allah said:

(...after that, either you retain her on reasonable terms or release her with kindness.) meaning, 'If you divorce her once or twice, you have the choice to take her back, as long as she is still in her `Iddah, intending to be kind to her and to mend differences. Otherwise, await the end of her term of `Iddah, when the divorce becomes final, and let her go her own way in peace, without committing any harm or injustice against her.' `Ali bin Abu Talhah reported that Ibn `Abbas said, "When the man divorces his wife twice, let him fear Allah, regarding the third time. He should either keep her with him and treat her with kindness, or let her go her own way with kindness, without infringing upon any of her rights."

### Taking back the Mahr (Dowry)

Allah said:

(And it is not lawful for you (men) to take back (from your wives) any of (the dowry) what you gave them,) meaning, you are not allowed to bother or pressure your wives to end this situation by giving you back the Mahr and any gifts that you have given them (in return for divorce). Similarly, Allah said:

(...and you should not treat them with harshness, that you may take away part of what you have given them, unless they commit open illegal sexual intercourse.) (4:19)

However, if the wife willingly gives back anything with a good heart, then Allah said regarding this situation:

(...but if they, of their own good pleasure, remit any part of it to you, take it, and enjoy it without fear of any harm.) (4:4)

### Allowing Khul` and the Return of the Mahr in that Case

When the spouses have irreconcilable differences wherein the wife ignores the rights of the husband, dislikes him and becomes unable to live with him any longer, she is allowed to free herself (from married life) by giving him back what he had given her (in gifts and Mahr). There is no sin on her in this case nor on him if he accepts such offer. This is why Allah said:

(And it is not lawful for you (men) to take back (from your wives) any of what you gave them, except when both parties fear that they would be unable to keep the limits ordained by Allah (e.g., to deal with each other on a fair basis). Then if you fear that they would not be able to keep the limits ordained by Allah, then there is no sin on either of them if she gives back.)

Sometimes, the woman has no valid reason and she still asks for her marriage to be ended. In this case, Ibn Jarir reported that Thawban said that Allah's Messenger said:

$$\text{«أَيُّمَا امْرَأَةٍ سَأَلَتْ زَوْجَهَا طَلَاقًا فِي غَيْرِ مَا بَأْسٍ، فَحَرَامٌ عَلَيْهَا رَائِحَةُ الْجَنَّةِ»}$$

(Any woman who asks her husband for divorce without justification, then the scent of Paradise will be forbidden for her.)

At-Tirmidhi recorded this Hadith and stated that it is Hasan.

Ibn Jarir said that the Ayah (2:229) was revealed about Thabit bin Qays bin Shammas and his wife Habibah bint `Abdullah bin Ubayy bin Salul. In his Muwatta', Imam Malik reported that Habibah bint Sahl Al-Ansariyah was married to Thabit bin Qays bin Shammas and that Allah's Messenger once went to the Fajr (Dawn) prayer and found Habibah bint Sahl by his door in the dark. Allah's Messenger said, "Who is this" She said, "I am Habibah bint Sahl, O Messenger of Allah!" He said, "What is the matter" She said, "I and Thabit bin Qays", meaning, (she can no longer be with) her husband. When her husband Thabit bin Qays came, Allah's Messenger said to him:

$$\text{«هذِهِ حَبِيبَةُ بِنْتُ سَهْلٍ قَدْ ذَكَرَتْ مَا شَاءَ اللهُ أَنْ تَذْكُرَ»}$$

(This is Habibah bint Sahl, she said what Allah has permitted her to say.)

Habibah also said, "O Messenger of Allah! I still have everything he gave me." Allah's Messenger said:

$$\text{«خُذْ مِنْهَا»}$$

(Take it from her.) So, he took it from her and she remained in her family's house."

This was reported by Ahmad, Abu Dawud and An-Nasai.

Al-Bukhari reported that Ibn `Abbas said that the wife of Thabit bin Qays bin Shammas came to the Prophet and said, "O Messenger of Allah! I do not criticize his religion or mannerism. But I hate committing Kufr in Islam (by ignoring his rights on her)." Allah's Messenger said:

$$\text{«أَتَرُدِّينَ عَلَيْهِ حَدِيقَتَهُ»}$$

(Will you give him back his garden)

She said, "Yes." Allah's Messenger said:

»اقْبَلِ الْحَدِيقَةَ وَطَلِّقْهَا تَطْلِيقَةً«

(Take back the garden and divorce her once.)

An-Nasa'i also recorded it.

### The `Iddah (Waiting Period) for the Khul`

At-Tirmidhi reported that Rubayi` bint Mu`awwidh bin `Afra' got a Khul` during the time of Allah's Messenger and the Prophet ordered her to wait for one menstruation period for `Iddah.

### Transgressing the set limits of Allah is an Injustice

Allah said:

(These are the limits ordained by Allah, so do not transgress them. And whoever transgresses the limits ordained by Allah, then such are the wrongdoers.)

This means that the laws that Allah has legislated are His set limits, so do not transgress them. An authentic Hadith states:

»إِنَّ اللهَ حَدَّ حُدُودًا فَلَا تَعْتَدُوهَا، وفَرَضَ فَرَائِضَ فَلَا تُضَيِّعُوهَا، وحَرَّمَ مَحَارِمَ فَلَا تَنْتَهِكُوهَا، وَسَكَتَ عَنْ أَشْيَاءَ رَحْمَةً لَكُمْ مِنْ غَيْرِ نِسْيَانٍ فَلَا تَسْأَلُوا عَنْهَا«

(Allah has set some limits, so do not transgress them; and commanded some commands, so do not ignore them; and made some things unlawful, so do not commit them. He has also left some matters (without rulings) as a mercy with you, not because He has forgotten them, so do not ask about them.)

### Pronouncing Three Divorces at the same Time is Unlawful

The last Ayah we mentioned was used as evidence to prove that it is not allowed to pronounce three divorces at one time. What further proves this ruling is that Mahmud bin Labid has stated - as An-Nasa'i recorded - that Allah's Messenger was told about a man who pronounced three divorces on his wife at one time, so the Prophet stood up while angry and said:

»أَيُلْعَبُ بِكِتَابِ اللهِ وَأَنَا بَيْنَ أَظْهُرِكُمْ«

(The Book of Allah is being made the subject of jest while I am still amongst you)

A man then stood up and said, "Should I kill that man, O Messenger of Allah"

### The Wife cannot be taken back after the Third Divorce

Allah said:

(And if he has divorced her (the third time), then she is not lawful for him thereafter until she has married another husband.)

This Ayah indicates that if the man divorces his wife for the third time after he divorced her twice, then she will no longer be allowed for marriage to him. Allah said:

(...until she has married another husband.) meaning, until she legally marries another man. For instance, if she has sexual intercourse with any man, even her master (if she was a servant), she would still be ineligible for marriage for her ex-husband (who divorced her thrice), because whomever she had sexual relations with was not her legal husband. If she marries a man without consummating the marriage, she will not be eligible for her ex-husband. Muslim reported that `A'ishah said that Allah's Messenger was asked about a woman who marries a man who thereafter divorces her (thrice). She then marries another man and he divorces her before he has sexual relations with her, would she be allowed for her first husband Allah's Messenger said:

«لَا، حَتَّى يَذُوقَ عُسَيْلَتَهَا»

(No, until he enjoys her `Usaylah (sexual relation).) Al-Bukhari also reported this Hadith.

Imam Ahmad recorded that `A'ishah said, "The wife of Rifa`ah Al-Qurazi came while I and Abu Bakr were with the Prophet and she said, `I was Rifa`ah's wife, but he divorced me and it was an irrevocable divorce. Then I married `Abdur-Rahman bin Az-Zubayr, but his sexual organ is minute like a string.' She then took a small string of her garment (to resemble how small his sexual organ was). Khalid bin Sa`id bin Al-`As, who was next to the door and was not yet allowed in, said, `O Abu Bakr! Why do you not forbid this (woman) from what she is revealing frankly before the Prophet' The Prophet merely smiled. Then, Allah's Messenger asked her:

«كَأَنَّكِ تُرِيدِينَ أَنْ تَرْجِعِي إِلَى رِفَاعَةَ، لَا، حَتَّى تَذُوقِي عُسَيْلَتَهُ، وَيَذُوقَ عُسَيْلَتَكِ»

(Do you want to remarry Rifa`ah You cannot unless you experience his `Usaylah and he experiences your `Usaylah (i.e., had a complete sexual relation with your present husband).)"

Al-Bukhari, Muslim, and An-Nasa'i also recorded this Hadith. Muslim's wording is "Rifa`ah divorced his wife for the third and final time."

The word `Usaylah mentioned in the Hadith means sexual intercourse. Imam Ahmad and An-Nasa'i reported that `A'ishah said that Allah's Messenger said:

$$«أَلَا إِنَّ الْعُسَيْلَةَ الْجِمَاعِ»$$

(`Usaylah is sexual intercourse.)

### The Curse on the Participants of Tahlil/Halalah

The reason for the woman (who was divorced thrice) to marry another man must be that the man desires her and has the intention of having an extended married life with her. These are the legal goals and aims behind marriage. If the reason behind the second marriage was to make the woman eligible for her ex-husband again, then this is the Tahlil that the Hadiths have cursed and criticized. In addition, when the reason behind this marriage (if it was Tahlil) is announced in the contract, it would make the contract invalid according to the majority of the scholars.

Imam Ahmad reported that `Abdullah bin Mas`ud said, "Allah's Messenger cursed the one who does Tahlil, the one in whose favor it is done, those who eat Riba (usury) and those who feed it (pay the usury)." At-Tirmidhi and An-Nasa'i reported this Hadith and At-Tirmidhi said, "This Hadith is Hasan." He said, "This is what is acted upon according to people of knowledge among the Companions, among whom are `Umar, `Uthman and Ibn `Umar. It was also the saying of the scholars of Fiqh among the Tabi`in (second generation of Islam). And it has been reported from `Ali, Ibn Mas`ud and Ibn `Abbas".

In his Mustadrak, Al-Hakim reported that Nafi` said: "A man came to Ibn `Umar and asked him about a man who divorced his wife three times. Then, his brother married her to make Tahlil for his brother, without the brother knowing this fact. He then asked, "Is she allowed for the first (husband)" He said, "No, unless it is a marriage that involves desire. We used to consider this an act of adultery during the time of Allah's Messenger ." Al-Hakim said, "This Hadith has a Sahih chain although they (Al-Bukhari and Muslim) did not record it."The wording of this Hadith indicates that the ruling came from the Prophet . Abu Bakr bin Abu Shaybah, Al-Jawzjani, Harb Al-Kirmani and Abu Bakr Al-Athram said that Qabisah bin Jabir said that `Umar said, "If the participants to Tahlil are brought to me, I will have them stoned."

## When does a Woman who was divorced Three Times become Eligible for Her First Husband

Allah said:

(And if he has divorced her) meaning, the second husband after he had complete sexual relations with her,

(it is no sin on both of them that they reunite) meaning, the wife and her first husband,

(provided they feel that they can keep the limits ordained by Allah.) meaning, they live together honorably. Mujahid said, "If they are convinced that the aim behind their marriage is honorable." Next, Allah said:

(These are the limits of Allah,) His commandments and legislation,

(He makes plain)

(for the people who have knowledge.)

### Surah: 2 Ayah: 231

﴿ وَإِذَا طَلَّقْتُمُ ٱلنِّسَآءَ فَبَلَغْنَ أَجَلَهُنَّ فَأَمْسِكُوهُنَّ بِمَعْرُوفٍ أَوْ سَرِّحُوهُنَّ بِمَعْرُوفٍ وَلَا تُمْسِكُوهُنَّ ضِرَارًا لِّتَعْتَدُواْ وَمَن يَفْعَلْ ذَٰلِكَ فَقَدْ ظَلَمَ نَفْسَهُۥ وَلَا تَتَّخِذُوٓاْ ءَايَـٰتِ ٱللَّهِ هُزُوًا وَٱذْكُرُواْ نِعْمَتَ ٱللَّهِ عَلَيْكُمْ وَمَآ أَنزَلَ عَلَيْكُم مِّنَ ٱلْكِتَـٰبِ وَٱلْحِكْمَةِ يَعِظُكُم بِهِۦ وَٱتَّقُواْ ٱللَّهَ وَٱعْلَمُوٓاْ أَنَّ ٱللَّهَ بِكُلِّ شَىْءٍ عَلِيمٌ ﴿٢٣١﴾ ﴾

231. And when you have divorced women and they have fulfilled the term of their prescribed period, either take them back on reasonable basis or set them free on reasonable basis. But do not take them back to hurt them, and whoever does that, then he has wronged himself. And treat not the Verses (Laws) of Allâh as a jest, but remember Allâh's Favors on you (i.e. Islâm), and that which He has sent down to you of the Book (i.e. the Qur'ân) and Al-Hikmah (the Prophet's Sunnah - legal ways - Islâmic jurisprudence.) whereby He instructs you. And fear Allâh, and know that Allâh is All-Aware of everything.

### Transliteration

231. Wa-itha tallaqtumu alnnisaa fabalaghna ajalahunna faamsikoohunna bimaAAroofin aw sarrihoohunna bimaAAroofin wala tumsikoohunna diraran litaAAtadoo waman yafAAal thalika faqad *th*alama nafsahu wala tattakhithoo ayati Allahi huzuwan waothkuroo niAAmata Allahi AAalaykum wama anzala

AAalaykum mina alkitabi waalhikmati yaAAithukum bihi waittaqoo Allaha waiAAlamoo anna Allaha bikulli shay-in AAaleemun

## Tafsir Ibn Kathir

### Being Kind to the Divorced Wife

This is a command from Allah to men that when one of them divorces his wife with a reversible divorce, he should treat her kindly. So when her term of `Iddah (waiting period) nears its end, he either takes her back in a way that is better, including having witnesses that he has taken her back, and he lives with her with kindness. Or, he should release her after her `Iddah finishes and then kindly asks her to depart from his house, without disputing, fighting with her or using foul words. Allah then said:

(But do not take them back to hurt them,)

Ibn `Abbas, Mujahid, Masruq, Al-Hasan, Qatadah, Ad-Dahhak, Ar-Rabi` and Muqatil bin Hayyan said that a man used to divorce his wife, and when her `Iddah came near its end, he would take her back to harm her and to stop her from marrying someone else. He then divorced her and she would begin her `Iddah and when her `Iddah term neared its end, he would take her back again, so that the term of `Iddah would be prolonged for her. After that, Allah prohibited this practice. Allah has also threatened those who indulge in such practices, when He said;

(...and whoever does that, then he has wronged himself.) meaning, by defying Allah's commandments. Allah then said:

(And treat not the verses (Laws) of Allah in a jest,)

Ibn Jarir said that Abu Musa (Al-Ash`ari) narrated that Allah's Messenger once became angry at the Ash`ari tribe. Abu Musa went to him and said, "O Messenger of Allah! Are you angry with the Ash`ariyyin" The Prophet said:

«يَقُولُ أَحَدُكُمْ: قَدْ طَلَّقْتُ، قَدْ رَاجَعْتُ، لَيْسَ هَذَا طَلَاقُ الْمُسْلِمِينَ، طَلِّقُوا الْمَرْأَةَ فِي قُبُلِ عِدَّتِهَا»

(One of you says, `I divorced her' -then says- `I took her back!' This is not the appropriate way Muslims conduct divorce. Divorce the woman when she has fulfilled the term of the prescribed period.)

Masruq said that the Ayah refers to the man who harms his wife by divorcing her and then taking her back, so that the `Iddah term is prolonged for her. Al-Hasan, Qatadah, `Ata' Al-Khurasani, Ar-Rabi` and Muqatil bin Hayyan said, "He is the man who divorces his wife and says, `I was joking.' Or he frees a servant or gets married and says, `I was only joking.' Allah revealed:

(And treat not the verses (Laws) of Allah in a jest,)

Then such men were made to bear the consequences of their actions.

Allah then said:

(...but remember Allah's favors on you,) meaning, by His sending His Messenger with the right guidance and clear signs to you:

(...and that which He has sent down to you of the Book (i.e., the Qur'an) and Al-Hikmah) meaning the Sunnah,

(...whereby He instructs you.) meaning, commands you, forbids you and threatens you for transgressing His prohibitions. Allah said:

(And fear Allah) meaning, concerning what you perform and what you avoid,

(and know that Allah is All-Aware of everything.) none of your secret or public affairs ever escapes His knowledge, and He will treat you accordingly.

## Surah: 2 Ayah: 232

﴿ وَإِذَا طَلَّقْتُمُ ٱلنِّسَآءَ فَبَلَغْنَ أَجَلَهُنَّ فَلَا تَعْضُلُوهُنَّ أَن يَنكِحْنَ أَزْوَٰجَهُنَّ إِذَا تَرَٰضَوْاْ بَيْنَهُم بِٱلْمَعْرُوفِ ۗ ذَٰلِكَ يُوعَظُ بِهِۦ مَن كَانَ مِنكُمْ يُؤْمِنُ بِٱللَّهِ وَٱلْيَوْمِ ٱلْأَخِرِ ۗ ذَٰلِكُمْ أَزْكَىٰ لَكُمْ وَأَطْهَرُ ۗ وَٱللَّهُ يَعْلَمُ وَأَنتُمْ لَا تَعْلَمُونَ ﴾

232. And when you have divorced women and they have fulfilled the term of their prescribed period, do not prevent them from marrying their (former) husbands, if they mutually agree on reasonable basis. This (instruction) is an admonition for him among you who believes in Allâh and the Last Day. That is more virtuous and purer for you. Allâh knows and you know not.

### Transliteration

232. Wa-itha tallaqtumu alnnisaa fabalaghna ajalahunna fala taAAduloohunna an yankihna azwajahunna itha taradaw baynahum bialmaAAroofi thalika yooAAa*th*u bihi man kana minkum yu/minu biAllahi waalyawmi al-akhiri thalikum azka lakum waatharu waAllahu yaAAlamu waantum la taAAlamoona

### Tafsir Ibn Kathir

## The Wali (Guardian) of the Divorced Woman should not prevent Her from going back to Her Husband

`Ali bin Abu Talhah reported that Ibn `Abbas said, "This Ayah was revealed about the man who divorces his wife once or twice and her `Iddah finishes. He later thinks about taking her back in marriage and the woman also wishes that, yet, her family prevents her from remarrying him. Hence, Allah prohibited her family from preventing her." Masruq, Ibrahim An-Nakha`i, Az-Zuhri and Ad-Dahhak stated that this is the reason behind revealing the Ayah (2:232). These statements clearly conform to the apparent meaning of the Ayah.

### There is no Marriage without a Wali (for the Woman)

The Ayah (2:232) also indicates that the woman is not permitted to give herself in marriage. Rather, she requires a Wali (guardian such as her father, brother, adult son, and so forth) to give her away in marriage, as Ibn Jarir and At-Tirmidhi have stated when they mentioned this Ayah. Also, a Hadith states that:

«لَا تُزَوِّجُ الْمَرْأَةُ الْمَرْأَةَ، وَلَا تُزَوِّجُ الْمَرْأَةُ نَفْسَهَا، فَإِنَّ الزَّانِيَةَ هِيَ الَّتِي تُزَوِّجُ نَفْسَهَا»

(The woman does not give another woman away for marriage and the woman does not give herself away in marriage, for only the adulteress gives herself away for marriage.)

Another Hadith states:

«لَا نِكَاحَ إِلَّا بِوَلِيِّ مُرْشِدٍ وَشَاهِدَيْ عَدْلٍ»

(No marriage is valid except with the participation of a mature Wali and two trustworthy witnesses.)

### The Reason behind revealing the Ayah (2:232)

It was reported that this Ayah was revealed about Ma`qil bin Yasar Al-Muzani and his sister. Al-Bukhari reported in his Sahih, when he mentioned the Tafsir of this Ayah (2:232), that the husband of the sister of Ma`qil bin Yasar divorced her. He waited until her `Iddah finished and then asked to remarry her, but Ma`qil refused. Then, this Ayah was sent down:

(...do not prevent them from marrying their (former) husbands.)

Abu Dawud, At-Tirmidhi, Ibn Abu Hatim, Ibn Jarir and Ibn Marduwyah and Al-Bayhaqi reported this Hadith from Al-Hasan from Ma`qil bin Yasar. At-Tirmidhi rendered this Hadith authentic and in his narration, Ma`qil bin Yasar gave his sister in marriage for a Muslim man during the time of Allah's Messenger . She remained with him for a while and he divorced her once and did not take her back until her `Iddah finished. They then wanted to get back with each other and he came to ask her for marriage. Ma`qil said to him, "O ungrateful one! I honored you and married her to you but you divorced her. By Allah! She will

# Chapter 2: Al-Baqarah (The Cow), Verses 142-252

never be returned to you." But Allah knew his need for his wife and her need for her husband and He revealed:

(And when you have divorced women and they have fulfilled the term of their prescribed period, ) until He said:

(...and you know not.)

When Ma`qil heard the Ayah, he said, "I hear and obey my Lord." He then summoned the man and said, "I will honor you and let you remarry (my sister)." Ibn Marduwyah added (that Ma`qil said), "And will pay (the expiation) for breaking my vow."

Allah said:

(This (instruction) is an admonition for him among you who believes in Allah and the Last Day.) meaning, prohibiting you from preventing the women from marrying their ex-husbands, if they both agree to it,

(among you) O people,

(who believes in Allah and the Last Day.) meaning, believes in Allah's commandments and fears His warnings and the torment in the Hereafter. Allah said:

(That is more virtuous and purer for you.) meaning, obeying Allah's Law by returning the women to their ex-husbands, and abandoning your displeasure, is purer and cleaner for your hearts,

(Allah knows) the benefits you gain from what He commands and what He forbids.

(and you know not) the benefits in what you do or what you refrain from doing.

## Surah: 2 Ayah: 233

﴿ ۞ وَٱلْوَٰلِدَٰتُ يُرْضِعْنَ أَوْلَٰدَهُنَّ حَوْلَيْنِ كَامِلَيْنِ ۖ لِمَنْ أَرَادَ أَن يُتِمَّ ٱلرَّضَاعَةَ ۚ وَعَلَى ٱلْمَوْلُودِ لَهُۥ رِزْقُهُنَّ وَكِسْوَتُهُنَّ بِٱلْمَعْرُوفِ ۚ لَا تُكَلَّفُ نَفْسٌ إِلَّا وُسْعَهَا ۚ لَا تُضَآرَّ وَٰلِدَةٌۢ بِوَلَدِهَا وَلَا مَوْلُودٌ لَّهُۥ بِوَلَدِهِۦ ۚ وَعَلَى ٱلْوَارِثِ مِثْلُ ذَٰلِكَ ۗ فَإِنْ أَرَادَا فِصَالًا عَن تَرَاضٍ مِّنْهُمَا وَتَشَاوُرٍ فَلَا جُنَاحَ عَلَيْهِمَا ۗ وَإِنْ أَرَدتُّمْ

أَن تَسْتَرْضِعُوٓا۟ أَوْلَٰدَكُمْ فَلَا جُنَاحَ عَلَيْكُمْ إِذَا سَلَّمْتُم مَّآ ءَاتَيْتُم بِٱلْمَعْرُوفِ وَٱتَّقُوا۟ ٱللَّهَ وَٱعْلَمُوٓا۟ أَنَّ ٱللَّهَ بِمَا تَعْمَلُونَ بَصِيرٌ ﴿٢٣٣﴾

233. The mothers shall give suck to their children for two whole years, (that is) for those (parents) who desire to complete the term of suckling, but the father of the child shall bear the cost of the mother's food and clothing on a reasonable basis. No person shall have a burden laid on him greater than he can bear. No mother shall be treated unfairly on account of her child, nor father on account of his child. And on the (father's) heir is incumbent the like of that (which was incumbent on the father). If they both decide on weaning, by mutual consent, and after due consultation, there is no sin on them. And if you decide on a foster suckling-mother for your children, there is no sin on you, provided you pay (the mother) what you agreed (to give her) on reasonable basis. And fear Allâh and know that Allâh is All-Seer of what you do.

### Transliteration

233. Waalwalidatu yurdiAAna awladahunna hawlayni kamilayni liman arada an yutimma alrradaAAata waAAala almawloodi lahu rizquhunna wakiswatuhunna bialmaAAroofi la tukallafu nafsun illa wusAAaha la tudarra walidatun biwaladiha wala mawloodun lahu biwaladihi waAAala alwarithi mithlu thalika fa-in arada fisalan AAan taradin minhuma watashawurin fala junaha AAalayhima wa-in aradtum an tastardiAAoo awladakum fala junaha AAalaykum itha sallamtum ma ataytum bialmaAAroofi waittaqoo Allaha waiAAlamoo anna Allaha bima taAAmaloona baseerun

### Tafsir Ibn Kathir

#### The Suckling Period is only Two Years

This is a direction from Allah to the mothers to suckle their infants through the complete term of suckling, which is two years. Hence, suckling after two years is not included in this address. Allah said:

(...who desire to complete the term of suckling,)

Therefore, the suckling that establishes Tahrim (prohibition, i.e., one cannot marry his mother or sister from suckling) is what occurs before the two years end. If the infant is suckled only after two years of age, then no Tahrim will be established. At-Tirmidhi under Chapter: `Suckling establishes Tahrim within the first two years,' reported that Umm Salamah narrated that Allah's Messenger said:

«لَا يَحْرُمُ مِنَ الرَّضَاعِ إِلَّا مَا فَتَقَ الْأَمْعَاءَ فِي الثَّدْيِ وَكَانَ قَبْلَ الْفِطَامِ»

(Suckling establishes Tahrim if it is on the breast and before Fitam (before weaning, i.e., before the end of the first two years).)

At-Tirmidhi said, "This Hadith is Hasan Sahih. The majority of the people of knowledge among the Companions of Allah's Messenger and others acted upon this, that is that suckling establishes Tahrim (prohibition in marriage) before the end of the two years and that whatever occurs after that does not establish Tahrim". At-Tirmidhi is alone in recording this Hadith and the narrators in its chain meet the criteria of the Sahihayn. The Prophet's statement:

«إِلَّا مَا كَانَ فِي الثَّدْيِ»

(On the breast) refers to the organ of suckling before the two years. Imam Ahmad reported a Hadith in which Al-Bara' bin `Azib narrated, "When Ibrahim, the Prophet's son, died, the Prophet said:

«إِنَّ ابْنِي مَاتَ فِي الثَّدْيِ، إِنَّ لَهُ مُرْضِعًا فِي الْجَنَّةِ»

(My son has died on the breast and he has someone to suckle him in Paradise.)

Furthermore, Ad-Daraqutni related that Ibn `Abbas said that Allah's Messenger said:

«لَا يَحْرُمُ مِنَ الرَّضَاعِ إِلَّا مَا كَانَ فِي الْحَوْلَيْنِ»

(Suckling establishes Tahrim only within the (first) two years.)

Imam Malik reported this Hadith from Thawr bin Zayd who narrated that Ibn `Abbas related it to the Prophet . Ad-Darawardi reported this Hadith from Thawr who narrated it from `Ikrimah who narrated it from Ibn `Abbas. In this narration, which is more authentic, he added:

«وَمَا كَانَ بَعْدَ الْحَوْلَيْنِ فَلَيْسَ بِشَيْءٍ»

(Whatever occurs after the two years is not considered.)

### Suckling beyond the Two Years

It is reported in the Sahih that `A'ishah thought that if a woman gives her milk to an older person (meaning beyond the age of two years) then this will establish Tahrim. This is also the opinion of `Ata' bin Abu Rabah and Layth bin Sa`d. Hence, `A'ishah thought that it is permissible to suckle the man whom the woman needs to be allowed in her house. She used as evidence the Hadith of Salim, the freed slave of Abu Hudhayfah, where the Prophet ordered Abu

Hudhayfah's wife to give some of her milk to Salim, although he was a man, and ever since then, he used to enter her house freely. However, the rest of the Prophet's wives did not agree with this opinion and thought that this was only a special case. This is also the opinion of the majority of the scholars.

## Suckling for Monetary Compensation

Allah said:

(...but the father of the child shall bear the cost of the mother's food and clothing on a reasonable basis.) meaning, the father of the baby is obliged to provide for the expenses of the mother and to buy her clothes, in reasonable amounts usually used by similar women in that area, without extravagance or stinginess. The father spends within his means in this case. Allah said in another Ayah:

(Let the rich man spend according to his means; and the man whose resources are restricted, let him spend according to what Allah has given him. Allah puts no burden on any person beyond what He has given him. Allah will grant after hardship, ease.) (65:7)

Ad-Dahhak commented, "If the husband divorces his wife, with whom he had a child, and she suckles that child, he is required to provide for the mother's expenses and clothes within reason."

## No Darar (Harm) or Dirar (Revenge)

Allah said:

(No mother shall be treated unfairly on account of her child,) meaning, the mother should not decline to rear her child to harm its father. The mother does not have the right to refrain from suckling the child after giving birth, unless she suckles him/her the milk that is necessary for his/her survival. Later on, she is allowed to give up custody of the child as long as she does not do that intending to harm the father. In addition, the father is not allowed to take the child from his mother to harm the mother. This is why Allah said:

(...nor father on account of his child.) meaning, by taking the child from its mother intending to harm the mother. This is the Tafsir of Mujahid, Qatadah, Ad-Dahhak, Az-Zuhri, As-Suddi, Ath-Thawri and Ibn Zayd, and others on this Ayah.

Allah then said:

(And on the (father's) heir is incumbent the like of that (which was incumbent on the father).) meaning, by refraining from harming the relative (of the father, i.e., his infant), as Mujahid, Ash-Sha`bi and Ad-Dahhak stated. It was also reported that (the Ayah requires) the inheritor (of the father) to spend on the mother of the child, just as the father was spending, and to preserve her rights and refrain from harming her, according to the Tafsir of the majority of the scholars. We should state that Ibn Jarir has explained this subject in detail in his Tafsir and that he also stated that suckling the child after the second year might harm the child's body and mind. Sufyan Ath-Thawri narrated that `Alqamah asked a woman who was suckling her child after the second year ended, not to do that.

### Fitam (weaning) occurs by Mutual Consent

Allah said:

(If they both decide on weaning, by mutual consent, and after due consultation, there is no sin on them.)

This Ayah indicates that if the father and the mother decide on the Fitam (weaning) before the two years (of suckling) end, and for a benefit that they duly discuss and agree upon, then there is no sin in this case. So, the Ayah indicates that one parent is not allowed to make this kind of decision without duly consulting the other parent, as stated by Ath-Thawri. The method of mutual consultation protects the child's interests. It is also a mercy from Allah to His servants, for He has legislated the best method for parents to rear their children, and His legislation guides and directs the parents and the children to success. Similarly, Allah said in Surat At-Talaq (chapter 65 in the Qur'an):

(Then if they give suck to the children for you, give them their due payment, and let each of you accept the advice of the other in a just way. But if you make difficulties for one another, then some other woman may give suck for him (the father of the child).) (65:6)

Allah then said:

(And if you decide on a foster suckling-mother for your children, there is no sin on you, provided you pay (the mother) what you agreed (to give her) on a reasonable basis.) meaning, if the mother and the father both agree that the father assumes custody of the child due to a circumstance that compels her or allows him to do so, then there is no sin in this case. Hence, the mother is allowed to give up the child and the father is allowed to assume custody of the child. The father should kindly give the mother her expenses for the previous period (during which she reared and suckled the child), and he should seek other women to suckle his child for monetary compensation. Thereafter, Allah said: (And fear Allah) meaning, in all of your affairs, (And know that Allah is All-Seer of what you do.) meaning, none of your affairs or speech escapes His perfect Watch.

## Surah: 2 Ayah: 234

﴿ وَٱلَّذِينَ يُتَوَفَّوْنَ مِنكُمْ وَيَذَرُونَ أَزْوَٰجًا يَتَرَبَّصْنَ بِأَنفُسِهِنَّ أَرْبَعَةَ أَشْهُرٍ وَعَشْرًا ۖ فَإِذَا بَلَغْنَ أَجَلَهُنَّ فَلَا جُنَاحَ عَلَيْكُمْ فِيمَا فَعَلْنَ فِىٓ أَنفُسِهِنَّ بِٱلْمَعْرُوفِ ۗ وَٱللَّهُ بِمَا تَعْمَلُونَ خَبِيرٌ ﴾

234. And those of you who die and leave wives behind them, they (the wives) shall wait (as regards their marriage) for four months and ten days, then when they have fulfilled their term, there is no sin on you if they (the wives) dispose of themselves in a just and honorable manner (i.e. they can marry). And Allâh is Well-Acquainted with what you do.

### Transliteration

234. Waallatheena yutawaffawna minkum wayatharoona azwajan yatarabbasna bi-anfusihinna arbaAAata ashhurin waAAashran fa-itha balaghna ajalahunna fala junaha AAalaykum feema faAAalna fee anfusihinna bialmaAAroofi waAllahu bima taAAmaloona khabeerun

### Tafsir Ibn Kathir

#### The `Iddah (Waiting Period) of the Widow

This Ayah contains a command from Allah to the wives whose husbands die, that they should observe a period of `Iddah of four months and ten nights, including the cases where the marriage was consummated or otherwise, according to the consensus (of the scholars).

The proof that this ruling includes the case where the marriage was not consummated is included in the general meaning of the Ayah. In a narration recorded by Imam Ahmad and the compilers of the Sunan, which At-Tirmidhi graded Sahih, Ibn Mas`ud was asked about a man who married a woman, but he died before consummating the marriage. He also did not appoint a Mahr (dowry) for her. They kept asking Ibn Mas`ud about this subject until he said, "I shall give you my own opinion, and if it is correct then it is from Allah, while if it is wrong it is because of my error and because of (the evil efforts of) Satan. In this case, Allah and His Messenger are innocent of my opinion. She has her full Mahr." In another narration, Ibn Mas`ud said, "She has a similar Mahr to that of the women of her status, without stinginess or extravagance." He then continued, "She has to spend the `Iddah and has a right to the inheritance." Ma`qil bin Yasar Ashja`i then stood up and said, "I heard Allah's Messenger issue a similar judgment for the benefit of Barwa` bint Washiq." `Abdullah bin Mas`ud became very delighted upon hearing this statement. In another narration, several men from Ashja` (tribe) stood up and said, "We testify that Allah's Messenger issued a similar ruling for the benefit of Barwa` bint Washiq."

As for the case of the widow whose husband dies while she is pregnant, her term of `Iddah ends when she gives birth, even if it occurs an instant (after her husband dies). This ruling is taken from Allah's statement:

(And for those who are pregnant, their `Iddah is until they lay down their burden.) (65:4)

There is also a Hadith from Subay`ah Al-Aslamiyah in the Two Sahihs, through various chains of narration. Her husband, Sa`d bin Khawlah, died while she was pregnant and she gave birth only a few nights after his death. When she finished her Nifas (postnatal period), she beautified herself for those who might seek to engage her (for marriage). Then, Abu Sanabil bin Ba`kak came to her and said, "Why do I see you beautified yourself, do you wish to marry By Allah! You will not marry until the four months and ten nights have passed." Subay`ah said, "When he said that to me, I collected my garments when night fell and went to Allah's Messenger and asked him about this matter. He said that my `Iddah had finished when I gave birth and allowed me to get married if I wished."

## The Wisdom behind legislating the `Iddah

Sa`id bin Musayyib and Abu Al-`Aliyah stated that the wisdom behind making the `Iddah of the widow four months and ten nights is that the womb might contain a fetus. When the woman waits for this period, it will become evident if she is pregnant. Similarly, there is a Hadith in the Two Sahihs narrated by Ibn Mas`ud stating:

«إِنَّ خَلْقَ أَحَدِكُمْ يُجْمَعُ فِي بَطْنِ أُمِّهِ أَرْبَعِينَ يَوْمًا نُطْفَةً، ثُمَّ يَكُونُ عَلَقَةً مِثْلَ ذَلِكَ، ثُمَّ يَكُونُ مُضْغَةً مِثْلَ ذَلِكَ، ثُمَّ يُبْعَثُ إِلَيْهِ الْمَلَكُ فَيَنْفُخُ فِيهِ الرُّوحَ»

((The creation of) a human being is put together in the womb of his mother in forty days in the form of a seed, and next he becomes a clot of thick blood for a similar period, and next a morsel of flesh for a similar period. Then, Allah sends an angel who is ordered to breathe life unto the fetus.)

So, these are four months and ten more days to be sure, as some months are less (than thirty days), and the fetus will then start to show signs of life after the soul has been breathed into it. Allah knows best.

## The `Iddah of the Slave Mother whose Master dies

We should state here that the `Iddah of the slave mother is the same in the case of death, as the `Iddah of the free woman. Imam Ahmad reported that `Amr bin Al-`As said, "Do not confuse the Sunnah of our Prophet for us. The

'Iddah of the mother, who is also a servant, when her master dies, is four months and ten nights."

## Mourning is required during the `Iddah of Death

Allah said:

(...then when they have fulfilled their term, there is no sin on you if they (the wives) dispose of themselves in a (just and) honorable manner (i.e., they can marry). And Allah is well-acquainted with what you do.)

This Ayah indicates that mourning for the dead husband is required until the `Iddah is finished. It is also reported in the Two Sahihs that Umm Habibah and Zaynab bint Jahsh narrated that Allah's Messenger said:

«لَا يَحِلُّ لِامْرَأَةٍ تُؤْمِنُ بِاللهِ وَالْيَوْمِ الآخِرِ أَن تُحِدَّ عَلَى مَيِتٍ فَوْقَ ثَلَاثٍ، إِلَّا عَلَى زَوْجٍ أَرْبَعَةَ أَشْهُرٍ وَعَشْرًا»

(It is not lawful for a woman who believes in Allah and the Last Day to mourn for more than three days for any dead person except her husband, for whom she mourns for four months and ten days.)

It is reported in the Two Sahihs that Umm Salamah said that a woman said, "O Messenger of Allah! My daughter's husband died and she is complaining about her eye, should we administer kohl in her eye" He said, "No," several times upon repeating this question. He then said:

«إِنَّمَا هِيَ أَرْبَعَةُ أَشْهُرٍ وَعَشْرٌ، وَقَدْ كَانَتْ إِحْدَاكُنَّ فِي الْجَاهِلِيَّةِ تَمْكُثُ سَنَةً»

(It is four months and ten (nights)! During the Jahiliyyah, one of you would mourn for an entire year.)

Zaiynab the daughter of Umm Salamah said (about the pre-Islamic era of ignorance), "When the woman's husband died, she would go into seclusion and would wear the worst clothes she has. She would refrain from wearing perfume or any adornments until a year passed. She would then come out of seclusion and would be given dung that she would throw. Then an animal would be brought out, a donkey, a sheep, or a bird. Then some blood would be drained from it, usually resulting in its death."

In short, the mourning required from a wife whose husband dies, includes not using beautification aids, such as wearing perfume and the clothes and jewelry that encourage the men to seek marriage from the woman. All widows must observe this period of mourning whether they are young, old, free, servant, Muslim or disbeliever, as the general meaning of the Ayah indicates.

Allah also said:

(...then when they have fulfilled their term) meaning, when the `Iddah finishes, according to Ad-Dahhak and Ar-Rabi` bin Anas.

(there is no sin on you) Az-Zuhri said, "Meaning her Wali (guardian)."

(if they (the wives) dispose) meaning, the women whose `Iddah has finished. Al-`Awfi said that Ibn `Abbas said, "If the woman is divorced or if her husband dies and then her `Iddah term ends, there is no sin that she beautifies herself, so that she becomes ready for marriage proposals. This is the way `that is just and honorable'." It was reported that Muqatil bin Hayyan gave the same explanation. Ibn Jurayj related that Mujahid said:

(...there is no sin on you if they (the wives) dispose of themselves in a just and honorable manner.) "refers to allowed and pure (honorable) marriage." It was also reported that Al-Hasan, Az-Zuhri and As-Suddi said the same.

### Surah: 2 Ayah: 235

﴿ وَلَا جُنَاحَ عَلَيْكُمْ فِيمَا عَرَّضْتُم بِهِۦ مِنْ خِطْبَةِ ٱلنِّسَآءِ أَوْ أَكْنَنتُمْ فِىٓ أَنفُسِكُمْ ۚ عَلِمَ ٱللَّهُ أَنَّكُمْ سَتَذْكُرُونَهُنَّ وَلَٰكِن لَّا تُوَاعِدُوهُنَّ سِرًّا إِلَّآ أَن تَقُولُوا۟ قَوْلًا مَّعْرُوفًا ۚ وَلَا تَعْزِمُوا۟ عُقْدَةَ ٱلنِّكَاحِ حَتَّىٰ يَبْلُغَ ٱلْكِتَٰبُ أَجَلَهُۥ ۚ وَٱعْلَمُوٓا۟ أَنَّ ٱللَّهَ يَعْلَمُ مَا فِىٓ أَنفُسِكُمْ فَٱحْذَرُوهُ ۚ وَٱعْلَمُوٓا۟ أَنَّ ٱللَّهَ غَفُورٌ حَلِيمٌ ﴿٢٣٥﴾

235. And there is no sin on you if you make a hint of betrothal or conceal it in yourself, Allâh knows that you will remember them, but do not make a promise of contract with them in secret except that you speak an honorable saying according to the Islâmic law. And do not consummate the marriage until the term prescribed is fulfilled. And know that Allâh knows what is in your minds, so fear Him. And know that Allâh is Oft-Forgiving, Most Forbearing.

### Transliteration

235. Wala junaha AAalaykum feema AAarradtum bihi min khitbati alnnisa-i aw aknantum fee anfusikum AAalima Allahu annakum satathkuroonahunna walakin la tuwaAAidoohunna sirran illa an taqooloo qawlan maAAroofan wala taAAzimoo AAuqdata alnikahi hatta yablugha alkitabu ajalahu waiAAlamoo

anna Allaha yaAAlamu ma fee anfusikum faihtharoohu waiAAlamoo anna Allaha ghafoorun haleemun

## Tafsir Ibn Kathir

### Mentioning Marriage indirectly during the `Iddah

Allah said:

(And there is no sin on you) meaning, to indirectly mention marriage to the widow during the term of `Iddah for her deceased husband. Ath-Thawri, Shu`bah and Jarir stated that Ibn `Abbas said:

(And there is no sin on you if you make a hint of betrothal) "means saying, `I want to marry and I am looking for a woman whose qualities are such and such,' thus talking to her in general terms in a way that is better." In another narration (by Ibn `Abbas), "Saying, `I wish that Allah endows me with a wife,' but he should not make a direct marriage proposal." Al-Bukhari reported that Ibn `Abbas said that the Ayah:

(And there is no sin on you if you make a hint of betrothal) means, "The man could say, `I wish to marry,' `I desire a wife,' or, `I wish I could find a good wife'." Mujahid, Tawus, `Ikrimah, Sa`id bin Jubayr, Ibrahim An-Nakha`i, Ash-Sha`bi, Al-Hasan, Qatadah, Az-Zuhri, Yazid bin Qusayt, Muqatil bin Hayyan and Al-Qasim bin Muhammad and several others among the Salaf and the Imams said that one is allowed to mention marriage indirectly to the woman whose husband died. It is also allowed to indirectly mention marriage to a woman who had gone through final, irrevocable divorce. The Prophet ordered Fatimah bint Qays to remain in the house of Ibn Umm Maktum for `Iddah when her husband Abu `Amr bin Hafs divorced her for the third time. He said to her:

《فَإِذَا حَلَلْتِ فَآذِنِينِي》

(Inform me when your `Iddah term ends.)

When she finished the `Iddah, Usamah bin Zayd, the Prophet's freed slave asked to marry her, and the Prophet married her to him. As for the divorced wife (not irrevocably divorced), there is no disagreement that it is not allowed for other than her husband to mention marriage proposals to her directly or indirectly (before the `Iddah finishes). Allah knows best.

Allah said:

(...or conceal it in yourself,) meaning, if you hide the intention of seeking marriage with them. Similarly, Allah said:

(And your Lord knows what their breasts conceal, and what they reveal) (28:69) and:

(...while I am All-Aware of what you conceal and what you reveal.) (60: 1) So, Allah said here:

(Allah knows that you will remember them) meaning, in your hearts, so He made it easy for you. Allah then said:

(...but do not make a promise (of contract) with them in secret)

`Ali bin Abu Talhah reported that Ibn `Abbas said that

(but do not make a promise (of contract) with them in secret) means do not say to her, "I am in love (with you)," or, "Promise me you will not marry someone else (after the `Iddah finishes)," and so forth. Sa`id bin Jubayr, Ash-Sha`bi, `Ikrimah, Abu Ad-Duha, Ad-Dahhak, Az-Zuhri, Mujahid and Ath-Thawri said that it (meaning of the Ayah) means taking the woman's promise not to marry someone else.

Afterwards, Allah said:

(...except that you speak an honorable saying.)

Ibn `Abbas, Mujahid, Sa`id bin Jubayr, As-Suddi, Ath-Thawri and Ibn Zayd said that the Ayah means to indirectly refer to marriage, such as saying, "I desire someone like you." Muhammad bin Sirin said: I asked `Ubaydah about the meaning of Allah's statement:

(...except that you speak an honorable saying.) He said, "He says to her Wali, `Do not give her away (in marriage) until you inform me first'." This statement was narrated by Ibn Abu Hatim.

Allah then said:

(And do not be determined on the marriage bond until the term prescribed is fulfilled.) meaning, do not make marriage contracts before the `Iddah finishes. Ibn `Abbas, Mujahid, Ash-Sha`bi, Qatadah, Ar-Rabi` bin Anas, Abu Malik, Zayd bin Aslam, Muqatil bin Hayyan, Az-Zuhri, `Ata' Al-Khurasani, As-Suddi, Ath-Thawri and Ad-Dahhak said that:

(until the term prescribed is fulfilled.) means, `Do not consummate the marriage before the `Iddah term finishes.' The scholars agree that marriage contracts during the `Iddah are invalid.

Allah then said:

(And know that Allah knows what is in your minds, so fear Him.) warning the men against the ideas they conceal in their hearts about women, directing them to think good about them rather than the evil, and Allah would not let them despair of His mercy, as He said:

(And know that Allah is Oft-Forgiving, Most Forbearing.)

## Surah: 2 Ayah: 236

$$ \lJ \text{جُنَاحَ عَلَيْكُمْ إِن طَلَّقْتُمُ ٱلنِّسَاءَ مَا لَمْ تَمَسُّوهُنَّ أَوْ تَفْرِضُواْ لَهُنَّ فَرِيضَةً ۚ وَمَتِّعُوهُنَّ عَلَى ٱلْمُوسِعِ قَدَرُهُ وَعَلَى ٱلْمُقْتِرِ قَدَرُهُ مَتَٰعًا بِٱلْمَعْرُوفِ ۖ حَقًّا عَلَى ٱلْمُحْسِنِينَ} $$

236. There is no sin on you, if you divorce women while yet you have not touched (had sexual relation with) them, nor appointed unto them their Mahr (bridal-money given by the husband to his wife at the time of marriage). But bestow on them ( a suitable gift), the rich according to his means, and the poor according to his means, a gift of reasonable amount is a duty on the doers of good.

### Transliteration

236. La junaha AAalaykum in tallaqtumu alnnisaa ma lam tamassoohunna aw tafridoo lahunna fareedatan wamattiAAoohunna AAala almoosiAAi qadaruhu waAAala almuqtiri qadaruhu mataAAan bialmaAAroofi haqqan AAala almuhsineena

### Tafsir Ibn Kathir

#### Divorce before consummating the Marriage

Allah allowed divorce after the marriage contract and before consummating the marriage. Ibn `Abbas, Tawus, Ibrahim and Al-Hasan Al-Basri said that `touched' (mentioned in the Ayah) means sexual intercourse. The husband is allowed to divorce his wife before consummating the marriage or giving the dowry if it was deferred.

#### The Mut`ah (Gift) at the time of Divorce

Allah commands the husband to give the wife (whom he divorces before consummating the marriage) a gift of a reasonable amount, the rich according to his means and the poor according to his means, to compensate her for her loss. Al-Bukhari reported in his Sahih that Sahl bin Sa`d and Abu Usayd said that Allah's Messenger married Umaymah bint Sharahil. When she was brought to the Prophet he extended his hand to her, but she did not like that. The Prophet then ordered Abu Usayd to provide provisions for her along with a gift of two garments.

## Surah: 2 Ayah: 237

$$ \{ \text{وَإِن طَلَّقْتُمُوهُنَّ مِن قَبْلِ أَن تَمَسُّوهُنَّ وَقَدْ فَرَضْتُمْ لَهُنَّ فَرِيضَةً فَنِصْفُ مَا فَرَضْتُمْ إِلَّا أَن يَعْفُونَ أَوْ يَعْفُوَاْ ٱلَّذِي بِيَدِهِ عُقْدَةُ ٱلنِّكَاحِ ۚ وَأَن} $$

تَعْفُوا۟ أَقْرَبُ لِلتَّقْوَىٰ ۚ وَلَا تَنسَوُا۟ ٱلْفَضْلَ بَيْنَكُمْ ۚ إِنَّ ٱللَّهَ بِمَا تَعْمَلُونَ بَصِيرٌ ﴿٢٣٧﴾

237. And if you divorce them before you have touched (had a sexual relation with) them, and you have appointed unto them the Mahr (bridal-money given by the husbands to his wife at the time of marriage), then pay half of that (Mahr), unless they (the women) agree to forego it, or he (the husband), in whose hands is the marriage tie, agrees to forego and give her full appointed Mahr. And to forego and give (her the full Mahr) is nearer to At-Taqwa (piety, righteousness). And do not forget liberality between yourselves. Truly, Allâh is All-Seer of what you do.

### Transliteration

237. Wa-in tallaqtumoohunna min qabli an tamassoohunna waqad faradtum lahunna fareedatan fanisfu ma faradtum illa an yaAAfoona aw yaAAfuwa allathee biyadihi AAuqdatu alnnikahi waan taAAfoo aqrabu lilttaqwa wala tansawoo alfadla baynakum inna Allaha bima taAAmaloona baseerun

### Tafsir Ibn Kathir

### The Wife gets half of Her Mahr if She is divorced before the Marriage is consummated

This honorable Ayah is not a continuation of the Mut`ah (gift) that was mentioned in the previous Ayah (i.e., divorce before the marriage is consummated). This Ayah (2:237) requires the husband to relinquish half of the appointed Mahr if he divorces his wife before the marriage is consummated. If it was discussing any other type of gift, then it would have been mentioned that way, especially when this Ayah follows the previous Ayah related to this subject. Allah knows best. Giving away half of the bridal-money in this case is the agreed practice according to the scholars. So, the husband pays half of the appointed Mahr if he divorces his wife before consummating the marriage.

Allah then said:

(unless they (the women) agree to remit it,) meaning, the wife forfeits the dowry and relieves the husband from further financial responsibility. As-Suddi said that Abu Salih mentioned that Ibn `Abbas commented on Allah's statement:

(unless they (the women) agree to remit it,) "Unless the wife forfeits her right."Furthermore, Imam Abu Muhammad bin Abu Hatim said that it was reported that Shurayh, Sa`id bin Musayyib, `Ikrimah, Mujahid, Ash-Sha`bi, Al-Hasan, Nafi`, Qatadah, Jabir bin Zayd, `Ata' Al-Khurasani, Ad-Dahhak, Az-Zuhri, Muqatil bin Hayyan, Ibn Sirin, Ar-Rabi` bin Anas and As-Suddi said similarly.

Allah then said:

(...or he (the husband), in whose hands is the marriage tie, agrees to remit it.)

Ibn Abu Hatim reported that `Amr bin Shu`ayb said that his grandfather narrated that the Prophet said:

«وَلِيُّ عُقْدَةِ النِّكَاحِ الزَّوْجِ»

(The husband is he who has the marriage tie.)

Ibn Marduwyah also reported this Hadith, and it is the view chosen by Ibn Jarir. The Hadith states that the husband is the person who really holds the marriage tie in his hand, as it is up to him to go on with the marriage or end it. On the other hand, the Wali of the wife is not allowed to give away any of her rightful dues without her permission, especially the dowry.

Allah then stated:

(And to remit it is nearer to At-Taqwa (piety, righteousness).)

Ibn Jarir said, "Some scholars said that this statement is directed at both men and women." Ibn `Abbas said:

(And to remit it is nearer to At-Taqwa (piety, righteousness).) indicates that the one who forgives, is nearer to At-Taqwa (piety)." A similar statement was made by Ash-Sha`bi and several other scholars.

Mujahid, An-Nakha`i, Ad-Dahhak, Muqatil bin Hayyan, Ar-Rabi` bin Anas and Thawri stated that `liberality' mentioned in the Ayah refers to the woman giving away her half Mahr, or the man giving away the full Mahr. This is why Allah said here:

(And do not forget liberality between yourselves.) meaning, kindness (or generosity), as Sa`id has stated. Allah said:

(Truly, Allah is All-Seer of what you do.) meaning, none of your affairs ever escapes His perfect Watch, and He will reward each according to his deeds.

### Surah: 2 Ayah: 238 & Ayah: 239

﴿ حَـٰفِظُوا۟ عَلَى ٱلصَّلَوَٰتِ وَٱلصَّلَوٰةِ ٱلْوُسْطَىٰ وَقُومُوا۟ لِلَّهِ قَـٰنِتِينَ ﴾

238. Guard strictly (five obligatory) As-Salawât (the prayers) especially the middle Salât (i.e. the best prayer - 'Asr). And stand before Allâh with obedience

# Chapter 2: Al-Baqarah (The Cow), Verses 142-252

﴿ فَإِنْ خِفْتُمْ فَرِجَالًا أَوْ رُكْبَانًا فَإِذَا أَمِنتُمْ فَاذْكُرُوا اللَّهَ كَمَا عَلَّمَكُم مَّا لَمْ تَكُونُوا تَعْلَمُونَ ﴾

239. And if you fear (an enemy), perform Salât (pray) on foot or riding. And when you are in safety, offer the Salât (prayer) in the manner He has taught you, which you knew not (before).

### Transliteration

238. Hafi*th*oo AAala alssalawati waalssalati alwusta waqoomoo lillahi qaniteena
239. Fa-in khiftum farijalan aw rukbanan fa-itha amintum faothkuroo Allaha kama AAallamakum ma lam takoonoo taAAlamoona

### Tafsir Ibn Kathir

Allah commands that the prayer should be performed properly and on time. It is reported in the Two Sahihs that Ibn Mas`ud said, "I asked the Prophet, `Which deed is the dearest (to Allah)' He replied:

«الصَّلَاةُ عَلَى وَقْتِهَا»

(To offer the prayers at their fixed times.) I asked, `What is the next (in goodness)' He replied:

«الْجِهَادُ فِي سَبِيلِ اللهِ»

(To participate in Jihad (religious fighting) in Allah's cause.)" I again asked, `What is the next (in goodness)' He replied:

«بِرُّ الْوَالِدَيْنِ»

(To be good and dutiful to your parents.) `Abdullah then added, "The Prophet told me these words, and had I asked more, the Prophet would have told me more."

### The Middle Prayer

Furthermore, Allah has specifically mentioned the Middle prayer, which is the `Asr prayer according to the majority of the scholars among the Companions, as At-Tirmidhi and Al-Baghawi have stated. Al-Qadi Al-Mawardi added that the majority of the scholars of the Tabi`in also held this view. Al-Hafiz Abu `Umar bin `Abdul-Barr said that this is also the opinion of the majority of the scholars of the Athar (i.e., the Hadith and the statements of the Salaf). In addition, Abu Muhammad bin `Atiyah said that this is the Tafsir (of the Middle prayer) of the majority of scholars. Al-Hafiz Abu Muhammad `Abdul-Mu'min bin Khalaf Ad-Dumyati stated in his book on the Middle prayer that it is the `Asr prayer and mentioned that this is the Tafsir of `Umar, `Ali, Ibn Mas`ud, Abu Ayyub, `Abdullah bin `Amr, Samurah bin Jundub, Abu Hurayrah, Abu Sa`id, Hafsah, Umm Habibah, Umm Salamah, Ibn `Abbas and `A'ishah. This is also the Tafsir of `Ubaydah, Ibrahim An-Nakha`i, Razin, Zirr bin Hubaysh, Sa`id bin Jubayr, Ibn Sirin, Al-Hasan, Qatadah, Ad-Dahhak, Al-Kalbi, Muqatil, `Ubayd bin Abu Maryam, and others.

### The Proof that the `Asr Prayer is the Middle Prayer

Imam Ahmad reported that `Ali narrated that Allah's Messenger said during the battle of Al-Ahzab (the Confederates):

«شَغَلُونَا عَنِ الصَّلَاةِ الْوُسْطَى، صَلَاةِ الْعَصْرِ، مَلَأَ اللهُ قُلُوبَهُمْ وَبُيُوتَهُمْ نَارًا»

(They (the disbelievers) busied us from performing the Middle prayer, the `Ar prayer, may Allah fill their hearts and houses with fire.)

He performed the `Asr prayer between Maghrib and `Isha'. Muslim and An-Nasa'i recorded this Hadith. In addition, the Two Shaykhs, Abu Dawud, At-Tirmidhi An-Nasa'i and several other collectors of the Sunan recorded this Hadith using different chains of narrators to `Ali. The Hadith about the battle of Al-Ahzab, when the Mushriks prevented Allah's Messenger and his Companions from performing the `Asr prayer, has been narrated by several other Companions. We only mentioned the narrations that stated that the Middle prayer is the `Asr prayer. Furthermore, Muslim reported similar wordings for this Hadith from Ibn Mas`ud and Al-Bara' bin `Azib.

In addition, Imam Ahmad reported that Samurah bin Jundub said that Allah's Messenger said:

«صَلَاةُ الْوُسْطَى صَلَاةُ الْعَصْرِ»

(The Middle prayer is the `Asr prayer.)

In another narration, Allah's Messenger mentioned:

(Guard strictly (five obligatory) As-Salawat (the prayers) especially the Middle Salah) and stated that it is the `Asr prayer. In another narration, Allah's Messenger said:

«هِيَ الْعَصْرُ»

(It is the `Asr prayer.) and Ibn Ja`far mentioned that the Prophet was then being asked about the Middle prayer. At-Tirmidhi reported this Hadith and said, "Hasan, Sahih." In addition, Abu Hatim bin Hibban reported in his Sahih that `Abdullah said that Allah's Messenger said:

«صَلَاةُ الْوسْطَى صَلَاةُ الْعَصْرِ»

(The Middle prayer is the `Asr prayer.)

At-Tirmidhi reported that Ibn Mas`ud narrated that Allah's Messenger said:

«صَلَاةُ الْوسْطَى صَلَاةُ الْعَصْرِ»

(The `Asr prayer is the Middle prayer.)

At-Tirmidhi then stated that this Hadith is of a Hasan, Sahih type. Muslim reported the Hadith in his Sahih and his wordings are:

«شَغَلُونَا عَنِ الصَّلَاةِ الْوسْطَى صَلَاةِ الْعَصْرِ»

(They (disbelievers) busied us from performing the Middle prayer, the `Asr prayer.)

These texts emphasize the fact (that the `Asr prayer is the Middle prayer). What further proves this fact is that, in an authentic Hadith, Allah's Messenger emphasized the necessity of preserving the `Asr prayer, when he said, as Ibn `Umar narrated:

«مَنْ فَاتَتْهُ صَلَاةُ الْعَصْرِ فَكَأَنَّمَا وُتِرَ أَهْلَهُ وَمَالَهُ»

(Whoever misses the `Asr prayer will be like who has lost his family and money.)

It is reported in the Sahih that Buraydah bin Al-Husayb said that the Prophet said:

«بَكِّرُوا بِالصَّلَاةِ فِي يَوْمِ الْغَيْمِ، فَإِنَّهُ مَنْ تَرَكَ صَلَاةَ الْعَصْرِ، فَقَدْ حَبِطَ

«عَمَلُهُ»

(On a cloudy day, perform the (`Asr) prayer early, for whoever misses the `Asr prayer, will have his (good) deeds annulled.)

## The Prohibition of speaking during the Prayer

Allah said:

(And stand before Allah with obedience.) meaning, with humbleness and humility before Him (i.e., during the prayer). This command indicates that it is not allowed to speak during the prayer, as speaking contradicts the nature of the prayer. This is why the Prophet refused to answer Ibn Mas`ud when he greeted him while he was praying and said afterwards:

«إِنَّ فِي الصَّلَاةِ لَشُغْلًا»

(The prayer makes one sufficiently busy.) (i.e., by the various actions of the body, tongue and heart involved during the prayer.)

Muslim reported that the Prophet said to Mu`awiyah bin Hakam As-Sulami when he spoke during the prayer:

«إِنَّ هَذِهِ الصَّلَاةَ لَا يَصْلُحُ فِيهَا شَيْءٌ مِنْ كَلَامِ النَّاسِ، إِنَّمَا هِيَ التَّسْبِيحُ وَالتَّكْبِيرُ وَذِكْرُ اللهِ»

(The ordinary speech people indulge in is not appropriate during the prayer. The prayer involves only Tasbih (praising Allah), Takbir (saying Allahu Akbar, i.e., Allah is the Most Great) and remembering Allah.)

Imam Ahmad reported that Zayd bin Arqam said, "One used to address his friend about various affairs during the prayer. Then when this Ayah was revealed:

(And stand before Allah with obedience.) we were ordered to refrain from speaking." The Group (i. e., the Hadith collections), except Ibn Majah, reported this Hadith.

## The Fear Prayer

Allah said:

(And if you fear (an enemy), (perform Salah) on foot or riding. And when you are in safety, then remember Allah (pray) in the manner He has taught you, which you knew not (before).)

After Allah commanded His servants to perform the prayer perfectly and emphasized this commandment, He mentioned the situation where the person might not be able to perform the prayer perfectly, during battle and combat. Allah said:

(And if you fear (an enemy), perform Salah on foot or riding.) meaning, pray in the appropriate manner under these circumstances, whether on foot or riding and whether facing the Qiblah or otherwise. Imam Malik reported that Nafi` related that Ibn `Umar used to describe the Fear prayer when he was asked about it and would then add, "If there is intense fear, pray on foot, riding, facing the Qiblah and otherwise." Nafi` commented, "I think that he related that to the Prophet ." Al-Bukhari and Muslim reported the Hadith.

Muslim, Abu Dawud, An-Nasa'i, Ibn Majah and Ibn Jarir reported that Ibn `Abbas said, "Allah has ordained the prayer by the words of your Prophet : four (Rak`ah) while residing, two Rak`ah while traveling and one Rak`ah during times of fear." This is also the view of Al-Hasan Al-Basri, Qatadah, Ad-Dahhak, and others.

In addition, Al-Bukhari has entitled a Chapter: `Prayer while confronting the Forts and facing the Enemy'. Al-Awza`i said, "If the victory seems near and the Muslims are unable to perform the prayer (in the normal manner), they should pray by nodding each by himself. If they are unable to nod, they should delay the prayer until fighting is finished. When they feel safe, they should pray two Rak`ah. If they are unable, they should then pray one Rak`ah that includes two prostrations. If they are unable, then Takbir alone does not suffice, so they should delay the prayer until they are safe." This is the same view that Makhul held. Anas bin Malik said, "I participated in the attack on the fort of Tastar, when the light of dawn started to become clear. Suddenly, the fighting raged and the Muslims were unable to pray until the light of day spread. We then prayed (the Dawn prayer) with Abu Musa and we became victorious. I would not have been pleased if I were to gain in the life of this world and whatever is in it instead of that prayer." This is the wording of Al-Bukhari.

**Prayer during the Times of Peace is performed normally**

Allah said:

(And when you are in safety, then remember Allah (pray)) meaning, `Perform the prayer as I have commanded you by completing its bowing, prostration, standing, sitting, and with the required attention (in the heart) and supplication.' Allah said:

(in the manner He has taught you, which you knew not (before).) meaning, just as He has endowed you, guided you and taught you about what benefits you in this life and the Hereafter, so thank and remember Him. Similarly, Allah said after He mentioned the prayer of Fear,

(...but when you are free from danger, perform As-Salah. Verily, As-Salah (the prayer) is enjoined on the believers at fixed hours.) (4:103)

We will mention the Hadiths about the prayer of Fear and its description in Surat An-Nisa' while mentioning Allah's statement:

(When you (O Messenger Muhammad ) are among them, and lead them in As-Salah (the prayer).) (4:102)

### Surah: 2 Ayah: 240, Ayah: 241 & Ayah: 242

﴿ وَٱلَّذِينَ يُتَوَفَّوْنَ مِنكُمْ وَيَذَرُونَ أَزْوَٰجًا وَصِيَّةً لِّأَزْوَٰجِهِم مَّتَٰعًا إِلَى ٱلْحَوْلِ غَيْرَ إِخْرَاجٍ ۚ فَإِنْ خَرَجْنَ فَلَا جُنَاحَ عَلَيْكُمْ فِى مَا فَعَلْنَ فِىٓ أَنفُسِهِنَّ مِن مَّعْرُوفٍ ۗ وَٱللَّهُ عَزِيزٌ حَكِيمٌ ﴾

240. And those of you who die and leave behind wives should bequeath for their wives a year's maintenance and residence without turning them out, but if they (wives) leave, there is no sin on you for that which they do of themselves, provided it is honorable (e.g. lawful marriage). And Allâh is All-Mighty, All-Wise.

﴿ وَلِلْمُطَلَّقَٰتِ مَتَٰعٌۢ بِٱلْمَعْرُوفِ ۖ حَقًّا عَلَى ٱلْمُتَّقِينَ ﴾

241. And for divorced women, maintenance (should be provided) on reasonable (scale). This is a duty on Al-Muttaqûn (the pious - see V.2:2).

﴿ كَذَٰلِكَ يُبَيِّنُ ٱللَّهُ لَكُمْ ءَايَٰتِهِۦ لَعَلَّكُمْ تَعْقِلُونَ ﴾

242. Thus Allâh makes clear His Ayât (Laws) to you, in order that you may understand.

### Transliteration

240. Waallatheena yutawaffawna minkum wayatharoona azwajan wasiyyatan li-azwajihim mataAAan ila alhawli ghayra ikhrajin fa-in kharajna fala junaha AAalaykum fee ma faAAalna fee anfusihinna min maAAroofin waAllahu AAazeezun hakeemun   241. Walilmutallaqati mataAAun bialmaAAroofi haqqan AAala almuttaqeena   242. Kathalika yubayyinu Allahu lakum ayatihi laAAallakum taAAqiloona

## Tafsir Ibn Kathir

### Ayah (2:240) was abrogated

The majority of the scholars said that this Ayah (2:240) was abrogated by the Ayah (2:234), what Allah said:

(...they (the wives) shall wait (as regards their marriage) for four months and ten days.) (2:234)

For instance, Al-Bukhari reported that Ibn Az-Zubayr said: I said to `Uthman bin `Affan:

(And those of you who die and leave wives behind them) was abrogated by the other Ayah (2:234). Therefore, why did you collect it (meaning, in the Qur'an)" He said, "O my nephew! I shall not change any part of the Qur'an from its place."

The question that Ibn Az-Zubayr asked `Uthman means: `If the ruling of the Ayah (2:240) was abrogated to four months (the `Iddah of the widow, and refer to 2:234), then what is the wisdom behind including it in the Qur'an, although its ruling has been abrogated If the Ayah (2:240) remains (in the Qur'an) after the Ayah that abrogated it (2:234), this might imply that its ruling is still valid.' `Uthman, the Leader of the faithful, answered him by stating that this is a matter of the revelation, which mentioned these Ayat in this order. `Therefore, I shall leave the Ayah where I found it in the Qur'an.'

Ibn Abu Hatim reported that Ibn `Abbas said about what Allah said:

(And those of you who die and leave behind wives should bequeath for their wives a year's maintenance (and residence) without turning them out, ) "The widow used to reside, and have her provisions provided for her for a year, in her deceased husband's house. Later, the Ayah that specified the inheritance (4:12) abrogated this Ayah (2:240), and thus the widow inherits one-fourth or one-eighth of what her (deceased) husband leaves behind."

Ibn Abu Hatim also related that `Ali bin Abu Talhah stated that Ibn `Abbas said, "When a man died and left behind a widow, she used to remain in his house for a year for her `Iddah, all the while receiving her provisions during this time. Thereafter, Allah revealed this Ayah:

(And those of you who die and leave wives behind them, they (the wives) shall wait (as regards their marriage) for four months and ten days.) (2:234)

So, this is the `Iddah of the widow, unless she was pregnant, for her `Iddah then ends when she gives birth. Allah also said:

(In that which you leave, their (your wives') share is a fourth if you leave no child; but if you leave a child, they get an eighth of that which you leave.) (4:12)

So Allah specified the share of the widow in the inheritance and there was no need for the will or the Nafaqah (maintenance) which were mentioned in (2:240)."

Ibn Abu Hatim stated that Mujahid, Al-Hasan, `Ikrimah, Qatadah, Ad-Dahhak, Ar-Rabi` and Muqatil bin Hayyan said that the Ayah (2:240) was abrogated by:

(four months and ten days.) (2:234)

Al-Bukhari reported that Mujahid said that:

(And those of you who die and leave wives behind them) (2:234) used to be the `Iddah, and the widow had to remain with her (deceased) husband's family (during that period, i.e., four months and ten days). Then, Allah revealed:

(And those of you who die and leave behind wives should bequeath for their wives a year's maintenance (and residence) without turning them out, but if they (wives) leave, there is no sin on you for that which they do of themselves, provided it is honorable (e.g., lawful marriage).)

So, Allah made the rest of the year, which is seven months and twenty days, as a will and testament for her. Consequently, if she wants, she could use her right in this will and remain in the residence (for the rest of the year). Or, if she wants, she could leave the (deceased husband's) house after the four months and ten days have passed. This is the meaning of what Allah said:

(...without turning them out, but if they (wives) leave, there is no sin on you.)

Therefore, the required term of `Iddah is still unchanged (refer to 2:234).

`Ata' quoted Ibn `Abbas, "This Ayah (2:240) has abrogated (the requirement that) the widow spends the `Iddah with his (i.e., her deceased husband's) family. So, she spends her `Iddah wherever she wants. This is the meaning of what Allah said:

(without turning them out,)."

`Ata' also said: "If she wants, she spends the `Iddah with his family and resides there according to the will (meaning the rest of the year). If she wants, she is allowed to leave, for Allah said:

(there is no sin on you for that which they do of themselves,)."

`Ata' then said: "Then (the Ayah on) the inheritance (refer to 4:12) came and abrogated the residence. Hence, the widow spends her `Iddah wherever she wants and does not have the right to residence any more."

The statement of `Ata' and those who held the view that the Ayah (2:240) was abrogated by the Ayah on the inheritance (4: 12), is only valid for more than the four months and ten days (required in 2:234). However, if they mean that the four months and ten days are not required from the deceased husband's estate, then this opinion is the subject of disagreement among the scholars. As proof, they said that the widow is required to remain in her (deceased) husband's house (for four months and ten days) according to what Malik reported from Zaynab bint Ka`b bin `Ujrah. She said that Fari`ah bint Malik bin Sinan, the sister of Abu Sa`id Al-Khudri, told her that she came to Allah's Messenger asking him to return to her family's residence with Banu Khudrah. Her husband had pursued some of his servants who ran away, but when he reached the area of Al-Qadum, they killed him. She said, "So I asked Allah's Messenger if I should stay with my family in Banu Khudrah, for my (deceased) husband did not leave me a residence that he owns or Nafaqah (maintenance). Allah's Messenger answered in the positive. While I was in the room, Allah's Messenger summoned me or had someone summon me and said:

《《كَيْفَ قُلْتِ》》

(What did you say) I repeated the story to him about my (deceased) husband. He said:

《《امْكُثِي فِي بَيْتِكِ حَتَّى يَبْلُغَ الْكِتَابُ أَجَلَهُ》》

(Stay at your home until the term reaches its end.) So I remained through the `Iddah term for four months and ten days in my (deceased husband's) house. Thereafter, `Uthman bin `Affan sent for me during his reign and asked me about this matter and I told him what happened. He made a judgment to the same effect." This Hadith was also collected by Abu Dawud, At-Tirmidhi, An-Nasa'i and Ibn Majah. At-Tirmidhi said, "Hasan Sahih".

### The Necessity of the Mut`ah (Gift) at the Time of Divorce

Allah said:

(And for divorced women, maintenance (should be provided) on reasonable (scale). This is a duty on Al-Muttaqin (the pious).)

`Abdur-Rahman bin Zayd bin Aslam said that when Allah's statement:

(...a gift of reasonable amount is a duty on the doers of good) (2:236) was revealed, a man said, "If I want, I will be excellent and if I do not, I will not." Thereafter, Allah revealed this Ayah:

(And for divorced women, maintenance (should be provided) on reasonable (scale). This is a duty on Al-Muttaqin (the pious).)

The scholars who ruled that the Mut`ah (reasonable gift) at the time of divorce is required for every divorced woman, whether she had a bridal-money appointed for her or not, and whether the marriage was consummated or not, relied on this Ayah (2:241) when they issued their ruling. This is the view taken on this subject by Sa`id bin Jubayr and several others among the Salaf and also Ibn Jarir. Hence, Allah's statement:

(There is no sin on you, if you divorce women while yet you have not touched (had sexual relation with) them, nor appointed for them their due (dowry). But bestow on them (a suitable gift), the rich according to his means, and the poor according to his means, a gift of reasonable amount is a duty on the doers of good.) (2:236) only mentions some specifics of this general ruling.

Allah then said:

(Thus Allah makes clear His Ayat (Laws) to you,) meaning, what He allows, forbids, requires, His set limits, His commandments and His prohibitions are all explained and made plain and clear for you. He did not leave any matter in general terms if you needed the specifics,

(in order that you may understand.) meaning, understand and comprehend.

### Surah: 2 Ayah: 243, Ayah: 244 & Ayah: 245

﴿ ۞ أَلَمْ تَرَ إِلَى ٱلَّذِينَ خَرَجُواْ مِن دِيَٰرِهِمْ وَهُمْ أُلُوفٌ حَذَرَ ٱلْمَوْتِ فَقَالَ لَهُمُ ٱللَّهُ مُوتُواْ ثُمَّ أَحْيَٰهُمْ إِنَّ ٱللَّهَ لَذُو فَضْلٍ عَلَى ٱلنَّاسِ وَلَٰكِنَّ أَكْثَرَ ٱلنَّاسِ لَا يَشْكُرُونَ ﴾

243. Did you (O Muhammad (peace be upon him)) not think of those who went forth from their homes in thousands, fearing death? Allâh said to them, "Die". And then He restored them to life. Truly, Allâh is full of Bounty to mankind, but most men thank not.

﴿ وَقَٰتِلُواْ فِى سَبِيلِ ٱللَّهِ وَٱعْلَمُوٓاْ أَنَّ ٱللَّهَ سَمِيعٌ عَلِيمٌ ﴾

244. And fight in the Way of Allâh and know that Allâh is All-Hearer, All-Knower.

﴿ مَّن ذَا ٱلَّذِى يُقْرِضُ ٱللَّهَ قَرْضًا حَسَنًا فَيُضَٰعِفَهُۥ لَهُۥٓ أَضْعَافًا كَثِيرَةً ۚ وَٱللَّهُ يَقْبِضُ وَيَبْصُۜطُ وَإِلَيْهِ تُرْجَعُونَ ﴾

245. Who is he that will lend to Allâh a goodly loan so that He may multiply it to him many times? And it is Allâh that decreases or increases (your provisions), and unto Him you shall return.

## Transliteration

243. Alam tara ila allatheena kharajoo min diyarihim wahum oloofun hathara almawti faqala lahumu Allahu mootoo thumma ahyahum inna Allaha lathoo fadlin AAala alnnasi walakinna akthara alnnasi la yashkuroona  244. Waqatiloo fee sabeeli Allahi waiAAlamoo anna Allaha sameeAAun AAaleemun  245. Man tha allathee yuqridu Allaha qardan hasanan fayudaAAifahu lahu adAAafan katheeratan waAllahu yaqbidu wayabsutu wa-ilayhi turjaAAoona

## Ibn Kathir's Tafsir

### The Story of the Dead People

Ibn Abu Hatim related that Ibn `Abbas said that these people mentioned herein, were the residents of a village called Dawardan. `Ali bin `Asim said that they were from Dawardan, a village several miles away from Wasit (in Iraq).

In his Tafsir, Waki` bin Jarrah said that Ibn `Abbas commented,

(Did you (O Muhammad ) not think of those who went forth from their homes in thousands, fearing death) that they were four thousand persons who escaped the plague (that broke out in their land). They said, "We should go to a land that is free of death!" When they reached a certain area, Allah said to them:

("Die.") and they all died. Afterwards, one of the Prophets passed by them and supplicated to Allah to resurrect them and Allah brought them back to life. So, Allah stated:

r(Did you (O Muhammad ) not think of those who went forth from their homes in the thousands, fearing death)

Furthermore, several scholars among the Salaf said that these people were the residents of a city during the time of the Children of Israel. The weather in their land did not suit them and an epidemic broke out. They fled their land fearing death and took refuge in the wilderness. They later arrived at a fertile valley and they filled what is between its two sides. Then Allah sent two angels to them, one from the lower side and the other from the upper side of the valley. The angels screamed once and all the people died instantly, just as the death of one man. They were later moved to a different place, where walls and graves were built around them. They all perished, and their bodies rotted and disintegrated. Long afterwards, one of the Prophets of the Children of Israel, whose name was Hizqil (Ezekiel), passed by them and asked Allah to bring them back to life by his hand. Allah accepted his supplication and commanded him to say, "O rotted bones, Allah commands you to come together." The bones of every body were brought together. Allah then commanded him to say, "O bones, Allah commands you to be covered with flesh, nerves and skin." That also happened while Hizqil was watching. Allah then commanded him to say, "O souls, Allah commands you to return, each to the body that it used to inhabit." They all came back to life, looked around and proclaimed, "All praise is due to You (O Allah!) and there is no deity worthy of worship except You." Allah brought them back to life after they had perished long ago.

We should state that bringing these people back to life is a clear proof that physical resurrection shall occur on the Day of Resurrection. This is why Allah said:

(Truly, Allah is full of bounty to mankind,) meaning, in that He shows them His great signs, sound proofs and clear evidences. Yet,

(but most men thank not.) as they do not thank Allah for what He has given them with in their worldly life and religious affairs.

The story of the dead people (2:244 above) also indicates that no caution can ever avert destiny and that there is no refuge from Allah, but to Allah Himself. These people departed from their land fleeing the epidemic and seeking to enjoy a long life. What they earned was the opposite of what they sought, as death came quickly and instantaneously and seized them all.

There is an authentic Hadith that Imam Ahmad reported that `Abdullah bin `Abbas said that `Umar bin Al-Khattab once went to Ash-Sham (Syria). When he reached the area of Sargh, he was met by the commanders of the army: Abu `Ubaydah bin Jarrah and his companions. They told him that the plague had broken out in Ash-Sham. The Hadith then mentioned that `Abdur-Rahman bin `Awf, who was away attending to some of his affairs, came and said, "I have knowledge regarding this matter. I heard Allah's Messenger say:

«إِذَا كَانَ بِأَرْضٍ وَأَنْتُمْ بِهَا فَلَا تَخْرُجُوا فِرَارًا مِنْهُ، وإِذَا سَمِعْتُمْ بِهِ بِأَرْضٍ فَلَا تَقْدَمُوا عَلَيْهِ»

(If it (the plague) breaks out in a land that you are in, do not leave that land to escape from it. If you hear about it in a land, do not enter it.)

`Umar then thanked Allah and went back. This Hadith is also reported in the Sahihayn.

### Abandoning Jihad does not alter Destiny

Allah said:

(And fight in the way of Allah and know that Allah is All-Hearer, All-Knower.)

This Ayah indicates that just as caution does not alter destiny, abandoning Jihad will neither bring the appointed term closer nor delay it. Rather, destiny and the appointed provisions are fixed and shall never be changed or altered, neither by addition nor deletion. Similarly, Allah said:

((They are) the ones who said about their killed brethren while they themselves sat (at home): "If only they had listened to us, they would not have been killed." Say: "Avert death from your own selves, if you speak the truth.") (3:168)

Allah said:

(They say: "Our Lord! Why have you ordained for us fighting Would that you had granted us respite for a short period" Say: "Short is the enjoyment of this world. The Hereafter is (far) better for him who fears Allah, and you shall not be dealt with unjustly even equal to the Fatila (a scalish thread in the long slit of a date stone). Wheresoever you may be, death will overtake you even if you are in fortresses built up strong and high!") (4:77, 78)

Abu Sulayman, Khalid bin Al-Walid, the commander of the Muslim armies, the veteran among Muslim soldiers, the protector of Islam and the Sword of Allah that was raised above His enemies, said while dying, "I have participated in so-and-so number of battles. There is not a part of my body, but suffered a shot (of an arrow), a stab (of a spear) or a strike (of a sword). Yet, here I am, I die on my bed just as the camel dies! May the eyes of the cowards never taste sleep." He, may Allah be pleased with him, was sorry and in pain because he did not die as martyr in battle. He was sad that he had to die on his bed!

**The Good Loan and its Reward**

Allah said:

(Who is he that will lend to Allah a goodly loan so that He may multiply it to him many times)

In this Ayah, Allah encourages His servants to spend in His cause. Allah mentioned this same Ayah in several other parts of His Glorious Qur'an. The Hadith that mentions that Allah descends (every night down on the nearest heaven to us when the last third of the night remains) states that Allah says:

«مَنْ يُقْرِضُ غَيْرَ عَدِيمٍ وَلَا ظَلُومٍ»

(Who would give a loan to He Who is neither poor nor unjust.)

Allah's statement:

(He may multiply it to him many times), is similar to His statement:

(The likeness of those who spend their wealth in the way of Allah, is as the likeness of a grain (of corn); it grows seven ears, and each ear has a hundred grains. Allah gives manifold increase to whom He wills.) (2:261)

We will mention this Ayah later on. Allah then said:

(And it is Allah that decreases or increases (your provisions), ) meaning, `Spend (in Allah's cause) and do not be anxious.' Certainly, Allah is the Sustainer Who increases or decreases the provisions to whomever He wills among His servants. Allah's wisdom is perfect, and,

(and unto Him you shall return.) on the Day of Resurrection.

### Surah: 2 Ayah: 246

﴿أَلَمْ تَرَ إِلَى ٱلْمَلَإِ مِنْ بَنِىٓ إِسْرَٰٓءِيلَ مِنْ بَعْدِ مُوسَىٰٓ إِذْ قَالُواْ لِنَبِىٍّ لَهُمُ ٱبْعَثْ لَنَا مَلِكًا نُّقَٰتِلْ فِى سَبِيلِ ٱللَّهِ ۖ قَالَ هَلْ عَسَيْتُمْ إِن كُتِبَ عَلَيْكُمُ ٱلْقِتَالُ أَلَّا تُقَٰتِلُواْ ۖ قَالُواْ وَمَا لَنَآ أَلَّا نُقَٰتِلَ فِى سَبِيلِ ٱللَّهِ وَقَدْ أُخْرِجْنَا مِن دِيَٰرِنَا وَأَبْنَآئِنَا ۖ فَلَمَّا كُتِبَ عَلَيْهِمُ ٱلْقِتَالُ تَوَلَّوْاْ إِلَّا قَلِيلًا مِّنْهُمْ ۗ وَٱللَّهُ عَلِيمٌ بِٱلظَّٰلِمِينَ ﴾

246. Have you not thought about the group of the Children of Israel after (the time of) Musâ (Moses)? When they said to a Prophet of theirs, "Appoint for us a king and we will fight in Allâh's Way." He said, "Would you then refrain from fighting, if fighting was prescribed for you?" They said, "Why should we not fight in Allâh's Way while we have been driven out of our homes and our children (families have been taken as captives)?" But when fighting was ordered for them, they turned away, all except a few of them. And Allâh is All-Aware of the Zâlimûn (polytheists and wrong-doers).

### Transliteration

246. Alam tara ila almala-i min banee isra-eela min baAAdi moosa ith qaloo linabiyyin lahumu ibAAath lana malikan nuqatil fee sabeeli Allahi qala hal AAasaytum in kutiba AAalaykumu alqitalu alla tuqatiloo qaloo wama lana alla nuqatila fee sabeeli Allahi waqad okhrijna min diyarina waabna-ina falamma kutiba AAalayhimu alqitalu tawallaw illa qaleelan minhum waAllahu AAaleemun bialththalimeena

## Ibn Kathir's Tafsir

## The Story of the Jews Who sought a King to be appointed over Them

Mujahid said that the Prophet (mentioned in the Ayah 2:246 above) is Shamwil (Samuel). Wahb bin Munabbih said: The Children of Israel remained on the straight path for a period of time after Moses. They then innovated in the religion and some of them even worshipped the idols. Yet, there were always Prophets sent among them who would command them to work righteous deeds, refrain from doing evil and who would rule them according to the commands of the Torah. When they (Israelites) committed the evil that they committed, Allah caused their enemies to overwhelm them, and many fatalities fell among them as a consequence. Their enemies also captured a great number of them, and took over large areas of their land. Earlier, anyone who would fight the Israelites would lose, because they had the Torah and the Tabut, which they inherited generation after generation ever since the time of Moses, who spoke to Allah directly. Yet, the Israelites kept indulging in misguidance until some king took the Tabut from them during a battle. That king also took possession of the Torah, and only a few of the Israelites who memorized it remained. The prophethood halted among their various tribes and only a pregnant woman remained of the offspring of Lavi (Levi), in whom the prophethood still appeared. Her husband had been killed, so the Israelites kept her in a house so that Allah may give her a boy, who would be their Prophet. The woman also kept invoking Allah to grant her a boy. Allah heard her pleas and gave her a boy whom she called `Shamwil' meaning `Allah has heard my pleas.' Some people said that the boy's name was Sham`un (Simeon), which also has a similar meaning.

As that boy grew, Allah raised him to be a righteous person. When he reached the age of prophethood, Allah revealed to him and commanded him to call (his people) to Him and to His Tawhid (Oneness). Shamwil called the Children of Israel (to Allah) and they asked him to appoint a king over them so that they could fight their enemies under his command. The kingship had also ended among them. Their Prophet said to them, "What if Allah appoints a king over you, would you fulfill your vow to fight under his command"

(They said, "Why should we not fight in Allah's way while we have been driven out of our homes and our children") meaning, `After our land had been confiscated and our children had been taken from us' Allah said:

(But when fighting was ordered for them, they turned away, all except a few of them. And Allah is All-Aware of the wrongdoers) meaning, only a few of them kept their promise, but the majority abandoned Jihad and Allah has full knowledge of them.

### Surah: 2 Ayah: 247

﴿ وَقَالَ لَهُمْ نَبِيُّهُمْ إِنَّ ٱللَّهَ قَدْ بَعَثَ لَكُمْ طَالُوتَ مَلِكًا قَالُوٓاْ أَنَّىٰ يَكُونُ لَهُ ٱلْمُلْكُ عَلَيْنَا وَنَحْنُ أَحَقُّ بِٱلْمُلْكِ مِنْهُ وَلَمْ يُؤْتَ سَعَةً مِّنَ ٱلْمَالِ ۚ قَالَ إِنَّ ٱللَّهَ ٱصْطَفَىٰهُ عَلَيْكُمْ وَزَادَهُۥ بَسْطَةً فِى ٱلْعِلْمِ وَٱلْجِسْمِ ۖ وَٱللَّهُ يُؤْتِى مُلْكَهُۥ مَن يَشَآءُ ۚ وَٱللَّهُ وَٰسِعٌ عَلِيمٌ ﴾ ﴿٢٤٧﴾

247. And their Prophet (Samuel (peace be upon him)) said to them, "Indeed Allâh has appointed Talût (Saul) as a king over you." They said, "How can he be a king over us when we are better fitted than him for the kingdom, and he has not been given enough wealth." He said: "Verily, Allâh has chosen him above you and has increased him abundantly in knowledge and stature. And Allâh grants His Kingdom to whom He wills. And Allâh is All-Sufficient for His creatures' needs, All-Knower."

### Transliteration

247. Waqala lahum nabiyyuhum inna Allaha qad baAAatha lakum taloota malikan qaloo anna yakoonu lahu almulku AAalayna wanahnu ahaqqu bialmulki minhu walam yu/ta saAAatan mina almali qala inna Allaha istafahu AAalaykum wazadahu bastatan fee alAAilmi waaljismi waAllahu yu/tee mulkahu man yashao waAllahu wasiAAun AAaleemun

### Ibn Kathir's Tafsir

When the Israelites asked their Prophet to appoint a king over them, he appointed Talut (Saul), who was then a soldier. But, Talut was not a descendant of the house of kings among them, which was exclusively in the offspring of Yahudha (Judah). This is why they said:

(How can he be a king over us) meaning, how can he be the king for us,

(when we are fitter than him for the kingdom, and he has not been given enough wealth) They said that Talut was also poor and did not have the wealth that justifies him being king. Some people stated that Talut used to bring water to the people, while others stated that his profession was dyeing skins. The Jews, thus, disputed with their Prophet while they were supposed to obey him and to say good words to him.

Their Prophet answered them:

(Verily, Allah has chosen him above you) meaning, `Allah chose Talut from amongst you while having better knowledge about him.' Their Prophet stated, "I did not choose Talut to be your king on my own. Rather, Allah has commanded that upon your request." Further:

# Chapter 2: Al-Baqarah (The Cow), Verses 142-252

(...and has increased him abundantly in knowledge and stature.) meaning, `Talut is more knowledgeable and honorable than you, and stronger and more patient during combat, and has more knowledge of warfare. In short, he has more knowledge and is stronger than you are. The king should have sufficient knowledge, be fair looking and should have a strong soul and body.' He then said:

(And Allah grants His kingdom to whom He wills.) meaning, Allah Alone is the Supreme Authority Who does what He wills and no one can ask Him about His actions, while they will be asked (about their actions by Him). This is because Allah has perfect knowledge, wisdom and kindness with His creation. Allah said:

(And Allah is All-Sufficient for His creatures' needs, All-Knower.) meaning, His favor is encompassing and He grants His mercy to whom He wills. He also knows those who deserve to be kings and those who do not deserve it.

### Surah: 2 Ayah: 248

﴿ وَقَالَ لَهُمْ نَبِيُّهُمْ إِنَّ ءَايَةَ مُلْكِهِ أَن يَأْتِيَكُمُ ٱلتَّابُوتُ فِيهِ سَكِينَةٌ مِّن رَّبِّكُمْ وَبَقِيَّةٌ مِّمَّا تَرَكَ ءَالُ مُوسَىٰ وَءَالُ هَٰرُونَ تَحْمِلُهُ ٱلْمَلَٰٓئِكَةُ إِنَّ فِى ذَٰلِكَ لَءَايَةً لَّكُمْ إِن كُنتُم مُّؤْمِنِينَ ﴿٢٤٨﴾ ﴾

248. And their Prophet (Samuel (peace be upon him)) said to them: Verily! The sign of His Kingdom is that there shall come to you At-Tâbût (a wooden box), wherein is Sakinah (peace and reassurance) from your Lord and a remnant of that which Musâ (Moses) and Hârûn (Aaron) left behind, carried by the angels. Verily, in this is a sign for you if you are indeed believers.

### Transliteration

248. Waqala lahum nabiyyuhum inna ayata mulkihi an ya/tiyakumu alttabootu feehi sakeenatun min rabbikum wabaqiyyatun mimma taraka alu moosa waalu haroona tahmiluhu almala-ikatu inna fee thalika laayatan lakum in kuntum mu/mineena

### Ibn Kathir's Tafsir

Their Prophet then proclaimed, "The sign of the blessings of Talut's kingship over you is that Allah will give you back the Tabut (wooden box) that has been taken from you." Allah said:

(wherein is Sakinah from your Lord) meaning, peace (or grace) and reassurance. `Abdur-Razzaq stated that Qatadah said:

(wherein is Sakinah) means grace. In addition, Ar-Rabi` said that Sakinah means mercy. This is also the meaning given by Ibn `Abbas, as Al-`Awfi narrated.

Allah then said:

(...and a remnant of that which Musa (Moses) and Harun (Aaron) left behind,)

Ibn Jarir related that Ibn `Abbas said about this Ayah:

(...and a remnant of that which Musa (Moses) and Harun (Aaron) left behind, ) Meaning, Moses' staff and the remnants of the Tablets. This is the same Tafsir of Qatadah, As-Suddi, Ar-Rabi` bin Anas and `Ikrimah, who added, "And also the Torah." `Abdur-Razzaq said that he asked Ath-Thawri about the meaning of,

(...and a remnant of that which Musa (Moses) and Harun (Aaron) left behind,)

Ath-Thawri said, "Some said that it contained a pot of manna and the remnants of the Tablets, while some others said that it contained (Moses') staff and two shoes (and refer to 20:12)."

Allah then said:

(...carried by the angels.)

Ibn Jurayj stated that Ibn `Abbas said, "The angels came down while carrying the Tabut between the sky and the earth, until they placed it before Talut while the people were watching." As-Suddi said, "The Tabut was brought to Talut's house, so the people believed in the prophethood of Sham`un (Simeon) and obeyed Talut"

The Prophet then said:

(Verily, in this is a sign for you) testifying to my truth in what I was sent with, my prophethood, and my command to you to obey Talut,

(if you are indeed believers. ) in Allah and the Hereafter."

### Surah: 2 Ayah: 249

﴿ فَلَمَّا فَصَلَ طَالُوتُ بِالْجُنُودِ قَالَ إِنَّ ٱللَّهَ مُبْتَلِيكُم بِنَهَرٍ فَمَن شَرِبَ مِنْهُ فَلَيْسَ مِنِّى وَمَن لَّمْ يَطْعَمْهُ فَإِنَّهُ مِنِّى إِلَّا مَنِ ٱغْتَرَفَ غُرْفَةً بِيَدِهِۦ فَشَرِبُواْ مِنْهُ إِلَّا قَلِيلًا مِّنْهُمْ فَلَمَّا جَاوَزَهُ هُوَ وَٱلَّذِينَ ءَامَنُواْ مَعَهُۥ قَالُواْ لَا طَاقَةَ لَنَا ٱلْيَوْمَ بِجَالُوتَ وَجُنُودِهِۦ قَالَ ٱلَّذِينَ يَظُنُّونَ أَنَّهُم

مُّلَـٰقُوا۟ ٱللَّهِ كَم مِّن فِئَةٍ قَلِيلَةٍ غَلَبَتْ فِئَةً كَثِيرَةً بِإِذْنِ ٱللَّهِ ۗ وَٱللَّهُ مَعَ ٱلصَّـٰبِرِينَ ﴿٢٤٩﴾

249. Then when Talût (Saul) set out with the army, he said: "Verily! Allâh will try you by a river. So whoever drinks thereof, he is not of me, and whoever tastes it not, he is of me, except him who takes (thereof) in the hollow of his hand." Yet, they drank thereof, all, except a few of them. So when he had crossed it (the river), he and those who believed with him, they said: "We have no power this day against Jalût (Goliath) and his hosts." But those who knew with certainty that they were to meet their Lord, said: "How often a small group overcame a mighty host by Allâh's Leave?" And Allâh is with As-Sâbirûn (the patient).

### Transliteration

249. Falamma fasala talootu bialjunoodi qala inna Allaha mubtaleekum binaharin faman shariba minhu falaysa minnee waman lam yatAAamhu fa-innahu minnee illa mani ightarafa ghurfatan biyadihi fashariboo minhu illa qaleelan minhum falamma jawazahu huwa waallatheena amanoo maAAahu qaloo la taqata lana alyawma bijaloota wajunoodihi qala allatheena yathunnoona annahum mulaqoo Allahi kam min fi-atin qaleelatin ghalabat fi-atan katheeratan bi-ithni Allahi waAllahu maAAa alssabireena

### Ibn Kathir's Tafsir

Allah states that Talut, the king of the Children of Israel, marched forth with his soldiers and the Israelites who obeyed him. His army was of eighty thousand then, according to As-Suddi, but Allah knows best. Talut said:

(Verily, Allah will try you) meaning, He will test you with a river, which flowed between Jordan and Palestine, i.e., the Shari`ah river, according to Ibn `Abbas and others. He continued,

(So whoever drinks thereof, he is not of me;) meaning, shall not accompany me today,

(and whoever tastes it not, he is of me, except him who takes (thereof) in the hollow of his hand.) meaning, there is no harm in this case. Allah then said:

(Yet, they drank thereof, all, except a few of them.)

Ibn Jurayj stated that Ibn `Abbas commented, "Whoever took some of it (the river's water) in the hollow of his hand, quenched his thirst; as for those who drank freely from it, their thirst was not quenched."

Ibn Jarir reported that Al-Bara' bin `Azib said, "We used to say that the Companions of Muhammad who accompanied him on the battle of Badr were more than three hundred and ten, just as many as the soldiers who crossed the river with Talut. Only those who believed crossed the river with him." Al-Bukhari also reported this.

This is why Allah said:

(So when he had crossed it (the river), he and those who believed with him, they said: "We have no power this day against Jalut (Goliath) and his hosts.")

This Ayah indicates that the Israelites (who remained with Saul) thought that they were few in the face of their enemy who were many then. So, their knowledgeable scholars strengthened their resolve by stating that Allah's promise is true and that triumph comes from Allah Alone, not from the large numbers or the adequacy of the supplies. They said to them:

("How often has a small group overcome a mighty host by Allah's leave" And Allah is with As-Sabirin (the patient).)

### Surah: 2 Ayah: 250, Ayah: 251 & Ayah: 252

﴿ وَلَمَّا بَرَزُواْ لِجَالُوتَ وَجُنُودِهِ قَالُواْ رَبَّنَآ أَفْرِغْ عَلَيْنَا صَبْرًا وَثَبِّتْ أَقْدَامَنَا وَٱنصُرْنَا عَلَى ٱلْقَوْمِ ٱلْكَـٰفِرِينَ ﴾

250. And when they advanced to meet Jalût (Goliath) and his forces, they invoked: "Our Lord! Pour forth on us patience and make us victorious over the disbelieving people."

﴿ فَهَزَمُوهُم بِإِذْنِ ٱللَّهِ وَقَتَلَ دَاوُۥدُ جَالُوتَ وَءَاتَىٰهُ ٱللَّهُ ٱلْمُلْكَ وَٱلْحِكْمَةَ وَعَلَّمَهُۥ مِمَّا يَشَآءُ وَلَوْلَا دَفْعُ ٱللَّهِ ٱلنَّاسَ بَعْضَهُم بِبَعْضٍ لَّفَسَدَتِ ٱلْأَرْضُ وَلَـٰكِنَّ ٱللَّهَ ذُو فَضْلٍ عَلَى ٱلْعَـٰلَمِينَ ﴾

251. So they routed them by Allâh's Leave and Dawûd (David) killed Jalût (Goliath), and Allâh gave him (Dawûd (David)) the kingdom

﴿ تِلْكَ ءَايَـٰتُ ٱللَّهِ نَتْلُوهَا عَلَيْكَ بِٱلْحَقِّ وَإِنَّكَ لَمِنَ ٱلْمُرْسَلِينَ ﴾

252. These are the Verses of Allâh, We recite them to you (O Muhammad (peace be upon him)) in truth, and surely, you are one of the Messengers (of Allâh).

### Transliteration

250. Walamma barazoo lijaloota wajunoodihi qaloo rabbana afrigh AAalayna sabran wathabbit aqdamana waonsurna AAala alqawmi alkafireena 251. Fahazamoohum bi-ithni Allahi waqatala dawoodu jaloota waatahu Allahu almulka waalhikmata waAAallamahu mimma yashao walawla dafAAu Allahi

alnnasa baAAdahum bibaAAdin lafasadati alardu walakinna Allaha thoo fadlin AAala alAAalameena 252. Tilka ayatu Allahi natlooha AAalayka bialhaqqi wainnaka lamina almursaleena

### Ibn Kathir's Tafsir

When the faithful party, who were few under the command of Talut, faced their enemy, who were many under the command of Jalut,

(they invoked: "Our Lord! Pour forth on us patience...") meaning, send down patience on us from You.

(and set firm our feet) meaning, against the enemy and save us from running away and from feebleness,

(and make us victorious over the disbelieving people.)

Allah said:

(So they routed them by Allah's leave) meaning, they defeated and overwhelmed them by Allah's aid and support. Then,

(and Dawud killed Jalut)

Israelite accounts claimed that (Prophet) David killed Goliath with a slingshot that he had, which he launched at Goliath causing his death.

Talut promised that whoever killed Jalut, would marry his daughter and would share his kingship and authority. He kept his promise. Later, the kingship was transferred to Prophet Dawud in addition to being granted Prophethood by Allah. So, Allah said: (...and Allah gave him (Dawud) the kingdom) that Talut had and, (and Al-Hikmah) that comes with the prophethood, meaning, after Shamwil. )Allah then said:(

(and taught him of that which He willed.) meaning, what He willed of the knowledge that He bestowed on (Prophet) Dawud.

Next, Allah said:

(And if Allah did not check one set of people by means of another, the earth would indeed be full of mischief.)

This Ayah indicates that if it were not for the fact that Allah checks one set of people with another, such as when Talut and the bravery of Dawud helped the Children of Israel (against Goliath), then people would have perished. Similarly, Allah said:

(For had it not been that Allah checks one set of people by means of another, monasteries, churches, synagogues, and Masjids, wherein the Name of Allah is mentioned much, would surely, have been pulled down.) (22:40)

Allah then said: (But Allah is full of bounty to the `Alamin (mankind, Jinn and all that exists)) meaning, by His mercy and favor He fixes some of them by some others. Surely, Allah has the wisdom, the supreme authority and the clear proof against His creation in all of His actions and statements. Allah said: (These are the verses of Allah, We recite them to you (O Muhammad ) in truth, and surely, you are one of the Messengers (of Allah).)

This Ayah states, `These Ayat (verses) of Allah that We have narrated for you in truth conform to the exact manner that these stories have occurred and to the truth that still remain in the (Divine) Books that the scholars of the Children of Israel have and know. Allah said: O Muhammad, (you are) (one of the Messengers (of Allah)) emphatically stating the truth of his prophethood)

### Ibn Kathir's Tafsir

## Neither Repentance of the Disbeliever Upon Death, Nor His Ransoming Himself on the Day of Resurrection Shall be Accepted

Allah threatens and warns those who revert to disbelief after they believed and who thereafter insist on disbelief until death. He states that in this case, no repentance shall be accepted from them upon their death. Similarly, Allah said, (And of no effect is the repentance of those who continue to do evil deeds until death faces one of them) (4:18).

This is why Allah said, (never will their repentance be accepted. And they are those who went astray.) to those who abandon the path of truth for the path of wickedness. Al-Hafiz Abu Bakr Al-Bazzar recorded that Ibn `Abbas said that some people embraced Islam, reverted to disbelief, became Muslims again, then reverted from Islam. They sent their people inquiring about this matter and they asked the Messenger of Allah . On that, this Ayah was revealed, (Verily, those who disbelieved after their belief and then went on increasing in their disbelief never will their repentance be accepted). The chain of narration is satisfactory. Thereafter, Allah said, (Verily, those who disbelieved, and died while they were disbelievers, the (whole) earth full of gold will not be accepted from anyone of them even if they offered it as a ransom.)

Those who die while disbelievers, shall have no good deed ever accepted from them, even if they spent the earth's fill of gold in what was perceived to be an act of obedience. The Prophet was asked about `Abdullah bin Jud`an, who used to be generous to guests, helpful to the indebted and who gave food (to the poor); will all that benefit him The Prophet said, (No, for not even one day during his life did he pronounce, `O my Lord! Forgive my sins on the Day of Judgment.)

Similarly, if the disbeliever gave the earth's full of gold as ransom, it will not be accepted from him. Allah said, (...nor shall compensation be accepted from him, nor shall intercession be of use to him,)(2:123), and (...on which there will be neither mutual bargaining nor befriending.) (14:31), and, (Verily, those who disbelieve, if they had all that is in the earth, and as much again therewith to ransom themselves thereby from the torment on the Day of Resurrection, it would never be accepted of them, and theirs would be a painful torment) (5:36).

This is why Allah said here, (Verily, those who disbelieved, and died while they were disbelievers, the (whole) earth full of gold will not be accepted from anyone of them if they offered it as a ransom). The implication of this Ayah is that the disbeliever shall never avoid the torment of Allah, even if he spent the earth's fill of gold, or if he ransoms himself with the earth's fill of gold, - all of its mountains, hills, sand, dust, valleys, forests, land and sea.

Imam Ahmad recorded that Anas said that the Messenger of Allah said, (A man from among the people of Paradise will be brought and Allah will ask him, "O son of Adam! How did you find your dwelling" He will say, "O Lord, it is the best dwelling." Allah will say, "Ask and wish." The man will say, "I only ask and wish that You send me back to the world so that I am killed ten times in Your cause," because of the honor of martyrdom he would experience. A man from among the people of the Fire will be brought, and Allah will say to him, "O son of Adam! How do you find your dwelling" He will say, "It is the worst dwelling, O Lord." Allah will ask him, "Would you ransom yourself from Me with the earth's fill of gold" He will say, "Yes, O Lord." Allah will say, "You have lied. I asked you to do what is less and easier than that, but you did not do it," and he will be sent back to the Fire.) This is why Allah said, (For them is a painful torment and they will have no helpers.) for they shall not have anyone who will save them from the torment of Allah or rescue them from His painful punishment.

www.ingramcontent.com/pod-product-compliance
Lightning Source LLC
Chambersburg PA
CBHW081106080526
44587CB00021B/3471